Torah Insights

Divrei Torah on the Parshiot Hashavua by leading rabbis and teachers

Edited by

**Rabbi Bertram Leff
and Yisroel Epstein**

Published by the

Insights

Divrei Torah on the Parshiot Hashavua by leading rabbis and teachers

TORAH INSIGHTS
© *Copyright 2000*
by Union of Orthodox Jewish Congregations of America
11 Broadway / New York, N.Y. 10004 / (212) 563-4000 / *www.ou.org*

FIRST EDITION
First Impression . . . August 2000

Distributed by
MESORAH PUBLICATIONS, Ltd.
4401 Second Avenue
Brooklyn, New York 11223

Distributed in Europe by
LEHMANNS
Unit E, Viking Industrial Park
Rolling Mill Road
Jarow, Tyne & Wear NE32 3DP
England

Distributed in Israel by
SIFRIATI / A. GITLER — BOOKS
10 Hashomer Street
Bnei Brak 51361

Distributed in Australia & New Zealand by
GOLDS BOOK & GIFT CO.
36 William Street
Balaclava 3183, Vic., Australia

Distributed in South Africa by
KOLLEL BOOKSHOP
Shop 8A Norwood Hypermarket
Norwood 2196, Johannesburg, South Africa

ISBN
1-57819-542-X (hard cover)
1-57819-543-8 (paperback)

Printed in The United States Of America by
Noble Book Press Corp., New York, NY

Established 1898

Orthodox Union

Union of Orthodox Jewish Congregations of America • איחוד קהילות האורתודוקסים באמריקה

11 Broadway • New York, NY 10004 • Tel: (212) 563-4000 • Fax: (212) 564-9058 • www.ou.org

RABBI RAPHAEL B. BUTLER
Executive Vice President

בס״ד

At the start of his presidency, Dr. Mandell I. Ganchrow encouraged us to create a broad Torah study opportunity to introduce our constituency worldwide to the inspiring work of Rabbanim, Roshei Yeshiva, educators, thinkers, and distinguished laity. Under the guidance of Rabbi Bertram Leff, then National Director of Synagogue Services, and Rabbi Yitzchak Rosenberg, Director of Synagogue Programs, we began to disseminate to member synagogues "Torah Insights," *divrei Torah* relating to the *parsha* of the week and the festivals. This volume represents a compilation of many of those essays.

Concurrent with Dr. Ganchrow's initiative was the desire of Rabbi Leff to create a forum for the many students of the Rav, Rabbi Joseph B. Soloveichik זצ"ל, to present commentary on Torah that they had either heard from the Rav or culled from his teachings. Thus, a preponderance of the material in this volume offers another portal of appreciation for the Rav's depth of scholarship and profundity of thought, and allows an ever burgeoning Torah community to draw further guidance and inspiration from his thoughts.

We thank Yisroel Epstein who had co-edited this work from its inception. He was assisted in its preparation by Elissa Epstein, Laura Berkowitz, Phyllis Meiner and Myra Lee Cohen.

Rabbi Moshe D. Krupka and his Department of Synagogue Services continue to expand the avenues of Torah opportunities for our community. This volume represents another such effort.

May the messages that this volume offers fuel passions for further study and increase the appreciation for the contemporary relevance of our treasured Torah.

Rabbi Raphael B. Butler

ᥲᔓ Preface

Upon his election, one of the first projects that the administration of Dr. Mandell I. Ganchrow, president of the Orthodox Union, embarked upon, was the publication of *Torah Insights,* encompassing a *devar Torah* on the *parshah* of the week. We have been privileged to serve as the editors of *Torah Insights* from its inception.

Much time and effort was expended to present an attractive and engaging publication so that the reader would be drawn to its words. Our desire was to engage as wide an audience as possible in the richness of our Torah tradition. Many of the *Torah Insights* contain the comments of Rav Yosef Dov Soloveitchik, *zt"l.* It is our hope that this volume will contribute to the wider dissemination of the Rav's *divrei Torah* to the broader Jewish community.

We endeavored to include in the collection messages from rabbis who serve Orthodox Union congregations, prominent educators, and community leaders. No distinction was made between male and female, young and old, well known and unknown. Each, in his or her own way, made a contribution to *Torah Insights.*

We would like to express our gratitude to all our contributors without whom this volume would not have been possible. We wish to acknowledge our appreciation for the support and encouragement of Dr. Ganchrow, Rabbi Raphael Butler, executive vice president of the Orthodox Union and Rabbi Moshe Krupka, national director of synagogue services for the Orthodox Union.

It is our prayer that this collection of *divrei Torah* will inspire all who read its words. It is our sincerest wish that these *Torah Insights* will add meaning to their daily lives and further their spiritual quests.

Rabbi Bertram Leff, Editor
Yisroel Epstein, Associate Editor

July 2000

❧ Table of Contents

Bereishis

Vayikra

Bamidbar

Devarim

Yamim Tovim

Sefer Bereishis

פרשת בראשית
Parshas Bereishis

_____ *Rabbi Emanuel Holzer*

ON THE SIXTH DAY OF CREATION, AFTER G-D CREATED MAN, THE
Torah records that "G-d saw everything that He made — *vehinei
tov meod* — and behold it was very good." G-d saw the completeness,
the harmony that united everything that He had created.

The Midrash interprets this verse to mean that both the *yeitzer hatov,*
man's good inclination, and the *yeitzer hara,* man's evil inclination, are
part of the complete goodness of this world.

How can this be? How can the evil inclination be included in the
statement, *"vehinei tov meod"*? After all, G-d does not foist evil upon
man.

In explaining the Midrash, Rav Yosef Dov Soloveitchik, *zt"l,* taught
that everything G-d created was good, not evil. When man makes use
of the gifts G-d set forth on the earth in their proper manner, they
are good. But when we take those gifts to the extreme, when we aren't
satisfied with good and try to make them *very* good, they can become
evil.

Man's physical desire to eat is good and necessary; but when he goes
to one extreme or the other, either gorging himself or fasting, he plays
into the hands of the *yeitzer hara.* In all avenues of life, when we overdo
or overeat or overreact, when we turn *tov* into *tov meod,* we turn ourselves over to the *yeitzer hara.*

Man, said Aristotle, should not feel or express great joy or great sorrow, since neither extreme is beneficial for him. In contrast to Aristotle's

golden mean, which leaves man devoid of emotion, the Rambam understood that man needs to express great joy and great mourning in their proper times. Nevertheless, man must always be in control of these emotions.

When we view emotions from the Torah's viewpoint, explains Rav Soloveitchik, we can not allow our emotions to run rampant. To sanction such behavior is to sanction excessive hate and self-abuse. The Torah requires us to control our emotions, not to squelch them. In mourning, we express sadness, but when Shabbos or the holidays arrive, we are required to limit our expressions of grief. The Torah commands us to regulate feelings of love, hate and sorrow. Emotions are only noble when controlled.

The Rambam, in describing the Tree of Knowledge that knew good and evil, explains that the knowledge the tree offered was the gamut of human emotion and drive, giving man the potential to either do the will of G-d or to go against His will.

If we use this potential wisely, we will learn when to say when, practicing moderation in all areas of life and insuring that we settle for *tov* and do not chase after *tov me'od*.

_____ *Rabbi Yosef Viener*

CHAG HASUCCOS IS A SPECIAL TIME OF *SIMCHAH*. THE *MITZVAH* OF "*Vesamachta* — And you shall rejoice" is stressed more on Succos than on any other holiday because Succos follows Rosh Hashanah and Yom Kippur, a time when one is at peace with oneself and with Hashem. Only at such time can true happiness be felt. Having worked earnestly during the days of awe to improve ourselves and having asked G-d to help us on the proper path, we entered Succos with the ability to enjoy our newfound closeness to Hashem.

Succos taught us two great lessons. First, to try to perform the *mitzvos* we do throughout the year with a greater sense of joy. Just as we enjoyed shaking the *lulav* and sitting in the *succah,* so too should we take pleasure in the *mitzvos* we do year around.

Second, to elevate all the aspects of our life, even those that do not fit the strict definition of *mitzvos.* Just as we enjoyed the days of Yom Tov in a physical sense, with good food, drink and companionship, so too should we find opportunities throughout the year to bring holiness into the temporal aspects of our lives.

Judaism believes that all natural things are inherently positive and were created for constructive use in the service of *Hakadosh Baruch Hu.* If the physical pleasures we enjoy help put us in a relaxed yet expansive state of mind, which makes us better able to serve G-d, we have taken the mundane and made it holy.

With these lessons in hand we come to the end of the holiday season, prepared to launch the new year. Thus we rejoice with the Torah, on Shemini Atzeres and Simchas Torah, at the end of Succos. Our ability to begin the year on a positive, joyous note comes only after the High Holy Days and Succos. With our newly acquired spiritual station, we begin the Torah anew.

The word *bereishis* reflects not only the dawn of creation, but also the renewal of our commitment to Torah and its values. Our dedication to the study of Torah and to the fulfillment of its *mitzvos* must be with *simchah* and enthusiasm.

The hope and prayer of every Jew is that the new year bring health, happiness and spiritual fulfillment. A vital sign of spiritual success is the ability to learn G-d's Torah with joy and satisfaction. This is the first challenge we face as we begin the new year.

_____ *Rabbi Shaya Sackett*

M OST EVERY SCHOOLCHILD WOULD TRANSLATE *"BEREISHIS BARA Elokim"* as "In the beginning, G-d created...." While this would, of course, be correct, Rashi offers a slightly different approach to understanding these first words of our Torah. *"Bereishis,"* Rashi translates, "For the sake of the Torah, which is called *Reishis,* G-d created the heavens and the earth."

It is one thing to know the story of Creation — what was created and on which day it was created. It is quite another to understand the purpose of Creation. This comment of Rashi helps us understand that the Torah, its study and observance, is the entire reason G-d created the world and everything in it, including mankind.

The Jewish people are fortunate. We acknowledge many new beginnings over the course of time. We just celebrated Rosh Hashanah, the Jewish New Year. We were presented with an opportunity to begin anew, to wipe the slate clean from our past indiscretions and to uninhibitedly begin fulfilling our purpose in creation.

This Shabbos we also mark a new beginning. We begin the new cycle of Torah readings. This timely opportunity, coupled with the message of the first words of the Torah as explained by Rashi, should motivate every one of us to study the weekly Torah portion regularly.

If it is your first time working through the text, a simple reading of the words will get you started. There are several good English translations and commentaries. If you are more experienced, studying the portion with Rashi's commentary is recommended. Have a bit more time? Pick a particular commentary that appeals to you and follow it through the entire cycle. It is amazing how many new insights you will discover each time you re-examine the Torah portion.

Additionally, while Torah study for its own sake is of the highest priority, the Talmud emphasizes the importance of study as a forerunner to proper behavior. Contained within our holy Torah are the principles for living in a manner befitting human beings and benefiting all of human society. Studying, absorbing and applying Torah principles to every aspect of our lives will bring us to the fulfillment of our purpose in creation.

_____ *Rabbi Jonathan Glass*

E VERY CHILD KNOWS THE STORY OF CREATION. THE TORAH GIVES US a day-by-day account, describing how G-d, in His omnipotence, benevolently brought forth all that we know — light and darkness, dry land and sea, trees and plants, stars and planets, animal and man. The text reads so simply and orderly that one is tempted to skim through it to get to the "meat" of the *parshah* — the story of Adam and Eve. The story of Creation remains an introduction, one that poses little difficulty for believers.

But Rashi, the great commentator, does not see it that way. He says that the opening sequence cries out for interpretation. It can not be that these verses are telling us about the chronology of Creation, he writes, for the Torah's second verse tells of G-d's Presence "hovering on the face of the water," before any account of G-d's creating water is given.

Rashi, therefore, does not subscribe to the popular translation of the opening verse of the Torah, "In the beginning, G-d created heaven and earth." Instead, he renders the words to leave open the possibility that water was created prior to heaven and earth. What looked like a neat and clear account of Creation turns out to be full of mystery. And the Torah beginning with mystery is important — it reveals the very nature of Creation and of the Torah itself.

We tend to feel a need to clarify and understand the world around us, to grasp and digest every experience we have. But we must never lose track of the mystery that pervades all of Creation. A sense of wonder is necessary in this world. We must know that we are part of something much larger than ourselves and our personal experiences, something we may never fully be able to understand.

The works of Creation refer to science, according to some Talmudic Sages. Science, too, resides in the tension between the known and the mysterious. In our century, particularly, with the discovery of subatomic particles, the science of Creation has become more mysterious than ever. Those very mysteries of our origin make us cognizant of the contemporary wonders around us today.

The Torah is also telling us about life itself. We don't need to have all the answers. A good question often serves us better than a mediocre answer. Even our great Sages were occasionally unable to answer questions of *Halachah* and left them for Eliyahu Hanavi to answer.

In the meantime, we are not threatened. Life, in fact, becomes more meaningful. Rather than trying to deny the existence of phenomena that don't fit neatly into our categories of thought, we are prepared to acknowledge an element of mystery, live with it, and be enriched by it.

פרשת נח
Parshas Noach

_____ *Rabbi Abner Weiss*

THE CONCLUSION OF THE NOACH NARRATIVE IS TRAGIC. HAVING BEEN described as righteous and unblemished in his generation and having been spared along with his family from death in the deluge, Noach, immediately after the Flood, plants a vine and gets drunk.

More tragic, though, is the Rabbinic interpretation of the behavior of his son, Cham, who finds Noach drunk and naked. Clearly, Cham did something more heinous than merely looking at his father's naked body. Such an act may well have provoked indignation, but could hardly justify the curse that Noach uttered against him. Rashi cites the Sages: according to one view he castrated Noach; according to another, he sodomized him.

The Rabbinic tradition appears to have run wild. But it is almost a truism that the more fantastic the Midrash, the more profound the truth it conceals. One may suggest, therefore, that this Midrash contains the Rabbinic view of human response to holocaust.

The destruction by deluge had been enormous. Apart from one family and the animals herded onto the ark, no life was left on earth. Everything was destroyed. Imagine the horrified reaction of that single human family. Nothing familiar to them remained. Their friends were dead, their civilization washed away, countless dreams dashed, hopes evaporated. Cosmos had become chaos.

Against a backdrop of this desolation and despair we must view the sin of Cham; his behavior can be seen as a response to holocaust.

According to the opinion that he castrated his father, his behavior may owe to his conviction that bringing children into a world vulnerable to death and destruction is wrong.

This viewpoint was fairly common among survivors of Hitler's Holocaust. Decent men and women, who had witnessed the murder of beloved spouses and children, determined that a world in which a Hitler could exterminate little children was no place for another generation of potential victims. Better to have no life, they reasoned, than to have life snuffed out.

The second Rabbinic interpretation has Cham guilty of an incestuous, homosexual act. He behaved as if all taboos were dismissed, as if no limits were placed on the pleasures of the flesh, as if instant gratification was all that mattered. This, too, was a response to the Holocaust. Surrounded by evidence that life is without meaning, many people felt that to limit their enjoyment of life's fleeting pleasures made no sense. Cham's behavior is simply a recasting of the classic adage, "Eat, drink and be merry, for tomorrow we die."

Both interpretations of Cham's behavior stem from the same premise. Each denies that life has meaning. Each negates the purpose of life.

Happily, there is a third response to holocaust—that of Cham's brothers. They refused to let go of principle in the face of hopelessness. They adhered to standards of decent social conduct in the face of death and destruction. They affirmed life even in the depths of the valley of the shadow of death. Each affirmed life in his own way. Yefes, the father of aesthetics, insisted that beauty and harmony can exist even in a world that is defined by destruction and death.

Sheim, the forebear of the Jewish people, asserted that life is affirmed by insisting on decency, justice and civilized moral standards. Even though man is vulnerable and the future is always uncertain, the present must be made as meaningful as possible.

The human response to holocaust, insecurity and vulnerability can be to deny life and human values. But it can also be to reaffirm them, to insist that there is a value in bringing children into the world so long as the time that is allotted to them is filled with transcendent meaning. This is the Jewish response. This is the lesson taught by the Sages in the Midrash.

T
HE TALMUD ACKNOWLEDGES THAT AVRAHAM OBSERVED THE ENTIRE
Torah, not only the Written Law but the Oral Law as well, as it
states: "Avraham listened to My voice and kept My charges, My com-
mandments, My statutes and My laws (*toros*)." "*Toros,*" plural, refers to
Torah Shebikesav, the Written Law, and *Torah Shebaal Peh,* the Oral
Law.

Avraham's observance raises all kinds of questions regarding his
status. Although he is the father of the Jewish people, the first Patriarch,
Avraham was not a Jew technically, since the Jewish nation first came
into existence centuries later at Sinai. How are we to understand the
spiritual status of our forefathers? Were the Patriarchs and their descendants expected to live lives based on Torah principles, or were they
restricted only by the *sheva mitzvos bnei Noach,* the seven Noachide
laws?

Furthermore, the Talmud rules that it is a capital crime for a non-
Jew to observe the Shabbos. For this reason, candidates for conversion
to Judaism, who are taught the *mitzvos* and begin to observe them, are
nevertheless careful to turn on a light on Shabbos or to violate the
Shabbos in some other way until they are actually converted. This being
so, how could generations prior to *mattan Torah* observe the Shabbos,
when they were not considered Jewish?

This principle also presents a practical problem, which was posed to
Rav Yosef Dov Soloveitchik, *zt"l.* Each year a number of babies are
abandoned and left as wards of the state. In which religion are they to be
raised? The Rav maintained that children found in Jewish neighborhoods should be considered Jews, and children found in non-Jewish
neighborhoods should be considered non-Jews.

But what of children who are found in neighborhoods where Jews
and non-Jews live side by side? The Rav argued that the restrictions
of both Jew and non-Jew be placed upon the child. Where, then, does
that leave the child in relation to Shabbos? Does such a child observe
Shabbos as a Jew, or, as a possible non-Jew, must he violate the Shabbos?

There are several ways around the problem. One solution, cited by the *Binyan Tziyon,* is based on the fact that the non-Jews follow a solar schedule while the Jewish nation follows a lunar schedule. Thus, the Jewish Shabbos begins Friday night and ends Saturday night. Non-Jews, who are tied to a solar calendar, can refrain from *melachah* on the Jewish Shabbos and still violate the seventh day — their seventh day — by working on Saturday night.

The *Minchas Chinuch* offers another solution. The Torah gives certain measurements necessary in order for a violation of Shabbos to occur. For example, a Jew who cooks on Shabbos is only culpable if he cooked something the size of an olive or greater. Anything less is not considered cooking.

But the Rambam maintains that these measurements do not apply to non-Jews. Thus, a non-Jew who cooked even one grain of rice on Shabbos has violated it. Accordingly, one could desecrate the Shabbos as a non-Jew, while simultaneously upholding it as a Jew.

The special status of Shabbos prevents it from being celebrated by the rest of the world. Shabbos belongs solely to *Am Yisrael,* "a sign between [G-d] and the children of Israel."

Through our observance of Shabbos, our special *tefillos* on Shabbos, and our added opportunities to study Torah on Shabbos, we proclaim that special sign that separates our nation from the nations of the world.

_____ *Rabbi Aaron Borow*

T HE ALMIGHTY IS AN *AV HARACHAMAN,* A MERCIFUL FATHER, WHO sustains the whole world. We turn to Him, especially during times of crisis, to show us His mercy and compassion. Yet Hashem destroyed the world in the days of Noach "because all flesh had corrupted their way upon the earth." How terrible was their corruption that G-d could not tolerate it?

Rabbi Eliyahu Ki Tov, *zt"l,* describes the behavior of that generation as told in the Midrash. The people "wanted to build a world that was entirely evil and allowed a person maximum pleasure and benefit for the present and the future." They wanted to live only for their own pleasure and joy, and so they freed their consciences not by simply sinning but by enacting laws that made sinning mandatory. Their society didn't tolerate sinning, it insisted on it.

First, they did away with clothing. As the climate in those days was warm, the only reason people wore clothes was out of modesty, and so "they went and stripped themselves of all boundaries of modesty in clothing. The leaders initiated and were followed by the rest of the nation."

What followed was a free-for-all. Once they lost their modesty, they were able to abandon all the rules of sexual morality. Men and women freely exchanged partners. Homosexuality was rampant and bestiality became the fashion. Marriage contracts were made between males and also between humans and animals. Our Sages teach that Hashem is slow to anger except when it comes to acts of sexual immorality. Noach's generation crossed that line by leaps and bounds.

But why didn't Noach pray to G-d on behalf of the people as Avraham and Moshe did in later generations?

The Zohar explains. When Noach left the ark he saw a world destroyed. Nothing was left — no trees, no vegetation, no animals, no human beings. Everything was gone. "Master of the world," he cried, "You are merciful and compassionate. Why didn't you show compassion to Your creations?"

The Almighty responded, "Noach, why didn't you say this to Me when I said, 'I have found you to be a *tzaddik,* a righteous person in this generation,' and afterwards, when I said, 'I am bringing a flood, make for yourself an ark.' I said all of these things to you, Noach, hoping that you would petition Me for mercy on the world! When you heard that you would be saved, you didn't think of saving others. You just entered the Ark. Now that the world is wasted, you come with petitions?!"

Why didn't Noach appeal to G-d *before* it was too late? Rabbi Ki Tov answers: Noach believed that the people of his time were too far gone. They were beyond salvation. They had no respect for their own humanity or for that of others. Among all those who lived in his time, Noach could not find even a *minyan* of good people. Nonetheless, for all their evil, Hashem takes Noach to task for not defending them, for not taking their case.

One lesson of this *parshah* is that we have no right to give up on people. Even if we believe they are beyond salvation, we must still extend a helping hand and pray to G-d for their salvation.

THE DELUGE THAT DESTROYED THE WORLD IN THE TIME OF NOACH caused a major upheaval in the physical makeup of the world. The geological and archeological evidence of these changes has baffled many a scientist — so much so that even skeptical scientists argue that some fossilized discoveries may be attributed to the Flood. Not only did the Flood leave its indelible mark on the contours of the planet, but, the Torah tells us, it changed the very physics of the world.

Hashem was deeply saddened by the immorality that had pervaded His world and to insure that it would not happen again, He did not simply destroy the world but changed its structure. After Noach and his family left the confines of their protective ark, they entered a new world order.

Noach had a very difficult year in the ark. He had to provide for and tend to the ark's menagerie. Each animal required its own diet and each had its own schedule. "During the twelve months that Noach was in the ark, he did not taste sleep," the Midrash tells us. Noach's natural environment was suspended for that time. In fact, but for three exceptions, everyone's nature changed while in the ark. Only the dog, the raven and Cham, Noach's son, functioned normally in the ark.

What motivated these three to be different? Why couldn't they suspend their personal needs during this time of universal tragedy? The answer is found in their very nature. Dogs are arrogant, the prophet Yeshayah states. They are selfish and uncaring. They must be well trained before they can become "man's best friend."

The raven is known for its cruelty. When Noach released the raven to see the conditions outside the ark, it came upon a human corpse on top of a mountain. After satisfying itself, the raven returned to Noach with no information for the inhabitants of the ark.

Cham, son of Noach, also submitted to his baser instincts. He totally ignored the suffering around him and allowed himself the pleasures of his indulgences. This selfishness did not go unnoticed by Hashem. Cham and his descendants were punished forever.

What a lesson for us. Are we so uncaring that the experiences of the world around us go unnoticed? Are we oblivious? Can we continue to go about "life as normal," without seeing and learning important lessons about compassion, morality and decency?

We must emulate the good we see and eliminate the bad we see. The spiritual nature of the world was changed after the Flood's destruction. It is up to us to sustain the world by avoiding the mistakes of the past.

פרשת לך לך
Parshas Lech Lecha

_____ Rabbi Yoel Schonfeld

THE *PARSHAH* OF *LECH LECHA* INTRODUCES THE CONCEPT OF THE Jewish homeland. Rav Yosef Dov Soloveitchik, *zt"l,* points to the Torah's succinct manner in announcing G-d's first communication concerning this cornerstone of Jewish destiny: "And G-d said to Avram, Go for yourself from your country, from your birthplace and from your father's house to the land that I will show you."

Herein lies the beauty of the Torah, the Rav would say, such a lofty concept with such majestic implications in the most modest of terms. This *pasuk* not only begins the designation of *Eretz Yisrael* as the Jewish homeland but it also initiates the debate as to the validity of a Jewish state there. Does the Land of Israel function merely as the dwelling place of its Jewish inhabitants regardless of a sovereign Jewish state, or is the idea of Jewish statehood integral to the spirit of our people and indispensable to Jewish survival?

This debate has come into sharp focus over the last hundred years with the advent of modern Zionism. The writings of some of the *gedolei Yisrael* indicate where they stood on the issue. Many supported the *Chovevei Tziyon* movement which was, arguably, a forerunner of modern political Zionism. Rav Samson Raphael Hirsch, in his commentary on this *parshah* and elsewhere in his writings, articulates his position on the matter. Regarding the relationship between Torah observance and the Land of Israel, Rav Hirsch writes, "The Torah was given in the wilderness to teach that it was not in any particular age or land to which the elevation of the human race is attached." Further along he writes that the Holy Land to which Avraham had relocated "had been promised to him for the future of his people, and the first experience he made there was: *famine*, and the second: *war*. Neither material abundance nor political independence was inherent in the land itself."

What emerges from Rav Hirsch's writings is the distinct impression that had he lived to see the development of the Zionist movement he would have been one of its fiercest opponents. This is no secret to anyone devoted to his works. (It may well be that had he witnessed the destruction of European Jewry, his thoughts on the matter would have changed. But that is a mere conjecture.) Nonetheless, it is important to recognize that Rav Hirsch's feelings about an independent State of Israel are not the result of negativism, but come rather from an abiding faith in the unique relationship the Jewish people have with G-d.

Rav Hirsch points out that whereas all other religions sprang from constitutions composed by man, "Jewish Law — the Torah — is the only one that did not emanate from the people whose constitution it was to form."

"Therefore," Rav Hirsch concludes, "all other religions and laws... must change, advance and progress with time.... But the Jewish 'religion' and the Jewish Law did not emanate from the contemporary convictions of human beings.... They are given by G-d and contain that, which, according to the Will of G-d, should be man's conviction in all ages." To Rav Hirsch, loyalty to Torah is the defining issue, at the core of the Jewish people. All else is secondary.

Following this line of thought one concludes that, no matter what position the various Torah-observant camps hold on Zionism, secular studies and other wrenching issues, our common love for Torah unites us. The overriding bond of Torah should put all other issues at a distant second. Circumstances in Israel force us to realize more than ever that Torah must be our blueprint for survival. May we merit to see the cherished prize of *achdus* in our time.

Rabbi Jonathan I. Rosenblatt

THE BIRTH OF YITZCHAK IS ANTICIPATED WITH PRAYERS, PROPHECIES and Divine promises. Moreover, his birth and upbringing are prefigured by the trials and errors of his father's two earlier son figures

—one a nephew and the other a concubine's child. The patterns and mistaken assumptions which cost Avraham the fidelity of both Yishmael and Lot also served as parenting instructors. The course adjustments in the wake of these disappointments contributed to the excellence of the third attempt. And although there can be no doubting the primacy of transmission through Yitzchak, the Torah's deference to Yishmael and to Lot's descendants suggests that even a failed son of Avraham is esteemed.

A careful reading of a small passage in *Lech Lecha* may illustrate how a crucial element in faith-training is discovered. Early in the *parshah*, Avraham answers the Divine call: "And Avram went as the Lord had spoken to him, and Lot went with him (*ito*)." When Avram moves to Canaan, Lot is carried along by the very same verb which carries Sarai.

Then comes the famine which drives the holy couple down to Egypt, testing their faith in the G-d who had just promised them Canaan. Beside the traumatic encounter with Pharaoh, the Egyptian detour rattles Avraham's security in his mission. The Abarbanel notes that despite the vast wealth — accounted in flocks and silver and gold — the *nefesh,* the proselytes, are missing.

For this reason, the Patriarch hastens to his earlier altar and to the work of calling out the name of the true G-d. He returns *"lemaasav,"* which the Malbim understands to refer to his regular missionary circuit.

Then the Torah moves to pick up another thread: the fortunes of Lot. Though Avraham returns safely to his mission and his G-d, the Torah subtly notes that his sojourn in Egypt did have one casualty: Lot. *"Vegam leLot haholeich es Avram."* A distance has grown between the nephew and his uncle, the Netziv notes. All they share in common now is rich holdings of property. The disputes between their shepherds is a projection of their own loss of spiritual kinship, and until Lot has gone his own way the Heavenly voice is absent from Avraham's camp.

The mature Avraham was able to put the blandishments of Egypt's rich, sensuous civilization in perspective. He remained steadfast and unblemished. But the young disciple, his roots yet shallow in the soil of faith, was not so lucky. True, he dutifully returned to Canaan with his uncle (for which the Abarbanel applauds him). Nevertheless, when his eyes scanned the landscape of the Promised Land, it was clear what he was searching for — Egypt! "And Lot lifted up his eyes and saw all the plain of the Jordan, that it was all well watered — like a garden of the L-rd, *like the land of Egypt*." The eyes which chose Sodom and Amorrah were no longer the eyes of a son of Avraham.

The lesson of environmental influence was not wasted. Yitzchak was destined to live out his entire life in the Land of Israel as an *olah temimah*. Avraham did not repeat the mistake that had cost him his precious nephew. There would be other lessons — the inexorable influence of Noach's designations of blessing and curse, the absolute necessity of righteous parenting from both father *and* mother, the existence of many ways in the service of Hashem beside the way of *chessed*. All these lessons would accrue, through painful experience and absolute devotion, to the eternal credit of the future generations which twinkled as stars in Avraham's heaven, to us.

_____ *Rabbi Reuven Tradburks*

MINHAGIM, JEWISH CUSTOMS, HAVE SUBTLE MEANINGS, AND THOSE meanings often contain nuances that ought not be overlooked. Two aspects of the blessings of the *haftarah* reading, for example, have always struck me as unusual. The blessing before the *haftarah* is sung in the minor key — a reflective, serious tone. Yet the blessings chanted after the *haftarah* are sung in the major key — bright and joyful.

Furthermore, four blessings are recited after the reading of the *haftarah*. However, only one blessing is said beforehand. During the Torah reading, too, only one blessing is recited both before and after each section. Why are the blessings after the *haftarah* sung in a bright and cheerful tone? And why do we conclude with three extra blessings?

The answer, I believe, stems from the prophecies recorded in the *haftaros*. The Torah, by contrast, doesn't generally deal with prophecy. Aside from the predictions in *Parshas Bechukosai* and *Parshas Ki Savo* of our punishment and exile from the Land resulting from our lack of loyalty to the Torah, there is very little prediction of the future in the Torah.

The *haftaros*, however, are entirely different. Most are taken from the great books of the Prophets and relate to the future redemption of our people, our return to the Land and our overt perception of the Divine in that time. They engage our *emunah,* our trust in Hashem. The *haftaros* paint all sorts of pictures for the future of mankind in general and the Jewish people in particular. In order to express our confidence in these Divine promises, we sing the blessings in a confident and joyful tune.

The blessings themselves speak of these promises. The first two blessings after the *haftarah* praise G-d as trustworthy. We believe in these prophecies, and through their reading and the blessings that follow we amplify that belief. We are confident that all of G-d's promises will be fulfilled. Our confidence in Divine predictions is what connects us to Avraham Avinu, who never saw the fulfillment of Hashem's promise to him that his descendants would inherit the Land of Canaan.

Avraham was given other promises by Hashem that he did see — you will be famous, you will be wealthy, you will have children. But the one that was the essence of his relationship with Hashem — the promise of the Land — was never realized in his lifetime. In fact, Hashem told him this; he would not live to see it happen. This is one of the great images of Avraham —the one who trusted in the promises of Hashem, knowing that he would never see their fulfillment.

We, who have lived to see the fulfillment of many promises, have much more reason to sing the blessings of the *haftarah* in a joyful manner, confident that many more promises will yet be fulfilled.

_____ *Rabbi Howard Zack*

"AND G-D SAID TO AVRAM: GO FOR YOURSELF FROM YOUR LAND, from your birthplace and from your father's house, to the land that I will show you."

How Avraham ascended to the stage where Hashem appeared to him is not mentioned in the Torah, but the Midrash is full of stories of a youthful Avraham's journey, how he studied nature and local social practices until he became convinced of Hashem's existence. The Midrash gives many accounts of Avraham's debates with the people of his generation regarding his newly discovered G-d. They did not take kindly to his pronouncements and ultimately threw him into a fiery furnace — from which he emerged, miraculously, unscathed.

None of this background, however, is recorded in the actual text of the Torah. Instead, we find Hashem commanding a 75-year-old man to uproot himself from familiar ground and undertake an undefined journey. Why does the Torah choose to introduce us to our Patriarch in this manner?

Allow me to suggest that Hashem wanted to clarify at the very outset that Judaism is fundamentally different from other faiths. In Judaism, deed takes precedence over creed; action is more important than belief. Faith is not the goal of Judaism — it is an assumption, a foundation upon which our religious lifestyle is built. Faith is not the end result of Judaism; it is the beginning.

In Judaism, salvation comes through action and correct behavior. Perhaps that is why there is only one *mitzvah* of belief among the 613 Biblical commandments. It is the first of the Ten Commandments, "I am the L-rd your G-d." All the rest are commandments of action or inaction.

It follows, therefore, that while Avraham became the very epitome of human faith in G-d, he is introduced as a simple man of action. His faith is already there and secured. How did he arrive at it? For Avraham, it was as obvious as creation. He saw it in the rising and setting of the sun, in the cycles of nature and in the order of life.

But beyond faith is action. Now it is time to go forward, Hashem tells Avraham. "Go for yourself from your land and from your birthplace." *Targum Onkelos* translates this last phrase, "Go from your youth." It is time to move on. Faith is indeed the primary prerequisite for a religious personality; but only correct action makes a person pious.

פרשת וירא
Parshas Vayeira

_____ *Rabbi Moshe Bomzer*

EVERY TIME I RELEARN THE STORY OF THE *AKEIDAH,* I AM PERPLEXED by Avraham's response to G-d's command that he take his son, Yitzchak, and sacrifice him. The normally dialogical, reactive Avraham remains silent. Not a word of question or protest. Why?

Rav Yosef Dov Soloveitchik, *zt"l,* suggests a reason for Avraham's silence by distinguishing between two kinds of prayer: community prayer and personal prayer. These two types of prayer are illustrated in the manner Moshe Rabbeinu approaches G-d. When it comes to the needs of the Jewish people, as after the sin of the Golden Calf, Moshe remains in Heaven forty days and forty nights until G-d assures him, "I have forgiven them." But when it comes to his personal needs, as when his sister, Miriam, fell ill, Moshe utters only five words: "O G-d, please heal her."

What is true of Moshe is true of Avraham as well. When it comes to the destruction of Sodom, with the possibility that innocent men, women and children will die, Avraham confronts G-d and asks, "Will the Judge of the world not act justly? Will the Almighty destroy the innocent together with the wicked?" For the community, Avraham musters all his rhetorical skills to reverse the verdict. But when it comes to his personal fate, he remains silent, accepting.

The Rav goes one step further. Avraham, perhaps, felt he had brought this situation upon himself, as the *Akeidah* follows Avraham's run-in with Avimelech, king of Gerar. Avimelech, having been told that Avraham's wife, Sarah, was his sister, brings her into his harem. G-d then visits him in a dream and informs him that he is dealing with a married woman. Avimelech asks Avraham why he hadn't told him the truth. "Because surely the fear of G-d is not in this place," Avraham responds. He had suspected they would kill him to get to his wife, so he lied.

Avimelech gives Sarah back to Avraham and makes him a rich man and "Avraham remained in the land of Gerar many days." But why did Avraham choose to stay in a society that he described as lacking fear of G-d? Would he not be affected by such an environment?

Avraham, therefore, had to be tested to prove that he still feared G-d. His submission to the command of the *Akeidah* accomplished this. "For now I know," the angel tells him after the event, "that you fear G-d."

"Avraham Avinu was tested with ten trials and he passed them all," states the Mishnah in *Avos*, "to show how much love Avraham Avinu had" for G-d.

Fear of G-d and love of G-d are the two fundamental attitudes one needs in approaching the Almighty. Only an individual who combines both can become the father of the Jewish nation. Our actions, we hope, will present us as those who love and revere G-d, and the tests of the personal *Akeidahs* in our lives will stand us in good stead in the Heavenly court.

_____ *Rabbi Berel Wein*

Parshas *Vayeira* contains the episode of *Akeidas Yitzchak*, the seeming martyrdom of Yitzchak in fulfillment of G-d's command to his father, Avraham. Even though martyrdom and the history of the Jewish people are inextricably linked, actual martyrdom is not the preferred goal of Jewish life. Rather, the Torah bids Jews "*Vechai bahem,*" to live by the precepts of Torah and to attempt to avoid having to die because of them.

Thus, the Talmud and Jewish law prescribe the actual circumstances where voluntary martyrdom (an oxymoron, if there ever was one) is permitted. Maimonides, in his famous code of Jewish law, *Mishneh Torah,* states that one has no right to give up one's life, even for what one feels to be valid and moral reasons, if the circumstances of the situation are not in exact conformance with the halachic norms established in the Talmud.

Dying for the sake of Torah and the G-d of Israel is considered a *kiddush Hashem,* a sanctification of G-d's name. However, living for the sake of Torah and the G-d of Israel is an even greater *kiddush Hashem.* Nevertheless, throughout the centuries, millions of Jews have died for being Jews. This ocean composed of the blood and tears of Jewish martyrs reached flood tide in our century.

A history professor of mine once characterized Jewish history to me as "martyrdom and books" but that is a distorted and dangerous over-simplification. Even in the midst of martyrdom, the Rabbis of Israel laid stress upon life and not death, upon surviving and prospering and not succumbing and disappearing.

In the *parshah,* we see this emphasis on life. After the *Akeidah,* Avraham and Yitzchak renew their efforts at spiritual attainment and positive influence in their society. Instead of being paralyzed and traumatized by the *Akeidah,* Avraham and Yitzchak view their Divine deliverance from actual martyrdom as a call to greater efforts on their part to increase life and to improve its spiritual and moral quality.

Avraham and Yitzchak are prepared for martyrdom if that is G-d's demand, but they see their future accomplishments in perpetuating-family, society, righteousness and holiness through living. As such, they are the archetypical "martyrs" of Jewish existence.

The Talmud relates to us that when the great sage of Israel, Rabbi Chanina ben Tradyon, was executed by the Romans for the crime of teaching Torah, he was wrapped in a *Sefer Torah* and set ablaze. Yet he proclaimed, "The parchment burns but the letters float undamaged in the air." Parchment burns, bodies decay, empires fall, civilizations wither, but the "letters" — the sanctity of life and human values, of G-dly precepts and holy traditions — are indestructible.

Jewish history is not only martyrdom and books; it is life and energy, creativity and holiness, service to G-d and man, Torah and tradition. It is that sort of life and history that makes the *Akeidah* so memorable and relevant to Jews of all times and circumstances. Certainly our generation, raised in the shadow of the most fearsome *Akeidah* in Jewish history, should rededicate itself to the strengthening of Jewish family, community, Torah and life. The G-d of Avraham and Yitzchak will not allow us lesser goals.

PARSHAS VAYEIRA RELATES THAT AVRAHAM AVINU, UPON HEARING that G-d was planning to destroy the cities of Sodom and Amorrah, proceeded to pray and beg Hashem to spare the cities. Why, ask many of the commentators, did Avraham cry out on behalf of the people of Sodom and Amorrah? The Rambam, in *Hilchos Teshuvah,* clearly states that the scales of Divine judgment apply to cities and countries and, in fact, to the entire world, just as they do to humans. Surely Avraham knew that cities as debauched as Sodom and Amorrah deserved to be destroyed!

Furthermore, we are taught that Avraham embodied the essence of kindness. Sodom was unquestionably the antithesis of Avraham's *raison d'etre.* It would seem that nothing should have given Avraham more satisfaction than seeing these cities destroyed. And yet, he prayed for their salvation.

Rabbi Noson Tzvi Finkel, *zt"l,* points out that for Avraham to feel satisfaction in the destruction of these people would only prove that he himself had adopted their ways — the very nature that he so detested. Avraham's wish was that the *wickedness* of Sodom be destroyed, not the people.

At the start of every month we repeat the words of the Psalmist, asking G-d, "*Yitamu chata'im min ha'aretz,*" normally translated as "May sinners cease from the world." But that's not correct. In the Talmud, Bruria points out, "*Chotim lo ne'emar*" — the verse does not ask for sinners to be destroyed, but for *chata'im* to be destroyed. It is the sin that is detested, not the sinner.

Our forebears established the Jewish spiritual DNA, the template for the soul of every Jew who followed. The remarkable sensitivity and concern that was the essence of Avraham has been one of the defining characteristics of Jews throughout the millennia. But something seems to have changed. We are living in a time of unprecedented arrogance. A half a century ago, when European Orthodoxy went up the chimneys of Auschwitz, American Orthodox Jews were skeptical of their future. Never did they imagine that fifty years later there would be more Jews studying in yeshivos then ever before.

Never would they have imagined that fifty years later *The Wall Street Journal* would run a front-page article declaring that the only movement in Judaism showing vibrancy, growth and long-term viability is the Orthodox community. The arrogance is well earned, yet it is out of place for the children of Avraham. We have no spiritual leeway for arrogance. Our Sages teach, in a play on words, that the splendor (*gayus*) of Torah can easily slip into arrogance (*ga'avah*). That arrogance distorts the Torah to the point that a young man can decide that it is okay to kill another Jew based on his own perverted understanding of *Halachah*. That arrogance distorts the Torah to the point that an Orthodox man in the street, upon being asked by a CNN reporter to respond to the murder, can say, "I wish it had happened sooner."

Arrogance and insensitivity are character traits that are not inherently Jewish. We are, by nature, the very opposite of those features. Our nature is to be like Avraham, to be concerned with the fate of every person in the world, certainly with the fate of every Jew, Orthodox, Conservative, or Reform. We must re-train ourselves to feel anguish, not anger, when we see *chilul Shabbos*. We have to cease seeing the Jewish world as a collection of political and theological camps, and see it as a nation of Jews. Period.

Strident opposition to non-Torah "movements" is a given. However, we can't lose sight of the fact that a Jew is a Jew is a Jew. If Avraham Avinu could find it in his heart to care about the fate of the people of Sodom, is it too much for us to care about each other — regardless of affiliation?

Let us commit ourselves to redoubling our efforts on behalf of our people, to strengthening the Avraham Avinu that is in each and every one of us, through sensitivity and care for each and every Jew. And as a result may we be granted a year of peace and unity, one which will herald the arrival of the *Mashiach,* swiftly, in our days.

_____ *Rabbi Chaim Steinmetz*

WHY DO CERTAIN NATIONS THRIVE WHILE OTHERS DISAPPEAR? PUNdits and historians will tell you about political, economic and military factors. However, our Torah informs us that ethical factors are far more consequential. Powerful nations fall if they are immoral, while weak ones succeed if they maintain moral excellence.

The Hebrew word *tzachak*, meaning to laugh, is employed several times in *Parshas Vayeira*, most notably in relation to the birth and naming of our Patriarch Yitzchak. The term is also used when Lot tells his sons-in-law that their home city of Sodom is about to be destroyed. They do not believe him, for his words are "like a joke (*kimitzacheik*) in their eyes."

To a social or political scientist, the possibility that a wealthy super-power like Sodom will disappear or that an elderly couple will produce the future regional superpower seems ludicrous. But this strange outcome is precisely what occurs. Avraham and Sarah have a child, through whom they become the ancestors of *Klal Yisrael.*

Meanwhile, the mighty city of Sodom is destroyed. The double reference to laughter demonstrates that both events are improbable to the point of being funny. Why were Avraham and Sarah chosen and Sodom condemned? What factor gave rise to one and led to the other's destruction?

The Torah points to hospitality: Avraham invites nomads, who turn out to be angels, into his home and is told of his future as the father of the Jewish people. Lot, too, invites angels into his home and is saved from destruction. But the people of Sodom, who sought to abuse Lot's guests, are destroyed. Even Lot's wife, who was half-hearted in her hospitality, does not survive.

The citizens of Sodom not only act violently toward strangers; they express contempt for justice as well. "Are you, the stranger, going to judge us?" one of the Sodomites asks Lot.

Avraham, on the other hand, demonstrates his just behavior by arguing with G-d over His decision to destroy Sodom. Hospitality and justice elevate Avraham and Sarah to the beginnings of a great nation, while intolerance and misanthropy destroy Sodom.

It is "not strength, not might, but G-d's spirit," in the words of the prophet Zachariah, that lifts and lowers nations. The moral and spiritual course chosen by a people, and nothing else, determines its future. The Torah realizes that this sounds funny, but funny is also the name of the first Jewish child, Yitzchak.

פרשת חיי שרה
Parshas Chayei Sarah

_____ Rabbi Dale Polakoff

T HE OPENING *PESUKIM* OF *PARSHAS CHAYEI SARAH* DESCRIBE AVRA-
ham's reaction to his wife, Sarah's, death. The Torah records that
he "came to eulogize Sarah and to cry for her." This order is intriguing
in the light of a statement by the Talmud in *Moeid Katan.* Analyzing the
pasuk in *Yirmiyahu,* "Cry not for the dead and do not bemoan him," the
Talmud concludes that there is an appropriate period of mourning —
three days of crying, seven days of eulogy — beyond which one should
not mourn.

From the Talmud it is apparent that crying is the more immediate
response to death, but the order describing Avraham's behavior is
precisely the opposite. How is one to understand Avraham's reaction?
The Talmud directs us based on the normal cycle of mourning. As
crying is our immediate reaction to loss, a burst of emotional grief,
it comes first. One cries even before the full weight of loss has sunk
in.

Eulogy is the next step. It is one of perspective, of trying to fully grasp
what has been lost and of trying to convey that loss to others. If crying is
inwardly directed, then eulogy is outwardly directed. When one mourns,
his emphasis is first on himself, through crying, then on others, through
eulogy.

Avraham's order was different. He realized the importance of con-
veying to others the meaning of Sarah's life, and he did so even before acknowledging his own personal grief. At her death, he had an

opportunity to continue to teach and inspire others through her life's story. Thus, "Avraham came to eulogize Sarah" first, and then "to cry for her."

Following Avraham's example, Rav Yosef Dov Soloveitchik, *zt"l,* saw the teaching of social justice and moral consciousness at every opportunity as one of the prime responsibilities of Jewish leadership. In a *shiur* describing the responsibilities of the *Kehunah,* the Priesthood, which included teaching moral consciousness, the Rav related a story about his grandfather, Rav Chaim Brisker, *zt"l.*

The renowned rav of a certain community died on the same day as a poor woman. According to *Halachah,* she should have been buried first, but the winter days were short and the second burial would not take place until evening, minimizing the number of people who could come. Since few people would come for the poor woman's burial anyway, it was reasoned that she be buried after the rav.

Rav Chaim was adamant. Though the late rav was a great supporter of his and had played a role in installing him as rav of Brisk, Rav Chaim insisted that the *chevra kadisha* bury the poor woman first. Such was his dedication to social justice and moral consciousness.

Every Jew, the Rav believed, has the capacity to achieve the level of responsibility placed upon the *Kehunah.* Each of us has in our lives opportunities to teach others lessons of moral responsibility and social justice. The challenge, which Avraham met, is to rise to those occasions.

_____ *Betty Ehrenberg*

P ARSHAS CHAYEI SARAH IS A DRAMA-FILLED ACCOUNT OF THE STEPS taken to insure the transmission of Sarah Imeinu's legacy to the next generation. Not only are many of the larger issues highlighted (such as land rights in Israel, the acquisition of *me'aras hamachpeilah,* and its significance to our people), but many of the personal ones as well. The criteria by which one chooses a mate are borne out by the account of the search for Yitzchak's bride.

Many of the commentaries ask the question: why did Avraham Avinu instruct his trusted servant Eliezer to find a suitable match for Yitzchak from among the people of his birthplace, Charan, while simultaneously warning him against choosing a Canaanite woman? While it was true that the Canaanites were idolaters, weren't the dwellers of Charan idolaters as well?

Many, including the Ran and the Sochatchover, point out that Avraham rejected the Canaanites because, unlike the people of Charan, they were morally corrupt in addition to being idolaters. Hashem had willed *Eretz Yisrael* to Avraham and his descendants, the *Meshech Chachmah* adds, on the condition that the Jewish people live according to the high moral standards of the Torah. Avraham could not allow the assimilation of Canaanite values and their sinful way of life into his family. Yitzchak, in turn, commands Yaakov not to take a Canaanite wife so that he too may merit the inheritance of *Eretz Yisrael*.

Other commentaries note that Avraham was concerned about the proximity of the Canaanites. If Yitzchak married a Canaanite woman, she would continue to live near her family and would still be exposed to the influences of *avodah zarah*. A bride from a distant land, such as Charan, however, would be separated from her family and their customs and would live according to Avraham and Yitzchak's standards. Eliezer prays for specific signs to identify the young woman, signs of a kind heart, a generous spirit, a concern for others and a willingness to go out of her way to help.

Significantly, this *shidduch* fulfilled the expectations of both sides. Rivkah and her family knew of Avraham and Yitzchak's greatness and the privilege of marrying into their family. Rivkah, herself, immediately recognizes Yitzchak's strong spiritual presence and impressive personality, even from a distance.

And Yitzchak loves Rivkah when he sees her greatness. The Brisker Rav, *zt"l,* quotes Onkelos's translation of the verse: "And Yitzchak brought her to the tent of Sarah, his mother, and he took Rivkah as a wife." Yitzchak took Rivkah as his wife after he saw that her deeds, her goodness and kindness, matched those of Sarah.

Eliezer had already recounted to Yitzchak all the marvels and miracles that happened on his trip. Indeed, as Rashi explains, the entire mission was a litany of miracles; his journey to Charan was shortened; Rivkah appeared immediately; she possessed the noble character he sought; Besuel, her father, who had tried to delay her departure, was killed by the Angel of Death, fulfilling Avraham's words, "And [G-d] will send His angel ahead and you shall take a wife for my son from there." Yet, in spite of all these miracles, when did Yitzchak marry Rivkah? Only after he saw that she was a *tzadeikes* like his mother. Only then.

The story of this *shidduch* and its lessons continue to be transmitted to us, Yitzchak and Rivkah's children. Their legacy — their Torah way of life — is our inheritance.

_____ *Rabbi Shlomo Horowitz*

T OWARD THE END OF *PARSHAS CHAYEI SARAH,* THE TORAH TELLS US that "Yitzchak went out *lasuach* — to meditate — in the field before evening." Our Sages comment that Yitzchak went to the fields in order to pray *("Sichah,"* our Sages say, "refers only to prayer"), and thus was instituted *Tefillas Minchah,* the afternoon prayer that all Jews are obliged to recite daily.

But why did Yitzchak turn to the fields in order to pray? ask the commentaries. Didn't he have a house in which to pray? *Tosafos* answers that the field in which Yitzchak prayed was no ordinary field. It was on Mount Moriah, first designated as a place of prayer by Adam Harishon and later consecrated by Yitzchak at the *Akeidah,* where he perceived the *Shechinah.* Centuries later it became the site of the *Beis Hamikdash.*

No ordinary field was this field, no ordinary prayer was this prayer. The Talmud advises us to be especially vigilant about praying *Tefillas Minchah,* for G-d is especially attentive to our prayers in the afternoon. Eliyahu's plea to Hashem was answered only in the afternoon. Why is *Tefillas Minchah* so important and what makes it so effective?

The *Tur* links *Minchah's* prominence to its timing. It comes at a time when people are most apt to be preoccupied with their daily work and business affairs. In order to pray, one has to pause and concentrate on his dependence upon the Creator, Who is the source of all blessing.

This abrupt suspension of daily activity is far from easy to do. It is much easier to pray in the morning before one starts out for work. We wake up refreshed, happy in the thought that we have been granted yet another day of life. We are in the proper mood for prayer and offer thanksgiving for our very existence on earth. This is the meaning of the *pasuk* in *Eichah, "Chadashim labekarim rabbah emunasecha."* Our faith in Hashem is greatest at the renewal of life every morning. Likewise, at night, with a productive day behind us, it is easy to take a few moments to thank G-d for the blessings of the day.

In the afternoon, the situation is much different. We are, like Yitzchak, in the fields, in the middle of our work with its attendant 101 problems, frustrations and aggravations. Then, in the midst of it all, we are called upon to pray — to interrupt the pursuit of our livelihood, to suspend our seeming dependence on the strength of our hands. We instead turn to Hashem in prayer.

Tefillas Minchah testifies to man's humility in the presence of G-d. This offering of worship and devotion also accounts for the prayer's name. Some assume that the word *minchah* means afternoon. This isn't so. The word, used often in the Torah, means a gift, an offering. Indeed, a prayer recited in the afternoon is a precious gift, readily accepted by G-d.

This is the legacy of Yitzchak Avinu — in the field. Whether you are in your office, at your shop, on the road, or at home, stop and take a break of inspiration. Pray *Minchah* with *kavannah* and then be confident that Hashem will hearken to your *tefillah*.

_____ *Rabbi Yitzchak Chinn*

PARSHAS CHAYEI SARAH PROVIDES THE BLUEPRINT FOR JEWISH MARriage, telling generations of Jews what to search for in a proper mate. The *parshah* begins with Avraham purchasing (*"vayikach"*) a field from Ephron the Hitite, which contained the cave in which he would bury his beloved wife, Sarah. This verse is used in the Talmud to help define the legal contract of marriage, which is introduced with the phrase, *"Ki yikach ish ishah* — When a man takes a wife. . ."

This word, *kichah,* establishes a permanence: Just as the money exchanged gave Avraham the field for all times, so too does the gift to the bride create a marriage, hopefully for all times. Even death does not end the bond between man and wife. Avraham wanted a burial plot big enough for himself and his family. He wanted to be buried next to his wife. As they shared this world, so too they share the next.

Marriage has permanence. Avraham's respect for his wife Sarah is evident in this *chessed shel emes,* this true kindness he shows her after death. His concern for her eternity is as strong as it was when she was alive. Fittingly, the next verses detail Avraham's search for a wife for his son, Yitzchak. Having experienced life under his parents' marriage, Yitzchak is now ready for his own partnership.

What is the obligation of parents in finding a proper match for their children? Alas, so many children think they can do it alone, and they make horrible blunders because of their personal subjectivity.

When my children were ready for marriage, I asked Rav Yaakov Kamenetsky, *zt"l,* "Rebbe, what should I look for in a mate for my children?"

His wise and thoughtful answer was, "They should have two qualities, *gezunt un gut,* health and goodness, for these are the two things we give over to our children."

Reb Yaakov was telling me the lesson of this *parshah.* Avraham knows the rock from whence he was hewn. His family has the physical strength to endure life's challenges. Avraham and Sarah also have the quality of goodness, of embracing and welcoming strangers into their home. They have compassion and pity — essential ingredients for building a Jewish home.

Avraham sought the same for his son. Though Rivkah's family worshipped idols, Avraham understood that *midos* are more important than ideology. Mind-sets can be changed. Ideas can be changed. Philosophies can be changed. Rav Shraga Feivel Mendlowitz, *zt"l,* often used the phrase "the mind is elastic." The mind can be stretched from one extreme to another.

Midos, however, are another matter. Rav Yisroel Salanter taught that changing one *midah* is harder then mastering the entire Talmud.

It is easier to change ideology than to change *midos.* Avraham knew that Rivkah possessed good *midos* and would fit the requirements of Jewish marriage, a bond that goes even beyond the grave. The home a couple builds, the children they raise is for eternity.

In our age of semipermanence, in which there are too many disrupted families, a generation that Dr. Abraham Twerski calls "the throw-away generation — if it doesn't work, don't fix it; just throw it away and get a new one," in these times and in this atmosphere, *Chayei Sarah* comes as a refreshing lesson of endurance.

פרשת תולדות
Parshas Toldos

_____ *Rabbi Shalom Baum*

O F THE THREE PATRIARCHS, YITZCHAK IS THE MOST CRYPTIC. Much of his life is clouded by mystery, for, in contrast with his father, Avraham, and his son, Yaakov, relatively little space in the Torah is dedicated to his life. And even when the events of his life are detailed, he is usually not the main character. The *Akeidah,* for example, is re-called more commonly to dramatize the greatness of Avraham than that of Yitzchak.

One story the Torah does tell is in *Parshas Toldos,* where Yitzchak reopens the wells that his father once dug. But this event gives us little insight into his personality; its relevance is, on the surface, ques-tionable. Nonetheless, Rav Yosef Dov Soloveitchik, *zt"l,* argues that the amount of text dedicated to Yitzchak should be viewed not as a diminu-tion of his greatness, but rather as an indication of his unique service to G-d.

Kabbalah assigns to each of the Patriarchs one of G-d's attributes: Avraham represents *chessed,* kindness; Yaakov represents *emes,* truth; and Yitzchak represents *gevurah,* strength. Avraham's trait, kindness, the Rav points out, expresses itself in expansion. Kindness is a move-ment away from oneself and toward others.

Yitzchok's trait, strength, by contrast, is a retreat into a private world — with G-d as one's companion. Yitzchak remained in private commu-nion with G-d for much of his life and because much of his life was concealed from the masses, the Torah tells us little about him.

Then Yitzchak marries Rivkah. Yitzchak waited until after the *Akeidah* to marry because until that moment he belonged exclusively to G-d. Once he was offered on the altar, his relationship with G-d reached its peak, and the man of *gevurah* could expand outside his insular world. At this point, says the Rav, Yitzchak begins to be less private. He still retains his *gevurah* but now an element of *chessed,* the trait that defined his father, becomes apparent.

The Torah tells the story of the wells, writes the Ramban, even though it appears to be of no benefit to the reader or to the honor of Yitzchak. But the significance of this account becomes clearer as one looks at the expansion of Yitzchak's personality. When Avraham lived with the Philistines, he had dug many wells, but the Philistines plugged up those wells. Yitzchak not only reopened those wells, but also restored their names according to the names Avraham had given them. Yitzchak's actions signified his transition to a more public role, continuing the legacy of this father.

Yitzchak also dug three new wells. The Philistines objected to the first two, and so he called them *Eisek,* meaning contention, and *Sitnah,* meaning enmity. But the third well caused no controversy and he called it *Rechovos,* meaning spacious. These three names allude to the three Temples, writes the Ramban. The first two were destroyed by our enemies because of contention and enmity, but the third will be built with no opposition. Then G-d will make our borders more spacious.

The once private Yitzchak not only reached out to a spouse but has offered hope to hundreds of generations.

_____ *Nathan J. Diament*

P ARSHAS TOLDOS INTRODUCES OUR PATRIARCH YAAKOV AS WELL AS his brother Eisav, and, from the outset, tips us off to the coming conflict between them. The Torah tells of their "struggle" within their mother's womb, and, as young adults, describes them very differently. Eisav is "a hunter, a man of the field," while Yaakov is "*ish tam,* who sits in tents." These textual descriptions, Rashi and Ibn Ezra point out, indicate that Eisav is a "trickster," a man not to be trusted, while Yaakov is a "simple" or "naive" shepherd, who spends his days studying Torah.

Yet, the comments of these *Rishonim* (which echo those of our Sages) seem to be at odds with the simple understanding of the narrative. Consider, as events of the *parshah* unfold, who is the trickster and who is the victim.

Even as they were being born, Yaakov grasped Eisav's ankle, trying to force his way out of the womb first. Later, as young adults, Eisav returns from a day of hunting famished and exhausted, begging his brother for food. Yaakov demands Eisav's birthright in exchange for some soup. Then, when Rivkah proposes that Yaakov disguise himself as Eisav in order to "steal" his blessing from Yitzchak, Yaakov protests — not because of the deception involved, but because he fears getting caught and consequently cursed by his father.

Nevertheless, despite these indications of Yaakov's trickery and Eisav's victimhood, our Sages find indications of Eisav's evil. They point to his readiness to sell the birthright as well as to the wives he took, who aggravated his mother, Rivkah. Thus it seems all the more amazing in light of our Sages's insights that Yitzchak seems oblivious to Eisav's evil and Yaakov's goodness such that he sought to confer his blessing upon Eisav.

How are we to understand Yaakov's early actions, Yitzchak's plan to bless Eisav, Yaakov's theft of the blessing, and the subsequent confrontation that he faced — all in a manner that gives us insight into this Patriarch and leaves us, his children, with a message?

As noted by the Netziv, Yitzchak proposed to bless Eisav with *birkas ha'aretz* — physical plenitude and mastery over the physical world. Reserved for Yaakov, and conferred upon him by Yitzchak before he fled to Lavan's house, was *birkas Avraham* — the blessing that Avraham received ensuring that his descendants would be Hashem's chosen nation.

Yitzchak had no reason to think that one of his sons would be rejected; he believed they would both lead this chosen nation as partners, with Eisav as general, mastering the physical world, and Yaakov as high priest, carrying on the spiritual legacy. However, Rivkah, the mother of these two brothers and, importantly, reared as the sister of Lavan (as emphasized in the second verse of the *parshah*), knew that such a partnership was impossible. She understood that

Yaakov needed both blessings — to combine spiritual strength with mastery over the physical world — in order to be the father of the Jewish nation.

Accordingly, she orchestrated the "theft" of the physical blessing in a context wherein Yaakov would be introduced to his destiny — to be a person with "the voice of Yaakov" but also with "the hands of Eisav." She thus wanted Yaakov to undergo an apprenticeship with her brother, Lavan, the master trickster, so that he would know how to combine these traits. He achieved mastery over the physical world, the *Kli Yakar* points out, when he surpassed Lavan's ability to beguile his adversaries.

After this "education," the fully developed Yaakov is commanded by Hashem to return to Canaan, whereupon he wrestles with Eisav's angel and is given a new name: Yisrael. This new name demonstrates his completed evolution, a name by which we, his descendants, are called: *Bnei Yisrael.* We too must struggle to achieve this synthesis, to master the physical world while remaining true to the spiritual legacy of our Patriarchs — to combine the "the voice of Yaakov" with "the hands of Eisav."

_____ *Rabbi Evan Shore*

MANY TIMES IN THE TORAH, THE SIMPLE EXPLANATION OF A VERSE only scratches its surface. A deeper meaning lies below. In *Parshas Toldos,* Eisav sells his firstborn rights to his younger brother Yaakov, saying, "Behold I am going to die, so what does a birthright do for me?" He saw the birthright as so inconsequential that he sold it for a bowl of beans.

From the beginning, Eisav had doubts whether his birthright would be an aid or a hindrance to him. Would it extend his life or end it prematurely? Rashi tells us that Yaakov told him of the punishments and deaths that are dependent upon the birthright. Eisav replied, "If I am going to die because of it, why would I desire it?"

But why was Eisav fearful of an early death? He was, as the Torah says, "a man of the field," who lived by the sword. The Talmud tells us that on the day Eisav came home weary and tired, he committed five transgressions: he cohabited with an engaged woman; he killed a human being; he denied the existence of G-d; he denied the tenet of the revival of the dead; and he spurned his birthright. These actions describe a person who lived a dangerous life with little fear of death. To Eisav, the mere fact that the birthright came with serious obligations and severe punishments should have been of no consequence.

Thus, there must be a deeper meaning behind Eisav's decision to turn his back on his birthright. The *Daas Zekeinim Mebaalei Tosafos* tells us Eisav returned home weary that day because he had killed none other than the mighty hunter, Nimrod. Eisav wanted to hunt in Nimrod's fields and was told to leave immediately. This was unacceptable to him and he sought his father, Yitzchak's, advice. Yitzchak told his eldest son that as long as Nimrod lived and wore clothing proclaiming his dominance over all others, Eisav would never be able to overcome him. So Eisav killed him.

What was Eisav's real motive for murdering Nimrod? Not wealth, but power and prestige. For the very same reason, Eisav sold his birthright. Rav Nosson Margolies explains that the Torah's emphasis on Eisav's feelings of being doomed to die accounts for why he sold his birthright. For should he die, the birthright would pass to his children. But Eisav did not care for what he would leave future generations; his only concern was for the here and now — "so what does a birthright do for me?"

Eisav surmised that the birthright was not worth anything because it contained no promise of, or even hope for, lasting power. He needed — he thrived upon — power. He needed to know that he was in a position to exercise control over all those who came into contact with him. To Eisav the birthright had to have both rank and influence. Since it possessed neither, it was, sadly, worthless in his eyes.

As children of Yaakov, we, the *Bnei Yisrael,* are the rightful heirs of the birthright. We understand its value and the influence it gives us in this world. The power and privilege of the *bechorah* lies in its responsibilities, in its sense of duty and destiny. Our mission, to serve our Creator through the performance of *mitzvos* and adherence to His Torah, is here and now. But its powerful effect goes far, far into the future.

T HE TORAH'S STATEMENT IN *PARSHAS TOLDOS* THAT "YITZCHAK
prayed across from (*lenochach*) his wife" raises several questions.
Rabbi Eliyahu Mizrachi asks: How could Yitzchak pray in front
of Rivkah? He would seem to be praying not to G-d but to his wife.
The Maharal of Prague raises the issue of his being distracted by
his wife. Furthermore, why would Yitzchak need to pray across from his
wife? Does G-d need Yitzchak to point out Rivkah?

Rashbam answers that Yitzchak prayed *for* his wife — about her,
but not necessarily in her presence. He did not pray at or to her.
Sforno and Redak maintain that Yitzchak simply stood across from
her when he prayed. Redak claims that he did so in order to stir his
emotions as he prayed. Just as visiting the sick stimulates one's compassion to pray for them, so too did Yitzchak feel that by being in the
presence of Rivkah he would feel more compassion for her and pray
with more devotion.

We are always encouraged to pray for all Jews; there are hardly any
prayers, in fact, that are just for an individual. This fits well with the
notion that prayer replaces the communal sacrifices brought in the
Temple. The daily sacrifice was brought on behalf of all Israel. We too
should pray for all of Israel together.

However, we also are taught that prayers were instituted by our
forefathers, centuries before the Temple. This conception of prayer
addresses the need for individual prayer for individual circumstance.
Jewish prayers emphasize the community over the individual. Our overriding concerns for the Jewish people and the State of Israel often
distract us from the needs of the individual. Our challenge is to maintain our interest and concern for the individual within our universal and
broader concerns.

We have to continue to be concerned with our own personal needs
and the personal needs of others, and not get lost in broad generalities.
We can not allow our communally oriented prayers to distract our
heartfelt concerns for those who are *nochachim,* who stand opposite us
in our own families. We must follow the advice of the Talmud, which

states, "One who has a sick person in his home says [a prayer for him] in the blessing for healing." We need to add our own private prayers to our communal prayers and we must never shy away from pleading the case of the individual within the context of the community.

פרשת ויצא
Parshas Vayeitzei

_____ *Gloria C. Leff*

THE RAMBAN, IN DISCUSSING YOSEF'S EFFORTS TO FIND HIS BROTH-
ers, quotes the maxim, "The decree is true and the diligence is
false" — the efforts of man are in vain if G-d has not decreed their
fulfillment. Nowhere is this statement more in evidence than in *Parshas
Vayeitzei*.

Yaakov meets Rachel at the well and falls in love with her. He agrees
to work for Lavan for seven years for his beloved. Then, on his fateful
wedding night, Leah becomes his wife, and Yaakov has to work another
seven years before he can marry Rachel.

Leah conceives and bears children, while Rachel remains barren. In
his commentary, *Oznayim Latorah*, Rav Zalman Sorotzkin, *zt"l*, points
out that Hashem deliberately opened Leah's womb to notify Yaakov
that Leah was not guilty of deception, that she rightfully deserved to be
his wife. Hashem willed her to be the mother of half of Israel's tribes.

But if Hashem was determined to have Yaakov marry Leah, why did
He not arrange for them to be wed in the natural course of events? Why
was this marriage forced upon Yaakov?

Rav Yosef Dov Soloveitchik, *zt"l*, postulates that Leah could not be
left out of the picture, because she had certain innate characteristics,
which when joined with those of her sister Rachel, would develop and
mold the people of Israel. Leah had a strong, independent personality,
says the Rav. She was a woman with defined goals who would actively
seek their realization. She was not going to wait passively until Yaakov
came to her; she would go to him.

Parshas Vayeitzei / 41

Leah is the paragon of determination and courage. She, as Lavan's eldest daughter, was to have married Eisav, Yitzchak's eldest son, a fate any other woman would have accepted. But she refused. Hashem wanted her to achieve her dream — but to achieve it through great effort, to rise above her name, Leah, meaning wearied, and become Leah Imeinu, our Matriach, a woman of strength, of valor. Only a woman of such resoluteness would have dared to enter the bridal tent in place of her sister.

Rachel, the Rav continues, symbolizes the *midah* of *chessed*, a quiet, reserved, modest woman. She is prepared to give up all for the sake of something greater. Her fate is to prepare the road, through loneliness, trials and tribulations, for another. Rachel, says the Rav, opens the door to victory, but the victory belongs to another, to Leah. Their qualities would be transmitted to their sons. *Gevurah*, valor, and *chessed*, self-sacrifice, would be the pillars upon which *Kenesses Yisrael* would be built.

All Israel awaits the day when Rachel's descendant, the *Mashiach ben Yosef*, will pave the way for the *Mashiach ben David*, Leah's descendant, who, with determination, strength and courage, will establish *Kenesses Yisrael* in *Eretz Yisrael*.

_____ *Rabbi Elazar Lew*

ONE IS OVERWHELMED BY THE DESCRIPTION OF YAAKOV'S DREAM: a ladder standing upon the earth, its top reaching the heavens, with angels ascending and descending it. This vision transcends all generations, as it teaches us how to live our daily lives.

A ladder raises its user to a higher level. This teaches us to improve our religious observance by increasing our religious standards. Not only should we elevate our own standards, but we should assist our fellow Jews to raise their religious levels as well. Like Yaakov's ladder, we must be straight and far reaching in understanding that religious principles can never be compromised. We must be unbendable in living Torah-observant lives.

Moreover, a ladder's rungs are also used to go down. The description of Yaakov's dream teaches that it isn't enough to "hide in the clouds" spiritually; one must find a way to attach Heaven to earth. We must keep our feet firmly planted on the ground and apply our knowledge of the Torah, which came down from above, to our everyday living here below. We must live Torah-observant lives from top to bottom.

A noteworthy part of Yaakov's adventure, quoted by Rashi from the Talmud, is the quarrel that took place among the stones that Yaakov's head rested upon. Each stone pleaded, "Upon me shall this righteous man rest his head." Hashem combined them into one large stone, quieting them.

The Jewish nation, represented by the stones, is composed of different types of individuals, each with his own ideas, his own thoughts, his own beliefs and his own opinions. Each thinks that only his ideas are worthy of consideration. Yet, we must be able to combine all these different opinions into one common force with one purpose in mind — the growth of religious observance in the Jewish community.

The *Baal Haturim* points out that the word for ladder, *sulam,* is numerically equivalent to *Sinai,* both numbering 130. The Torah given at Sinai is a bridge from Heaven to earth.

May all of *Klal Yisrael* be worthy always of remaining strong and upright as a ladder in observing the ideals handed down from Mount Sinai. This, combined with the individual Jew remaining an observant piece of "the rock," will surely hasten the coming of *Mashiach.*

_____ *Rabbi Shlomo Crandall*

THE PASSOVER *HAGGADAH* TEACHES THAT YAAKOV'S FATHER-IN-law, Lavan, was far more evil than Pharaoh, the king of Egypt. How so? Pharaoh's solution to the Jewish problem was to kill all Jewish males. Lavan's strategy was to kill all Jews, male and female. Lavan's scheme was also qualitatively different. The commentaries point out that he did not intend to kill them physically but rather to erase them through love, by drawing them so close that their uniqueness would disappear.

These two approaches to destroying the Jewish nation became the paradigms for future attempts. Fifty years ago, we witnessed the

Pharaoh model in Germany's final solution. Today, the freedoms of America follow Lavan's method. But the intended results are the same: No more Jews.

The one question that remains to be answered is how our Sages knew of Lavan's plan. Though he is clearly described in *Parshas Vayeitzei* as a trickster and a dishonest person, nowhere is it written of a plan to destroy his daughters' family. From where does the notion come that Lavan wanted to eradicate the Jewish people?

When a discussion in *Parshas Vayeitzei* between Yaakov and Lavan is looked over carefully, a clearer picture of Lavan's intention emerges. Toward the end of the *parshah,* Yaakov Avinu runs away from Lavan. When Lavan catches up to him, he challenges him with the words, "Your sons are mine; your daughters are mine."

Immediately after making that audacious claim to Yaakov, Lavan makes the following proposal. "Let us make a covenant, a treaty." A treaty can bring friends closer or it can simply be a pact agreeing not to go to war against each other. It was the latter that Yaakov agreed to.

Lavan, dissatisfied with Yaakov's understanding of the treaty, points out to him that they speak the same language. He builds a monument and calls it *yegar sahadusa* (Aramaic for "testimony monument"). Yaakov quickly responds, I once spoke Aramaic, but my language is now Hebrew. And Yaakov called it *Galeid* (Hebrew for "testimony monument").

A few verses later, Lavan reminds Yaakov that he can not deny that they share the same grandfather, Avraham Avinu. They have the same roots. Maybe so, responds Yaakov, but I received the *mesorah* from my father, Yitzchak. Yaakov slaughters an animal and partakes of it without Lavan and his entourage. This tells Lavan that Yaakov can not even break bread with him. For the Jewish people to assimilate with him will bear no fruit. Lavan relents. He kisses his daughters goodbye and leaves.

The enemies of Israel are many and their strategies come in different forms. In our generation, we must be on the lookout for Lavan, who is trying ever so hard to weave us into the fabric of western civilization. With G-d's help his efforts will ultimately bear little fruit.

(Based on Leil Shimurim, by Rabbi Zvi Dov Kanotopsky, zt"l.)

P ARSHAS VAYEITZEI SPANS THE TWENTY YEARS SPENT BY YAAKOV
Avinu — the quintessential *ish tam,* man of integrity — in the
inhospitable company of his sinister uncle, Lavan, a master of manipu-
lation, deceit and double-talk. From his initial embrace of Yaakov,
which, Rashi notes, is actually a search for concealed valuables, Lavan
is bent on exploiting Yaakov for his own purposes. Barely a month had
passed when Lavan beguiles Yaakov into tending his flock and agrees
to offer the hand of his younger daughter, Rachel, in exchange for seven
years of labor.

But after the allotted time, Lavan surreptitiously substitutes his
eldest daughter, Leah, for Rachel and justifies his chicanery by invoking
local custom. In order to claim his rightful bride, Yaakov has
no choice but to commit himself to an additional seven years of
servitude. During the final six years of Yaakov's stay, Lavan's deception
becomes routine; he repeatedly reneges on his agreements. Yaakov's
fortunes nevertheless soar despite his uncle's machinations, and an
embittered Lavan comes to view himself as victim rather than aggres-
sor.

The full measure of Lavan's hatred does not become apparent until
the disappearance of his cherished *terafim* coupled with Yaakov's clan-
destine departure. Infuriated, Lavan engages in hot pursuit, intent on
destroying Yaakov's entire family — Lavan's own daughters and grandchildren. Bloodshed is averted only through Divine intervention, a
frightful warning issued to Lavan in the dead of night.

Despite unrelenting exploitation, Yaakov maintains his faith and
equanimity. This is most evident in his impassioned response to Lavan's tirade, in which Yaakov offers stirring testimony to twenty years of
unwavering loyalty and meticulous honesty. Yaakov's defense is
as dignified as his labor — firm, but devoid of bitterness. Without engaging in personal attacks on Lavan, he eloquently places blame for
the conflict where it belongs. As the Midrash insightfully comments,
"Better the grievances of the Patriarchs than the humility of the offspring."

Not withstanding his inspired appeal, Yaakov's words make no discernible impression upon Lavan, whose callous response is, "All that you see is mine."

As the two part, the Torah notes that Lavan returns "to his place" — morally as well as geographically. For Lavan there is only stagnation. Yaakov, however, goes "on his way" — rising to new spiritual heights. Perhaps Yaakov's greatest achievement from his years with Lavan was his ability to confront *sheker* with *emes.* This was to become Yaakov's proud declaration to his brother Eisav: "I managed to live with Lavan for twenty years, remaining faithful to the letter and spirit of the *mitzvos,* without succumbing to his evil ways."

"*Maaseh avos siman labanim*" — the experiences of the Patriarchs provide inspiration to their progeny. Yaakov's moral triumph serves as a model for the Jew throughout history. In our own time, the Israeli government, Jewish leadership, as well as individuals in their professional and personal relationships are confronted by a sea of *sheker.* While we may not change the Lavans of the world, our challenge is to engage them in the spirit of "Yisrael Saba," with firmness, integrity and dignity.

פרשת וישלח
Parshas Vayishlach

_____ *Rabbi Elazar Muskin*

T WENTY YEARS HAD PASSED SINCE YAAKOV RAN FOR HIS LIFE, FROM
the hands of his brother Eisav. In *Parshas Vayishlach,* Yaakov prepares, with bated breath, for his reunion with Eisav, hoping against all
odds that time will have tempered his brother's wrath.

As the story unfolds, the Torah recounts each move Yaakov makes
and every strategy he uses in preparation for this encounter. But before
he actually faces Eisav, the story is interrupted with a new one. The
Torah tells how Yaakov transfers his family and possessions across the
Yabbok River, in the middle of the night. Then, "Yaakov remained
alone, and a man wrestled with him until daybreak." Why did Yaakov
remain alone on one side of the river in the middle of the night? What
was so urgent that required him to endanger himself?

Rashi, quoting the Talmud, states, "He had forgotten some small jars
and returned for them." But we are still left wondering why Yaakov would
risk his life to fetch such mundane and trivial articles as small jars.

Rav Yosef Dov Soloveitchik, *zt"l,* explains that the encounter of Yaakov and Eisav is not simply a story of the reunion of two estranged brothers, but rather serves as a paradigm for all Jews in in their relationship
with the non-Jewish world. This is demonstrated, notes the Rav, by the
exact words Yaakov tells his messengers to relay to Eisav. Yaakov anticipated that Eisav would ask his messengers three questions. The first
was, "Whose are you?" and the second, "Where are you going?" To these
inquiries, Yaakov provides the answer: "To your servant, to Yaakov."

These two questions and their answers can be reinterpreted by contemporary Jewry as, "To whom do you pledge ultimate loyalty?" and "What are your spiritual goals?" In other words, the non-Jewish world of Eisav wants to know who our G-d is and what path in life have we chosen. Our reply, like Yaakov's, must be bold, clear and precise. We must enunciate our commitment to a unique Jewish destiny that is not open to dialogue or debate.

Then there is the third question, "And whose are these [gifts] before you?" Here, Eisav addresses a totally different issue. Are we willing to contribute our talents, capabilities and material resources toward the cultural and technological development of the world? Are we going to be partners with the non-Jewish world in developing a productive society?

"It is a present sent to my lord, to Eisav," Yaakov responds. Yes, we are determined to participate in civic, scientific and political enterprises for the welfare of the general community. We are obligated to enrich the society we live in with our creative talents.

With this background one can understand what our Sages meant when they said that Yaakov crossed back over the river to retrieve small jars. These jars represented the material welfare of mankind, and in order to retrieve them, Yaakov first had to struggle. This "man" with whom he struggled, the Midrash reports, was Eisav's guardian angel. The angel wrestled with Yaakov's spiritual identity, hoping that he would surrender his spiritual obligations and remain interested only in the material "small jars." Yaakov, though, did not succumb, for he knew that the Jew must combine his social responsibilities with an uncompromising commitment to Judaism.

The struggle Yaakov faced is one that confronts every observant Jew who participates as a member of society. We must remember that Yaakov was victorious and the angel changed his name to Yisrael — "for you have contended with G-d and with man, and you have prevailed." We, too, must prevail in our struggle, for we are the children of Israel.

_____ *Rookie Billet*

THE SUSPENSEFUL STORY OF YAAKOV AND HIS FAMILY'S ESCAPE FROM Lavan and their journey to *Eretz Yisrael* continues to unfold in the opening verses of *Parshas Vayishlach*. On the verge of a confrontation with his brother Eisav, whose terrible anger at Yaakov for intercepting the blessings intended for him still burned, Yaakov sends him messengers.

The message is addressed to "the land of Sei'ir, the fields of Edom," and it states: I lived with Lavan and tarried until now. I have material wealth, which I send to my master to find favor in his eyes.

Rav Yosef Dov Soloveitchik, *zt"l,* finds Yaakov's message perplexing. Why does the Torah repeat Eisav's location, first as Sei'ir, then as Edom? Second, why does Yaakov need to tell him he was with Lavan all these years? Moreover, Rashi explains that within Yaakov's message that he lived (*"garti"*) with Lavan is the encoded message that he kept all 613 (*taryag*) commandments of the Torah. Why the need to employ this anagram? Of what relevance is Yaakov's Torah observance? Finally, why does Yaakov conclude with a list of his material blessings? How do these points serve the goal of his message — to assuage Eisav's anger and to find favor in his eyes?

The Rav reconstructs Yaakov's stream of consciousness in light of the brothers' last encounter twenty years previous. For a score of years, Eisav's angry words rang in Yaakov's ears. "You deceived me — *"vayaakveini"* — twice, "first taking my birthright and then taking my blessing." Eisav plays on Yaakov's name to imply that he is the very essence of deception!

In truth, Yitzchak blessed Yaakov twice. Posing as Eisav, Yaakov intercepted the blessing, intended for his brother, for material wealth and comfort. But Yaakov received another blessing — to serve G-d and inherit the Land of Israel — given to him openly and freely by Yitzchak, who knew at that point which son he was blessing. Furthermore, Yaakov knew that Eisav thought the blessing for the Land of Israel was contingent upon his not marrying a Canaanite woman. Hence, Eisav's marriage to Yishmael's daughter.

The Rav reconstructs Yaakov's message to incorporate these ideas. "You may be wondering if I still qualify to inherit the Land of Israel," Yaakov is saying to his brother. "Let me first remind you, your address is still the land of Sei'ir, the fields of Edom. I repeat so that you make no mistake. Furthermore, I have fulfilled the contingency to serve G-d. I may have lived with the evil Lavan, but I nevertheless observed the *taryag mitzvos.* I fulfilled the other stipulations by marrying into my mother's family and not Canaanites. And yes, while the material blessings have also arrived, they mean nothing to me. I give them to you freely."

Yaakov continues this line of thinking when Eisav offers to escort him back to the land of their father. Knowing he must keep his distance from Eisav, Yaakov declines, explaining that his children are weak and slow. "Let us go at our own pace," Yaakov is saying. "You return to Sedei Edom and allow me to achieve my destiny as I bring my family home to Israel."

In our times as well, the temptations of Eisav's world are powerful and dangerous. Our children are also young and vulnerable. The modern house of Jacob needs to strengthen itself through Jewish education in the home, the school and the *shul*. We must fortify ourselves and our children with *yiras Shamayim* and *shemiras hamitzvos*. We must avoid the insidious influences of Eisav's world and involve ourselves in *tikun olam*. We must remind ourselves that even when G-d bestows upon us material blessings, they are not the essence of life, for as a nation, our goal is to be worthy of the *birkas Avraham* — to be *ovdei Hashem* and heirs to the Land of Israel.

_____ *Rabbi Daniel Korobkin*

THE TORAH SPENDS SEVERAL PARAGRAPHS IN *PARSHAS VAYISHLACH* listing Eisav's descendants. Rashi points out several instances of incestuous relationships, which polluted Eisav's line. One such example is in the verse, "These are sons of Tzivon, Ayah and Anah. He is Anah who found the *yeimim* in the desert while tending the donkeys of his father Tzivon."

What are *yeimim*? Mules, explains Rashi. Anah bred horses with donkeys to produce mules. Of what relevance is this to the story line? "He was a bastard and he brought illegitimacy to the world." The mule, the *midrash* maintains, was Anah's invention.

Yet, an earlier *midrash* indicates that Eisav's father, Yitzchak, owned mules — well before Anah. On the verse, "The man [Yitzchak] became very great," the *midrash* relates, "People used to say, 'Rather the manure of Yitzchak's mules than the silver and gold of Avimelech.' " How can Anah have invented mules when Yitzchak was famous for his mules years earlier? Furthermore, what is the meaning of this curious *midrash*? How can manure be preferable to gold and silver?

The Shelah Hakadosh explains. Scoffers of the time used to say that Yitzchak's father was not really Avraham, but Avimelech, who took Yitzchak's mother, Sarah, into his home for a night because he was told she was Avraham's sister. People had good reason to think Yitzchak was illegitimate. Look at his son Eisav, an unscrupulous and immoral person, whose family is filled with bastardy. After all, they reasoned, the apple doesn't fall far from the tree.

To respond to these critics, the Torah tells us that Yitzchak became quite wealthy in *Eretz Yisrael*. The Land of Israel, which is completely holy and pure, produces wealth only for one who is also holy and pure. (Eisav, by contrast, was rejected by the land and eventually left.)

Even his most mundane possessions were proof of Yitzchak's purity and holiness. G-d gave Yitzchak creatures that looked like a cross between a horse and a donkey, the Shelah writes, but these "mules" were not the product of crossbreeding. Rather, Hashem provided Yitzchak with them, indicating "that even something that naturally contains illegitimacy came into his possession without crossbreeding."

If this was true of his animals, how much more did it apply to the man himself. This is what is meant by the verse, "The man [Yitzchak] became very great." Even the scoffers came to recognize Yitzchak's greatness, that he was indeed from holy stock. They therefore stated that the manure from these mules testified to Yitzchak's holiness more than Avimelech's silver — the money that Avimelech had attempted to give Sarah as "hush money" after he realized that she was a married woman — testified to Yitzchak's supposed illegitimacy.

In order to succeed in Israel, we must be, like our forefather Yitzchak, of pure heart and spirit. Only then can we look towards the Almighty to provide us with prosperity in the Holy Land.

_____ *Rabbi Yehoshua S. Hecht*

PARSHAS VAYISHLACH BEGINS WITH YAAKOV ANTICIPATING AN AT-tack from his brother Eisav and preparing for this confrontation in three ways. First, Yaakov sends Eisav gifts of goats, ewes, rams and camels, hoping that this elaborate gesture will placate his brother's jealousy and hatred. Yaakov goes so far as to specify the exact words of greetings his messengers are to say to Eisav on his behalf. Next, Yaakov prays. He cries out to G-d, "Rescue me, please, from the hand of my brother, from the hand of Eisav, for I am afraid, lest he come and strike me down, mother and children."

Last, Yaakov sends half his family across the Yabbok River reasoning that "if Eisav comes to one camp and smites it, the camp that is left will escape." Yaakov does not count on goodwill or his Divine merits to deliver him. In addition to praying and placating, he splits the camp. He does everything in his power to save his children and family.

After making these arrangements, "Yaakov was left alone and wrestled with a man until the break of dawn." The *midrash* identifies this "man" as the archangel of Eisav, who dislocates Yaakov's right thigh in the scuffle. The Talmudic Sage Rav Yehoshua ben Levi states that this cosmic confrontation between Yaakov and the angel of Eisav kicked up a dust storm that reached all the way up to the Divine throne. How did this angel appear to Yaakov?

Rav Shmuel bar Nachman explains that he appeared in the guise of a heathen. The *Halachah* states that a Jew who is joined by a heathen on the road should make sure that the heathen is to his right side, so that if the heathen attacks him, the Jew will be able to ward him off with his stronger hand. Hence, Yaakov's right side was closest to the angel and his right hip was dislocated by him.

Rav Shmuel bar Acha, recording the opinion of Rabba bar Ulla, disagrees. The angel appeared to Yaakov in the guise of a scholar, he maintains. The law is that whoever walks to the right of his teacher is considered ignorant. Hence, Yaakov — having assumed the man was a scholar — positioned himself to the left of the angel.

What impelled our Sages to describe the appearance of this angel? What difference does it make? What lesson does it impart to us, the grandchildren of Yaakov?

Historically, Jews have had to contend with two very different types of threats to our survival. One is the brute force of a heathen, when our enemies seek to wrestle us to the ground. At such moments, we must defend ourselves to protect Jewish lives.

At other times, however, our enemies threaten us not with physical attacks, but with spiritual ones. These bombardments come from so-called enlightened individuals, who attack the beliefs and practices of Torah Judaism with sarcasm and ridicule. They kick up a storm of confusion and doubt in the minds of the children of Yaakov. This is the other face of Eisav, the one that poses as a scholar and attempts to wrestle the Jew, intellectually and emotionally, to the ground.

We, Yaakov's descendants, have wrestled and continue to wrestle with both of these dangers — from without and from within — through the long, dark night of exile. Our response, like that of our forefather Yaakov, must be threefold. We must take the high road and, while maintaining our integrity and principles, make appropriate gestures toward Eisav.

At the same time, we must strategize within our own camp to fend off the attacks — both overt and insidious — of secular society. We do not live in a vacuum. We exist in this world and in its cultures. But we must nevertheless maintain our unique identity and treasure our unique values. We must "split the camp" and live in this world while simultaneously remaining apart.

And we must pray. We must pray for ourselves and for our children, for our community and for the greater community of *Klal Yisrael,* for those who observe and for those who do not yet observe. Ultimately, our fate rests in the Hands of our Creator, and we must turn to Him to bring an end to our exile and redeem us, finally and completely, from all the angels of Eisav.

פרשת וישב
Parshas Vayeishev

_____ Rabbi Bertram Leff

PARSHAS VAYEISHEV CONTINUES THE BIOGRAPHY OF YOSEF. HE IS incarcerated in the Egyptian king's prison, where he encounters two royal prisoners, the baker and the cupbearer of Pharaoh. As captains, neither one prepared the food or drink that he served; others did the actual work, while they supervised. What were their crimes? The cupbearer, says the Midrash, was held accountable for a fly found in Pharaoh's goblet, and the baker was responsible for a pebble discovered in his bread.

Which of these offenses was more severe? At first glance, the cupbearer appears more guilty. With his own eyes he could have seen the fly in the goblet before serving it. All he had to do was look. The baker, on the other hand, having not been involved in its preparation, could not have known of the pebble in the bread. He could not see through the bread. Yet the baker was hanged and the cupbearer, after a prison term, was released and restored to his position. How is one to understand these punishments?

Their crime, the Malbim explains, was one of responsibility. The cupbearer's error was relatively minor; a harmless fly fell into the king's cup at the last minute, an accident that is understandable. The baker's sin was more grievous. The presence of a pebble in the bread is dangerous and could only happen as a result of negligence. As captain, the baker was responsible for insuring against just that sort of thing, and he neglected that responsibility — a sin greater than committing the act

54 / TORAH INSIGHTS

itself. Responsibility is the key to understanding how the punishment fit the crime.

It is no coincidence, says Rav Yosef Dov Soloveitchik, *zt"l,* that this lesson in responsibility is read in close proximity to the holiday of Chanukah, for the theme of responsibility forms the essence of the holiday; it is at the core of what we celebrate. The miracle of Chanukah, teaches the Rav, is not only that our nation defeated the Greeks in war, but that the Hasmoneans arose to take on the responsibility to fight our enemies — both from without and from within. They did not isolate themselves. With great courage, they stood up and demonstrated the principle of *kol Yisrael areivim zeh bazeh,* declaring that all Jews are responsible for one another.

The Hasmoneans were the teachers of their time, teaching through their actions the essence of the Chanukah miracle — national responsibility. Such individuals arose in other eras of Jewish history, and such individuals continue to arise in times where the spiritual survival of Israel is at stake.

In our era, the concept of *areivus,* responsibility, is the prime mover of the Torah community's outreach activities. Like the *Chashmona'im* of old, each and every one of us must take upon himself the responsibility of teaching and transmitting Torah knowledge and expanding the observance of *mitzvos* in our communities.

During the year we have the opportunity to fulfill that responsibility by inviting the unaffiliated to our Shabbos tables. Invite a neighbor or a business acquaintance who is not yet observant to join you for Shabbos. Be a teacher of Torah Judaism through your *Kiddush,* your *zemiros,* your *divrei Torah,* your *bentching.* Join the community of *Chashmona'im* who take seriously their responsibility for other Jews, and thereby become a part of the contemporary miracle of Chanukah.

 *Rabbi Mordecai E. Feuerstein*

T HERE IS A THEMATIC LINK BETWEEN THE STORY OF YOSEF, IN THIS week's *parshah,* and the story of Chanukah: man's realization that G-d's "Unseen Hand" is guiding history. When Yosef goes in search of his brothers, an anonymous "man" meets him in Shechem and directs him toward Dosan. Thus begins the chain reaction that sends Yosef to Egypt as a slave and culminates in his ascension to Egypt's throne.

"The Torah incorporates Yosef's encounter with the anonymous man," explains the Ramban, "in order to teach the fundamental principle that in determining the real cause of history's events, *hacharitzus sheker vehagezeirah emes* — man's industriousness is false and G-d's decree is true." Sensitivity to this truth grew within Yosef until, many years later when it was time to reveal his identity to his brothers, he was able to say, "It was not you who sent me here, but G-d."

It was this same awareness that motivated the *Chashmona'im*. They understood that in all their accomplishments, G-d's *gezeirah* was *emes* and their *charitzus* was secondary.

The recognition suggests an answer to the well-known questions regarding the flask of pure oil found by the *Chashmona'im*. The law of *tumah hutra betzibbur* establishes that, when there is no alternative, a communal offering is acceptable even if it is in an impure state. Since the oil used to kindle the Temple menorah was considered a communal offering, it would therefore be covered by this rule and, had the *Chashmona'im* not found the flask of pure oil, they would have been permitted to kindle the menorah with impure oil.

Why, then, did the *Chashmona'im* insist on using ritually pure oil for the menorah when all they had was one small flask? To have lit the menorah with pomp and ceremony only to have it go out after just one day would have certainly exposed them to ridicule from the Hellenists and a dubious public.

In seizing the very first opportunity to light the menorah and in insisting on pure oil no matter what the risks, the *Chashmona'im* were making a statement. Surely their military success was striking. But was it an undeniable miracle? Was it the "Unseen Hand"? Could it not have been argued that Judah Maccabee was a master military tactician with a highly motivated guerrilla force, who succeeded in humbling an occupying superpower — as have many such groups in history?

What is crucial to the festival of Chanukah is the Maccabees' conviction that G-d's miraculous intervention was responsible for whatever they had achieved militarily. *Hacharitzus sheker vehagezeirah emes.* Their capacity to sense the "Unseen Hand" behind the unfolding events generated a profound sense of thanks to G-d Who was responsible for their victories. Rav Yosef Dov Soloveitchik, *zt"l,* once said that this appreciation distinguished the lighting of the menorah by the *Chashmona'im* from the lighting which would occur in the Temple daily for the next two hundred years.

Theirs was not only a *halachic* performance but a unique and extraordinary expression of *hakaras hatov* to the Almighty. Other ways could have been found to stretch the small flask of oil — by dividing it into eight smaller parts or by using thinner wicks — until new, pure oil could be produced. But the flame would have been dim and unimpressive. Such an impoverished light would have failed to convey the profound gratitude that drove the *Chashmona'im* to rekindle the menorah at the very first opportunity and in the most beautiful manner possible.

_____ *Rabbi Chaim Landau*

UPON REVIEWING THE STORIES OF TWO OF YAAKOV'S TWELVE SONS, Yosef and Yehudah, one may wonder why Yehudah's descendants were ultimately crowned with the kingship of Israel rather than those of Yosef. Stories regarding their chastity are told of both. After her first and second husbands died (both sons of Yehudah), Tamar dresses as a prostitute and seduces her former father-in-law.

Yosef, on the other hand, when confronted by his master Potiphar's wife, who propositioned him in the privacy of her mansion, runs away. Yehudah accedes to temptation; Yosef resists.

Earlier in the *parshah* the Torah tells us that Yosef is thrown into a pit by his brothers and going to be killed. What does Yehudah do? He suggests that the brothers sell Yosef to a passing caravan of Ishmaelite merchants. Though he is the leader of the brothers, he does not recommend that Yosef be retrieved from the pit and brought back to their father.

Moreover, Yehudah, according to a certain *midrash,* married a Canaanite woman at a time when his family was anxious about the children intermarrying, Why, one wonders, was Yehudah rewarded with the sovereign leadership of Israel?

A good leader is not one who is perfect, but one who falters and finds the strength of purpose to make a fresh start through repentance and improved actions. The Talmud tells us, "Four died through the serpent's machinations" — that is, they died because all people are doomed to die and not on account of their personal sins: Binyamin, Amram, Yishai and Caleiv. Binyamin was the most perfect of Yaakov's sons, but he was never featured as a leader. The son accepted as leader, by the brothers and their father, was Yehudah.

Yehudah's public admission of his relations with Tamar made a great impact in Heaven. Following G-d's forgiveness of him, the angels pronounced the blessing (which later formed part of the *Amidah*), "Blessed are You, Lord, Who is gracious and forgives repeatedly." While the sincere confession acknowledges imperfection, it demonstrates moral maturity and responsibility.

The *baal teshuvah* has the courage to admit his failures and uses those setbacks to better himself. Leaders are not born perfect, but they constantly strive toward that goal. This is Yehudah and his claim to royalty.

_____ *Rabbi Michael Fine*

W HEN YOSEF'S BROTHERS THROW HIM INTO A DANGEROUS PIT, THE Torah records: "And Reuven heard, and he saved him from their hands."

"If Reuven had known that Hashem would write [this verse] concerning him," the *midrash* observes, he would have done much more. "He would have carried Yosef on his shoulder back to his father."

Why is this so? Is it possible that Reuven would have been galvanized by an exalted place in history? Unthinkable, *Yalkut Yehudah* insists. "It would be impossible to say that *tzaddikim* such as these were motivated by considerations of honor." The *midrash's* assessment of Reuven must be viewed in the proper light.

Undoubtedly, Reuven, like the classic *tzaddikim* of *Klal Yisrael,* had within him a profound sense of humility. Good character requires a firm sense of humility. One must always keep in mind that "man does, but Hashem accomplishes," in the words of Rav Yisroel Salanter. Reuven surely understood that his capacities, his talents, his strengths were the designs of Hashem. Had he realized that Hashem considered him Yosef's savior, he would have felt a sublime sense of spiritual satisfaction, and he would have gone further to enhance his estimation in G-d's — not history's — eyes.

Sometimes people confuse this all-important trait of humility with insignificance. One must always remember how important he is and how significant all his thoughts, statements and actions are. To this end, our Sages say that a person is obligated to declare, "The world was created for me." This balance between humility and pride, between self-effacement and self-esteem, is critical to the fine-tuned Torah Jew. He must never overestimate himself, yet never underestimate his significance.

We find this precise balance in some of the statements ascribed to Rav Moshe Feinstein, *zt"l.* It is reported that Rav Moshe's wife once urged him to sleep later than his customary 4 a.m. rising. He responded that if he got up any later, his Torah learning would suffer and he would remain ignorant. This statement came at a point in his life when he had the entire world's respect as a *gadol hador,* a leader of the generation.

Rav Moshe understood that even he needed to strive continually, and that no success comes automatically. Yet, at the same time, Rav Moshe recognized the significance of his personal Torah study. He knew the meaning of the world having been created for him—and he urged others to recognize this truth and act upon it.

The first man was called *Adam,* from the root *adamah,* meaning ground. Just as the ground we live upon is basis for life and the medium for development, so too, man is the essence of potential, says Rabbi Yaakov Moshe Charlap, *zt"l.*

Our sense of significance is meant to fuel our growth and development, while our sense of humility guides us in a constructive path. With the proper balance, Adam emerges as an *ish,* a man, a credit to himself and to his Creator.

פרשת מקץ
Parshas Mikeitz

_____ *Rabbi Basil Herring*

IN *PARSHAS VAYEISHEV,* RASHI COMMENTS THAT YOSEF'S FACE REFLECT-
ed that of his father. This resemblance, Rav Ahron Soloveichik,
shlit"a, points out, is illustrated not only in their both having dreamed
prophetic dreams, but in the similarity of those dreams. The ladder in
Yaakov's dream reached the heavens while planted solidly on the
ground, representing his lofty idealism, his striving to transform the
mundane into the transcendental while still maintaining a sense of
practical realism.

So too, Yosef's two dreams, taken together, follow his father's. The
sheaves in the field point to a groundedness, a this-world reality, and
the sun, moon and stars bespeak a lofty aspiration to reach beyond the
here and now. (No wonder his brothers are envious only after Yosef's
second dream. His first dream refers only to material domination, but
his second vision completes the Jacobean circuit by incorporating a
spiritual element. Yosef's aspirations for their father's mantle, the brothers reckoned, may come at their expense; hence, their anger and their
envy.)

The duality of Yaakov's and Yosef's dreams reflects the ethos of the
Jewish, as opposed to the Greek, outlook. The Greek Hellenist places
the highest value on preserving reality, Change and movement, to the
classic Greek mind, is necessarily regression and dissolution leading to
chaos.

Judaism insists the contrary. While respecting the facts "on the ground," one should strive to slowly and carefully transform G-d's Creation, reaching ever higher. Set high spiritual goals, Judaism teaches, but never lose sight of the human political dimension at your feet. Always treat people with sensitivity and respect, for their good and for your own.

This approach is the basis for Yosef's understanding of Pharaoh's dream: the lean cows in the dream are not satiated by a one-time feeding frenzy — they eat the fat cows yet remain emaciated. Yosef recognizes that the same would be true of Egypt as a nation. Salvation and success would only come via a strategically planned, carefully implemented, sometimes painful, long-term approach. His fourteen-year plan brings blessing and salvation to both friend and foe.

The underlying principle of Yosef's policy, says Rav Ahron Soloveichik, shlit"a, is the Torah's rejection of radical change, of apocalyptic thinking not grounded in gradual growth and transformation (represented by the rungs of the ladder in Yaakov's dream). In any endeavor, one must take a full account of the human condition, of current realities and the limitations they impose.

Hence, the necessity for only one vial of oil as the basis of the Chanukah miracle, and the gradual, eight-day progression of light and power — corresponding to the growing military and political strength of the Chashmona'im — in our contemporary kindling of the menorah.

In our days, we have sadly seen firsthand the consequences of ignoring Yaakov and Yosef's vision. Extreme solutions to difficult and painful problems must be rejected. In our earnest hopes to bring the Mashiach, to transform the Jewish people, to redeem Eretz Yisrael, and to establish communities suffused with the spirituality of Torah, we dare never neglect modalities that comprise the totality of derech eretz — the moral and political virtues that are the foundation for all that we do as bnei and bnos Torah.

Only by following the methods of our ancestors will we deserve to see the chanukas habayis has.helishi, the rebuilding and dedication of the third Temple, at which time, beshuv Hashem es shivas Tziyon, hayinu kecholmim, when Hashem will return the captivity of Zion, we will be as dreamers — following in the footsteps of Yaakov and Yosef.

THE TORAH DESCRIBES, IN VIVID DETAIL, YOSEF'S INCREDIBLE RISE to power through his correct interpretation of Pharaoh's dreams. But why, ask various commentators, including _Akeidas Yitzchak_ and Abarbanel, was the Egyptian monarch so willing to listen to the interpretation of this foreign convict, not only to accept it as a theoretical possibility, but to actually give it such credence as to determine the economic policy of his entire nation?

To be sure, Pharaoh had received word that this prisoner had successfully interpreted the dreams of the chief butler and the chief baker. He had been put to the test before, and had responded with a fully accurate prediction of the events to come.

Yosef seemed worthy of Pharaoh's ear. Nonetheless, why would Pharaoh put such trust in a stranger who had met the challenge on but one occasion, when he had at his side the wisdom of Egypt — his trusted advisors, who for years had successfully guided his political and religious life, and secured his status as sovereign and god of the ancient world?

In fact, as the _midrash_ reports, his advisors were far from dumbstruck by the dreams: "Rabbi Yehoshua of Sichinin said in the name of Rabbi Levi, They interpreted [the dreams] for him, but their voices did not enter his ears. [They told him,] 'The seven goodly cows — you will have seven daughters. And the seven sickly cows — you will bury seven daughters.' And they also said, 'The seven goodly stalks — you will conquer seven provinces. And the seven sickly stalks — seven provinces will rebel against you.' "

Our question, therefore, persists: If alternative explanations were advanced by his most trusted ministers, why did Pharaoh choose Yosef, an unknown entity?

Nechama Leibowitz, _a"h,_ points to a closer reading of the text, which reveals that although Pharaoh had two distinct dreams — one of the cows; one of the stalks — and his advisors explained them as two dreams with two meanings, Pharaoh, the text informs us, "told them of his _dream._ " Pharaoh refers to his dreams as one dream and understood them to convey a single meaning. His directive to Yosef confirms this approach: "I have dreamed a dream and there is no one who can interpret it."

Because Pharaoh was convinced of the oneness of his visions, he rejected the efforts of his trusted ministers and turned instead to Yosef. Rav Yosef Dov Soloveitchik, *zt"l,* describes Yosef as a visionary, who had the ability to see beyond what others saw, particularly beyond that which his brothers could see. The Rav, another Yosef, envisioned the founding of a Jewish state differently from his "brothers" in Torah, by welcoming it and seeing it as an act of Divine providence and religious import.

In expanding upon this approach, we have seen that Yosef again saw a vision different from that of those who surrounded him. They saw two dreams; he saw one. And so in our time, the Rav, in the spirit of his namesake, with an interpretation that differed from those around him, envisioned philosophical commitments and aspirations not as separate, disparate entities. The relationship of Torah and *Eretz Yisrael* were to be interpreted, in his passionate and intellectual vision, as one. Let us remain steadfast to that vision.

פרשת ויגש
Parshas Vayigash

_____ *Esther Krauss*

T HE STORY OF YOSEF AND HIS BROTHERS IS THE STORY OF A FAMILY torn apart by internal strife, later reunited to fulfill its destiny and become G-d's chosen people. It is the story of leadership emerging from within a family through the intricate process of *teshuvah.*

Yosef, with his princely coat and fateful dreams, achieves executive powers in Egypt. His brothers come down to Egypt and bow before him. But it is, in fact, Yehudah who emerges as the acknowledged leader of the brothers, receiving his father's deathbed blessing of eternal leadership. The future kings of Israel descend from him.

Yehudah is not only the spokesman and catalyst for the reunification of his family, but is also at the center of a personal transformation that proclaims him worthy of kingship. His defining quality (which also characterizes his descendant, King David) is his ability to admit to fault, to confess to wrongdoing. This crucial element of *teshuvah* catapults him to greatness.

The story of Yehudah and Tamar, which interrupts the narrative of Yosef and his brothers and seems unrelated, is actually closely connected to it. Yehudah rises from the lowest point in his life by confessing to his relationship with Tamar. His princely ability to know himself, to understand the consequences of his actions and to take full responsibility for them, is perhaps most strikingly conveyed in a statement he makes at two critical junctures in the story.

Yehudah convinces his reluctant father to allow Binyamin to go with the other brothers to Egypt by guaranteeing the boy's safety. He promises Yaakov that, should he fail, "I will have sinned to you all the days." He later reveals this vow to Yosef, inducing him to drop his mask and reveal himself to his brothers.

Nechama Leibowitz, a"h, cites the *Peirush Eim Lemikra,* which derives from Yehudah's statement a profound principle regarding the wages of sin: Punishment is not a price paid for sin, but inherent in sin. "The punishment is not outside sin; the sin is itself the punishment."

In a similar analysis of sin and repentance, Rav Yosef Dov Soloveitchik, zt"l, distinguishes between the natures of *kapparah,* acquittal, and *taharah,* purification. *"Kapparah,"* says the Rav, "removes the need for punishment." But while the offender is forgiven, his crime does not go away. "Sin also has a polluting quality," the Rav explains, which remains even after *kapparah.* Transgression sullies the transgressor, driving a wedge between him and G-d, and only *taharah,* purification, can fully restore him.

Before Yehudah spoke, his older brother, Reuven, tried to convince Yaakov to let Binyamin travel with them to Egypt, guaranteeing the boy's safety. "Kill my two sons if I do not bring him back to you," Reuven tells Yaakov. But Yaakov refused.

While most commentators concede that Reuven spoke figuratively, his words are telling. In the Rav's terms, his offer was an effort to achieve *kapparah,* an attempt to expiate his sin by repaying the debt it would incur. But Yehudah understood that Binyamin's loss would cause irreparable damage; his father would never recover from it and, consequently, *taharah* would be impossible. Yehudah would forever remain a sinner to his father. In his words, "I will have sinned to you all the days." Yaakov allows him to take Binyamin along.

Yehudah's remarkable growth in this story can be measured by contrasting his deception of his father regarding Yosef's fate with his sensitivity to him regarding Binyamin's fate. Yehudah, who was directly responsible for selling one brother into slavery, offers himself as a slave in place of another brother, in order to prevent his father's pain and suffering. Yosef recognizes this change and is convinced that both *kapparah* and *taharah* have been achieved. The time is ripe for the family to be reunited.

Rabbi Yitzchok A. Breitowitz

Y OSEF'S INTERACTION WITH HIS BROTHERS IS ONE OF THE MOST PER-
plexing stories in the Torah, one that has puzzled generations of
readers for thousands of years. Why does Yosef conceal his identity?
Why did he wait so long to tell his father that he was in Egypt?

Even if one follows the view of the Abarbanel, that, as a slave, Yosef
had no means of informing Yaakov and, after his ascension to political
power, he still could not do so lest he be accused of disloyalty, questions abound. How do we explain his demand that the brothers bring
Binyamin down from Israel? Why did he falsely accuse Binyamin of
being a thief and sentence him to slavery, when he knew the news would
devastate Yaakov and perhaps kill him? In Yosef, we are not simply
dealing with a victim who finds himself in a position to take revenge.
And even if we were, why would he want to exact vengeance on his
father?

The Ramban states that Yosef perceived his dreams as a Divine mandate. His dream, years earlier, that eleven stars bowed to him made it
essential for Binyamin, the eleventh brother, to descend to Egypt as
well and acknowledge him as the ruler. Moreover, since Yosef also
dreamt that the sun and moon bowed before him (presumably representing his parents), Yaakov needed to join them. Yosef, therefore,
imprisoned Binyamin in order to draw his father down to Egypt.

Many commentators question the Ramban's view. Is it Yosef's job to
manipulate his family through fraud and misrepresentation just to fulfill
his dreams? Do the ends justify the means? Is it not G-d's job to insure
that His prophecies are carried out?

One possible explanation can be found in Yosef's understanding that
his descent to Egypt was a prelude to the enslavement of the Jewish
people there. As such, his Divinely ordained mission was to pave the
way for his brethren by giving them the tools they would need to survive
this exile, to retain their faith in Hashem in a hostile and decadent
environment, and not to assimilate.

Every step of his life demonstrated _"Ani Yosef."_ I remain Yosef. Whether one is at the pinnacle of greatness or at the nadir of persecution —

Yosef embodied both extremes — one can always be a Yosef, faithful to the Torah and to the Jewish people. This is why we bless our children to be like Ephraim and Menashe, Yosef's children, who grew up in an exile with few role models, yet remained faithful to G-d.

Nevertheless, during 210 years of Egyptian exile, the Jewish people descended to the forty-ninth level of impurity, the Arizal teaches. Most Jews were idolaters, did not practice circumcision and were generally "naked and bare" from any *mitzvos*. Yet they had some merits — their empathy, their concern and their unity. They kept their distinct Jewish names and clothing, did not inform on each other, and did not intermarry. These qualities, while insufficient, are a necessary start on the road back, for our Sages teach that no individual Jew is redeemed except to the extent that he identifies with the future and destiny of *Klal Yisrael*.

With their animosity toward Yosef, the brothers demonstrated the opposite capacity. They sent him into slavery, and thus they too were exiled.

It was indeed Yosef's Divinely ordained mission to insure that the hatred that led to his enslavement was gone and the rift was healed. The children of Leah were not only protective of Binyamin, the presumptive last child of Rachel, but were willing to give up their lives to insure his safe return. They had come full circle. Their *sinas chinam* turned into an *ahavas chinam,* and, in Hashem's manner of providing the cure before the illness, the seeds of redemption were planted before the exile was allowed to commence.

The Vilna Gaon teaches that the Egyptian exile was the prototype for future exiles. Just as community and solidarity were necessary prerequisites for redemption then, so too are they necessary now, for if we are consumed by hatred and polarization, how can our people survive this hostile *galus*?

_____ *Rabbi Ephraim Slepoy*

FOR THOSE WHO LIVE WITH THE WEEKLY TORAH PORTION, THESE PAST few weeks have been emotionally trying. We have been reading of the trials and tribulations of Yosef, whose problems compound in episode after episode. He is held captive by his jealous brothers, then sold to a caravan of traders. After being transported to Egypt, he is sold into slavery and later jailed.

Nonetheless, through Divine providence, he rises to become ruler of Egypt, second in command to the Pharaoh. And, in this week's *parshah*, he comes full circle to be reunited with his brothers and his father in one of the most poignant and emotionally charged chapters of the Torah.

Yosef Hatzaddik unequivocally forgives his brothers for their crime against him. He does not harbor the slightest ill feeling toward them, attributing all that he went through to the hand of G-d. Even his seemingly cruel decision to withhold his identity from his brothers and frame Binyamin is, in fact, motivated by his genuine desire to find forgiveness for them. He jails Binyamin to put his brothers in a situation identical to the one they put themselves in years earlier when they abandoned him. By enabling his brothers to return to the scene of their crime, Yosef gives them the opportunity to reconcile their mistake and to achieve full penance.

However, even with Yosef's total forgiveness and his brothers' full repentance, the episode of Yosef's kidnapping manages to come back and haunt the Jewish people.

Toward the end of the *Mussaf* service on Yom Kippur there is a prayer which is one of the emotional highlights of the day's services. (A different version of the prayer is part of the *Kinos* recited on Tishah B'Av morning.) It is the story of the Ten Martyrs, which graphically and movingly tells the story of ten great Sages of the *Mishnaic* period (including Rabbi Akiva, Rabban Shimon ben Gamliel and Rabbi Elazar) who were brutally and mercilessly put to death at the anti-Semitic whim of the capricious Roman government.

Why were ten sages of Israel chosen to be slaughtered at this time?

A lecturer on the history of anti-Semitism once began by stating, "As long as there have been Jews, there have been anti-Semites; and as long as there have been anti-Semites, there have been theories of anti-Semitism."

In their book, "Why the Jews?", Dennis Prager and Joseph Telushkin thoroughly explore the many varied reasons for anti-Semitism. In our Yom Kippur prayer, *"Eileh Ezkerah,"* a rather novel and somewhat ironic explanation is given. The Roman ruler opened up the Book of *Shemos* to the *parshah* of *Mishpatim,* where the law regarding kidnapping is found. He then posed this question to the Sages: "What is the law, if a man is found to have kidnapped one of his Jewish brethren and he enslaved him and sold him?"

"The kidnapper is to die," the Sages replied.

The Roman ruler asked, "Then what about your ancestors who sold their brother Yosef to a caravan of Ishmaelites? They were never punished as is required by your own Torah. And so you ten [corresponding to the ten brothers] must accept the Heavenly judgment upon yourselves."

The Roman idea of judgment included unspeakable torture and horrible deaths. These ten martyrs were slaughtered under the pretext of exacting "justice" for a crime committed over sixteen centuries earlier! How utterly preposterous! But then, isn't all anti-Semitism absurd? Furthermore, isn't all *sinas chinam* — senseless hatred — irrational?

Looking into the story of Yosef and his brothers, we find that the reason they sold him into slavery was jealousy and *sinas chinam* — the very same senseless hatred that the Talmud tells us caused the destruction of the *Beis Hamikdash* two thousand years ago. It is that very same senseless hatred that prevents it from being rebuilt today.

We look sadly at the news making headlines around the world, from Germany to Bosnia to Somalia, and we can't help but wonder, "When will mankind ever learn?" Then we look at the news that we Jews are making — the pronouncements, the statements, the internal strife and discord — and we must ask ourselves, "When will *we* learn?"

Rabbi Myron Rakowitz

S URELY, YOU HAVE PERSONALLY SAID OR HEARD SOMEONE ELSE say, "I am proud to be a Jew." We always hear, "I am proud to be a Jew." But how come we never hear, "I am proud to be an Israelite," or "I am proud to be a Hebrew"? In fact, we speak of Judaism, never of Israelism or Hebrewism. What makes "Jewish" stick?

The name "Jew" comes from Yehudah, whose eloquent plea on behalf of his brother, Binyamin, opens this week's *parshah.* In the subsequent *parshah,* Yaakov blesses him: "Yehudah — your brothers know you." It is Yehudah in whom we take special pride.

But what is the special quality that distinguishes Yehudah from his brothers — the quality for which he is chosen by his father to precede the family to Goshen and establish a Jewish presence in Egypt?

A young man once interviewed for a job. Toward the end of the interview he was asked, "Are you a responsible person?"

"Of course," he said. "In my last job, everything that went wrong, they held me responsible."

Responsibility. That is Yehudah's prime quality. Yehudah's words resound through history, "I have taken responsibility for the youth." Yehudah would guarantee his family's and his people's future. This guarantee, this commitment to the future, is the hallmark of Jewish living.

A Chasidic Rebbe extracts from Yehudah's protection of Binyamin the ultimate quest in life — the quest for continuity, for a learned and observant youth to carry on future generations. "How can I return to my father and the lad is not with me?" Yehudah asks Yosef. The Rebbe replays this very question to our generation: "How can I face my Heavenly Father if I do not bear responsibility for our youth?"

We are Jewish because we are like Yehudah. We are responsible.

פרשת ויחי
Parshas Vayechi

_____ *Rabbi Feivel Wagner*

I T HAS BEEN SAID THAT WE LIVE IN AN AGE OF SPECIALIZATION. OVER THE past few decades, society has seen an increase in people who know more and more about less and less. The concentration of one's energies on a particular area is especially evident in the medical field and seen in other professions as well. How should this trend impact upon Jewish living? Does the Torah desire specialization in one area or does it prefer well-roundedness?

The *mishnah* tells us that "Rabbi Chanina ben Akashia says, The Holy One, Blessed is He, wished to confer merit upon Israel; therefore, He gave them Torah and *mitzvos* in abundance." Yet, in giving us more *mitzvos* and more opportunities for merit, G-d also made our job more challenging. If we had only ten *mitzvos* to concentrate on, we could probably do a better job of fulfilling them.

The first Gerer Rebbe, known as the *Chiddushei Harim,* explains that the 613 *mitzvos* that G-d gave us cover every aspect of human endeavor and relate to every facet of human personality. We are asked to be merciful yet firm, kind yet strong, emotional yet intellectual, spontaneous yet disciplined. The Torah asks us to call on every part of our makeup in serving Hashem.

But while we must use every aspect of ourselves to serve Him, we should also find one area in which we excel, from where we can draw a particular talent from our deepest reservoir of resources for the glory of our Creator. Since each human being is unique, Hashem provides many *mitzvos* so that each can find his niche, a place to excel. Every Jew can enhance his general practice with excellence in one specialized area.

At the end of *Parshas Vayechi,* our ancestor, Yaakov, who understood this principle, blessed his children fittingly — "Each man according to his blessing he blessed them." Rashi notes the shift in pronoun from singular to plural. The connotation, he says, is that although Yaakov blessed each of his sons individually, he included all of them in every blessing. Each son received all the blessings, but with special reference to one specific area.

A practical application of this lesson addresses a common, even tragic, misconception. The partnership of Yissachar and Zevulun finds itself at the center of Jewish living to this day: the commerce of Zevulun supporting the Torah study of Yissachar. But Zevulun, while specializing in the support of Torah, understood that he had an obligation to study as well. Just as his work did not absolve him from keeping kosher or putting on *tefillin,* it did not absolve him from his daily obligation to personally study Torah.

Even if we are not Yissachars, we must be proper Zevuluns, setting times for our own Torah study even while excelling at supporting those whose lives are totally immersed in Torah. If we neglect our own learning time, we lose a crucial aspect in our development as complete Torah Jews, regardless of the amount of resources we devote to the support of Torah.

_____ *Rabbi Yaakov Pollak*

HOW MUCH IMPORTANCE DO WE ATTACH TO BLESSINGS THAT WE RECEIVE from others? How seriously do we take them? Our Sages established that "everything depends upon the one who gives the blessing and the one who receives it." What if G-d Himself gives the blessing?

A deeper significance to the concept of blessings is found in the Almighty's declaration to Avraham, "*Veheyei berachah*—You will be a blessing." This gave Avraham the Divine authority to bless anyone else he wanted, according to Rashi. The Ramban explains that Avraham became the model through whom other people blessed each other.

But there is another way to understand "*Veheyei berachah.*" The Torah tells us that Avraham Avinu, just before his death, "gave Yitzchak all that he possessed. And to the children of his concubines, Avraham gave gifts." But how did he give his many other children gifts, if he bequeathed it all to Yitzchak?

"All that he possessed," the *midrash* writes, does not simply refer to Avraham's material wealth, but also to his spiritual wealth, his essence, his very being. Avraham's personality and demeanor, his perspective on life—these he bestowed solely upon Yitzchak. One dare not equate material riches of cattle and oil with the spiritual riches secured by Avraham and passed on to Yitzchak.

Yaakov, too, in *Parshas Vayechi,* wishes to bestow blessings upon his children as a last will and testament. The Torah states, "Each man according to his blessing he blessed them." Yaakov individualized each of his blessings for each of his sons, Rashi writes. But Rav Yosef Dov Soloveitchik, *zt"l,* explains that "according to his blessing" does not necessarily refer to the blessings' recipients, his sons, but could, in fact, refer to Yaakov himself. Yaakov blessed them with *his* blessing—that is, with his essence, with his very being. In addition to tailoring each *berachah* to the personality and temperament of each of his sons, Yaakov gave them all a common *berachah,* one that he had received from Yitzchak, who, in turn, had received it from Avraham.

Parents have always made every effort to bless their children with estates of material wealth. Some are even judged by how much they've left for their children. The meaning of "*Veheyei berachah*" shouts out to us. You will be a blessing! How much of *you* did you bequeath to your children? How much of your Torah and moral character, how much of your spiritual legacy will your children inherit? Let us be sure to answer those questions.

_____ *Rabbi Jacob J. Greenberg*

BEFORE HIS DEATH, YAAKOV BLESSED HIS GRANDSONS, THE TWO SONS of Yosef. "*Becha,*" he told them, "With you will Israel bless [its children], saying, 'May G-d make you like Ephraim and Menashe.' " In his *sefer, Be'er Yosef,* Rav Yosef Tzvi Salant asks, why *Becha,* the singular tense, is used when the subjects of the blessing seem to be the two grandsons. Shouldn't the plural tense, *Bachem,* be used?

Rav Salant explains that Ephraim and Menashe, as sons of a powerful leader, had opportunities not available to the general public. Menashe became managing director of the viceroy's household, while Ephraim studied Torah at the highest levels. Who could ask for a better package of *Yiddishe nachas*?

How is it possible, therefore, for people who are poor and downtrodden or who are far from the halls of Torah to conceptualize the blessing of Ephraim and Menashe? How might it apply to them? Even someone of modest means may feel that the fulfillment of these blessings is far beyond his reach. Why has this blessing become so essential that we utilize it every Friday evening to bless our children?

The answer, Rav Salant notes, becomes clear when we come to appreciate all that transpired to Yosef. He rose to great heights despite everything he went through — the horror and degradation of being sold as a slave, the accusation of sexual harassment, the prison sentence. From these dismal depths of despair did he rise to greatness. He became viceroy of Egypt, second only to Pharaoh — a model for his people and for all times. Yes, it is possible to reach great heights, even from the lowliest of circumstances.

This is what Yaakov meant when he blessed Yosef's children. *Becha,* through you, because of you, Yosef, will all the children of Israel, even those in adverse circumstances, be comfortable in reciting this blessing. The grandfather blesses his grandchildren through his son. The *chut hameshulalsh,* the cord of continuity, will never be torn asunder.

If we reach for the highest goals and apply ourselves with diligence we can attain a level far beyond those who are satisfied with less. In every generation, our blessing is appropriate: "May G-d make you like Ephraim and Menashe."

_____ *Rabbi Moshe Hauer*

T WICE DAILY, IN OUR PRAYERS, WE RECALL THE EXODUS FROM EGYPT, affirming our faith by remembering the miracles that demonstrated G-d's power over nature. Less remembered, however, is an earlier attempt at exodus, detailed in *Parshas Vayechi,* that would have appeared entirely natural. After the death of Yaakov, Yosef and his brothers ask Pharaoh to allow them to go to the Holy Land to bury him.

Pharaoh grudgingly allows them to go — but only the adults; their children and property were left behind as a guarantee for their return. Apparently, the brothers had been looking to make this their final departure from Egypt, to take their families to the Holy Land for good. Pharaoh said no. But what if Pharaoh *had* allowed them all to go? Would this have been a suitable time for redemption, for *Yetzias Mitzrayim?*

Redemption has one critical condition: It must demonstrate G-d's strength as the force behind it. This goal of achieving revelation through redemption is repeatedly emphasized throughout the story of the Exodus, which stresses that the miracles of *geulah* produced an appreciation of G-d's dominant strength.

In the story of Yosef and his brothers, as well, revelation is a dominant theme. Yosef's wisdom is consistently seen as imbued with the G-dly spirit, as he repeatedly invokes G-d as the engineer of the complex set of circumstances that brought him to his high position in Egypt. His brothers, on the other hand, see things differently. They perceive Yosef's turbulent experiences as a result of their own bad behavior. The element of redemption is eclipsed by the glare of their own cruelty and its painful consequences for Yosef. In a series of events so dominated by the hateful and harmful hands of man, they do not perceive the gentle hand of G-d.

This lack of perception is highlighted when Hashem ruefully contrasts His method of involvement with the Israelites of Egypt to the way He had related to their forefathers. As Rabbi Yehudah Haleivi explains in his *Kuzari,* G-d had not revealed miracles to the forefathers, as their faith did not require it. But to the entirety of *Klal Yisrael,* it had become necessary to bring about redemption through miraculous means. For the new generation, not sensitive to the subtleties of G-d's hand in nature, a flash of brilliance was needed. It takes far greater perception and sensitivity to see G-d in the ordinary.

Tradition teaches that the final redemption will come in two stages, the first achieved through *Mashiach ben Yosef* and the second through *Mashiach ben David.* The Gaon of Vilna teaches that the first stage will be accomplished with Yosef's approach, through natural means, while the second stage will be built on miracles. Perceptive people will merit to see G-d's redemptive presence in His hidden hand in history, long before the rest of us recognize it from the miraculous events that even the blind can see.

One can only wonder: Had all the brothers shared Yosef's perception, had they seen in this story the *geulah* that Yosef saw, would the subsequent era of slavery have been necessary? Could this journey to bury Yaakov have been the final trip to Israel, culminating in the triumphant acknowledgment of exceptionally ordinary G-dliness?

And are we perhaps failing to notice the same thing: the final chapters of redemption as they occur in our own lives and in the national life of *Klal Yisrael*?

Sefer Shemos

פרשת שמות
Parshas Shemos

Dr. Michelle Levine

T HE STORY OF THE EGYPTIAN EXILE, RECOUNTED IN *PARSHAS SHEMOS,* marks the beginning of a new era in the history of *Bnei Yisrael,* culminating in their miraculous redemption and in the giving of the Torah at Sinai. But the second book of the Torah is not entitled *Sefer Hageulah,* the Book of Exodus, but *Sefer Shemos,* the Book of Names.

Furthermore, *Sefer Shemos* begins with the conjunctive letter, *vav,* "*Ve'eileh shemos — And* these are the names," implying that this second book of the Torah is a continuation of the narratives in *Sefer Bereishis.* In fact, the first six verses of *Shemos* briefly recapitulate an entire section from the end of *Sefer Bereishis* which lists the members of Jacob's family, who descended to Egypt.

Rashbam, Rashi's grandson, analyzes this repetition: "Because the Torah wishes to explain and say (in the seventh verse), "And the children of Israel were prolific and fertile," it had to repeat and say that upon their arrival to Egypt, they were but seventy people. In order to fully appreciate the impact of their proliferation, says Rashbam, one must be reminded of *Bnei Yisrael*'s meager number when they first entered Egypt.

Rashbam delivers a localized and internal link between this repetition and the upcoming events of *Sefer Shemos,* rather than connecting it to the narratives of *Sefer Bereishis.* In his view, the recapitulation serves as a literary device to move the narrative forward. However, if this were the sole purpose of the recap, why repeat the information in such detail? It could have been simplified. "And all of Jacob's issue who came to Egypt were seventy." Why does the text record not only their number but their individual names?

Rashi employs a *Midrashic* interpretation to unravel the deep significance of this recapitulation: "Although the Torah already enumerated them by name while they were living, it again enumerated them at the time of their deaths to show how dear they are [to G-d], for they are compared to the stars, which G-d brings out [at night] and brings in [in the morning] by number and by name."

In contrast to Rashbam, Rashi regards the recapitulation as an actual second counting of *Bnei Yisrael,* signifying G-d's deep love for His nation. This re-enumeration parallels the repeated countings of *Bnei Yisrael* after their exodus from Egypt, after the sin of the Golden Calf and following G-d's command to build the Tabernacle. In counting them by name and by number, G-d expresses his dual affection for them, as individuals and as members of a nation.

With this *Midrashic* comment, Rashi reveals the essence of *Sefer Shemos.* Although *Bnei Yisrael* are entering the darkness of exile, G-d's love for them is forever present and will ultimately be revealed at their redemption. Thus, G-d's love for them is compared to the stars of the night. The stars are "brought in" at dawn, by number and by name, but they do not cease to shine; they are only hidden from view.

So too, the tribes of Israel are recounted by number and by name on the eve of their existence. Though their light will be hidden during the long exile, it will continue to shine upon their future generations born in Egypt, and it will be displayed once again at their redemption.

G-d's special love can not be expressed merely by counting their number, but their names, their individual identities, must be singled out. For in *Sefer Shemos, Bnei Yisrael* forge their *sheim,* their essence, their unique form as a nation of G-d, which Pharaoh tried to eradicate. By applying an intrinsic meaning to the first verses of *Shemos,* rather than viewing them as a literary repetition, Rashi divulges G-d's special relationship to His nation and sets the tone for all of *Sefer Shemos,* the Book of Names.

ACCORDING TO THE _MIDRASH,_ THE ISRAELITES WERE SAVED FROM perpetual servitude in Egypt due to four things, one of which was that they did not change their Hebrew names. Yehudah remained Yehudah and did not become Leon; Reuven stayed Reuven and didn't switch to Rufus. In light of this inflexibility, one finds it ironic that Moshe Rabbeinu, who was chosen by Hashem to deliver the Jewish nation from Egyptian bondage, apparently had an Egyptian name.

When Pharaoh's daughter, Bisyah, retrieved a baby from the river, she called him Moshe, _"ki min hamayim mishisihu_ — for I drew him out of the water." The unlikelihood that Pharaoh's daughter was fluent enough in Hebrew to create a Hebrew name for her adopted son has led to various theories as to the origin of the name Moshe.

The _Chizkuni_ gives two explanations. One, there is a tradition that Bisyah converted and therefore, yes, she did know Hebrew. Two, it is possible that Moshe's mother, Yocheved, named him Moshe and Bisyah approved.

Nevertheless, it appears, from a simple reading of the text, that Moshe was indeed an Egyptian name. This notion is elaborated upon by the Malbim, who quotes Philo's explanation that Moshe is composed of _mo,_ Egyptian for water, and _sheh,_ meaning exiting or escaping in Egyptian. The name Moshe, according to the Malbim, means the same thing in both Hebrew and Egyptian.

The _Yalkut Shimoni_ offers a list of Moshe Rabbeinu's other names: "his father called him Chaver; his mother called him Yekusiel; his sister called him Yered; his brother called him Avi Zandach; his nurse called him Avi Socho; the Israelites called him Shemayah."

Nonetheless, Hashem always called him Moshe, the name that Bisyah gave him. With all of the various Hebrew alternatives, why did Hashem address Moshe exclusively by this name? Rav Yehudah Amital gives a novel explanation for this preference. Water, being a liquid, takes on the shape of the container into which it is poured. Having no shape of its own, water constantly adjusts to its surroundings. It represents the ultimate in conformity.

Moshe, as the leader of the Jewish people and as Hashem's agent for rescuing them from Egypt, was, literally, "the one who was drawn out from the water." He was the "anti-water," a living symbol of the behavior that preserved the Israelites during their decades of bondage in Egypt. By maintaining their beliefs, language, customs and mode of dress in the face of ever-changing surroundings — by not conforming — the Jewish people were redeemed.

Their attitudes and actions serve as a model for Jewish survival always, in various exiles and under various oppressive regimes. By not being bound to outside influences and pressures, by remaining distinct no matter what the surroundings, Jews survive and flourish.

Indeed, the Exodus from Egypt culminates with the entire Jewish nation enacting this idea, as they pass through the waters of Yam Suf to emerge a free and independent people, with the strength and conviction to face whatever challenges may lie ahead.

_____ *Rabbi Gershon Sonnenschein*

THE BOOK OF *SHEMOS* BEGINS WITH THE STORY OF THE EXODUS, INtroducing Moshe and the unique qualities that make him worthy of leading the redemption. G-d tells Moshe to go to Pharaoh and demand the release of his people — but Moshe is reluctant. He hesitates to go for two reasons: one, he doubts his stature is great enough to appear before Pharaoh, and two, he questions the possibility of the people actually being redeemed.

Moshe's reaction is troubling. One can understand his apprehension about facing Pharaoh, the Midrash tells us, because he had run away from the royal house after killing an Egyptian. But how could Moshe doubt the actual redemption? How could Moshe second-guess the wishes of G-d?

Our Sages teach that there are two types of redemption. The ideal form of redemption is not an escape from adverse circumstances, but simply a progression to greater circumstances. Even in an exile that is not dark and repressive, redemption is still the desired goal. The other form of redemption is one that is mandated by harsh circumstances. Due to the duress of situations and surroundings, redemption becomes the desired goal.

The distinction between the two is essential to a clear appreciation of what redemption has to offer us. When conditions in the Diaspora are such that life is good, that all our needs are filled, that nothing is lacking, many are not willing to strive toward a greater spiritual redemption. As soon as they encounter difficulties, they stop everything and remain content with their present situation.

But the individual who senses a deeper redemption desires the ideal. No matter how comfortable his circumstances, no matter what the obstacles are, nothing will stop him from achieving his goal.

There was never any doubt that Moshe wanted redemption for the Jewish nation, but he wanted them to leave Egypt under ideal circumstances. He knew that if they left with the attitude that they were fleeing from persecution, they would encounter difficulties later on. Sure enough, their complaints led to the construction of the Golden Calf.

Moshe sought to avoid this by postponing the redemption until the Jewish nation was prepared to leave in a frame of mind that would bring them gracefully into *Eretz Yisrael*. But Hashem does not consent. He tells Moshe that He suffers along with His nation, and while they do not recognize the magnitude of their suffering, G-d does. So He wants them taken out of Egypt under less-than-perfect circumstances, even though it will lead to problems down the road. They are judged by their present situation not by their future behavior.

Living in a world and a society such as ours, we sometimes forget our ultimate goals. May we be cognizant of who we are and who we ought to be.

_____ *Rabbi Herzel Kranz*

A T THE END OF *PARSHAS SHEMOS,* PHARAOH INCREASES THE WORK-load of the Jewish people, creating an environment of frustration and tension between Moshe and the Jewish people, including the Israelite leadership of the time.

The question persists: Why did Hashem appoint Moshe, someone almost unknown and totally out of the leadership structure of the Israelite society, to redeem them? Additionally, what happened to the Jewish leadership of the time, whose members were instructed to be partners with Moshe and Aharon in the process of redemption?

As we scan our national history we find that the ways of the Almighty in His relationship with His people do not fit any rational sequence that is readily understood at the time it takes place. From the selection of our father Avraham on down through the prophets, we see that G-d appoints unique souls, often outside the normal system, to further His intentions, to advance the destiny of the Jewish people and human civilization.

Moshe proved his authenticity to the Jewish leaders regarding the purpose of his mission. However, when the moment of truth came to confront Pharaoh, the Jewish leaders were nowhere to be found. The Midrash states, "The elders slipped away one by one from Moshe and Aharon until they were all gone before arriving at the palace, for they were afraid to go."

Conventional Jewish leaders do not always rise to the ultimate challenges.

We live in ominous times. Our people and the State of Israel face challenges and anxieties. Finding the right people with the courage necessary to deliver G-d's message to humanity will surely take an extraordinary act by Hashem.

פרשת וארא
Parshas Va'eira

_____ Rabbi Kenneth N. Hain

THE DEFINING QUALITIES OF JEWISH LEADERSHIP WAS A SUBJECT that fascinated Rav Yosef Dov Soloveitchik, _zt"l_. It is, to him, the obvious theme of _Parshas Behaalosecha_ and of _Parshas Korach_, but emerges also as a dynamic dialectic with broad contemporary implications from a brief comment by Rashi in _Parshas Va'eira_.

The _parshah_ opens with G-d's promise to rescue the Jews from "the burdens of Egypt." They are told that a glorious future awaits them after their liberation from slavery, culminating in their arrival "to the land that I raised my hand to give to Avraham, Yitzchak and Yaakov, and I shall give it to you as a heritage — I am G-d."

However, much to Moshe's dismay, when he presents this message to the Jews, "they did not listen to him." He is then ordered to speak to Pharaoh, but balks at the command, saying, "Behold, the children of Israel did not listen to me, so how will Pharaoh listen to me?" Nevertheless, Moshe and Aharon are "commanded regarding the children of Israel and Pharaoh, king of Egypt, to take the children of Israel out of Egypt."

At this crucial point in the narrative, the Torah digresses and presents the names of the leaders of the tribes of Israel, concluding with the names, _"Aharon uMoshe,"_ to which Rashi notes: "There are places [in the Torah] where Aharon precedes Moshe and there are places in the Torah where Moshe precedes Aharon, to tell us that they are equal in value." This comment is borne out in the very next verse, where the Torah reverses the order of their names.

The Rav understands Rashi's words to reflect more than simple lessons about textual sequence and the equality of Moshe and Aharon. To the Rav, this comment offers a basic insight into the requirements for Jewish leadership at crucial junctures in Jewish history.

Moshe and Aharon, in the view of our Sages, represent sharply contrasting qualities. The Talmud states "Moshe's guiding principle was that the strict law is immutable, but Aharon loved and pursued peace and sought to reconcile man with his neighbor." The Midrash further elaborates: "Kindness and peace, this is Aharon; truth and righteousness, this is Moshe."

These two approaches, the Rav points out, present the classic choice that Jewish leadership must make between *din*, law, and *rachamim*, compassion. Should it exercise the firm, uncompromising "truth" of Moshe, or the softer, more flexible "kindness" of Aharon?

This, then, is the great dilemma of *Parshas Va'eira*. At this crucial and transitional moment in our nation's early history, following the oppression in *Parshas Shemos* and still awaiting the redemption that begins in *Parshas Bo,* the need for leadership is enormous. During this interim period, between "darkness and light," doubt and confusion are rampant and the centrality of leadership is heightened.

But which kind of leadership — that of Moshe or that of Aharon? The stern, unwavering approach of *emes* or the loving embrace of *chessed*?

The answer is, unequivocally, both. Throughout our history, from *Parshas Va'eira* until contemporary times, when Jews are suffering, the quality of Aharon must be emphasized. They need to be cared for and loved unconditionally in the classic mold of the Chasidic rebbe.

But at the very same time, when liberation is imminent and freedom is around the corner, the principles of *Toras Moshe* must be affirmed. We may very well be living now in a *Va'eira* moment — neither fully oppressed nor fully redeemed — and we therefore need the duality of *emes* and *chessed* to be delicately applied. To reach the minds and hearts of our people, in the words of the Rav, Jewish leaders must combine the legacies of Moshe and Aharon and utilize law as well as love.

I N RESPONSE TO MOSHE RABBEINU'S COMPLAINT THAT ISRAEL'S CON-
dition has only worsened since the beginning of his mission to
Pharaoh, Hashem pronounces the four famous expressions of His redemption: _"Vehotzeisi," "Vehitzalti," "Vega'alti," "Velakachti."_

Rabbi Yisrael Lifshitz, the _Tiferes Yisrael,_ explains that these four
words represent the four aspects of enslavement to which the _Bnei
Yisrael_ were subjected and from which, consequently, they had to be
redeemed. Their suffering, he writes, was physical, material, psychological and spiritual.

In a recent speech, Natan Sharansky, the famed former Soviet dissident
and current Minister of the Interior for the State of Israel, movingly described his nine years in the Soviet gulag and how he survived the in-
cessant interrogations of the K.G.B. He drew strength, he said, from a
small book of _Tehillim,_ which had been sent by his wife, Avital, and that
allowed him to mentally prepare himself for the questions of his captors.

During these interrogations, he would tell the K.G.B. agents the latest
jokes circulating about Brezhnev. Sharansky would then explode in
laughter. His interrogators, too, wanted to laugh, but were forced to
stifle the urge. Sharansky would then tell them, "You see, you are really
the prisoners and I am the free one."

Though physically imprisoned, Natan Sharansky remained free psychologically.

In our Diaspora, we enjoy physical freedom, economic freedom, religious freedom. Yet, we risk being psychologically enslaved by the foreign culture in which we live. Our Sages have given us the formula to
remaining free — the _mitzvah_ of _arba kosos,_ the four cups of wine that
we drink at the _seder_ table.

Each of the _arba kosos_ corresponds not only to one of the four expres-
sions of redemption but also to an important element of the _seder._
Kiddush is recited over the first cup, the _Haggadah_ over the second,
Birkas Hamazon over the third and _Hallel_ over the fourth.

There is another aspect to these cups. They "must be properly
mixed," rules the Rambam in _Hilchos Chameitz Umatzah,_ "so as to be

pleasant to drink.... One who drank these four cups using concentrated wine," which is not pleasant, "fulfilled [the *mitzvah* of] the four cups but did not fulfill [the aspect of] freedom.... One who drank these four cups using [properly] mixed wine but drank them at once," and not in their proper sequence, "fulfilled [the aspect of] freedom but did not fulfill [the *mitzvah* of] the four cups."

Rav Yitzchak Ze'ev Soloveitchik, *zt"l,* the Brisker Rav, similarly splits the significance of the cups in two. One aspect is that they are *kosos shel berachah,* each having a blessing said over it. One who did not drink the four cups individually would not recite a separate blessing over each.

The second aspect, he says, is to display one's freedom by drinking the wine. If the cups' taste is unpleasant, they do not properly display freedom.

Jews must realize that Torah and *mitzvos* are *kosos shel berachah* — vehicles through which we are blessed. They are not a restrictive burden, but rather an extraordinary opportunity to lead a life of freedom, joy and fulfillment.

Second, Jews must display that freedom externally. We must wear our Jewishness with pride.

Rabbi Meir Simcha of Dvinsk, *zt"l,* in his great work, *Meshech Chochmah,* cites the famous *midrash* that the *Bnei Yisrael* were redeemed because "they did not change their names, their language or their clothes" while slaves in Egypt. Maintaining the external identity of a Jew, he writes, is more significant than the performance of *mitzvos* in preventing assimilation.

If we realize that the study of Torah and the performance of *mitzvos* are an incomparable *kos shel berachah,* and if we proudly exhibit our Jewish identity, we will remain free until the complete and ultimate redemption of our people, which we so eagerly await.

_____ *Rabbi Leonard Oberstein*

M Y LATE ROSH YESHIVA, RABBI YAAKOV YITZCHOK RUDERMAN, *ZT"L,* of Yeshivas Ner Israel, used *Parshas Va'eira* to demonstrate the importance of gratitude. In this *parshah,* Hashem tells Moshe that he should speak to Aharon and tell him to take his staff and strike the Nile River. Moshe wasn't commanded to do the job himself, Rashi explains, "because the Nile protected Moshe when he was cast into the river; it was not to be smitten by his hand — not in the plague of blood and not in the plague of frogs."

This notion also held true for the plague of lice. Moshe was not to strike the earth to bring on the plague because that very earth had saved him when he used it to bury the Egyptian taskmaster whom he had killed. In this manner, the Torah is teaching us how deeply we must feel gratitude, not only to human beings who help us but even to inanimate objects such as water and sand.

The Rosh Yeshiva quoted a case from the *Shitah Mekubetzes.* A wealthy man lost his fortune and needed to sell his bathhouse to satisfy creditors. The famous rabbi, the Rif, lived in that city and was asked to assess its value, but declined to do so because he had personally benefited from the use of the bathhouse.

To this the *Shitah Mekubetzes* writes: "If this internal feeling of gratitude by the Rif applied to an inanimate bathhouse, how much more so should a person be sensitive to the feelings of a human being."

In *Bamidbar,* Moshe is commanded to take vengeance on the nation of Midyan, and while he did not hesitate to go into battle, he nonetheless did not lead the troops himself. Because he had lived in Midyan many years earlier and felt gratitude toward his former homeland, it would not be proper for him to personally fight this battle.

Rashi, at the beginning of the *Chumash,* tells us that the world was created for something called *reishis. Bikurim,* the first fruits of the harvest, are called *reishis,* and we can thus learn that the world was created so that one could bring these first fruits, which show appreciation for the bounty of the Almighty. One who displays the trait of gratitude fulfills the purpose of Creation.

One who shows ingratitude, on the other hand, is described by the Talmud as "an ingrate, son of an ingrate." This appellation was applied to the Jews who complained to Moshe in the Sinai Desert. They had, it seems, inherited their lack of appreciation for Hashem's favors from the first human, Adam, who, when asked why he ate the fruit of the tree of knowledge, told G-d, "The woman you placed beside me caused me to eat." Adam, in a sense, blamed Hashem for his own failings. Throughout history, man is confronted with the opportunity to show his gratitude or to deny his debt to another.

Rabbi Ruderman related that once a certain *bachur* came to the *Chafetz Chaim*'s yeshiva in Radin. The *Chafetz Chaim* personally arranged proper accommodations for the young boy. He explained that many years before, this boy's grandfather had been kind to him in Vilna and thus he showed the grandson his appreciation.

In our generation, much of the strife that is found can be traced to failing to display gratitude, especially toward spouses and other family members. One who develops this trait of gratitude is a much happier person and certainly sees more satisfaction in his interpersonal relationships.

_____ *Rabbi Bertram Leff*

A T THE BEGINNING OF *PARSHAS VA'EIRA* THE TORAH RECORDS: "G-D spoke to Moshe and said to him, 'I am Hashem.' " Rabbi Chaim Attar, in his commentary *Ohr Hachaim,* asks why G-d felt it necessary to make this declaration to Moshe, when He had already told him, "This is My name, that is Hashem, forever," at the very beginning of his mission to redeem the Jews from Egypt.

The *Ohr Hachaim*'s answer presents us with a lesson of faith. At the end of *Parshas Shemos,* Moshe and Aharon come to Pharaoh to plead their case on behalf of the Israelites. The king of Egypt rebuked them and not only continued the Jews' enslavement and persecution, but worsened their conditions.

The Israelites responded by complaining to Moshe and Aharon, who brought their plea before G-d. "Why have you done evil to this people? Why have you sent me?" Moshe asks. G-d's answer is our verse in question at the beginning of *Va'eira. Elokim,* representing G-d's attribute of judgment (*midas hadin*), spoke to Moshe and said to him, "I am Hashem" — the name that encompasses G-d's attribute of mercy and compassion (*midas harachamim*).

The inadequate human mind often sees G-d as *Elokim,* as a harsh G-d. But the reality is that everything G-d does is encapsulated in His *midas harachamim,* "I am Hashem — I am the G-d of mercy." Although Moshe seems to experience G-d through His *midas hadin,* in reality G-d's *midas harachamim* is being demonstrated, for "*Hashem Hu Ha'elokim.*"

In his essay, "*Kol Dodi Dofeik,*" Rav Yosef Dov Soloveitchik, *zt"l,* sums up this lesson in a most eloquent passage:

"Man's apprehension is limited and distorted.... As long as he perceives only isolated fragments of the cosmic drama and the mighty epic of history, he remains unable to penetrate into the secret lair of suffering and evil. To what may the matter be compared? To a person gazing at a beautiful tapestry, a true work of art, one into which an exquisite design has been woven, but looking at it from the reverse side. Can such a viewing give rise to a sublime aesthetic experience? We, alas, view the world from its reverse side. We are unable to grasp the all-encompassing framework of being. And it is only within that framework that it is possible to discern the Divine plan, the essential nature of the Divine actions."

Let us assimilate the lesson of faith that we draw from G-d's encounter with Moshe Rabbeinu and the Jewish people as they experience redemption from Egypt.

פרשת בא
Parshas Bo

_____ *Rabbi Nachman Kahane*

OVER THREE THOUSAND YEARS AGO, ON SHABBOS HAGADOL, THE Jews of Egypt asserted their independence by taking the Egyptian deity, the lamb, to bring as a sacrifice to Hashem. At that moment, the Jewish people came of age as a nation, making choices and forging a way of life. Their arrival is analogous to a young man becoming a *bar mitzvah,* who must now take the experience and education of his formative years and begin the initial steps of his own independent life, a life in which he is responsible for his actions and punishable for his misdeeds.

This comparison of our nation at the Exodus to a boy at his *bar mitzvah* is a central theme of the *Haggadah.* The *Haggadah* describes four sons — one wise, one evil, one simple and one ignorant — who question their father regarding the implications of the Exodus. Each of the four takes a unique approach, but the dialogue between the wise son and the father stands out as the most intriguing.

"What are these testimonies, commands and laws that the L-rd our G-d commanded you?" asks the wise son. It appears that he asks his father to reveal the entire Torah, an inquiry worthy of a wise son. But what does the father answer?

"One is prohibited from eating after the *afikomen*" — the last piece of matzah at the end of the *seder.* Is the father so oblivious to his son's request that his reply totally lacks pedagogical value?

As with most Rabbinic statements, however, the father's response conceals more than it reveals at first glance, for it must be understood in the context of our nation becoming *bar mitzvah* and asking our Father in Heaven for instruction.

The text of the *Haggadah* was finalized toward the end of the *Tannaic* period, when the Romans ruled *Eretz Yisrael.* At that time, the majority of Jews were dispersed throughout the Roman Empire and those who remained in the Holy Land suffered. People, such as the Christians, questioned our status as G-d's chosen people: Why was our fate so horrendous?

But our Sages knew that there would be a long period of *galus* for the Jewish nation. Thus, in the *Haggadah,* in the dialogue between the wise son and his father, our Sages set down the response to this claim that we are not G-d's chosen people.

The son is asking about the necessity of keeping the laws now that G-d has seemingly rejected the Jewish nation. The father replies surreptitiously (because of the dangers of stating it publicly) that just as the taste of the *afikomen* must linger throughout the night, so too does G-d's choice of the Jewish nation as His own linger forever, regardless of our status in society.

The most rudimentary concept of Judaism is that we are G-d's chosen people, and for this reason G-d gave us the Torah, the Holy Land, the Temple and the prophets. The greatest human experience is to be born a Jew — so much more so today, when, with a little sensitivity, one can see the Hand of G-d in historic events.

_____ *Rabbi Barry Freundel*

WE WATCH PHARAOH, OVER THE COURSE OF THE TEN PLAGUES, GO from being the ruler of the most powerful country in the world to being a veritable punching bag, taking blow after blow after blow. As his power diminishes, he resorts to more and more desperate attempts to maintain some measure of control in his confrontation with the Jews.

But after the eighth plague, Pharaoh explodes and threatens Moshe, ending their dialogue. No one has ever suggested that Pharaoh was anything less than a competent, perhaps even brilliant, leader, but cutting off his dialogue with Moshe appears counterproductive for him, making himself even more vulnerable. But he does it anyway.

Perhaps one can develop an explanation for Pharaoh's behavior by finding a pattern in the way the plagues are visited on the Egyptians. Many commentators, notably the Ramban, have described patterns that repeat throughout the various plagues, at particular intervals.

There are four plagues during which Pharaoh attempts to bargain with Moshe in one fashion or another, either to end a specific plague or to end the exile and all the plagues. In every one of these plagues, some reminder of the plague remains even after the plague is over.

The first is the plague of *tzefardei'a,* frogs. Pharaoh makes his first offer to let the Jews go and asks Moshe to pray for him that the plague end. Moshe, of course, agrees and the frogs die. The Egyptians, we are told, gather the dead frogs in heaps and, as expected, a terrible stench fills the land. The plague may be over, but not completely over.

The second of these "dialogue" plagues is *arov,* wild beasts. Pharaoh asks Moshe to pray for him and Moshe accedes to that request because again Pharaoh promises that the Jews will be allowed to go. When the plague ends, the beasts leave. Not a single one remains. Over the long term, however, this would have a negative effect on Egypt's ecosystem, as the lack of wild animals would cause overbreeding in other species. Thus there would still be a reminder of the plague after the plague.

In the third plague, *barad,* hail, the barley and flax crops were eradicated, but the wheat and spelt were not affected because they were late in ripening and were not yet grown. So each time the Egyptians looked at their fields, they saw the limited crops that remained (until the plague of locusts destroyed that too) and were reminded of what the hail had done.

Finally, the fourth plague, *arbeh,* locusts, ends when G-d brings a strong westerly wind to bear on Egypt, and, as a result, not a single locust remains within the entire borders of the land. This is remarkable. Not to have a single member of this species is a feat that modern science can not even begin to approximate. And since locusts may well have been an important food source, their absence hurt the Egyptians as well. The pattern is set. In each case, the plague continues in some way.

Following this pattern, at the plague of *choshech,* darkness, Pharaoh would have feared that some aspect of the darkness would remain. Even more frightening was the inability of the Egyptians to move during the plague of darkness, while the Jews could move about. The increasing weakness of the Egyptians was contrasted to the growing strength of the Jews. This realization must have hit Pharaoh very hard. He must have been truly demoralized by this turn of events.

I suspect that the combination of his realizing that he had nothing left with which to bargain coupled with his increasing awareness of the collapse of the Egyptian empire was too much for him. Continued dialogue meant continued punishment, which meant continued exposure of weakness. This was simply intolerable, and so he cut off all dialogue in a desperate attempt to break the cycle.

The only problem with his thinking is that shortly after the plague of darkness came a different kind of darkness, when in the middle of the night, G-d Himself descended on Egypt and killed the firstborn of every household, including Pharaoh's. In that sense, the plague of darkness continued too.

_____ *Rabbi Asher Vale*

B EFORE THE JEWS COULD LEAVE EGYPT, THEY HAD TO TAKE CARE OF one last piece of unfinished business. Generations earlier, the Almighty had told Avraham that his descendants would experience slavery and suffering. But He also assured him that they would emerge with great wealth. The time had now arrived for the fulfillment of this promise.

The Jews were instructed to approach the Egyptians and ask them for their valuables. To prevent the Egyptians from denying that they possessed any treasures, the Almighty put a foolproof plan into place. During the plague of darkness, while the Egyptians were completely immobilized, the Jews were free to roam around wherever they wanted.

The ancient Hebrews took advantage of this opportunity and entered their neighbors' homes, discovering the locations of all their valuables. If an Egyptian subsequently claimed to have nothing of value, the Jew would say to him, "What about the silver candelabra hidden in the back of the closet?" The amazed Egyptian would then hand over his precious possessions.

Nonetheless, why were the Egyptians willing to give up their personal treasures simply because they were impressed by their slaves' knowledge of the contents of their homes? Were they afraid of being struck by another plague as terrible as the first ten that had already decimated their country? Or, was this an admission that the Jews were the victors and as such were entitled to the spoils of war?

No, the Almighty had not cast some kind of spell over the Egyptians to make them suddenly like the Jews. There was a reason for their seeing the ancient Hebrews in such a favorable way. "Hashem gave the people *chein* in the eyes of the Egyptians," the Torah tells us. The *chein* — favor, grace, beauty, charm — of the Jews is what made the difference.

Rav Samson Raphael Hirsch explains that the Egyptians were amazed by the fact that the Jews hadn't removed a single item from their homes during their three days of unrestricted access. It was their ability to restrain themselves that impressed the Egyptians.

There are numerous ways in which we Jews can make a favorable impression upon the gentile world in which we live. Examples abound of Jews who have excelled in the arts and sciences. In the financial realm, too, many Jews have been extremely successful. We can highlight the disproportionately high number of Nobel prizes that have been won by people of our faith.

We learn from the experience of our ancestors, however, that our ability to be morally superior is what most impresses others. Our *chein,* the sweetness and charm of the Jewish people, is our best feature.

_____ *Rabbi Yaakov Luban*

PHARAOH'S BEHAVIOR DURING THE TEN PLAGUES SEEMS INCOMPRE-hensible. During several plagues, Pharaoh capitulates and agrees to let the Jewish people leave Egypt. Yet as soon as each plague ends, Pharaoh recants — even though he knows that his stubbornness will result in further punishment for Egypt.

Equally unfathomable is the indifference of the Egyptian population toward the exhortations of Moshe. After accurately predicting six plagues of doom, Moshe forewarns the people of the upcoming hail and tells them not to leave their slaves and animals out in the fields, lest they be killed. Nonetheless, the Torah reports, many Egyptians did just that, and their slaves and livestock perished. What accounted for their stubbornness?

The Kotzker Rebbe makes a striking observation. "Pharaoh rose in the night," the Torah reports, and Rashi comments that he rose from his bed. Imagine: after enduring nine terrible plagues, Moshe warns Pharaoh that at midnight every firstborn in the country would die. Pharaoh completely ignores this prophecy and goes to sleep! How could he be so relaxed in face of such compelling danger?

Seven days after this plague, another remarkable incident occurs. In perhaps the greatest miracle of human history, G-d splits the waters of the Red Sea, and the Jewish people pass through. The Egyptian army follows and, to nobody's surprise, G-d brings the waters crashing down on them. Why did the Egyptians think that G-d, Who had been defending the Jewish people all along, would suspend the waters' onslaught for the benefit of the Jews' enemies?

The Torah explains the mentality of Pharaoh and the Egyptian people simply: They "did not take to heart the word of G-d." Human beings are given the capacity to ignore even the most obvious truths, something psychologists call "denial."

With powerful symbolism, the ninth plague of darkness reflects this irrational behavior in the Egyptians. Our Sages tell us that when a Jew visited an Egyptian home, there was light for the Jew and darkness for the Egyptian. The very same spot was both light and dark, depending on the viewer's perception. The Jew saw the hand of G-d clearly revealed, but the Egyptian remained in the dark, seeing nothing at all. Thus, the plague of darkness preceded the final blow, providing the key psychological insight into the mental blindness that prevailed in Egypt.

There is an important lesson to be learned from these events: We all have traces of Pharaoh's personality lingering within us. We, too, sometimes deny self-evident truths and close our eyes to blatant realities.

Rabbi Moshe Chaim Luzatto, in his classic work of Jewish ethics, *Mesilas Yesharim,* instructs every human being to ask himself the question, *"Mah chovosi ba'olami?"* What is my obligation in life? Why did G-d create me with unique talents and abilities? What is the purpose of my existence? This inquiry is fundamental, yet many people live out their lives never once having pondered this question and its implications.

If the behavior of Pharaoh and the Egyptian people strikes us as absurd, perhaps we should look at ourselves and become inspired to open our souls, to see the light of the Almighty which illuminates the entire world.

פרשת בשלח
Parshas Beshalach

_____ *Rabbi Marc D. Angel*

A FTER MIRACULOUSLY CROSSING THE RED SEA, MOSHE AND THE children of Israel sing a beautiful song praising G-d. In the Torah scroll, this song is written in a special way. Its words do not run together as an uninterrupted block of text, but are arranged, rather, with a blank space following each clause. This style of gaps interspersed within the words implies that silence went together with song. The Torah wants us to consider the words of the Israelites, but also to ponder their unspoken thoughts and feelings. It wants us to value silence as well as words.

In life, too, we know that the words we speak represent but one level of our being; the silence that often surrounds those words represents another level. It is possible to speak words of happiness and encouragement with a broken heart. It is possible to express sadness and grief while feeling consolation and calmness within.

People operate on different levels. The wise among us know the meaning of their words and also the meaning of their silence.

Silent stirrings within a person must be recognized. For people to be spiritually and morally whole, they need to be closely attuned to their own hidden motives and meanings. To serve G-d *lishmah* requires the ability to purify one's heart and mind so that one's words are in consonance with a truly religious inner life.

In his monumental work, *Ish Ha-halakhah,* Rav Yosef Dov Soloveitchik, *zt"l,* writes: "Halakhic man does not quiver before any man; he does not seek our compliments, nor does he require public approval....

The old saying of Socrates, that virtue is knowledge, is strikingly similar to the stance of halakhic man."

The *halachic* individual, grounded in Torah teachings, has a rich inner life. He needs no external praise, for the silence within him sustains him and gives meaning to his words. Moreover, a true religious personality needs to be aware not only of his own silence and words, but also of the different dimensions in the personalities of others. One must always be attuned to the unstated feelings, fears and anxieties of those to whom he speaks — even when they criticize him.

Human communication is hampered most not when words are misunderstood, but when silent feelings and underlying motives go undetected. One can not truly understand a fellow human being without being prepared to invest the time and sensitivity to listen to his whole communication, verbal and non-verbal.

Rabbi Shimon ben Gamliel said: "All my days I have grown up among the Sages and I have found nothing better for a person than silence." Silence is the repository of our deepest feelings and thoughts.

Life, like the song of Moshe and the Israelites, is composed of both words and silence. Happy is the person who can control his words. Happy is the person who can understand and appreciate the value of silence, in himself and in others.

_____ *Rabbi Asher Bush*

FROM THE VERY START OF THEIR SOJOURNS IN THE WILDERNESS, THE Jewish people meet numerous challenges they never had to address in their days of slavery. Food, water, shelter and safety had been provided by their masters in exchange for their backbreaking labor.

It therefore comes as no surprise that each of these needs brings on a national panic and crisis of faith: How can they escape the oncoming Egyptian hordes at the Red Sea? Where will they find fresh water in the parched desert? What will they eat? How will 600,000 hungry families find meat?

Through each of these crises, Moshe sympathizes; the people's needs are real, their fears legitimate. Considering their past, what other reaction can he expect from them? Thus, throughout each crisis, Moshe speaks to the people calmly and reassuringly, expressing his deep faith in G-d, a faith he hopes they, too, will begin to develop.

Only once in *Parshas Beshalach* does Moshe get angry at them, only once does he feel the need to rebuke them for their complaints, only once does he turn to G-d in frustration—after they demand water for the second time and question G-d's supervision of them. Immediately, the Torah pronounces those ominous words: "*Vayavo Amaleik* — And Amaleik came and waged war on Israel."

But Amaleik does not simply come out of nowhere, as Rashi points out; he is brought on. *Bnei Yisrael's* lack of faith in G-d is only half the story. They also treat Moshe with great disrespect. They do not simply bring their grievance to Moshe, but actually fight with him over it.

Throughout *Parshas Beshalach,* G-d makes it clear to the Jewish people that He will take care of all their material needs, their food and water, their clothing and shelter. He asks for but one thing in return: that the Jewish people have complete faith in Him. Faith means that they can not demand things of G-d, nor can they test Him.

A faithful Jew would never need to fight with Moshe or yell at him to provide water. If G-d is the Provider, then there is no room to blame another person. Since our formation as a nation, G-d alone has provided for us and watched over us in every way possible. All we need to do is appreciate His gifts properly.

For this reason, in *Parshas Ki Seitzei,* the *mitzvah* to remember Amaleik's attack is placed beside the *mitzvah* to have honest weights and measures, for, as many of the commentaries point out, if we fail to treat each other with honesty and integrity, we invite Amaleik upon us. To have dishonest weights and measures, to cheat at business, is the surest sign that one does not really believe that G-d is providing one's livelihood. Otherwise, why break — why even bend — the rules?

If we do not demonstrate our faith in G-d, not only in our hearts but in our conduct, we risk forfeiting our special Providential care and make ourselves vulnerable to the harshness and brutality of Amaleik. When the people of G-d forget G-d, they encounter a people who are G-dless. When the Jewish people forget how to properly treat a brother, they are confronted by a people who know no brothers and show no compassion.

As the Jewish people prepare to depart from Egypt, each one busily gathering his belongings, only Moshe takes the time to fulfill the ancient promise made to Yosef, to carry his remains with them to be buried in the Holy Land. Moshe is motivated to personally uphold this vow because he knows that the Jewish people will be given the Torah and begin a new lifestyle that they are not accustomed to, and it will only be natural for them to question the viability of such a faith and such a lifestyle.

The remains of Yosef, which, the Talmud states, were transported beside the Holy Ark, served to remind this new nation of Yosef's abiding faith in G-d in all that he did and through all that he experienced. Yosef remained a moral man in a world of immorality. His example led the way for the Jewish people then and leads the way for the Jewish people today. As we move through this world, let us do so with honesty and integrity, raising the banner of our faith in the One True G-d.

_____ *Rabbi Abraham Halbfinger*

P ARSHAS BESHALACH TELLS TWO STORIES. IT BEGINS WITH THE PEOPLE of Israel leaving Egypt, journeying into the desert and through the Red Sea. It describes the Egyptians drowning, followed by the song of Moshe and the Jewish nation. The *parshah* ends with a description of Amaleik's attack upon the people of Israel, the battle that took place, and G-d's promise to obliterate the memory of Amaleik.

A look at the victories against these two enemies of Israel reveals a distinction. G-d alone defeated Egypt, as the Torah states, "The Lord will fight for you and you shall hold your peace." The battle with Amaleik, by contrast, was fought by the nation, albeit with G-d's miraculous help. Moshe commanded Yehoshua to choose elite soldiers and lead them into battle. Moshe stayed in the background and prayed, holding his hands high, begging G-d to forgive the Israelites and give them victory.

While Moshe's hands were raised Heavenward, the Torah tells us, the Jewish people prevailed. But when he put them down, they fell. The Talmud, questioning how it was that Moshe's hands determined success or failure, states that "as long as Israel looked to their Father in Heaven, they were victorious; but when they did not, they faltered."

In his splendid work, *Hadrash Veha'iyun,* the Raisher Rav, Rabbi Aaron Levine, *zt"l,* explains that Moshe's prayer came at a difficult time for Israel, for they did not deserve salvation — having just questioned G-d's presence among them and His concern for them. The war took place in Refidim, so called because the people of Israel loosened (*rafu*) their hands from Torah.

The battle with the Amalekites also marked the debut of Yehoshua as a leader of the nation. The Ramban notes that Yehoshua's position in the community was not only enhanced but firmly established as a result of his leadership in this battle. The Midrash states that Yehoshua was anointed with oil on that day, an inaugural procedure reserved for kings. (Even Moshe was not anointed.)

In directing Yehoshua, Moshe told him that the war would begin "tomorrow." The power of tomorrow is an important concept in Judaism. Moshe in particular looked forward to the anticipated accomplishments of the next day and those of the future. He spoke about the future destiny of our people as if this battle would secure our eternal relationship with G-d.

Parshas Beshalach speaks of the future of Israel and of our people's potential. Yehoshua came into his own, and the nation moved on to Sinai, recognizing the importance of their relationship with G-d.

_____ *Rabbi Saul Aranov*

T HE JEWISH NATION'S PASSAGE THROUGH THE SPLIT WATERS OF THE *Yam Suf* marked not only the final step of their Exodus from Egypt, but their first step toward becoming G-d's chosen people. In this manner, they followed in the footsteps of the Patriarchs.

Avraham, according to the *midrash,* was on his way to the *Akeidah* with Yitzchak, when the *Satan* took the form of a stream and blocked their path. Avraham pressed on and as he waded through, the water reached his neck. But his devotion to fulfill the Divine request to take Yitzchak to the *Akeidah* enabled him to safely pass through those threatening waters.

Yitzchak's similar devotion to Hashem enabled him to remain steadfast in Canaan, even during the famine there, and to re-open Avraham's wells, which the Philistines had stopped up. Yaakov, too, was tested at a body of water — the Yabbok River — where he wrestled with the angel of Eisav. The Israelites, confronted by a turbulent sea, acted with self-sacrifice by jumping into the *Yam Suf,* an act that propelled them forward with a new resolve, a new dimension of faith.

After crossing through the water, the Israelites express their new-found faith in song — the *Shiras Hayam,* the Song of the Sea. The *midrash* states that at Creation the angels declared, "What is man that we should make mention of him?" G-d replied, "Come observe the scene of the Song of the Sea." As soon as they heard the Israelites sing, the angels began to sing as well: "O G-d, how glorious is Your Name in all the earth."

Song, through which celestial beings praise the Almighty in the Heavenly abode, is the language of the soul. Song possesses therapeutic powers for those who are physically and mentally handicapped. Moshe, who suffered from a speech impediment, sang at the sea without obstructions. The Torah is called a *shirah,* a song. The Torah is also allegorically referred to as water for the parched soul. The combination of water and song at the *Yam Suf* brought the nascent Jewish nation one step closer, physically and spiritually, to their acceptance of the Torah and their embrace of the Divine mandate.

Our mission today remains that of our forebears — to swim in the "Sea of Torah," to drink from its waters, and to sing out gloriously to G-d for His generous, eternal gift to us.

פרשת יתרו
Parshas Yisro

Rabbi Kenneth Brander

T HE PROPHET YIRMIYAHU PROCLAIMS THE PASSIONATE COMMITMENT demonstrated by the Jewish people in accepting the Sinai covenant: "So says G-d, I remember the devotion of your youth, your love as a bride." His words are a poetic expansion on the verse in this week's *parshah,* where the Jewish people announce, "Everything that G-d has said we will do and we will obey."

Yet the Talmud records a more pessimistic account of the Jewish people's acceptance at Sinai: "Rav Avdimi bar Chama bar Chasa stated, The Holy One, Blessed is He, overturned the mountain above them like an inverted cask and stated, If you accept the Torah, good; if not, here will be your grave."

Which description is correct? Is the former account, expressed directly in the text of the Bible and Prophets, accurate, or the one described in the oral tradition of the Talmud? Is there a way to reconcile these two seemingly conflicting opinions?

One can perhaps reconcile the two with the understanding that each approach represents a dimension of the Jewish experience. There are times when one embraces the precepts of Judaism through a recognition of their relevance, their nurturing and enriching potential. An individual's journey in search of G-dliness compels one to passionately observe those *mitzvos* viewed as meaningful. At that moment, one experiences the *naaseh venishma* phenomenon. We will do and we will obey — without any need to intellectually digest all of the details.

However, there are also times when a particular *mitzvah* or set of *mitzvos* does not appear meaningful. How does one respond to a *mitzvah* that one views as uninspiring? What is one to do at that moment of metaphysical crisis?

This is the second dimension of the religious experience. A Jew's commitment to the Sinai covenant, to Torah and *mitzvos,* can not be limited to *mitzvos* that feel meaningful. There are times when one must re-experience the feeling that the mountain is overturned above him, when he must understand his obligation to observe the precept simply because it is G-d's will. Compliance is demanded regardless of emotional attachment. Observance celebrates the Jews' commitment to the eternal reality of Torah. Its norms and mores are a blueprint for an empowering lifestyle.

Both dimensions of the Jewish experience must be realized. We must observe the commandments that we have been endowed with through the Sinai experience and its continued *mesoratic* development.   At the same time, those precepts that do not presently speak to us must be studied, analyzed and researched. The Hebrew word for question — *she'eilah* — contains at its core the name of G-d. In every question, in every religious search, G-d is found — even in those questions that remain unanswered.

As we read the Ten Commandments, let us recommit ourselves to our covenantal relationship with G-d, acknowledging its pendulous motions between the above extremes and celebrating our willingness to embrace its religious experience *beleiv shaleim.*

_____ *Rabbi Bertram Leff*

T HE TEN COMMANDMENTS ARE INTRODUCED BY THE VERSE, "AND THE L-rd spoke all of these words, saying *(leimor)....*" According to the *midrash, leimor* denotes a verbal acceptance by the Children of Israel. How this acceptance was phrased is a source of debate between two *Tanna'im.*

Rabbi Yishmael was of the opinion that the Jewish people answered yes to each of the proactive commandments and no to each of the prohibitive commandments. Rabbi Akiva disagreed. The Jews answered yes to both. What is the source of their argument and what are its ramifications?

Rav Yosef Dov Soloveitchik, *zt"l*, explains that Rabbi Yishmael's view indicates an agreement on the part of the Jewish people. Yes, we accept the Divinity of G-d, the sanctity of Shabbos, the honor of our parents. And no, we reject murder, robbery, adultery.

Rabbi Akiva's view interprets the Jewish people's feeling as, Yes, we accept whatever G-d says, regardless of any doubts or questions. Even without rational explanation, we surrender our will to G-d's will and fulfill His laws. In fulfilling this type of *mitzvah*, called a *chok*, we do what He demands of us under all circumstances.

A *rasha*, an evil person, the Rav, *zt"l*, taught, is defined by his unwillingness to surrender to G-d. In the prayer, *"Aleinu,"* we proclaim that evil will no longer have a place in this world when, in the words of *Yeshayah*, "All the world's inhabitants will recognize and know that to You every knee should bend."

The average Torah Jew struggles every day to develop that level of *emunah*, to completely surrender to G-d and His will. The ultimate goal of every Torah Jew is to become a *"chok* Jew," a person whose knee is bent in submission to G-d and the Torah of Sinai; to respond as the Jews did, in Rabbi Akiva's fashion, to the commandments at Sinai.

We must be able to give a resounding "Yes" to all the *mitzvos*, whether they are rational and accepted in the world or questioned because their meaning eludes us.

May we struggle mightily and successfully each day to bend our knees and become *chukim* Jews.

Rabbi Melvin I. Burg

"AND MOSHE WENT UP TO G-D." THE GREAT EVENT, TOWARD WHICH all of creation moved from the hour of its inception, was about to take place. The entire universe was hushed and attentive to the sublime drama which was about to unfold in the wilderness of Sinai.

In view of the vivid circumstances surrounding the Divine Revelation, it is most disconcerting that its substance rapidly dissipated. For shortly after Sinai, the Hebrews create a golden calf and Moshe, learning of it from atop the mountain, shatters the tablets containing the Ten Commandments. What a magnificent beginning! What an abysmal ending!

Wherein lay the difference between the first set of tablets, which were broken, and the second set, which Moshe later fashioned and which remained whole? Why were the latter more enduring? Why were they received in sincerity by the Jewish nation?

Rashi comments that the first tablets, which were given amid tumult, thundering and a great assembly, were affected by the evil eye, whereas the second tablets, which were given under more modest circumstances, were able to endure. There is nothing more beautiful than modesty.

But while this teaching of Rashi contains a very important moral lesson, it still does not fully explain the circumstances surrounding the second tablets. Why did G-d command Moshe to hew these second tablets instead of giving them to him ready-made from Above, as He had with the first pair?

And if it was, for some reason, essential that Moshe hew them by himself, could he not have done so at the top of the mountain? Why did G-d instruct him to hew them at the foot of the mountain and carry them up to the top?

It is precisely this incident that explains the durability of the second tablets. The first tablets were given to Moshe ready-made by G-d. They were given from Above to be carried down. G-d made his revelation but the Jewish people were not spiritually prepared to fully appreciate and receive it. In a great moment of inspiration, they had exclaimed, "We will do and we will listen." But the moment passed. Backsliding was the result. Confusion and disgrace followed.

The second tablets, on the other hand, were brought up from below. They were hewed by the hand of man. The Jewish people, purged and cleansed by the unfortunate incident of the Golden Calf and its aftermath, were, at this point, spiritually ready to receive the message of the tablets. They had prepared themselves adequately for its reception. They elevated themselves to be suitable receptacles for the word of G-d. G-d inscribed the tablets, but Moshe prepared them and brought them up to be inscribed. These tablets could endure.

Frequently people complain, "Why is Judaism meaningless to me? It doesn't move me. I am not affected by its message. When I attend services, it leaves me cold. Nothing happens to me. The rabbi and the cantor do not inspire me sufficiently."

These people mistakenly view religion as something external to themselves, as something separate and apart. They do not realize that one must prepare himself to receive the message of G-d. "Hew for yourself" — make yourself a proper receptacle to receive G-d's word. Then it will affect you.

Attending services is not like attending a show or theater. Services require active participation, not merely passive observation. The rabbi and cantor can not pray and be devout for you. Prepare your own tablets and ascend the mountain. Then G-d will inscribe His word upon them.

_____ *Rabbi Mordechai Green*

AN ENTIRE *PARSHAH* IN THE TORAH IS NAMED IN HONOR OF YISRO, Moshe's father-in-law, for his major contribution to the Jewish people in suggesting that a judicial system be organized and adopted for the nascent nation. One wonders why Moshe, the Master Prophet, seemingly did not possess the foresight to do this on his own. Why did Yisro have to come along with this suggestion?

Yisro, who held a high position in Pharaoh's inner court, possessed the administrative skills of achieving judicial expediency. In order to be objective, balanced and efficient, justice, he believed, needed to be systematic.

Moshe, however, had his concerns with such a system. He did not want any systemized justice system interfering with individuality. After all, Moshe had just led the Jewish people out of an all-embracing system in Egypt which demonized and dehumanized them. Instituting a system, he feared, would sacrifice the *tzelem Elokim* of each person on the altar of efficiency.

Nonetheless, Yisro's suggestion had merit. "Moshe listened to the voice of his father-in-law" — he understood Yisro's intention and wrestled with the idea of how to establish a Divinely inspired judicial process without compromising the value of the individual. Moshe struggled to incorporate individualism into a system.

If one carefully studies the dialogue between Yisro and Moshe, it becomes evident that Yisro is sensitive to Moshe's concerns. A depersonalized system would not be appropriate. "And you shall make known to them the path on which they should walk and the actions that they should do," Yisro tells his son-in-law. The *hamtakas hadin,* the "sweetness of judgment," needed to be incorporated into the judicial process. Only then would the nation "come in peace."

What do we learn from *Parshas Yisro?* Systems are essential to expedite certain matters and resolve certain conflicts. And Jews must certainly learn to adapt to the social systems in which they find themselves. Nonetheless, Jews must maintain their Divinely inspired individual spirit, the spirit that bids them to hearken to G-d's commands, to the sweetness of His judgment.

We must develop our spirituality and loyalty to *mitzvos,* maintain compassion for others, meet our responsibilities to our communities and to the nation of Israel.

Though the mind-set of rugged capitalism and aggressive competition, which defines our time, leads to self-centeredness and even outright selfishness, the Jew must circumvent this social system and be free of it by entering the spiritual oasis of Torah life.

The challenge we face in our open society is spiritually similar to that which our forebears faced in the wilderness. Though our physical situation has radically changed, many of us remain chained, enslaved to the mind-set and culture of our times. At the same time, an ever-growing number of our people are developing a free spirit, hearkening to the call of *"Shema Yisrael"* and willingly and enthusiastically abiding by His bidding.

פרשת משפטים
Parshas Mishpatim

Rabbi Allen Schwartz

"AND THESE *(VE'EILEH)* ARE THE ORDINANCES THAT YOU SHALL PLACE before them."

Rashi notes that whenever the word *eileh* is preceded by the letter *vav*, the text that follows is connected to an earlier text. In this case, the earlier text is the Decalogue — the Ten Commandments — and *Ve'eileh* teaches that just as the Decalogue was revealed at Sinai, so too the ordinances that follow were given at Sinai.

The *Ohr Hachaim Hakadosh* asks why this *vav* is needed to teach that the laws of *Parshas Mishpatim* were revealed at Sinai. Was not the entire Torah revealed at Sinai? Why does this *parshah* require a special inference?

Rav Yosef Dov Soloveitchik, *zt"l,* answers that the ordinances of *Parshas Mishpatim,* which govern interpersonal relationships, do require a special reminder that they were also given at Sinai.

The Decalogue itself was inscribed on two tablets, the first governing a Jew's relationship to Hashem and the second prohibiting antisocial acts. There, too, the Rav points out, is an introduction: "And G-d spoke all of these words, saying..."

The inclusion of the word *all,* Rashi explains, is to teach that G-d pronounced all the words of the Decalogue in a single utterance. This means, says the Rav, that the Decalogue constitutes an indivisible entity. The faith mandated by the first tablet and the morality set down by the second are inseparable.

For this reason the word for the tablets, *Luchos,* is spelled in the Torah without the letter *vav* — *luchas* — as though the two tablets are a singular tablet. This bespeaks the equality of both aspects of our religious awareness.

Along these same lines, the Midrash teaches that when Moshe cast down the tablets from atop Mount Sinai, after seeing the Jewish people dancing before the Golden Calf, he had intended initially to cast only the first tablet. However, G-d advised that just as one can not be observed without the other, one can not be destroyed without the other.

Likewise, *Kli Yakar,* in an exercise of homiletic ingenuity, reads the verse, "These are the ordinances that you shall place before them," understanding the word *them* as referring to the Tabernacle and the sacrifices, which are described in detail in the ensuing *parshios* of the Torah. From here, he derives the primacy placed by the Torah of the interpersonal laws over the sacrificial order.

In the same vein, Rav Ovadia Bartenura explains why *Pirkei Avos* begins by tracing the origins of the Torah to Sinai — to acknowledge that the ethical teachings of the Torah are from the same G-dly source as the ritual and legal teachings.

One must remember that the Code of Hammurabi also addresses many of the cases found in *Parshas Mishpatim.* But our Torah is on a different plane. Though Hammurabi announced, in his prologue, that his man-written laws are meant only for him and his highest advisors, our Divine Torah is meant to be placed before all of us.

It is a tribute to the leadership and teaching of Moshe and to the tenacity of our *rabbanim* and teachers throughout the generations that more and more Jews today are advancing the holy cause of Torah, setting it before the masses in numbers greater than those at the Revelation at Sinai.

Everyone who does so testifies to that original encounter so long ago.

_____ *Rabbi Chaim Marder*

THE *BNEI YISRAEL*'S INITIAL RESPONSE TO MOSHE'S PRESENTATION OF the Divine Covenant in *Parshas Yisro* was to proclaim, "All that G-d has spoken we shall perform (*naaseh*)." Toward the end of *Parshas*

Mishpatim, Moshe presents to them "all of the words of Hashem and all of the judgments (*mishpatim*)," which they commit to perform, declaring once again, "*Naaseh.*"

Then, a few *pesukim* later, Moshe reads them the "Book of the Covenant" and their response is different: "*Naaseh venishma* — We shall perform and we shall hear." How does the reaction of the *Bnei Yisrael* in *Parshas Yisro* differ from their reaction in *Parshas Mishpatim*? What distinguishes *naaseh* from *naaseh venishma*?

Sinai, where the *Bnei Yisrael* proclaimed "*Naaseh venishma,*" is not just the place where the Torah was given, Rav Yosef Dov Soloveitchik, *zt"l,* explains; it was the moment of Divine Revelation. This revelation culminated not with the receiving of the Ten Commandments, he argues, but with the acceptance of their details, of the *mishpatim,* the Jewish civil code, which we read this week.

In the presentation of the covenant in *Parshas Yisro,* Hashem promises the children of Israel that they will be not only His "*am segulah,*" His cherished nation, but also a "*mamleches kohanim vegoy kadosh,*" — a kingdom of priests and a holy people." With their initial willingness, in *Parshas Yisro,* to accept the Torah — *naaseh* — the *Bnei Yisrael* became G-d's *am segulah.* With Moshe's presentation of the *mishpatim* in this week's *parshah,* and with the Jewish people's commitment to observe them, to listen and give their ear to His words — *naaseh venishma* — they became a *mamleches kohanim vegoy kadosh.*

This promotion, the Rav explains, came with the culmination of the *bris.* The Rambam teaches that every Jew has the potential to be a prophet and, consequently, has the obligation to pursue that which makes one worthy of being a prophet. As a holy nation of prophets, we are expected to attempt to come close to G-d, to reach toward Him, to comprehend Him on whatever level we are capable.

What is the significance of *naaseh venishma?* The Midrash quotes the following statement of Rav Simla'i: "It is written, '*Kol Hashem bako'ach* — the voice of the Lord is with power; that is, according to the power of each individual, according to the individual power of the young, the old and the very small."

Each Jew has a unique level of intensity to his Divine experience. Each individual comprehends Hashem in a different way. The nature of the voice of G-d is relative — *according to the power of each individual.*

Thus the dual nature of the Sinai revelation broadens the meaning of *naaseh venishma* as opposed to simply *naaseh*. First, a uniform set of principles for everyone (*naaseh*), expressed in the generalities of the Ten Commandments and the specifics of the *mishpatim*. Then, a second layer of the revelation was added, an awareness of and a connection to the Divine (*nishma*), with every Jew accessing his own personal window to Hashem, be it through *talmud Torah* (this avenue, explains the Rav, is why the yeshivos traditionally study the tractates of *Seder Nezikin*, which deal with the *mishpatim*), through *tefillah*, through communal activities involving charities or *Eretz Yisrael*.

Our challenge is to reconnect with that Sinai experience, to partake of the *bris*, to become — each of us in his or her own fashion — prophets, as we attempt to come close to the mountain. The more windows we access the more success we will have. When we appreciate the full extent of the commitment of *naaseh venishma* — we shall perform and we shall hear — we not only carry out our mandate as a holy nation of priests. We continue to experience that unique revelation that has guided us throughout the generations.

_____ *Rabbi Ezra Labaton*

P ARSHAS *MISHPATIM* CONTAINS, ACCORDING TO MAIMONIDES, FIFTY-four commandments, and rivals most other *parshios* as the basis for all Jewish legislation. There are different types of *mitzvos* in the *parshah*. First are those known as ritual laws, laws that seek to define the relationship between man and his Creator (*bein adam Lamakom*). Then there are civil laws, which define the legal relationship between man and his neighbor (*bein adam lachaveiro*).

Finally, there are laws that have a specific ethical dimension to them. In this context we enter into another realm wherein a person is viewed as having been created "in the image of G-d" (*tzelem Elokim*), codifying the way that we are to view all of mankind.

This concept is arguably the greatest teaching that Judaism has given the world. Every human being is created in the image of Almighty G-d and partakes in those essential, Divine values. As such, every human being is infinitely important, utterly unique and deserving of absolute respect. One dare not desecrate, for any reason, the *tzelem Elokim* of a fellow human being.

The *tzelem Elokim* aspect of man expresses itself in a unique fashion in our *parshah*. For example, the law states that one is obligated to loan a poor person money. Still, the lender has the right to ask for collateral. When evening comes, however, the lender must return the collateral. Why? "Because it is his only covering; it is the garment for his skin. In what will he sleep? And it will be when he cries out to Me that I shall listen, for I am compassionate."

Allowing this poor person to go through the night cold and miserable would violate his *tzelem Elokim*. Hence, even though the lender has the absolute right to collateral, he dares not use it to denigrate the *tzelem Elokim* of the borrower.

Halachah — Jewish Law — not only establishes our relationship to G-d, it forms the basis for all civilization. *Hakadosh Baruch Hu* revealed laws to sustain the entire world, not just the Jewish people. His system of law, which revolves around the twin poles of justice and righteousness, is rooted in the knowledge that man is *tzelem Elokim*. This point is brought out forcefully by Rav Yosef Dov Soloveitchik, *zt"l,* in his classic essay, *Ish Hahalakhah.* The Rav takes pains to point out the relationship between *Halachah* as an ideal construction, and the world.

"Halakhah," the Rav writes, "has a fixed *a priori* relationship to the whole of reality in all of its fine and detailed particulars. Halakhic man orients himself to the entire cosmos and tries to understand it by utilizing an ideal world, which he bears in his halakhic consciousness. All halakhic concepts are *a priori,* and it is through them that the halachic man looks at the world.... Halakhic man's ideal is to subject reality to the yoke of the halakhah."

Rabbi Soloveitchik provides a philosophy of *Halachah* in teaching us about the goal and overall thrust of the *halachic* system.

"Halakhic man implements the Torah without any compromises or concessions," he continues. "When a person actualizes the ideal halakhah in the very midst of the real world, he approaches the level of that godly man, the prophet — the creator of the worlds. He takes up his stand in the midst of the concrete world, his feet planted firmly on the ground of reality, and he looks about and sees, listens, hears, and publicly protests against the oppression of the helpless, the defrauding of the poor, the plight of the orphan. My uncle, R. Meir Berlin, told me that once R. Hayyim of Brisk was asked what the function of a rabbi is. R. Hayyim replied, 'to address the grievances of those who are abandoned and alone, to protect the dignity of the poor, and to save the oppressed from the hands of his oppressor.' The actualization of the ideals of justice and righteousness is the pillar of fire which halachic man follows, when he, as a Rabbi and teacher in Israel, serves his community."

Here the Rav tells us that *Halachah* is a Divine system of legislation that sees *tzelem Elokim* as its focal point. Every area of Jewish law — be it ritual, civil or ethical — is a manifestation of the Divine will and wisdom that has to be imposed upon this mundane world. All of Jewish law reflects the grandeur of the Creator.

_____ *Rabbi Kenneth Auman*

PARSHAS *MISHPATIM* AND *PARSHAS SHEKALIM* ARE FREQUENTLY READ on the same Shabbos, and though this may seem to be a random act of the Jewish calendar, a common thread does in fact connect these two Torah readings — money. *Parshas Mishpatim* deals with all sorts of monetary issues and is the source for much of Jewish jurisprudence. *Parshas Shekalim* deals with money as well — the half-shekel given yearly by every Jew for the census and for joint participation in the communal sacrifices brought in the Holy Temple.

There is a contrast between these two Torah readings, as well. Whereas *Mishpatim* deals with money as a source of conflict, and provides methods for resolution, *Shekalim* deals with money as a unifying factor, a means to allow each individual to be part of the community. The two readings therefore complement each other; money can be divisive, "the root of all evil," or it can draw people together for great and holy purposes.

Despite this contrast, we do find one aspect of money common to both *Mishpatim* and *Shekalim*: money as *kofer,* atonement. In *Mishpatim,* we read of an ox with a history of goring that kills a human being. "The ox shall be stoned, and also its owner shall be put to death."

However, the *parshah* continues, the owner can redeem himself through the payment of *kofer,* an atonement. "If an atonement is imposed upon him, he must give for the redemption of his soul whatever is imposed upon him."

In *Shekalim,* too, the Torah calls the half-shekel *kofer.* "When you take the count of the children of Israel according to their numbers, each will give to G-d an atonement for his soul."

Yet, there remain two basic differences between the *kofer* of *Mishpatim* and the *kofer* of *Shekalim.* First, the *kofer* of *Mishpatim* comes to atone for an act of negligence, while the *kofer* of *Shekalim* is incumbent upon everyone regardless of circumstance. Second, the *kofer* of *Mishpatim* is not a fixed amount, whereas the *kofer* of *Shekalim* is. Are these two completely different forms of *kofer* or are the two more similar than they appear to be?

Mishpatim defines for us the essence of *kofer:* an individual was negligent — so negligent that a life was lost. And the negligence stemmed from indifference. The ox's owner knew that his animal had a history of destruction, yet he remained indifferent to the threat. He must atone for his sin through *kofer.* The *kofer* of *Shekalim,* too, addresses this threat of indifference. People often feel insignificant when they consider themselves within the context of the larger group. And feelings of insignificance can quickly lead to feelings of indifference.

The individual often feels that he or she does not make a difference and consequently makes no attempts at civic participation. Such feelings are detrimental to the group as a whole, for it loses the opportunity to benefit from the strengths and talents of all. The Torah, therefore, requires *kofer* when counting the people — as an antidote to indifference. The payment is uniform, a half-shekel each, to indicate the equal significance of each.

One who pays *kofer* for his ox's attack will certainly take steps to prevent his animals from running wild. His concern for the public welfare will certainly intensify. But will the same hold true for the Jew who pays his annual half-shekel to the public coffer? Will that simple act foster feelings of concern for the nation?

Moshe Rabbeinu may have been troubled by precisely this question. Our rabbis relate, in the Jerusalem Talmud, that Moshe had difficulty envisioning the proper coin to be used for *machatzis hashekel,* so G-d showed him the fiery image of the coin. Did Moshe really have trouble picturing the coin? And if so, couldn't G-d have simply given such a coin to Moshe?

Perhaps Moshe was not troubled so much by the physical specifications of the coin, but by its effectiveness in fostering feelings of significance and concern in those who were to give it. Moshe was perhaps skeptical as to the value of this coin. Could it dispel indifference? Could it inspire caring?

Moshe was then shown a coin of fire. This demonstration told him that this simple coin did in fact contain the dramatic power to influence people. The combined strength of all Jews, coming together from far and wide, uniting in the service of G-d, has an influence far beyond that which we might expect.

פרשת תרומה
Parshas Terumah

Yisroel Epstein

M Y REBBE, RAV BEREL WEIN, *SHLIT"A* TELLS THE STORY OF THEODOR Herzl's family. Upon Herzl's death, in 1904, the World Zionist Organization went about setting up a fund to support his wife and three children. The WZO leadership chose to invest the monies they raised in gilt-edged bonds of the Austro-Hungarian empire, a decision that would have been supported by any investment strategist of the time. But within a decade, the First World War put an end to the Austro-Hungarian empire and, with it, the Herzl family's pension.

An understandable, if costly, misstep on the part of the Zionist elders. But why, asks my rebbe, didn't they even consider investing the money in the Jewish National Fund, the WZO's own bonds, which have been paying returns to this day? "Why don't we believe in ourselves?" he asks.

Rav Yosef Dov Soloveitchik, *zt"l,* brings home the point that every Jew must have *emunah Bekenesses Yisrael* — faith in the Congregation of Israel. The Talmud in *Sanhedrin* records a dispute as to whether the Mashiach's arrival is unconditional or dependent upon *Klal Yisrael*'s repenting. This dispute seems to have been settled, as Jews all over the world believe that the Mashiach's arrival is definite, if not imminent. We sing the words of the Rambam, from his Thirteen Principles of Faith, "*Ani maamin be'emunah sheleimah* — I believe with complete faith in the coming of the Mashiach."

Yet, in his legal code, *Yad Hachazakah,* the very same Rambam is unequivocal: "Israel will not be redeemed except through repentance."

If this is so, asks the Rav, how can one have "complete faith in the coming of the Mashiach"? If his arrival is conditional, dependent upon *Klal Yisrael*'s behavior, there is no guarantee that he will come!

Not quite. For the Rambam adds: "The Torah has already guaranteed that Israel will eventually repent at the end of their exile and will be redeemed immediately."

This, then, is the key, says the Rav. "Faith in the coming of the Mashiach is dependent upon our faith in *Kenesses Yisrael*." Moreover, "if we allow this faith to waiver, then our entire belief in the coming of the Mashiach is undermined."

In *Parshas Terumah*, G-d grants the Jewish people a special gift. "They will make for Me a sanctuary and I will dwell among them." "G-d did not rest His Presence on Israel until they engaged in work," states the *Tanna*, Rabbi Tarfon. The *Torah Temimah* explains: G-d did not need a Tabernacle or a Temple from the Jews; but he wanted them to labor on behalf of His Divine Name. G-d does not need our gifts, our tithes, our prayers or our Temples. He gives us opportunities to worship and serve Him for *our* benefit. When we seize those opportunities, G-d dwells among us.

After equating faith in the Final Redemption with faith in *Kenesses Yisrael,* the Rav notes the verse in *Devarim,* "If your outcasts are at the ends of the heavens — from there the L-rd your G-d will gather you and from there He will fetch you." This *pasuk,* he says, refers to the spiritual outcasts, the assimilated members of our nation. They are the ones whom G-d promises to gather; they are the ones whom G-d promises to fetch. God has not written them off and, consequently, neither can we.

In order to rebuild the Holy Temple, we must do what we can to bring about the Final Redemption. Reaching out to the millions of Jewish "outcasts" sometimes feels like a lost cause. But we must not get discouraged. As firm believers in the Mashiach, we must realize that that belief is bound up in the belief that all of Israel has the potential to return to Divine service.

It is not enough to believe in G-d's miraculous Redemption and in the rebuilding of the Holy Temple, soon and in our time. We must also believe in ourselves.

A YOUNG CHILD ASKS HIS MOTHER, "MOMMY, WHAT DOES HOLY MEAN?" The mother, uneasy with the complexity of the question, responds, "Holy means special."

The child looks up at his mother and says, "Mommy, you're holy." _Kadosh,_ holy, means separate from the ordinary, endowed with a special status. Hashem teaches us to recognize and participate in the sanctification by commanding us to observe the Shabbos "_lekadesho_ — to make it holy."

Hashem further commands us with the _mitzvah_ of _kiddush hachodesh,_ the sanctification of the new month. With this _mitzvah,_ the Jewish people set the Jewish calendar and the schedule of holidays. Our observance of the Shabbos and _Yamim Tovim_ give us an appreciation of the sanctity of time. During these days our lives are filled with a sense of _kedushah,_ of being special.

Just like time, space can also be endowed with _kedushah._ When Moshe first encountered the _Shechinah_ at the burning bush, G-d instructed him to remove his shoes, because he was standing on "_admas kodesh,_" holy ground. At Sinai, Israel as a people took on the status of a "_goy kadosh,_" a holy nation. Our lives, guided by the Torah, are different. We are special.

As we read _Parshas Terumah,_ the Jewish people have been freed from Egypt, they have seen G-d's Revelation at Sinai, and they have received the Torah with all its laws. Nevertheless, their redemption is not yet complete, the Ramban states, until they are "restored to the status of their fathers and returned to their place."

This return begins with G-d's command, "And they shall make for Me a _Mikdash,_ and I will dwell among them." Once this _Mikdash,_ the _Mishkan,_ is built, Hashem's glory fills it and the _Bnei Yisrael_ reach once more the status of their ancestors Avraham, Yitzchak and Yaakov.

The _Mishkan_ was to be a holy place within the camp of Israel, a portable Sinai, where the Jews had experienced G-d's Revelation and felt His Presence. Yet, it remains the deeds of the people that ensures the presence of the _Shechinah_ among _Klal Yisrael,_ as this week's _haftarah_ makes clear. Shlomo Hamelech builds a magnificent permanent structure in Jerusalem, the *Beis Hamikdash,* to replace the *Mishkan.* "Hashem comes to Shlomo saying, 'This Temple that you build — if you follow My decrees, perform My statutes and observe My commandments to follow them, then I shall uphold My word with you which I spoke to Dovid, your father. I shall dwell among the children of Israel and I shall not forsake the people of Israel."

The weight of our deeds is evident, as this *parshah* follows *Parshas Mishpatim,* which deals mainly with Jewish civil law. This teaches us, says the *Beis Halevi,* that even when giving to a sacred cause, one must be sure that there is no taint of illegality in his contribution. The holiness of the *Mikdash* must not be desecrated by a violation of Torah ethics.

Hashem's Presence, found equally in the modest Tabernacle that roamed the wilderness and in the grand and magnificent Temple of Solomon and in our contemporary synagogues, is conditioned upon our adherence to the Torah, both in our homes and in our businesses.

The Torah scrolls in the arks of our synagogue and the *sefarim* on the shelves of our *batei midrash* help us focus on the centrality of Torah study in our lives. The study of Torah gives us direction, allowing us to bring *kedushah* into every facet of life's experiences. When we achieve that degree of understanding, we are able to appreciate and respect that special quality of time, the sanctity of particular places, and the holiness of our lives.

_____ Rabbi Barry Hartman

THE *PARSHAH* OF *TERUMAH* DISCUSSES THE BUILDING OF THE *MISHKAN,* the portable Tabernacle that accompanied the Jews through their journey in the wilderness. Describing how the walls of the Tabernacle would stand, the text states, "The middle bar across the planks shall extend from end to end." The *Targum Yonasan* comments that this bar came from the tent of Avraham Avinu. In *Shai LaTorah,* Rabbi Shimon Miller, quoting his father, Rabbi Elimelech Miller, offers an insightful interpretation of this cryptic statement.

The Jews in the wilderness contributed gold and silver, wool and skins to build the *Mishkan* and all that it contained, but it was this middle bar, which came from the tent of Avraham, that ran through the walls and kept the structure standing.

In his time, Avraham was renowned for his *chessed,* his kindness, and he continues to be the paragon for that trait. That the bar which propped up the *Mishkan* came from his tent provides us with an important principle: the Tabernacle can only stand if its foundation is kindness. This concept is clearly laid out in a *mishnah* in *Avos,* which states: "The world rests upon three things — on the Torah, on the service of G-d and on acts of kindness."

The *Beis Hamikdash* had two of these pillars — the study of Torah and the Divine service of the priests — but the third pillar, the pillar of *chessed,* is also necessary for the structure to survive.

William F. Buckley, Jr., the famed social and political commentator, once wrote of how impressed he was by the activities of the Jewish community in the United States on behalf of Soviet Jewry. The Jews of America, he wrote, are not related, in a narrow biological framework, to the Jews behind the Iron Curtain, yet they work hard to help, in a variety of ways, their co-religionists in the Soviet Union.

What prompted the American Jew to demonstrate outside the Soviet Mission and the United Nations? What prompted him to visit Jews in the Soviet Union and bring packages? The answer is one word, *chessed.*

This principle must continue to be the guiding force of Jewish communal organizations and individuals. We must energize our efforts on behalf of others, constantly and consistently, and thereby rebuild the Holy Temple upon a foundation of *chessed.*

Rabbi Moshe A. Kasinetz

P ARSHAS TERUMAH BEGINS A SERIES OF *PARSHIOS* FOCUSED ON THE building of the Sanctuary in the wilderness to "house" the Divine presence. But how is this to be understood? How can finite people using finite materials construct a dwelling place for the Infinite? How can an area be defined for His presence when the prophet proclaims, "The entire world is filled with His glory"?

The *parshah*'s initial verse, "They shall make for Me a Sanctuary and

I will dwell among them," addresses this concern, informing us that this Sanctuary was not to simply be a tangible project, but develop into a metaphysical fixture of Jewish existence. G-d did not promise to live "in it" but "among them" — among the Jewish people, in each and every Jew for all time, according to the *Shaloh Hakadosh, zt"l.*

Thus, the Sanctuary is to be viewed not simply as a physical structure, but as a spiritual framework granted to each of us, an endowment from G-d to the Jewish people to fuse the spiritual and physical worlds. We are assured that by adopting the formula spelled out in the Torah we can create this Sanctuary within us. It is in our hands — based on our ability and on our commitment — to establish it. It is the very purpose of Creation, in the words of the Midrash, "to make this world a dwelling place for Almighty G-d."

The *parshah* lists fifteen items used in building and maintaining the Sanctuary. Rashi, however, writes that "the thirteen items under discussion were needed for the construction of the Sanctuary and the priestly garments."

The Biblical commentaries are left to wonder why Rashi says thirteen when the Torah lists fifteen. The *Tzemach Tzedek* points out that the Midrash in *Shir Hashirim* also lists thirteen items, omitting oil and spice.

Oil and spice were used on an ongoing basis as part of the Tabernacle service. That is why Rashi takes care to point out that the thirteen materials were for the structure and the priestly garments. The other two — oil and spice — were used continuously, and thus communicate a distinct message.

Oil symbolizes Torah, and spices were used as incense for the sacrificial offerings. Torah and sacrificial offerings — which in our times becomes Torah and *tefillah,* prayer. Once the structure of the Sanctuary is set, there is the need for precise services formulated by strict procedures. Only when Torah and *tefillah* are practiced do the other thirteen items compose a Sanctuary.

The Sanctuary that is within us is founded on the same premise. It can not be removed from us as long as we maintain our people's timeless program of Torah and *tefillah* in their precise formulation — not adulterated or tampered with. Only when we follow this blueprint can we bring the Divine presence into our physical environment. We can do it. We are given the power and the promise to succeed.

פרשת תצוה
Parshas Tetzaveh

_____ Rabbi Michael Azose

T HE *BAAL HATURIM* POINTS OUT THAT *TETZAVEH* IS THE ONLY *PAR-shah* in the *Chumash* that does not contain Moshe's name (except those *parshios* that discuss events before his birth and those that Moshe narrates in the Book of *Devarim*).

Why is his name left out? Because in next week's *parshah,* Moshe, in pleading with Hashem to forgive the Jewish people after they worshipped the Golden Calf, says, "And if not, blot me out of Your book that You have written." The words of a sage, even when conditional, have some effect and Moshe's name was therefore erased from the *Chumash* to some extent.

Still, out of all the *parshios* in the Torah, why was *Tetzaveh* chosen as the one in which to "blot out" Moshe's name? Because, the Vilna Gaon points out, this *parshah* is always read on the Shabbos following the seventh of Adar, the date of Moshe's birth and of his death. But why should these anniversaries correspond to Moshe's name being deleted from *Tetzaveh*?

Centuries after the Jewish nation traveled across the wilderness, the wicked Haman cast lots to determine when he should destroy the Jews. The month he got was Adar. Haman, the Talmud relates, "rejoiced greatly. He said, 'The lot has fallen for me on the month in which Moshe died.' But he did not know that Moshe...was [also] born on the seventh of Adar."

Parshas Tetzaveh / 125

The *midrash* reports that G-d found Haman's intentions absurd. G-d said to him, "I thought to destroy them and couldn't, as it were" — because of Moshe's protest — "yet you contemplate destroying them? I swear your head will be in place of theirs."

The *Torah Temimah* explains that the Jews of the time did, in fact, deserve severe punishment for joining in the feast of Achashveirosh. But they were able to expiate their sin by killing Haman, because in doing so they fulfilled the great *mitzvah* of destroying Amaleik, the nation from which Haman descended. "G-d has a war with Amaleik from generation to generation," and by fighting that war, the Jews of the time insured that Haman's head would be in place of theirs.

Parshas Zachor, which instructs the Jewish people to destroy the nation of Amaleik, is always read on *Parshas Tetzaveh* of a non-leap year. On leap years, when there are two Adars, *Zachor* is read either on *Parshas Vayikra* or *Parshas Tzav,* but always on the Shabbos following the seventh of Adar II. The connection between Moshe and *Zachor* is complete.

G-d was "unable" (in the words of the *midrash*) to destroy the Jewish people, but, in the process, blotted out Moshe's name from the *parshah.* Haman, too, could not destroy the Jewish nation and, in attempting to, was himself destroyed, helping to blot out the name of Amaleik.

The *midrash* on Esther says that Eliyahu Hanavi pleaded with Moshe to do something about G-d's initial acquiescence to Haman's decree to kill the Jews. Eliyahu insisted that, since Moshe had started the war with Amaleik, he should be the one to finish it. Moshe asked Eliyahu whether the decree was sealed in mud or in blood. If it was sealed in mud, Moshe maintained, the decree could be reversed. But if it was sealed in blood, no reversal would be possible.

The distinction between mud and blood, the *Mei'am Lo'eiz* explains, determined the spiritual level of the Jews. Had their degradation reached a level so low that they were assimilating — mixing blood — with the other nations, or had they merely been muddied by their sin of partaking from the feast of Achashveirosh? As the Jews' fate had only been sealed in mud, salvation was still possible. Mordechai and Esther were able to aid them in their regeneration.

Moshe's 120 years of life, the completeness of which reveals his righteousness, stands in the breach, as G-d's chosen one, to make us ever cognizant of G-d's promise to expiate our sins through the *mitzvah* of zachor.

THE GLEAMING ROCKET STANDS POISED ON ITS LAUNCH PAD, ITS cargo an interplanetary probe, prepared to embark upon a journey that will take years. But the slightest miscalculation in the launch trajectory, even by half a degree, will result in a mission failure of epic proportions. Space technology teaches the crucial importance of setting the direction accurately from the very start. This is true of life, too, as the _mitzvah_ of lighting the menorah teaches.

The Midrash draws an analogy between the light of the menorah and the light of the Torah. Just as the menorah's light dispels darkness and illumines the way, so too the Torah provides spiritual light and direction in life.

The Talmud teaches, "Even if a person only reads the _Shema_ once in the morning and once at night, he fulfills the Torah's injunction, 'This Torah shall not depart from your mouth, and you shall study it day and night.' " The question is obvious: How can a person, by reciting the _Shema_ in a few minutes, be considered to have spent the entire day from morning until evening immersed in Torah study?

The _Chiddushei Harim_ replies with a comparison to the menorah lit by the _Kohein Gadol_ in the _Mishkan._ When the _Kohein Gadol_ ignites the menorah, he is considered to have created "an eternal flame lit before Me [Hashem]."

Even though the _Kohein Gadol_ does not stand at the menorah applying the flame continuously, his one-time act of kindling creates "an eternal flame." Thus, the _Chiddushei Harim_ concludes, one moment of dedicated effort can affect the outcome of one's entire day.

Similarly, if one concentrates intently on the _Krias Shema,_ focusing upon its themes of _kabbalas ohl malchus Shamayim_ and _kabbalas ohl mitzvos,_ his entire day can be ignited by its inspiration. The _Shema,_ recited over a few intensive minutes, can provide proper spiritual direction for the whole day.

Similarly, a commitment to the Torah, its _mitzvos_ and its values provides direction in and throughout life enabling adherents to navigate through the spiritual darkness, decay, anarchy and chaos that surround us. This is essentially the call of the prophet Hoshea: "Return O Israel, *toward* the Lord, your G-d." If the direction is on target, the journey will be positive.

_____ *Rabbi Daniel Cohen*

WHAT IS THE RELATIONSHIP BETWEEN *PARSHAS TETZAVEH* AND THE upcoming holiday of Purim? At first blush, this week's subject, the inauguration of the Tabernacle, seems unconnected to the celebration of Purim. A brief analysis, however, shows that *Parshas Tetzaveh* underscores one of the themes of Purim.

People generally respond with greater enthusiasm to new experiences than to routine ones. How many of us have seen the glow of a *bar* or *bas mitzvah* on the day they celebrate their obligation to do *mitzvos*? But how many of us continue to perform our responsibilities every day with such joy?

Hashem understands this challenge to human nature, and, in *Parshas Tetzaveh,* He charges the Jewish people to overcome their listlessness. The *parshah* concludes with the inauguration of the *Mishkan* and Hashem's promise to reside amid the Jewish people. But positioned between these two related topics is the command to bring the daily sacrifice. What is the significance of its placement here?

Rabbi Samson Raphael Hirsch explains that the construction of the *Mishkan* did not by itself evoke Hashem's Divine Presence among the Jewish nation. That was only achieved by the daily offering, which reflected the devotion of the people to the ideals of G-d.

The spiritual health of the Jewish people requires more than a formal edifice, more than routine structure; it requires constant acts of heartfelt devotion. The holiday of Purim, too, epitomizes the challenge of infusing habitual *mitzvos* with energy and enthusiasm. The essence of Purim, explains Rav Moshe Sternbuch, is the cultivation of passion for serving Hashem. Two customs contribute to this: drinking and masquerading.

On the surface, such behavior seems out of character for the observant Jew. On Purim, though, Hashem motivates us to move beyond our external, often perfunctory, acts of devotion. The Talmud writes that a person should become so inebriated on Purim that he does not know the difference between Haman and Mordechai. But while one's senses are dulled to this extent, nevertheless, Rav Sternbuch writes, his love for Hashem should be so transformative that he can still *emotionally* distinguish between Haman and Mordechai.

The custom of masquerading reflects a similar ideal — moving from the external to the internal. Too often, we value what is superficial. Wearing a mask hides our identity and forces us to focus not on the external dimension of our personalities but on the internal dimension, our souls, which lie behind the masks.

Purim is a time to deepen our sense of spirituality. If we feel that our synagogues are places where our prayers ring hollow, we are missing valuable opportunities. We must transform our prayers through song, dance and a fuller understanding of the dynamics of *tefillah*. We must take seriously our synagogues' status as miniature Tabernacles.

May we utilize the upcoming holiday of Purim to reinvigorate ourselves with passion toward service of Hashem, and, in this merit, may He dwell once again in our midst.

_____ *Rabbi Bertram Leff*

I N 1940, THE AMERICAN AGUDATH ISRAEL ORGANIZATION CONVENED A memorial gathering upon the passing of the great rabbinic leader of Eastern Europe, Rabbi Chaim Ozer Grodzinski, *zt"l*. At the gathering, Rav Yosef Dov Soloveitchik, *zt"l*, described Rabbi Grodzinski's leadership of European Jewry by comparing it to the vestments of the *Kohein Gadol* described in our *parshah*.

The High Priest wore a golden headband *(tzitz)* engraved with the words, *"Kodesh LaHashem* — Holy to Hashem." The headband "shall be on his forehead always, to bring them favor before Hashem." Another essential component of the *Kohein Gadol's* vestments was the *choshen*, the breastplate that contained twelve stones representing each of the twelve tribes of Israel. The Breastplate of Judgment was to be "on Aharon's heart when he comes before Hashem, and Aharon shall bear the judgment of the children of Israel on his heart constantly before Hashem."

Rav Soloveitchik explained that the *tzitz*, the golden band worn on the forehead of the *Kohein Gadol*, represents the intellect, the knowledge of Torah that a leader of Israel must possess. The *choshen*, the breastplate, symbolizes the heart of love, commitment and devotion to *Klal Yisrael*, to the tribes of Israel.

Jewish leadership encompasses a love for each Jew and a concern for the needs of every segment of the Jewish people, represented by the names of each of the tribes engraved in each stone on the breastplate.

The *Kohein Gadol* of each generation, men such as Rabbi Chaim Ozer Grodzinski, the Rav said, integrated into their leadership the *tzitz* and the *choshen* — great intellectual knowledge of Torah coupled with a heart full of love and devotion to *Klal Yisrael*.

Shabbos Zachor is the Sabbath before the festival of Purim. If we were to analyze the leadership of Mordechai and Esther we would find that their leadership of the Jewish people reflected intellect and heart, Torah knowledge and compassion for the future of the Jewish nation.

G-d has given each of us the potential to be a spiritual *Kohein Gadol*, to combine both Torah learning and commitment to the Jewish people. In our daily lives we have the opportunity to wear the *tzitz*, the golden headband of the *Kohein Gadol*, and thereby, through the study of Torah, bring the holiness of Hashem into our daily existence.

In addition, we can place the *choshen*, the breastplate of the *Kohein Gadol*, on our hearts and strive to love every Jew. In this way we will merit to bring to fruition the glory that is Hashem's mission for the tribes of Israel.

פרשת כי תשא
Parshas Ki Sissa

THE INCLUSION OF THE FOUL-SMELLING INGREDIENT, *CHELBENAH,* IN the ritual incense, *ketores,* evokes an observation by Rabbi Shimon Chasida: "Any fast day that does not include sinners is not a [valid] fast, for *chelbenah* is malodorous and yet is counted among the spices of the *ketores.* " Far from being an isolated remark, this lesson is the culmination of a pattern of images that dates back to the Book of *Bereishis.*

Yosef's brothers sell him to a caravan of Ishmaelite traders and he is taken to Egypt along with a shipment of gum, balsam and resin. The only other time these three spices are mentioned in the Torah is when Yaakov instructs his sons to bring the Egyptian viceroy a gift of "a little balsam and honey, some gum and resin." All throughout the day, as the brothers awaited the denouement of their encounter with Yosef, they inhaled these fragrances.

Why were these spices, the very ones that accompanied Yosef on his descent into Egypt, picked? The answer may lie in the peculiar properties of aroma. More than any other sense, the sense of smell has the capacity to bring one back through vast gulfs of time and to trigger vivid memories. Perfume manufacturers know this fact well and have made fortunes exploiting it.

At the very moment that the brothers were propelled toward complete *teshuvah* — marked by their adamant refusal to allow Benjamin to suffer the same fate as Yosef by being incarcerated in the Pharaoh's

Parshas Ki Sissa / 131

prison — Divine Providence stepped in. While they waited to meet with Yosef, the brothers were transported back, by the scent of the spices, to the scene of the sale. This set the stage for the dramatic outcome with their brother.

Similarly, the Torah places emphasis on the aromatic nature of sacrifices — *rei'ach nicho'ach* — perhaps to express the hope that the pleasing aroma of the people's offering will symbolically transport G-d Himself back to the time before our sin, the time of first unsullied love.

The idea of leaping back in time past the iniquity is embodied in the *ketores,* the very essence of which is aroma. According to tradition, the first of the incense's eleven ingredients is *tzari,* evoking once more the sin of the sale of Yosef and the atonement for it. Moreover, the inclusion of *chelbenah* in the priestly ritual preserves eternally that painful time in *mitzvah* form.

The *ketores* speaks to every Jewish quorum, just as it did to that first *minyan* of Yaakov's sons. It warns that a congregation of ten can not declare themselves self-sufficient and sever an eleventh member for his outspoken views, can not deny a brother the purification the *klal* affords, can not deny the *klal* the contributions this member can make.

Who knows which eleventh member is really Joseph? Who knows which superficially unpleasant spice will serve to bind the rest together? Most sadly, what value can a festive table or ritual fast have when empty places only remind us of banished brothers?

_____ *Rabbi Jonathan Horowitz*

S IX SHORT WEEKS AFTER THE JEWISH PEOPLE REACH THE APEX OF their history, receiving the Torah at Sinai, they descend to the depths of spiritual degradation, fashioning the Golden Calf and indulging themselves in a wild orgy of idolatrous worship.

G-d is ready to annihilate the nation for its betrayal. But it is here that Moshe emerges as a great leader, issuing, on behalf of the Jewish people, a powerful plea for forgiveness. Yet, one wonders: If G-d is immutable, how could Moshe "convince" Him to change His mind, as it were?

Rav Yosef Dov Soloveitchik, *zt"l,* explains: It is the person praying, not G-d, who is transformed through prayer. In praying, man becomes a different person. He transcends his former self of sins and failures and stands before G-d as a new being.

And how Moshe changed! The privileged prince of Egypt could have enjoyed a career tending the sheep of his father-in-law, Yisro, in the lush land of Midyan. But Moshe observed the suffering of his people, the *midrash* records, and put aside the dignity of his position to help them with their backbreaking toil. When G-d saw Moshe, He saw a leader.

After the sin of the Golden Calf, Moshe eloquently prays for his people. "If You forgive them," he cries out, I am content to live. "But if not — please erase me from Your Book." The *Kli Yakar* writes that Moshe's words describe a man who identifies completely with his people. He lives through them. Moshe, who initially felt unsuited to represent the Jewish people before Pharaoh, becomes their fearless, articulate champion. His personality is transformed. His prayer is answered.

In Talmudic times, when agriculture was the main means of sustenance, rain was the lifeblood of the land. Small wonder that the Jew would turn Heavenward and pray for rain. When there was a severe drought, the rabbinic court would proclaim a fast day, and the greatest sages would lead the people in prayer. On one such occasion, the Talmud tells us, Rabbi Eliezer led the congregation in prayers, offering 24 blessings. But his prayers were not answered. Then Rabbi Akiva prayed, saying simply, "Our Father, our King, we have no king but You." And the rains came down. A Heavenly voice declared that it was not that one's prayer was greater than the other's, but that one transcended his own nature and the other did not.

Both Rabbi Eliezer and Rabbi Akiva were great scholars, and both were outstanding and devoted leaders. But Rabbi Akiva had, in his personal history, a struggle to change his whole character. Turning against his upbringing and background, he had redefined his goals and waged a battle against his inclinations to recreate himself. He had gone from being an ignorant shepherd to a spiritual giant. His prayers and wishes were thus fulfilled.

Prayer — especially sincere prayer on an everyday basis — runs contrary to human nature, for prayer reminds us of both our mortality and our helplessness. And prayer, especially communal prayer, is extremely difficult. It requires sacrifice and effort. It obligates us to leave the comforts of home, to pull away from the TV set, to leave our families and join the congregation in prayer.

But prayer offers us great opportunities to come closer to G-d through our membership in the community of Israel. Prayer helps us transcend human nature, allows us to leave behind human comforts and desires, asks us to sacrifice our egos — to change who we are — and cling to the eternal.

_____ *Rabbi Avram Bogopulsky*

K*I SISSA* TELLS OF THE GREATEST SIN IN ALL OF JEWISH HISTORY — the *chait ha'eigel,* the sin of the Golden Calf. Before ascending to the top of Mount Sinai, Moshe tells the *Bnei Yisrael* that he will be gone for forty days and forty nights. But the Jews miscalculate his absence by one day. When Moshe fails to return at the expected time, they turn to Aharon, Moshe's brother, to fill the void of leadership.

In an attempt to stall them for one more day, Aharon asks the people for their gold, hoping they will refuse. But they give enthusiastically, and so Aharon throws their gold into a fire from which arises the infamous Golden Calf. Moshe, meanwhile, is oblivious to all this until G-d tells him to go down from the mountain for the people are corrupt. Moshe descends and as he approaches the camp, he hears singing, dancing and rejoicing around the Golden Calf. "And Moshe turned and went down the mountain with the two Tablets of Testimony in his hand," is how the Torah describes it.

What is this "turning" that Moshe did? Why not simply write, "Moshe went down"? We find this word *vayifen* — "and he turned" — twice more in the Torah in connection with Moshe. Before the Exodus, Moshe came upon an Egyptian who was beating an Israelite. The Torah records that Moshe "turned this way and that way and he saw no man, so he smote the Egyptian and hid him in the sand." Then, at one point during his negotiations with Pharaoh over the people's release from Egypt, the Torah states that Moshe "turned and went out from before Pharaoh."

Why does the Torah continually stress this notion of turning — all in dealing with Moshe? All three instances testify to Moshe's turning not in a physical sense, but in a more dramatic way. Each case necessitated a spur of the moment decision — a turning point in his life and leadership.

The first act of leadership taken by Moshe was killing the Egyptian. Moshe could have sat back and waited to inherit the throne of Egypt. Instead, he took action on behalf of his brethren. His heroism necessitated his fleeing from Egypt and set the stage for his encounter with G-d.

His second "turn" was a dangerous one. Not giving proper respect and honor to the Pharaoh would normally be punished instantly with death, but Moshe wanted to show Pharaoh that he meant business. "Let my people go," he demanded, keeping in mind that with the king's honor and pride on the line, Pharaoh might never let the Jews go, despite the ten plagues. Looking back, when push came to shove, the shoving of Pharaoh's honor was the right choice.

Finally, the moment when Moshe threw down the tablets was the ultimate turn of events. He shattered the heart and soul of the Jewish people. Why? Moshe needed to shake up the people after they had committed such a horrendous sin.

In all cases Moshe acted properly. The first time led Moshe to the mantle of leadership. The second helped free the Jews from slavery. The third received the consent of the Almighty Himself.

The Ark that stood in the Tabernacle and later in the Temple contained the new tablets as well as the original, broken ones. This served to remind the Jews of the atrocious abomination of the Golden Calf. We should keep it as a constant reminder to us.

פרשת ויקהל-פקודי
Parshas Vayakheil-Pekudei

_____ *Rabbi Moshe D. Krupka*

I MAGINE OUR POTENTIAL AFTER EXPERIENCING A GENUINE YOM KIPPUR. What great achievements are we capable of after the Almighty has embraced us, forgiving our past indiscretions and providing us with an opportunity to grow?

The events of this week's *parshah,* Rashi explains, begin the morning after the very first Yom Kippur. On this day, G-d not only instructs the people with commandments to fulfill, but also provides them with a philosophy to follow and apply each and every day.

Parshas Vayakheil begins with Moshe relating to the *Bnei Yisrael* the Almighty's command to build the *Mishkan.* Before doing so, however, he reiterates the command to observe the Shabbos. It seems that Moshe did not simply join two separate, unrelated commands. As Rav Yosef Dov Soloveitchi, *zt"l,* points out, the *parshah* begins: "And Moshe assembled the entire Israelite community and said to them, 'These are the words that G-d has commanded [you] to do them.' "

The use of the plural form — "These are the words (*devarim*)" — makes it clear that Moshe is deliberately uniting both of the mandates that follow: observance of the Shabbos and construction of the *Mishkan.*

Moreover, the juxtaposition of Shabbos and *Mishkan* is found not only here; it is common in many other *parshios.* The repeated pairing of these two concepts confirms the idea that there is a relationship between them. For example, by virtue of this juxtaposition, Rashi points out, we deduce the *halachah* that the construction of the *Mishkan* does not override the sanctity of the Shabbos. Construction must be halted on Shabbos.

However, the Rav sees a deeper connection. Shabbos represents holiness in time. Six days are mundane; the seventh is holy. Shabbos represents a period within the weekly cycle when a person is able to come closer to *Hakadosh Baruch Hu.* Shabbos is a sanctuary of time placed beyond the physical world, where one may commune with Hashem, for He has imbued this day with His Presence.

In an analogous fashion, the *Mishkan* represents holiness of space. Of all the places in the world, Hashem's Presence is most felt in His sanctuary — the *Mishkan,* and, later, the *Beis Hamikdash.* It is there that one may seek to become closer to *HaKadosh Baruch Hu,* for it is there that the *Shechinah* resides.

On the morning after the first Yom Kippur, when, following a full pardon from the Almighty, the *Kenesses Yisrael* rose to unmatched spiritual strength, Moshe introduces the commandments of Shabbos and *Mishkan.* While he emphasizes the similarities of the two, he gives them a sequence. Sanctity of time takes priority to sanctity of space; to achieve *kedushah,* as well as to retain it, Moshe Rabbeinu asserts, one must first gain control over his time. Then he can attempt to seize control over his space.

All of us, within our communities, strive to perfect our synagogues, our *Mikdashei Me'at.* However, as the Rav explains, we must be equally diligent, if not more so, that our time — each moment of our lives — be properly focused on the ideals of Torah and *mitzvos.* Only then can we achieve our full potential, individually and communally.

_____ *Rabbi Shaya Kilimnick*

T HE TORAH READING RECALLS THE OFTEN EMPHASIZED THEME OF Jewish unity. The *Bnei Yisrael*'s eager contribution of materials for the construction of the *Mishkan,* chronicled in *Parshas Vayakheil,* and their annual half-shekel donation for its maintenance, recalled in the *maftir* of *Shekalim,* are among the finest examples of such *achdus,* unity.

Moshe Rabbeinu, who received the charge from G-d to build the *Mishkan* in the previous *parshios* of *Terumah* and *Tetzaveh,* now brings this command to the Jewish people. The way the Torah records these events is telling. In *Terumah,* Moshe is commanded, "Speak to the children of Israel and they will take (*veyikchu*) for Me a gift." When Moshe relays this to the community the reaction is such that "everyone whose heart motivated him brought (*heivi'u*)."

The same words are used in another passage: "Take (*kechu*) from yourselves a gift for Hashem; everyone whose heart motivates him should bring it (*yevi'ehah*)." Why, the commentaries wonder, does the verse begin with the word *take,* which connotes aversion, and then shift to the word *bring,* which connotes willingness?

Daas Sofer al Hatorah utilizes the Rambam's approach to a different issue to explain these verses. A *get,* a Jewish bill of divorce, must be given by the husband willingly. Nevertheless, it is permissible for the *beis din* to coerce a recalcitrant husband to give his wife a *get.* He is pressured until he says, "I want to."

Intrinsically, a Jew wants to do what's right. But often he is detoured by a preoccupation with his finite needs and desires. When the *beis din* coerces him, the Rambam explains, they are merely removing the negative barriers and facades which he has developed and which prevent him from pursuing the course of his Jewish life which he is indigenous to. His declaration of "I want to" is not fabricated, but rather is a genuine spirit he possesses, heretofore concealed by veils of vanity.

In the collection of *terumah,* as well, the *Bnei Yisrael* are first charged with *taking.* It is difficult to part with newly acquired possessions, such as those the *Bnei Yisrael* took from Egypt after 210 years of owning nothing. Nonetheless, given the opportunity to join with others to build Hashem's sanctuary and to atone for the communal sin of the Golden Calf, the *Bnei Yisrael* were eager to *give.* They quickly recognized that nothing was being taken from them; rather, they were being revitalized through their contributions.

Collectively they declared, "We want to." On top of the mandatory *terumah,* their hearts motivated them to bring more. It is the elevated spirit of the people that causes the *Shechinah* to dwell among them.

In our day, we, too, must be committed to our people who have become distanced from the contemporary *Mishkan* — our *shuls* and the *mitzvos* they contain, along with all the beauty and significance of Jewish living. Perhaps, there will be reluctance at first, but willingness will follow.

We must learn to take from ourselves — from our time, from our energy — and contribute to the unity of our people. This will ultimately bring our brothers and sisters — *kol Beis Yisrael* — to the threshold of the *Mishkan.*

The half-shekel each donates maintains and promotes our sacred unity. But we need *kol Beis Yisrael.* Until then, we are providing only half of what we can achieve.

_____ *Rabbi Bertram Leff*

P ARSHAS VAYAKHEIL TEACHES US ABOUT OUR RELATIONSHIP TO G-D through our observance of the holy Shabbos.

The Torah links Shabbos to the building of the Tabernacle, the *Mishkan.* Rav Yosef Dov Soloveitchik, *zt"l,* teaches: The nexus of the *Mishkan* and the Shabbos comes to emphasize the important concept that Shabbos is a *Mishkan* in its own right. The *Shechinah* — the Divine Presence of G-d — is present in the Shabbos just as the *Shechinah* was present in the *Mishkan.*

There is, however, one difference between the two. The *Shechinah* of the *Mishkan* was transcendental. In *Parshas Pekudei* we read that when the *Mishkan* was completed, a cloud of glory filled the Tabernacle. Even Moshe Rabbeinu could not enter the *Mishkan* at will. The Presence of G-d in the *Mishkan* was an experience that went beyond the laws of nature.

Shabbos, on the other hand, brings with it the Presence of G-d on a natural level. Through observance of Shabbos we naturally sense the intimate relationship we have with G-d. The beauty of Shabbos observance lies in its ability to cast the Divine light upon each of us.

To describe the *mitzvah* of Shabbos, "Moshe gathered the entire assembly of the children of Israel and said to them, 'On six days work may be done, but the seventh day shall be holy for you.' "

The Hebrew word for assembly, *adas,* is related to *eid,* witness. The term *eidah* refers to the aristocratic, historical community of Israel.

When we are faithful to the Shabbos we are a community of witnesses, whose Divine mission is to proclaim each week to the entire world that Hashem is the Creator and Master of the universe and we testify to His presence in human affairs.

On Shabbos we declare how intimately entwined His Presence is with our lives.

_____ *Rabbi Marvin Sugarman*

THE DOUBLE *PARSHAH* OF *VAYAKHEIL* AND *PEKUDEI* RECORDS THE completion of the Tabernacle constructed in the wilderness by the Jewish nation. In the preparation of the Tabernacle, the Torah relates that the people, in their zeal to have a share in this unique *mitzvah,* continued to offer gifts to Moshe, even after all the necessary materials were gathered. "Moshe commanded that they proclaim throughout the camp: 'Let no man or woman do any more work for the sanctified offering.' So the people ceased bringing."

Moshe only told the people to stop working; he never asked that the contributions be discontinued. Why did the people refrain from bringing further monetary gifts?

The Ramban, perhaps sensing this difficulty, writes simply, "Money is called work," and brings other verses to support this contention.

The first Belzer Rebbe, however, understands the word *melachah* in its common usage of "physical work," and explains the effect in psychological and emotional terms. Moshe did indeed suspend further man-made gifts, but when a person's labors are not welcome, he tends to reduce or even discontinue his financial commitments as well. Therefore, when the people were told that the toil of their hands was no longer needed, they stopped contributing money as well.

Centuries later, after celebrating the inauguration of the Holy Temple in Jerusalem for seven days, King Solomon and the Jewish nation celebrated for an additional seven days. Then, "on the eighth day he sent the nation [home] and they blessed the king and went to their tents joyful and glad of heart." "Joyful," the Talmud interprets, that they had enjoyed the radiance of the Holy Presence of G-d; and "glad of heart" that their wives conceived and bore them each a baby boy.

Those who participated in the dedication of the Temple became so infused with the Holy Presence that they returned home and impregnated their wives. Even those women who had been infertile became pregnant and gave birth to sons.

How are we to understand this statement of the Talmud? What is the connection between attending the inauguration of the Holy Temple and bearing sons?

Rav Yosef Dov Soloveitchik, *zt"l,* explains that the holiness of the Tabernacle, and later, the Temple, emanated from the Holy Ark, which contained the two *Luchos,* representing the Torah. Indeed, as the Ramban elucidates in his commentary, the purpose of the Tabernacle was to perpetuate the revelation of G-d's glory at Mount Sinai, where the Torah was given.

Hence, having shared in the dedication of the Temple, which is sacred by virtue of the Torah contained in its Holy of Holies, the Jewish people absorbed a portion of this holiness and immediately merited children who would become Torah scholars.

_____ *Rabbi Herschel Welcher*

T HE *SFORNO* OBSERVES THAT THE *MISHKAN* BUILT IN THE WILDERNESS was unique among the structures that *Am Yisrael* built throughout our history. Both of the *Batei Mikdash* were destroyed, but the *Mishkan* never fell into the hands of our enemies. Furthermore, unlike the *Batei Mikdash,* which needed renovations over time, the *Mishkan* never deteriorated. It remained in proper condition through all its years and through all its travels. Moreover, the holy vessels that were used in the *Mishkan* never fell into enemy hands either. Even the Holy Ark, which had been transported to the *Beis Hamikdash,* was hidden and spared capture when the *Beis Hamikdash* was overrun.

Why did the *Mishkan* escape the fate that befell both *Batei Mikdash?* A combination of four factors, the *Sforno* answers, endowed the *Mishkan* with a unique sanctity. It contained the *Luchos* that Moshe received at Mount Sinai; it was constructed under Moshe's leadership; it was assembled by the Levites; and it was crafted by artisans of spiritual distinction.

By contrast, the first *Beis Hamikdash,* built by Shlomo Hamelech, was constructed by non-Jewish craftsmen from the city of Tzor. The second *Beis Hamikdash* was also built by non-Jewish craftsmen and under the auspices of a non-Jewish king, Koresh. Consequently, the *Shechinah* did not dwell in the second *Beis Hamikdash.* Ultimately, both were destroyed.

The *Sforno* emphasizes that despite the greater amounts of wealth that were spent on the construction of both *Batei Mikdash,* neither was as sanctified as Moshe's *Mishkan.* Hashem is not impressed by the expense or the grandeur of the edifices that are dedicated to Him. Hashem cherished the *Mishkan* because it was constructed with spiritual distinction — and it was that special sanctity which protected it from our enemies.

This very same notion is found in the actions of Rabbi Chiya. The Talmud tells how he devised a plan to single-handedly restore Torah education to Jewish youth. He planted flax, which he then spun into linen and made a net. He used the net to capture deer, whose skins he turned into parchment. Upon these parchments he wrote the entire *Chumash.* He then taught the *Chumash* to a select group of young men, who, in turn, taught it to others. Why did Rabbi Chiya personally grow the flax and capture the deer? Why didn't he simply purchase skins from a dealer?

Rabbi Chiya recognized, the Maharsha explains, that to buy skins would necessarily commercialize, to some degree, his project. He wanted the scrolls to be fashioned exclusively for the sake of Torah study. Only if the children studied Torah from a *Chumash* made with absolutely pure intentions could he be sure that the Torah he taught them would endure.

In all of our Torah endeavors — and particularly those that we undertake on behalf of the community — it is necessary that we set the highest standards of integrity and operate purely *lesheim Shamayim.* The Torah teaches that the results we obtain are commensurate with the standards by which we act.

Sefer Vayikra

פרשת ויקרא
Parshas Vayikra

_____ Rabbi Moshe Faskowitz

"AND IF HIS OFFERING IS A SMALLER ANIMAL..."

Rashi, quoting the Midrash, explains that this section of the laws of offerings is a continuation of the previous one (which discussed offerings of cattle) but they were split into two sections to teach that Moshe was given time to pause and ruminate between the various topics as they were taught to him by the Almighty.

The Midrash continues: If Moshe Rabbeinu, who was blessed with Divine prophecy and was taught by G-d Himself, had to stop and contemplate one section at a time, certainly an ordinary man, who is taught by mere mortals, must pause and contemplate what he has learned and must not rush to the next topic.

But a question arises. If Moshe Rabbeinu, the prophet blessed with the most extraordinary wisdom, was instructed by G-d Himself, then there was no question as to the perfect clarity of explanation and interpretation. G-d's word was most certainly precise. There could not have been the slightest obscurity. Why then was it necessary for Moshe to pause? What could have been added by his personal contemplation?

The word the _midrash_ uses to describe Moshe's need to contemplate what he had learned is _hisbonenus,_ which denotes a process of examining in order to understand. To understand Torah, one must ponder, weigh and scrutinize. Uncovering the secrets of the Torah requires lengthy analysis and depth of perception.

All this thinking is necessary because the concepts themselves are so complex. Their lessons are often ambiguous and enigmatic. Esoteric ideas abound. Therefore, the topics themselves demand intensive examination. However, Torah is not merely an intellectual exercise. Even the erudite scholar who has mastered Torah methodology and who possesses a comprehensive knowledge of its teachings has achieved but the first level of *hisbonenus*.

The process of examining in order to understand extends beyond acquiring knowledge. It requires intense reflection as to how these acquired concepts can be expressed in one's personal life. How do the lessons of the Torah lead us through the obstacle course of day-to-day living? How does the study of the *korbanos*, described in this week's and next week's *parshios*, make us more faithful Jews and better people?

I would suggest that even Moshe Rabbeinu, after receiving the Torah directly from G-d, needed to pause and contemplate how these Divine lessons might alter his conduct. Through *hisbonenus* he learned how his life could reflect the glory of the Torah, how he could convert *Torah miSinai* into *Toras chaim*. Certainly then, as the *midrash* concludes, people such as ourselves must learn Torah not only to grasp its spiritual and intellectual beauty, but also with an eye toward its essence — the enhancement of life itself.

_____ *Rabbi Howard Kutner*

T HE MOST IMPORTANT TORAH READING OF THE YEAR, FROM A *HALA-chic* standpoint, is today's *maftir, Parshas Zachor*. It is a Biblical obligation to hear this *parshah* read, to hear the words, "*Zachor* — Remember — what Amaleik did to you on your way out of Egypt." This leads to another *mitzvah* to "wipe out the memory of Amaleik from under the heavens."

Curiously, we find a different command in the first account of this episode, in *Parshas Beshalach*, where Hashem declared, "I will surely wipe out the memory of Amaleik from under the heavens." One wonders: If G-d promises to take care of it, why does the Torah command *us*, in today's *maftir*, to do so? Whose responsibility is it to "wipe out the memory of Amaleik," ours or G-d's?

There exists a debate in the *midrash* as to whether Amaleik is compared to a mad dog, which barks and bites at everyone indiscriminately, or to a fly, which flies over an open wound or a heap of garbage. What is the meaning of this *midrash*?

Two types of anti-Semites exist. One will observe a Jew misbehave and cheat and his reaction will be to blame all Jews and spread news of their dishonesty to his friends. He is like the fly who flocks to the garbage and brings his friends along. He takes advantage of the dirt that exists but he has a rationale for why he's there.

The other anti-Semite hates Jews without cause or provocation. He is the mad dog that doesn't discriminate between people. All are attacked equally.

Amaleik may have been the father of anti-Semitism, but throughout the centuries he has had many children. According to Rav Chaim Brisker, *zt"l,* descendants of Amaleik, unlike those of the seven Canaanite nations and other nationalities mentioned in the Torah, are not biologically connected. Rather, they are defined by their *"simanim,"* characteristics, such as a lack of fear of G-d and a desire to destroy Jews.

Immediately preceding the account of Amaleik's attack, in *Parshas Ki Seitzei,* the Torah hands down guidelines for business practices and ethics. Rashi makes the connection; if we are dishonest in our business practices, we must beware of the enemy. Don't cheat, don't lie, don't defraud, the Torah warns us. Be honest, be straightforward. By dealing with society in a manner that will create a *kiddush Hashem,* we are doing our part to eradicate Amaleik. We are helping to destroy this form of anti-Semitism and fulfilling the command to "wipe out the memory of Amaleik."

If we do our part, then G-d will do His. "I will surely wipe out the memory of Amaleik from under the heavens." These are the "mad dogs," the hatemongers who need no reason or provocation for attack. G-d will handle these anti-Semites, but we must first deal with those whom we are responsible for. Hashem works together with His nation to eradicate evil and hatred from the world. G-d's Name and throne remain incomplete, the *midrash* points out, until Amaleik and all it represents are destroyed.

Each year, as we approach Purim, we must see to it that there is a little less Amaleik and a little more G-dliness in the world. When

Amaleik is eradicated, we will be able to sense the completeness of G-d's Name and His Throne, and see the perfection of the world under the reign of the Almighty.

_____ *Rabbi Alan M. Abramson*

THERE IS A FAMOUS DISPUTE BETWEEN THE RAMBAN AND THE RAMbam as to the meaning behind all the different animal sacrifices described in *Parshas Vayikra*. The Rambam in his *Moreh Nevuchim* posits that the sacrifices described in the Torah have as their forerunner the general sentiments of the time to bring sacrificial offerings, and Hashem elevated those sentiments through the *mitzvos* of the sacrifices.

The Ramban strongly disagrees. No *mitzvah* is a reaction to a generally accepted, standardized form of worship. He emphasizes the necessity to accept Hashem's *mitzvos* as original and not a product of or a concession to human frailty.

Perhaps one can understand the Rambam's view as underscoring the importance of sacrifices in human terms. For a sacrifice to be meaningful, one must give of himself that which is important. Thus, Cain's jealousy of Abel in the Book of *Bereishis* was a result of Abel's ability to give everything he had to Hashem through the medium of a sacrificial offering. Cain could not bring himself to do the same.

The Rambam reminds us that through an offering — *korban* in Hebrew, from the root *karov*, near — we achieve closeness to Hashem. Recognizing that everything belongs to Hashem tells us that we must give over, we must sacrifice, that which is meaningful rather than that which is insignificant. For the same reason, prior to the Exodus, the Jews were commanded to bring as a sacrifice the Egyptian god, a lamb, to teach them that everything belongs to Hashem.

Parshas Hachodesh represents these ideals as well. As the first *mitzvah* given collectively to the *Bnei Yisrael,* declaring the new month gives us the opportunity to participate in G-d's renewal of the world and brings us to an awareness of His majesty and greatness. No other *mitzvah* better brings to the fore the realization that Hashem is involved in our lives every day. Especially on the eve of Pesach, therefore, we need to rededicate our effort to be part of G-d's world.

We live in a society too riddled with divisiveness and pettiness. We recall through our daily prayers, themselves a commemoration of the korbanos of old, the importance of Hashem's world and we remember the Exodus from Egypt. We must not allow ourselves to be wrapped in our own obsessions and instead appreciate the potential each of us has to become close to Hashem.

——————————————————————— Rabbi Steven Weil

THE THEME OF *SEFER VAYIKRA* IS *KORBANOS,* THE ANIMAL SACRI-fices brought in the Tabernacle and, later, in the Temple. The Rambam, in his *Guide to the Perplexed,* writes, "The purpose of sacrifices being incorporated into the Divine service of the Jewish people was to accommodate the transition of the people going from the extreme falsehood of idol worship to the extreme truth of worshiping one true G-d. The Jewish people had been steeped in an idolatrous culture and could only free themselves from it by utilizing the same form of animal sacrifice that they were accustomed to. Now, through strict rules and regiments, they could direct it toward the service of God."

Unfortunately, this statement has been grossly misunderstood. The Rambam never meant to imply that *korbanos* were a temporary means of service, whose practice would be abandoned as soon as the Jewish people were weaned from their idolatrous ways. Noach and his sons offered *korbanos* after the Flood; Avraham offered various sacrifices. Neither of them needed to be weaned from idolatry.

Though the concept of animal sacrifices seems foreign, almost antithetical, to our notion of *avodas Hashem, korbanos* were offered in the Temple on a daily basis. The detailed rituals of sacrifices played an essential role in the celebration of each Yom Tov, and various sacrifices were offered to mark significant events in the lives of people. *Korbanos* obviously played a major role in *avodas Hashem.* How are we to understand that role?

The ultimate way to serve G-d and come closer to Him is through prayer and Torah study, for those methods involve one's heart and one's intellect. At the same time, we are created with physical drives, and we are therefore driven to relate to G-d in a physical, tangible way. Offering

Parshas Vayikra / 149

a *korban* (from the word *karov* — to come close) is a hands-on project. But this very human need is not given free reign; rather, the offering of sacrifices is governed by strict regulations, in order that we tangibly relate to G-d in a true, proper way.

Furthermore, *korbanos* address the human emotion of guilt. After a person sins, it is natural for him to feel guilty about having done wrong, having failed to live up to expected standards of behavior.

Instead of allowing a person to wallow in guilt, to feel disappointed and disillusioned and to succumb to a sense of hopelessness, the Torah requires the sinner to bring a sacrifice. He must purchase an animal — a living creature — bring it to the Temple, confess his sin, express a firm resolve never to repeat it, and then offer the sacrifice upon the altar.

These steps allow for the individual to express his natural guilt in a constructive manner, to improve and cleanse his character instead of tarnish it. Even in today's times, in absence of *korbanos,* the Torah continues to challenge us to use our *yeitzer hatov* to control our *yeitzer hara* — our physical and emotional drives — and always channel them to achieve a higher purpose, to relate to G-d in a way that allows us to grow and improve and approach perfection.

פרשת צו
Parshas Tzav

Rabbi Max N. Schreier

Pastebin...

ARSHAS TZAV BEGINS WITH HASHEM TELLING MOSHE RABBEINU TO command his brother Aharon to bring the *olah* offering. Rashi explains that the word *tzav*, command, is a term denoting "alacrity — immediately and for generations." What does he mean by the phrase "for generations"? Do the *korbanos* have relevance to *all* generations? What about today, when there is no *Beis Hamikdash*?

Rav Yosef Dov Soloveitchik, *zt"l*, refers to the Rambam's introduction to the *Mishnah Torah*, which begins, "All the *mitzvos* that were given to Moshe on Sinai were given with their explanations, for it is written, 'And I will give you the stone tablets and the Torah and the *mitzvah*.' 'Torah' means the Written Torah and 'the *mitzvah*' means its explanation. He commanded us to do the Torah according to the *mitzvah*. And *mitzvah* is what is called the Oral Torah."

By defining the term *mitzvah* as the Oral Law, the Rav explains, the Rambam is incorporating the idea of *mesorah* into every *mitzvah* — inherent in the *mitzvah* is the transmission of its law and meaning from one generation to the next. Consequently, the word *tzav* must also be understood in this context — as a directive of *mesorah*, a command to transmit Torah throughout the generations. This is what Rashi means by "for generations."

The Talmud in *Megillah* records that when G-d promised *Eretz Yisrael* to Avraham Avinu and his descendants, the following dialogue took place: "Avraham said, 'Sovereign of the universe, this is very well in

Parshas Tzav / 151

times when the Temple will be standing, but in times when the Temple will not be standing, what will befall them?' G-d said to him, 'I have already fixed for them the order of sacrifices. Whenever they read from [the sections describing] them, I will consider it as if they are bringing Me an offering, and I will forgive all their iniquities.' "

This statement of the Talmud enunciates the idea that "neshalmah parim sefaseinu" — our prayers substitute for the sacrifices in the Temple. We have fulfilled the mitzvos for the past 1900 years without interruption. We have put on tefillin, affixed mezuzos and observed the Shabbos. It is the miraculous power of our people that has enabled us to sustain the mitzvos for thousands of years; no other nation could have done it. And yet, we have not brought the twice-daily korban tamid even once during the time.

How have the korbanos stayed alive during the past two millennia? Through our prayers and our Torah study. We have incorporated into the siddur the sections of the Torah describing the Temple service. We read the parshios of the korbanos on their respective holidays. We study Seder Kodshim and learn the procedures of the Beis Hamikdash.

This is the point that the Talmud and the Rambam drive home. The Beis Hamikdash was destroyed physically, but its pesukim and halachos were not destroyed. Our contemporary share in the mitzvos of the korbanos comes from the transmission, the mesorah, of their laws. These laws, the Torah shebaal peh, of Kodshim have made it possible for us to carry on the work of the Beis Hamikdash to this day.

We, therefore, must not postpone the study of Kodshim or the parshios that deal with the korbanos. This is tzav ledoros — that the laws of the sacrifices have the same reality to us today as the laws of Shabbos do.

_____ *Rabbi Elihu Marcus*

INCANTATIONS, POTIONS AND SPELLS HAVE ALWAYS BEEN FROWNED upon by Rabbinic authorities. Torah, our total recipe for life, covers all needs and situations, leaving no room for superstition or legerdemain. Nevertheless, there is a tradition that particular pronouncements are helpful under certain conditions.

One of the great sages, the *Shaloh Hakadosh*, writes of a strange prescription for moral excellence and freedom from transgression. He quotes the great mystic, Rav Moshe Kordovero, who recommended the regular recital of the *pasuk* in *Tzav*: "An eternal flame shall burn on the altar; it shall never be extinguished."

The *Kesav Sofer* writes: "Anyone whose heart burns with an eternal flame for Hashem and whose veins pulse with the desire to fulfill Hashem's will to the best of his abilities — Hashem helps him and rescues him from foreign thoughts and surely prevents him from actively sinning, as our Sages said, 'A *mitzvah* protects and saves.' Behold, the altar is man himself, an altar of earth, and, therefore, the fire will not be extinguished. He who seeks purification is assisted. He who sanctifies himself below is further sanctified by the Heavenly fire of the altar above."

Rav Avraham Yitzchak Hakohein Kook, *zt"l*, writes in his epic work *Mussar Hakodesh*: "It is forbidden to extinguish the Divine thirst that burns and storms with a powerful flame in the heart. If one who dares extinguish a coal on the physical altar [of the Temple] violates the prohibition of "it shall never be extinguished," certainly one who extinguishes the lofty spiritual coal from the spiritual altar that fills the heart of a Jew with holiness [is guilty]."

Rav Lopian, *zt"l*, the late *rav* of Kfar Chassidim, once invited a colleague of his to spend the night at his home. His guest rose early the next morning, knowing that the *rav* went to pray at dawn. He hurried, washed his hands and face, and went into the kitchen. There the *rav* was standing at the window and whispering to himself. The guest listened and heard the *rav* saying the verse, "You shall not bring an abomination into your house."

He was confused. What was this strange preparation before the morning prayers? Rav Lopian promised to explain later. They walked out into the street, into the semidarkness. No one was in sight as they walked to *shul*. Then they saw a wagon approaching. A Jew was bringing his farm produce to sell at the central market. Seeing Rav Lopian, he stopped his wagon and bowed. "Good morning, honorable rabbi, good morning," he said.

Another wagon carrying milk passed. That driver, too, stopped his wagon, bowed, and said, "Good morning, honorable rabbi, good morning."

When they entered the *shul,* all who were there rose from their seats, bowed, and said, "Good morning, honorable rabbi, good morning."

On the way home, the rav turned to his guest and said, "Now you understand why I repeat that verse each morning. You've seen the honor that is paid to me each morning. I must accept it as part of my obligation as *rav.* Yet, I pray each morning to Hashem, 'Please let the fire of the altar burn within me, and let me not take these words and acts of homage into my house. Let me remain humble and bring the fires of the eternal flame and all of my people's offerings before Hashem.' "

_____ *Rabbi Lawrence S. Zierler*

MUCH CAN BE LEARNED, IN TERMS OF SOCIAL GRACES AND RELIGIOUS etiquette, from the *korban todah,* the thanksgiving offering detailed in the *parshah.* Rashi, basing his comment on the Talmud, lists the four who bring a *todah:* one who returns from travel at sea, one who returns from a journey in the wilderness, one who is released from prison, and one who recovers from an illness.

This comment of Rashi requires an explanation. We know that bringing a thanksgiving offering is not obligatory; it is a voluntary, heartfelt gesture. The priests and the courts could never demand that someone bring a *todah.* How can Rashi then imply that specific cases *require* one to offer an animal as evidence of his thanks?

We might better understand the *korban todah* as a moral requirement, not a legal one. Accordingly, the Talmud uses the term *tzrichin,* implying that one is expected to bring a *todah* as prescribed by the Talmud. If the intention was to obligate one to bring an offering in these four cases, the Talmud would have used the term *chayavim,* which indicates a *halachic* imperative.

This distinction notwithstanding, one can still claim that offering thanks is, in fact, required. Our need to thank Hashem and to be cognizant of His kindness in an actively expressive way is an ethically binding commitment. The *Chovos Halevavos* explains that the entire foundation of our service to G-d flows from our recognition that we owe the Almighty our thanks.

Although bringing this offering is not, in the formal sense, an obligation, it is nonetheless required as an expression of one's ethical personality.

Moreover, the *korban todah* — an expression of thanks for an event that assumes the importance of a miracle — was eaten only during the very day it was brought. As miracles occur daily for our benefit, the Gerer Rebbe explains, we must recognize and thank Hashem every day for His help. It is not sufficient that we gave thanks yesterday. Every day brings new opportunities to appreciate G-d's goodness to us, and we must express our thanks in a timely manner.

Furthermore, the Abarbanel notes, since the meat of the offering had to be eaten on that same day, the offerer was encouraged to invite relatives, friends and neighbors to eat and celebrate with him. They would be curious to know the reason for the celebration, and he would have the opportunity to share the great wonders of G-d that precipitated the offering. Such an experience would engender positive and fruitful discussion and involvement. If he had been given more time to eat the offering, he would have less incentive to share. Implied, then, is an added understanding of the adage, "A *mitzvah* that presents itself, do not let it sour."

By creating the need to share the *korban todah* experience, one shares the joy and the example of his appreciation, and thereby expands the faith of the community and its appreciation for G-d's grace and goodness.

פרשת שמיני
Parshas Shemini

_____ *Rabbi Fabian Schonfeld*

A T FIRST GLANCE THERE SEEMS TO BE NO CONNECTION BETWEEN THE *parshios* of *Shemini* and *Parah*. But seen through the eyes of our *gedolim* the connection becomes obvious and thought provoking. In *Shemini*, we read of the tragic deaths of the two sons of Aharon, Nadav and Avihu, whose crime was offering before G-d "a strange fire, which He had not commanded them" to bring. The *mefarshim* describe the brothers as great, pious men, who were obviously not offering some kind of pagan or heathen worship. What, then, was their sin?

The *Sefas Emes, zt"l,* offers the explanation that even though they were *tzaddikim gedolim,* and despite their intentions *lesheim Shamayim,* they originated a service in the *Mishkan* that Hashem *"lo tzivah osam"* — that G-d did not command. The idea behind this is that we Jews live by the *mitzvos,* by the commands that He gives us. That can not be altered. However thoughtful our intentions may be, however noble our purpose may be, our behavior is unacceptable if we do things that Hashem has not commanded.

This is the reason we bless Hashem *"asher kiddeshanu bemitzvosav vetzivanu"* before doing a *mitzvah* — to show that no matter how much we can rationalize the *mitzvah* and make it comprehensible to the intellect, we do it only because Hashem has commanded us. One should give *tzedakah,* not because it makes sense, not because it is just, but because Hashem commanded us to give charity.

156 / TORAH INSIGHTS

This principle also applies to prohibitions, the *Sefas Emes* continues. We must abstain from sin because Hashem commanded us to, not because it makes sense. We don't steal, not because it is morally wrong, but because Hashem ordered us, *"Lo signov* — Thou shalt not steal."

This concept, that we live by *tzivui Hashem,* G-d's command, is emphasized in *Parshas Parah,* explains Rav Yosef Dov Soloveitchik. The law of the *parah adumah,* the red heifer, is introduced with the words, *"Zos chukas HaTorah",* putting it in the category of *chukim,* which are usually defined as *mitzvos* without reasons. But there are reasons. In fact, Hashem said to Moshe, "To you I will reveal" the logic behind the *parah adumah.* There is logic behind the *mitzvah;* it does make sense. But only to someone on the level of Moshe Rabbeinu.

The Torah should have written, *"Zos chukas haparah."* Why does it say instead, *"Zos chukas Hatorah"*? The Rav explains that the Torah intends to show that even *mitzvos sichlios,* so-called rational *mitzvos* — giving *tzedakah,* visiting the sick, comforting mourners — must be treated the same way as *chukim,* as the law of the *parah adumah. "Zos chukas HaTorah"* — this is the statute of the Torah, the entire Torah, including the "rational" *mitzvos.* We should not really make a distinction between rational and non-rational *mitzvos.* To us the entire Torah is a *chok,* not just *parah adumah.* The entire Torah is a command of Hashem.

It is reassuring that the Rav's and the *Sefas Emes's* explanations are parallel, proving once again that *gedolei Yisrael,* be they *Chassidim* or *Misnagdim,* who walk in the way of the Torah's teachings and seek the truth in Torah, find themselves walking side by side. The words of the *Sefas Emes,* a *Chassidic* giant, and those of the Rav, a giant of Brisk, teach us that these two great luminaries saw the Torah in the same light.

This provides a valuable lesson: not to make distinctions between one kind of yeshiva and another kind of yeshiva. All *yeshivos* where Torah is taught are *yeshivos gedolos,* great institutions. That both the *Sefas Emes* and the Rav said essentially the same thing teaches us the importance of *achdus Yisrael.* May we live to see it materialize in our days.

O N ROSH CHODESH NISSAN THE TABERNACLE WAS DEDICATED WITH great joy and celebration. This sanctuary served as the focal point of the Children of Israel's prayers and service, for in this holy structure they brought sacrifices to mark every occasion — to express gratitude to Hashem, to celebrate joys and triumphs, to seek forgiveness for transgressions. The proper approach toward understanding the Tabernacle and, in later years, the Holy Temple in Jerusalem, is reflected in a Talmudic passage, which teaches how each of our three Patriarchs characterized the House of Hashem.

Avraham, when he took his son Yitzchak to the *Akeidah,* referred to the place where the Temple would eventually be built as a mountain. Yitzchak referred to that same place as a field, when he went to pray there prior to meeting his future wife, Rivkah. And Yaakov, upon recognizing that he had been sleeping atop the holy site of the Temple, called it a house.

The Talmud states that Yaakov's description, *bayis,* is the preferred term and in so stating, appears to convey a sense of how one should relate to G-d's dwelling in the midst of the Jewish people. Approaching G-d is not to be perceived as an overwhelming and frustrating challenge — as approaching a steep mountain. On the other hand, it is not to be perceived as a casual matter — as open and accessible as a field. Attaining proximity to Hashem is best seen as entering a house. One must develop a relationship with the owner and comply with his wishes in order to be welcome.

These two rejected concepts are similarly reflected in an interpretation offered by Rav Yosef Dov Soloveitchik, *zt"l,* regarding the sin offerings that were brought on the day of the Tabernacle's dedication. On that day, Aharon was instructed to bring a goat offering on behalf of the Jewish nation to atone for the sale of Yosef by his brothers, and a calf on his own behalf to atone for his complicity in the construction of the Golden Calf.

The Rav explains that these two different animals reflect the root causes of the sins for which they atoned. The Golden Calf was constructed because the people demanded that Aharon create for them a leader to substitute for Moshe. This demand manifested their overdependence upon the accessibility of G-d. Consequently, Aharon's designated sin offering was a calf, which follows its mother submissively, enjoying constant access.

In contrast, when the brothers sold Yosef, they manifested a rebellious instinct, overwhelmed by the challenge of submission which prevented them from accepting their father's choice of Yosef as leader of the family. Appropriately, the reluctant and brazen goat was designated as their sin offering.

Unfortunately, our generation has not as yet merited the rebuilding of the *Beis Hamikdash*. However, the lessons of old remain very relevant and critical to developing our own proper attitude in serving Hashem in our own time. We must work toward spiritual attainment, for it is not something that can be taken for granted. On the other hand, we can not become frustrated or overwhelmed, for if we make the effort Hashem will surely respond.

Rabbi Joel Tessler

NADAV AND AVIHU DIED, THE TORAH TELLS US, AFTER THEY "OFFERED a strange fire before the Lord, which He had not commanded them." It is not clear, though, what exactly these two sons of Aharon did to deserve such a dramatic death. Of the many possibilities offered, one stands out. *Midrash Rabbah* states that the brothers never married and had no children. Why were they killed for this? Our Sages explain that they felt they were too special to marry just any women. After all, they were the sons of Aharon, the nephews of Moshe.

Hakesav Vehakabalah further explains that the phrase in the verse describing their death by fire, "and it consumed them," does not refer to the fire itself but to their love of Hashem. They were consumed by a single-minded dedication to the performance of His *mitzvos*.

A danger lurks in such focused zealousness. The Lubavitcher Rebbe, *zt"l*, taught that even though a *tzaddik* is allowed to leave his physical reality and become totally absorbed in a *mitzvah*, he must nevertheless return to the "lower regions." A person must have his feet planted on the ground even as he ascends to the Heavens. Thus, before the *Kohein Gadol* entered the Holy of Holies on Yom Kippur, he brought an offering on behalf of himself and his family. At his moment of great spiritual elevation, he was still responsible to remember his human connections and familial obligations.

A story is told of a young man who was the finest student in his *kollel.* He had a brilliant mind and hoped to one day head his own yeshiva. He was married to a wonderful woman and had a number of children, but rarely helped with the housework. His wife was always overworked and tired. One day, she asked him to take out the garbage and he got angry with her. "You want me to take out the garbage?" he said. "Do you know who I am? I am a *talmid chacham* and you want me to take out the garbage? *Es past nit* — it is beneath me!"

His *rosh yeshiva* heard about the incident. The next morning the *rosh yeshiva* got up very early and proceeded to the apartment of this *kollel* family. He knocked and woke up the young student, who was shocked to see the *rosh yeshiva* at his door.

"Rebbe, what are you doing here?" he asked.

"I've come to take out the garbage," the *rosh yeshiva* told him. "For you, *es past nit,* but for me *es past.*"

Nadav and Avihu became so close to G-d that they died. They didn't feel anyone was worthy of marrying them. They forgot that they had to behave like men, not angels. We, too, are human beings who strive to be consumed with love, Hashem and Torah. May we all become big enough to take out the garbage for our wives. For *bnei Torah, es past*!

_____ *Rabbi Shlomo Hochberg*

THE TORAH FIRST INTRODUCES THE NOTION OF NATIONAL SANCTITY At Mount Sinai, where G-d commands the Jewish people to be a holy nation. Then, Hashem directs them to build a Sanctuary, in which His Divine Presence will reside. In *Parshas Shemini*, the Torah develops this theme, informing us of our potential for *personal* sanctity through our responsibilities as individual Jews, and instructing us on how to accomplish this.

The Torah's detailed delineation of kosher and non-kosher species culminates with the directive: "You shall make yourselves holy and you shall be holy, for I am holy." *Seforno* explains that this verse is not to be understood as saying that adherence to the laws of *kashrus* automatically endows us with holiness. Not so. It merely prepares us to acquire that holiness.

Hashem wants us to become holy, and to prepare ourselves for holiness. How then, according to *Seforno,* is holiness acquired?

Our ability to sanctify ourselves comes from the command, "*Vehalachta bidrachav* — You shall walk in His ways." Our emulation of G-d's traits brings sanctity upon us. Just as Hashem is merciful, so too should we be merciful. Just as Hashem is kind and patient, so too should we be kind and patient. In other words, holiness does not emanate merely from the ritual performance of *mitzvos bein adam Lamakom* — commands between man and G-d — such as *kashrus.*

Rather, these G-d-directed *mitzvos* prepare us for the performance of the interpersonal *mitzvos bein adam lachaveiro* — commands between man and his fellow. Hence, Rabbi Akiva's dictum that the foremost principle of the Torah is, "Love your neighbor as yourself," and Ben Azai's response that common respect for all people is even more important. Both Rabbi Akiva and Ben Azai focus upon the interpersonal dimensions of Torah and *mitzvos* and describe them as paramount to our mission as members of the Holy Nation.

Our Sages further explain that the duplicate phrasing, "You shall make yourselves holy and you shall be holy," indicates that our every movement toward sanctity is reciprocated with an amplified reaction by Hashem. First, one who sanctifies himself in a small way is sanctified, with G-d's help, in a much greater way. Second, one who sanctifies himself below, on earth, is sanctified from Above. And finally, one who sanctifies himself in this world will be sanctified by G-d in the World to Come.

Thus, Rav Yosef Dov Soloveitchik, *zt"l,* accentuates the ethical emphasis of Judaism. The Rav would quote his grandfather, Rav Chaim Brisker, that the function of *halachic* man is "to address the grievances of those who are abandoned and alone, to protect the dignity of the poor, and to save the oppressed from the hands of his oppressor."

Our attainment of holiness is predicated upon our *small* acts of kindness performed in *this* world. It is these interpersonal *mitzvos* that endow us with personal, individual sanctity and enable us to bond with the One Who Is All-Compassionate.

פרשת תזריע־מצורע
Parshas Tazria-Metzora

_____ Rabbi Joseph Grunblatt

PARSHAS TAZRIA DEALS WITH THE VARIOUS FORMS OF SKIN DISEASE
known as *nega'im* or *tzaraas.* At the conclusion of *Tazria,* we read
another section called *Parshas Hachodesh,* marking the start of the
month of Nissan, the month of our redemption from Egypt, and the first
month of the Jewish year. Seemingly these two themes have nothing in
common, the result of an accidental alignment of the calendar. Yet, a
clearer understanding of both *parshios* reveals, once again, that nothing
in Jewish life is purely coincidental.

Whether one views *tzaraas* as having natural or supernatural properties — the commentaries offer various opinions — there is no debate
that it is a form of Divine retribution for certain sins. Although *tzaraas* is
commonly associated with the sin of gossip — *lashon hara* — the Talmud lists six others: murder, false testimony, sexual immorality, arrogance, theft and miserliness.

Certainly miserliness is a long way off from murder, so what common
denominator links these seven? All are forms of antisocial behavior,
behavior deleterious to the welfare of the Jewish community. This is
why the *metzora* is banished from the community, the Talmud explains.
"He caused rifts between husband and wife, between man and his neighbor, therefore the Torah says, 'Alone he shall dwell ; outside the camp
shall be his living quarters.' " Furthermore, the *metzora* must announce
his condition wherever he goes — *"Tamei, tamei yikra."* The Talmud
elaborates: "He must inform the community of his pain, and the com-

munity will implore Hashem for compassion for him." Part of his reha-bilitation is reintroducing himself to the Jewish way of caring by experi-encing the compassion and concern of others for him.

The Jews spent centuries in Egypt under severe exilic conditions, oppressed and enslaved. Their plight, which Hashem foretold to Avra-ham, was presented almost as a prerequisite to their nationhood and their ultimate inheritance of the Holy Land. What was the purpose of this exile? What did Hashem wish for the Jewish people to achieve through this trying experience?

The Rav, Rav Yosef Dov Soloveitchik, zt"l, describes the centrality of the Egyptian experience in Jewish life:

> Whenever the Torah wishes to impress upon us the *mitzvah* of having compassion and sympathy for the oppressed in society, it reminds us of our similar helplessness and lowly status during our bondage in Egypt. The most defenseless elements in society are usually the slaves, strangers (proselytes), widows and orphans, and we are repeatedly enjoined by the Torah to be sensitive to their plight.
>
> ...The Egyptian experience may therefore be regarded as the fountainhead and moral inspiration for the teaching of compassion which is so pervasive in Jewish law. It sharpened the Jew's ethical sensitivity and moral awareness, The Midrash has R. Nehemiah say this explicitly: "The Egyptian bondage was of great value for us, since it served to implant within us the quality of kindness and mercy." Ours is a singularly ethical culture, which expresses itself through a heightened regard for human rights and dignity.

The first *mitzvah* given to the Jews was *kiddush hachodesh*, the sancti-fication of the new month. This first new month, the month of Nissan, marked not only the beginning of political freedom for the Jewish peo-ple, but also the start of their own unique lifestyle. Shortly thereafter they would receive the Torah, whose "ways are ways of sweetness, and all her byways are peace." A Torah lifestyle is built on caring, compas-sion and sensitivity for others.

A person who violates this heritage betrays this central tenet of Ju-daism and is thus dealt with measure for measure. By being driven into isolation, he feels the need for others and is guided back to the great lesson of the Egyptian experience, "the quality of kindness and mercy."

_____ *Rabbi Nisson E. Shulman*

THE TORAH STATES, "AND ON THE EIGHTH DAY HE SHALL BE CIRCUM-
cised." The *Baal Haturim* points out that the number of words
in this passage corresponds to the number of words in the passage
recited each Shabbos at the conclusion of the Friday-night services,
"*Vayechulu.*" The *midrash* makes a similar connection, citing the verse
in *Koheles*, "Give tribute to seven and also to eight." This verse, say our
Sages, refers to the connection between the seventh day, the Shabbos,
and the eighth day following the birth of a boy, the day of his *bris milah.*

What is the connection between these two themes?

At the *bris,* the child's father recites the blessing praising G-d, "Who
commanded us to enter him into the covenant of Avraham Avinu."
Avraham symbolizes the *mitzvah* of *chinuch,* Torah education, as the
Torah testifies, "For I know that [Avraham] will command his children
and his household after him to guard the way of G-d and walk according
to His commandments."

To inspire the next generation of Jews to walk in G-d's way has always
been the highest aspiration of the Torah community. No other nation
has raised the level of education to the extent that our nation has. The
first system of universal education was a Jewish invention. Our motto:
"Teach many students."

The commandment to teach children begins from the time of their
birth. And circumcision is the first step toward that goal. That is why all
assembled declare before the father, "Just as he entered into the covenant, so may he enter into a life of Torah, marriage and good deeds."

How does one continue to teach a child? Not only with words
and thoughts. Example is equally important, for without example
there is no aspiration. My late father-in-law, Rabbi Michael Kossowsky,
zt"l, rav for many years in Johannesburg, South Africa, writes in his
sefer, Tosafos Harim: "How does one fulfill the command of '*Veshi-
nantam levanecha* — You shall teach [the Torah] to your children'?
'*Beshivtecha beveisecha* — When you are sitting in your house.' Only by
observing proper Jewish conduct in the house can one be sure that the
lessons of the Torah will take root."

Parshas Tazria-Metzora / 165

The most potent example of Jewish conduct that creates a truly Jewish atmosphere is the Shabbos. The spirit of holiness that the Shabbos creates has the greatest affect on children and on their development.

"Give tribute to seven and also to eight." If you honor the Shabbos you will influence your child to continue in the fashion begun on the day he entered into the great covenant of *bris milah*. The words commanding the *mitzvah* of *milah* will thus correspond, as the *Baal Haturim* points out, to the number of words describing the Shabbos.

_____ *Rabbi Joseph S. Ozarowski*

THE OPENING VERSES OF *TAZRIA* DEAL WITH THE VARIOUS RITUALS A woman undergoes after childbirth. After the birth of a child she brings two offerings — a year-old lamb or a turtledove or a pigeon as an *olah,* a burnt offering; and a turtledove or a pigeon as a *chatas,* a sin offering. The Talmud questions the order of the offerings as they are described in the Torah, pointing out that when these two offerings are brought as a pair, the *chatas* is always offered first. Yet in these verses about childbirth, the *olah* is listed first. Rabbah maintains that, in fact, the *chatas* is brought first. Why, then, is it listed second?

Rabbi Menachem Sacks, *zt"l,* in his wonderful homiletic work, *Menachem Tziyon,* views this sequence as a message on how we ought to view our children's future. Parents continually sacrifice for their offspring, with their efforts, funds and time spread out on the altar of child development. The *olah* and the *chatas* symbolize the dual nature of parenting. The *olah,* considered the highest offering, symbolizes the high aspirations we parents have for our children. We expect great things from them in their Torah learning and personal piety, in their academic and financial pursuits, indeed, in almost everything they do. We want them to be great and we want them to be perfect.

And we want to be perfect parents. We want to give them everything they need to succeed and shelter them from any obstacles to success. But commonly it is the *chatas* which is brought for unintentional sins that more closely resembles our efforts. We make mistakes while parenting. We make mistakes raising and training our children. No parent can avoid this.

The Talmud's interpretation of the *pasuk* teaches a profound truth. The *olah* is listed first in the verse. When a child is born, we have high hopes and we should never give up those hopes and dreams; we must continue our struggles and efforts, so that our sons and daughters can be the best they possibly can be. We are bidden to dedicate all our efforts to this end, even though we know that, in reality, perfection is unattainable. We, as parents, can not always implement every one of our dreams. Thus the *chatas* is, in actuality, brought before the *olah*.

Rav Sacks points out that the *chatas* represents the Rambam's "golden mean." Reality may not equal the dream, but it can be quite good. If we keep our dreams in focus, we can reach many of them and enjoy satisfaction and *nachas* in seeing our children grow as Jews and as human beings.

_____ *Rabbi Jack Bieler*

T HE EXODUS TOOK PLACE ON A THURSDAY, THE TALMUD STATES; therefore, the ritual preparation of the paschal sacrifice must have been on a Wednesday, with the acquisition of the animals coming on the preceding Shabbos. The handling of these lambs for sacrifice was an abomination in the eyes of the Egyptians, who deified the creatures. Nevertheless, the preparation of the offerings proceeded without incident, yet another miracle on par with the series of plagues that had befallen Egypt over the previous several months. Thus the name: Shabbos Hagadol, The Great Shabbos.

Tosafos, however, tells a different story behind the name. Upon learning that they were going to be the target of the final plague, the firstborn Egyptians pleaded with their parents and with Pharaoh to acquiesce to Moshe's demands and release the Jewish nation. But when it became evident to them that the Egyptian ruling class was not going to be sympathetic to their fate, the firstborn rose up violently and many people were killed, marking Shabbos Hagadol as the beginning of the final plague, *makas bechoros.*

Hashem manipulated the minds of the Egyptians to generously give their possessions to the Jews just before the Exodus. Yet, in making the decision to give the Jews their freedom, only Pharaoh's mind, according to the literal text, was controlled by G-d. While the Torah repeatedly states that G-d prevented Pharaoh from allowing the Jews to leave during the final series of plagues, no such "hardening of the heart" occurred to the parents of the firstborn. That they, too, would turn a deaf ear to the pleas of their children is a remarkable notion.

While certain individuals did seem to communicate their consternation to Pharaoh, the average Egyptian felt helpless in trying to dissuade him from the self-destructive course he had set for the nation. History shows us that, at times, people get caught up in a series of events from which they simply do not believe they can extricate themselves, and they allow themselves to be carried along even when it is clear that the result will be tragic and devastating.

In this sense, it is striking that Shabbos Hagadol this year should coincide with the reading of *Parshas Metzora.* Rambam understands the effects of *tzaraas* on one's body, one's home and one's possessions to be designed by Hashem in order to get a person's attention, to snap him out of the reverie that causes people to slide down the slippery slope of iniquity without even realizing it. This recognition should lead us to view *tzaraas* as a Divine *chessed,* rather than a series of punishments and medical afflictions. Let us reflect upon the meanings of both Shabbos Hagadol and *Parshas Metzora* and think about how we should live our lives as *ovdei Hashem.*

_____ *Rabbi Yehoshua Berkowitz*

ONE OF THE MOST CONTROVERSIAL POINTS OF JEWISH LAW IS THE concept of *"Kofin oso ad sheyomar rotzeh ani,"* the charge to the Jewish court system to compel someone to obey the court's decision by "forcing him until he says, 'I want to.' " Whenever I review the laws of *gittin,* a majority of those in attendance are in disbelief that *Halachah* would permit this principle to be exercised, to apply severe physical duress, albeit only in certain situations, toward a person who refuses to give his wife a divorce.

This power of the courts seemingly violates an elementary principle of the *get,* namely, that the man divorce his wife willingly. Any type of coercion invalidates the process. The Rambam's famous answer to this conundrum is that the innate personality of every Jew is to do the right thing. The court merely assists him to act on his own natural impulses. *Halachah* maintains, in these instances, that it may take a series of lashes to the body to bring sense to the mind.

The court can be adequately assured that after a few lashes the Jew has become sufficiently "inspired" to remove the *yetzer hara* from his subconscious and do the right thing. He is now ready to perform a meritorious task, which, were it not for the impediment of an evil impulse, he would have been willing to do all along. What is the Biblical source for the Rambam's opinion?

Rav Yosef Dov Soloveitchik, *zt"l*, argues that the appearance of *tzaraas* is Biblical proof for the superficial nature of sin. *Tzaraas*, the leprosylike affliction that comes to punish such sins as slander and illicit relations, is a skin-deep spiritual malady and testifies to the sinner's lack of spiritual depth.

Introducing the laws of the sacrifices at the beginning of *Vayikra*, the Torah begins, "*Adam ki yakriv mikem....*" When the Torah reports on the punishment of a Jew, it begins with a similar phrase, "*Adam ki yihiyeh be'or besaro....*" But the word *mikem* is not used. For a Jew to elevate his soul, notes Rav Soloveitchik, the sacrifice he brings must come from within, *mikem*. But when he sins, it has its roots elsewhere. It never comes from within; it is not *mikem*.

This idea, said the Rav, also allows us to understand the *Kohein Gadol*'s request on Yom Kippur. He asks Hashem to forgive the Jewish people: *"Kaper na."* Why these words?

Because the expression *kaper* means to wipe away, without leaving any telltale marks. The sin of the Jew is merely on the surface, it can therefore be cleanly wiped away. The *Kohein Gadol* beseeches Hashem to use the mildest form of "detergent" in cleansing His nation. The *Kohein Gadol* knows that a mere "dusting" — a gentle reminder to do the right thing — and the pure, Jewish soul returns.

The principle of *kofin oso ad sheyomar rotzeh ani* is not so much a testimony to the power of the court as it is to the enduring purity of the Jewish soul. Our souls have been covered with a Divinely manufactured form of teflon. They can be soiled, but it doesn't take much to wipe away the sin, to make them as clean as they were when given to us by our Creator.

Parshas Tazria-Metzora / 169

I MMEDIATELY FOLLOWING A DETAILED DESCRIPTION OF THE RANGE OF sacrifices that the *kohanim* offered in the Tabernacle, and the laws that apply to the special status of the *kohanim* in the Household of Israel, the Torah embarks upon another aspect of their responsibility as leaders, arbiters and confidants, to whom all matters of Jewish life were brought for resolution.

The *kohein,* the Torah teaches in *Parshas Metzora,* was the person to whom the afflicted went if they discovered certain physical blemishes upon their bodies and houses. The *kohein* would determine if these marks were to be categorized as *tzaraas* — an act of G-d that set the individual apart from the community and left him in a state of spiritual contamination.

At the beginning of *Parshas Tazria,* the Torah introduces a different level of spiritual impurity which results from the joyous experience of birth. The description of the mother's impurity after childbirth is then followed by the command of circumcision, a *mitzvah* given such weight that it is performed even on Shabbos and Festivals.

New life comes as the result of compassionate sensuous contact between male and female. Although it may lead to the creation of another individual, who reflects G-d's presence on earth, the means of creation is still carried out in a physical way. Therefore, when a woman gives birth she remains spiritually unclean for a period set forth in Scripture. And if a male is born, he must be elevated — through the *mitzvah* of *milah* — from the mundane experience that made his birth possible.

This answers the question of the nonbeliever to Rabbi Akiva, quoted by the *midrash:* If circumcision enjoys such priority on the scale of Jewish observance, why wasn't Adam given this *mitzvah?*

Adam, created by G-d, was not exposed to the lower experiences of man and woman. He therefore did not require circumcision to elevate his status to the level of holiness. As a creation of G-d, he was endowed with completion.

In the course of life every one of us falls prey to the temptations that seek to interfere with the sanctity of the covenant of *milah.* As a sign, one of the three symbols of Judaism, along with Shabbos and *tefillin,* the *mitzvah* of circumcision raises one to the highest level of sanctity.

It is our duty to remain loyal to the totality of Judaism as represented by these three *mitzvos,* to pursue all that is sacred and holy, to be a *mamleches kohanim* — a nation of priests — to identify and uproot the spiritual blemishes in all of us. In this way we will help restore Israel to its birthright of holiness.

פרשת אחרי מות־קדושים
Parshas Acharei Mos-Kedoshim

_____ *Rabbi Zevulun Charlop*

THE TORAH READINGS FOR YOM KIPPUR — FOR BOTH *SHACHARIS* AND *Minchah* — are taken from the *parshah* of *Acharei Mos:* The morning's reading deals with the Yom Kippur service performed in the Temple's Holy of Holies by the *Kohein Gadol,* and the afternoon reading is, in the main, a long and forbidding litany of illicit sexual relationships. But there is another, less apparent connection between this *parshah* and Yom Kippur, which, in its own way, powerfully conveys the meaning of this holiest of days.

The *parshah*'s description of the Yom Kippur service begins: "*Bezos yavo Aharon el hakodesh* — With this Aharon shall enter into the Holies." The numeric value (*gematria*) of *zos* is 408. The three chief methods of repentance, pithily encapsulated in three words — *tzom,* fasting; *kol,* voice or prayer; and *mamon,* money or charity — also numerically total 408. In the *machzor,* one finds these three words printed parenthetically within the prayer, "*Unesaneh Tokef,*" which declares: "And repentance and prayer and charity annul the evil decree."

But beyond numerical symbolism, *bezos* conveys a message that speaks, possibly as no other instruction does, to Jewish survival and to its relentless adversaries.

There is no more heartrending moment on Yom Kippur than during the repetition of *Mussaf* when the congregation recites the martyrs' prayer, "*Eileh Ezkerah* — These I Will Remember." The vicious Roman tyrant, who then held sway in the land of our fathers, assembled ten of the *gedolei Yisrael* of that time and of all time. With ferocious directness he guided this incomparable complement of piety and genius into sweeping self-incrimination and moral indictment for crimes committed by their ancestors more than a millennia and a half earlier, and for which they themselves were not guilty; the kidnapping and sale of Yosef by his brothers.

The Roman had them acknowledge that the Torah calls for capital punishment for the kidnapping and selling of a Jew, and since Joseph's brothers were never formally punished for their crime, "it is now you who must atone for the iniquity of your fathers."

They turned to Rabbi Yishmael, the High Priest, and asked him to pronounce the Divine name and ascend on High to learn if the Roman's intention, indeed, was Divinely decreed. Rabbi Yishmael returned with the answer: "Submit, beloved saints, for I have heard from behind the curtain, *'Bezos atem nilkadim — With this* you are condemned.' " But what Heaven may also have been telling Rabbi Yishmael was: *Bezos atem nilkadim —* Your generation has also been caught up in this self-same sin that is captured by the word *bezos.*

When the brothers meet with the Egyptian viceroy, unaware that he is Yosef, he begins to plumb the depths of their beings — to take their moral measure. Have they truly repented their fraternal treachery? Have they genuinely banished from their hearts hatred of their brother? He exclaims, "*Bezos tibacheinu — With this* you shall be tested." And near the end of that verbal onslaught: "*Bezos ayda ki keinim atem — With this* I shall know that you are upright."

The ten martyrs were put to death not because of the sin that shamed their progenitors at the dawn of our national formation as G-d's people, but because that same sin, in a different guise, persisted throughout the centuries unabated. It was *sinas chinam,* causeless hatred, in fact, that brought in its wake the destruction of the Second Temple and, in its terrible aftermath, the miasma of persecution that overtook our people, including the martyrdom of the ten rabbis, whose sacred heroism reverberates down through the generations.

The Talmud in *Yevamos* states: "Rabbi Akiva had 12,000 pairs of disciples spread from Gevet to Antiperes, and all of them died in one span because they did not show proper respect to one another."

In *Kallah Rabbasi* it further states: "Why was Jerusalem destroyed? The first time because of idol worship and the second time because of causeless hatred. Causeless hatred is more grievous than idol worship, as it is written, 'Ephraim is joined to idols; let him alone.' When they are joined together, even to [worship] their idols, let them alone."

Their generation's failure of the test of *bezos,* not merely some egregious crime perpetrated long ago, compelled their martyrdom. This is what is also implied in the Torah's command, *"Bezos yavo Aharon el hakodesh."* *Bezos* — with this constant test measuring the texture and authenticity of our fraternal reality is what the *Kohein Gadol* takes with him as he enters into the sanctum, working atonement for his people. Appropriately, the first Yom Kippur begins with Aharon, the supreme *oheiv shalom verodeif shalom,* lover and pursuer of peace, whose pure heart was entirely unblemished by what often seems to be the irresponsible urge of jealousy and hatred of one's own kin and people.

_____ *Rabbi Moshe Morduchowitz*

NADAV AND AVIHU, TWO OF AHARON'S FOUR SONS, WERE KILLED, the Torah states, "when they came close before G-d." The Torah then goes on to describe the service performed by Aharon on Yom Kippur. Who were Nadav and Avihu, and what does their death have to do with Yom Kippur? Furthermore, why were they killed? Is it not the duty of every Jew to strive to come close to G-d?

Nadav and Avihu died during the sanctification of the *Mishkan.* "They offered before the L-rd an alien fire, which He had not commanded... and a fire came forth and consumed them." They were not just killed, they were consumed. Their death can be viewed as sacrificial. Describing their death, the Torah adds two words: They died "before G-d." G-d did not distance Himself from them, but reached down and brought them up.

"Bikerovai ekadeish — I will be sanctified through those who are close to me," G-d says of Nadav and Avihu. They were the *tzaddikim* of their generation and died attempting to find G-dliness and spirituality in their own way. By attempting to experience G-d in His fullness, they sanctified themselves; but their mere physicality could not endure it.

It is a lesson that we all must learn: it is part of the human condition that there are boundaries to everything, even to religiosity and spirituality. The ecstatic tragedy of Nadav and Avihu teaches us that one can only go so far. Our world is both physical and spiritual. The ideal of Judaism is to combine the two. Being clothed in human garb, we must recognize that there are limits on how we can achieve holiness and spirituality.

Thus, the story of Nadav and Avihu's death is real on Yom Kippur, for not only does the Yom Kippur service bring atonement to the people, the death of *tzaddikim* brings atonement as well. The tragedies of Jewish history have, unfortunately, introduced a slanted view of *kiddush Hashem,* sanctification of G-d's Name. The main *mitzvah,* as the Rambam codifies it, is not to die for the sake of G-d, but to live for the sake of G-d, to sanctify His Name through our actions. *Kiddush Hashem* involves doing heroic and wonderful things as a Jew, and to demonstrate collectively as a people that we are the people of G-d.

As Yom HaShoah approaches, let us appreciate that nearly half our people died *al kiddush Hashem.* Let us respond by living a life filled with *kiddush Hashem* to vindicate their sacrifice and make their deaths and our lives meaningful.

_____ *Rabbi Moshe Frank*

O UR SAGES OFFER SEVERAL REASONS FOR THE FATE OF AHARON'S two sons, Nadav and Avihu, who were killed *"bekorvasam lifnei Hashem vayamusu,* when they came close before G-d... and they died." This passage indicates that their fatal action reflected an unbridled quest for spirituality. They came too close.

A similar concept is introduced in the story of the *Akeidah.* On the morning that he was to offer his son, Yitzchak, as a sacrifice to G-d, Avraham, the *pasuk* tells us, rose early and saddled his donkey for the journey. This is notable because Avraham had many servants who could have done this for him, yet he chose to saddle his own donkey in order to personally tend to every detail of his Divinely ordained mission.

Under normal circumstances, Avraham ought not to have occupied himself with the animal, for it was beneath his stature to do so. But our Sages deemed Avraham's love and enthusiasm for the *mitzvah* great and praiseworthy. "Love [of G-d] rescinds the rules of dignified conduct."

Nonetheless, such unchecked emotion is sometimes inappropriate. If we overlook the fine, yet important, *halachic* details in our quest for spirituality, no matter how genuine our intentions, our behavior is unacceptable. Though some may argue that only the goal is important, and how one gets there is secondary (for example, encouraging people to come to *shul* on Shabbos even if it means condoning their driving there), the Torah does not approve of such priorities.

In Nadav and Avihu's noble quest to reach the Heavens, their service went up in smoke. In their desire to come very close to G-d, they overstepped their bounds. By not consulting Moshe and Aharon to see whether, in fact, their exuberance was acceptable, they brought about death and destruction.

Though Pinchas is praised in the Torah for upholding G-d's honor by slaying publicly two individuals who compromised the sanctity of the Jewish people, Shimon and Levi are criticized for a similar action, killing the people of Shechem after the rape of their sister. The difference? Shimon and Levi reacted without consulting their father, Yaakov, to determine if their actions were acceptable before G-d. Pinchas, on the other hand, did consult with Moshe, his teacher.

Even fighting for G-d's glory requires deliberation.

The story is told that Rav Chaim Volozhiner received a dubious response from his teacher, the Vilna Gaon, when he proposed opening a yeshiva in Volozhin. Consequently, Rav Chaim did not move ahead with the project. The next time Rav Chaim visited, the Vilna Gaon asked him if the yeshiva had opened. Rav Chaim told the Gaon that it had not, since his impression was that the Gaon was not in favor of the idea.

The Vilna Gaon responded, "When you came to me the first time, you were so excited about the idea that I wasn't certain as to the motive and origin of your fervor. Now that I see that you have harnessed your fire in anticipation of your Rebbe's approval, I know that your exuberance is authentic. You have my blessings for a successful venture."

Emotional highs are acceptable only if they are unadulterated, only if one's feelings are tempered by a total commitment to tradition in all its detail. We must strive every day to come closer and closer to G-d — by following the time-tested methods of the Torah.

_____ *Julius Berman*

T HE *SHULCHAN ARUCH* RULES THAT WHEN TWO *PARSHIOS* ARE READ together on the same Shabbos, the *haftarah* of the second *parshah* is subsequently read. There is one significant exception to this rule: when the *parshios* of Acharei Mos and *Kedoshim* are read together, the *haftarah* of the first, Acharei Mos, is read. Rav Yosef Dov Soloveitchik, *zt"l*, noting this exception, asks, "Why? What is special about the *haftarah* of Acharei Mos that requires that it always be read even when the *parshah* is combined with *Kedoshim*?"

The Rav points out that all *haftaros* have a connection to the *parshios* that they follow, but that the connection is not always obvious. In these two *parshios*, the Torah, for the first time, refers to the possibility that the Jewish people will be exiled from the Land of Israel after conquering and settling it. At the end of *Parshas Acharei Mos* the Torah sets forth prohibitions on homosexuality and bestiality, then goes on to say: "You shall keep My statutes and My laws and not do any of these abominations... so that the land will not expel you for defiling it, as it expelled the nation that was before you."

The same language is used in *Parshas Kedoshim:* "Keep all of My statutes and all of My laws and do them, and the Land to which I am bringing you there to reside therein will not expel you."

Since both *parshios* refer to the possibility of exile, says the Rav, the Sages wished to choose appropriate verses from the Prophets for the *haftarah* reading and focused upon the final words from the prophet Amos, who assures the Jewish people that, should they ever be banished from the land of Israel, their exile will only be temporary. Hashem promises that the Jewish people will eventually return to their land, this time for eternity: "I will return the captivity of My people, Israel, and they will build the waste cities and inhabit them; they will plant vineyards and drink their wine; they will make gardens and eat their fruit. And I will plant them upon their Land, and they shall no more be plucked up out of their Land that I have given them, says the L-rd, your G-d."

Our Sages wished to insure that we understand the inevitability of redemption and return, even in the face of *galus.* Thus whenever we read these two *parshios,* whether in combination or separately, and hear of the impending *galus,* we must also read the *haftarah* of *Amos* containing the promise that we shall be returned to our Land — permanently.

_____ *Rabbi Jacob S. Rubenstein*

WHATEVER RELIGIOUS TRAINING AND EDUCATION ONE RECEIVES, HE reaches a point in life when he forms an ideology and a position of how religion will play a part in his life. At that time, he also develops an idea of how a religious society should function and gravitates toward others who share his religious outlook. After all, who would want to live with people who, by word or example, criticize one's observance and condemn his *hashkafah*?

As a religious community has the right to assert what does and what does not conform to its tenets, it may declare a member's views unacceptable. Nonetheless, how is one to relate to another who does not share his views on G-d, Torah and religion? How is one to deal with someone who tramples his most revered beliefs and cherished traditions? And what if such people are from within one's own community? Should he take a passive approach and adopt a pluralistic posture or should he react with rejection and damnation?

The Torah states, "Be holy, because I, Hashem your G-d, am holy." This message from Sinai declares that if a Jew's behavior is disassociated from Hashem, it can not be considered holy. As such, how one relates to a fellow Jew who does not share his Torah view ultimately determines whether he is being guided by Hashem in fulfilling the mandate of Torah and holiness or not.

The Torah is clear that love and hate, rebuke and resolution are to be personified with G-d and holiness in mind. A lesson in "holy rebuke" was illustrated by Rav Avraham Yitzchak Hakohein Kook, *zt"l.* In 1912, two guards of the Shomer Society in Palestine were killed defending the Galilee, and Rav Kook was asked to offer a eulogy. He hesitated because the Shomer Society flouted Jewish tradition. The movement reeked of secular values.

But though they rejected the Torah, defied the Rabbinate and desecrated all religious expression in the land of Israel, Rav Kook reckoned that *Halachah* does not consider them apostates, as they gave their lives for the defense of the land and people of Israel. For this reason, he opined, it was permitted to mourn them. At the same time, Rav Kook listed the *halachic* principles that prohibited him from eulogizing these men.

Contradictory emotions raged within Rav Kook. In a sharp, paradoxical way, he expressed his intense feelings toward these antireligious pioneers. "My beloved but antagonistic brothers," he would write them, "my sacred-profane souls, woe, what has befallen us." His spirit and convictions were torn between an urge to love and an obligation to reject and abhor.

What did Rav Kook do? He stood by the coffins of those defending Israel, his heart bleeding, with tears in his eyes. But his lips were sealed. He refrained from delivering a eulogy. He could not speak because of his religious principles. But he was there. He marched with the procession. He showed his solidarity.

Rav Kook would not waver in his principles nor would he allow a situation to generate such hatred and hostility as to negate any hope of reconciliation. He did not agree with his antagonists. He abhorred those whose morality ran counter to the Torah. But he did not boycott. He suffered "unlimited agonies for His Name's sake and the love of the children of Israel," and he reminded people to be "conscious of the fact that we are fighting brothers and not enemies."

We must empathize with Rav Kook's feelings of love and reflection, hope and despair, idealism and disappointment. It is not easy, in dealing with people, to unite the law and its spirit, to harmonize the emotive with the *halachic* — to be holy in the face of adversity.

_____ *Rabbi Mordecai E. Zeitz*

WHEN REQUIRED, TORAH PORTIONS ARE JOINED TOGETHER, NOT simply to make up the necessary count but also because they possess a complimentary theme or subject matter. On the surface, this norm seems to be absent in the merger of *Acharei Mos* with *Kedoshim*. The themes of these portions seem out of sync with each other, as *Acharei Mos* deals with the high holiday of Yom Kippur and its service, and *Kedoshim* deals with low crimes, such as robbery, cheating and slandering, and matters of fair trade and compensation.

Two totally different aspects of life — the holy and the mundane — are linked in one Torah reading. What kind of combination of themes and subjects do we have here? Moreover, the title of the second portion, *Kedoshim,* denotes holiness. But its subject matter seems far from holy. What accounts for this designation?

Let us answer the question with a question: Who took care of the maintenance of the Holy of Holies, the cleaning, the washing, the repair, during the course of the year? Answer: Ordinary persons. This extraordinary place was tended to by ordinary individuals. By the same token, seemingly ordinary subjects and affairs have the potential to become extraordinary when they are tended to by individuals who are bound by the ethical and moral laws of the Torah. When done properly, even temporal dealings with neighbors and business associates become meaningful and holy.

When we are careful not to mislead people, not slander others, when we show love and respect to all, when we share our wealth with those of lesser means, when we do not allow hate to overcome us but instead show unlimited love even to those with whom we have disagreements — then we have brought the ordinary stuff of life into the Holy of Holies.

Jewish practice was never meant to be shut behind the closed doors of the Holy of Holies. Quite the reverse. The same sanctity and spirituality which we tend to feel on Yom Kippur in the presence of the Holy of Holies ought to be extended and applied the other 364 days of the year, out in the open, in the marketplace, in the home, in our daily lives.

As we apply the laws of *Kedoshim* to every aspect of living, making them meaningful and purposeful, each of us becomes a *Kohein Gadol* in his own right, transforming life into something extraordinary. The profound privilege and responsibility of being part of a "nation of priests" becomes clear in the most well-known pronouncement of our Torah reading: "*Ve'ahavta lerei'acha kamocha* — Love your neighbor as yourself." This pronouncement goes against every natural instinct we possess and even against basic Jewish law, as one may not forfeit his own life to save another.

What perhaps is being implied, therefore, is that one must love his neighbor no less and no more than himself. This assumes that one has a sense of value and self-worth, that one sees honor and purpose in his existence, recognizing the contributions he has to make to society and to the Jewish community. Recognizing your own value as a person, as a spouse, as a child, as a member of a community, you should expect no less from your neighbor.

In other words, you are charged to become the *Kohein Gadol,* restoring and enhancing the integrity of your neighbor on a regular basis, through every experience with which you relate to him. As the *Kohein Gadol* prays for the atonement of Israel one day a year, we are commanded to advance the integrity of our neighborhoods and communities each and every day of the year. *Acharai Mos* — after the passing of this one holy day of Yom Kippur, we take on the role of *kedoshim* — to make that one day everyday.

פרשת אמור
Parshas Emor

_____ *Rabbi Bertram Leff*

THE *PARSHAH* OF *EMOR* CONTAINS A CHAPTER DESCRIBING THE *mo'adim,* the festivals of the Jewish calendar. What is puzzling about this chapter, though, is that it includes a reference to Shabbos: "These are My appointed festivals (*mo'aday*): For six days labor may be done and the seventh day is a day of complete rest, a holy convocation; you shall not do any work — it is a Sabbath for G-d in all your dwelling places." The Torah then proceeds to list the various Festivals with their concomitant *mitzvos.* But what common denominator does Shabbos share with the *Yamim Tovim* that it too is described as a *mo'eid*?

Rav Yosef Dov Soloveitchik, *zt"l,* taught that the word *mo'eid* does not literally mean festival, but rather means an appointment, a meeting, as in the term *ohel mo'eid,* the tent of meeting, the designated place where Moshe Rabbeinu was summoned by G-d for instruction. Thus, the *pasuk* that refers to Shabbos as a *mo'eid* simply calls both Shabbos and *Yom Tov* appointments, encounters between Jew and *Shechinah.*

There is a difference, however, between our *mo'eid* with Hashem on *Yom Tov* and our *mo'eid* with Him on Shabbos. The Torah commands that on *Yom Tov* we travel to Jerusalem to meet G-d in His house, the *Beis Hamikdash.* A Jew was required, in Temple times, to make this pilgrimage, as it is written, "And you shall not appear before Hashem empty handed. Each [must bring] according to what he can give, according to the blessing that Hashem, your G-d, gave you."

On *Yom Tov,* each Jew is a guest in G-d's house and, like any guest, he brings a gift for his Host. But on Shabbos, although we also have an appointment with Hashem, an encounter with the *Shechinah,* we do not travel to His house. Rather, Hashem travels to us. On Shabbos, the *Shechinah* is the guest in every Jewish home. We welcome Him with a song, with *"Lecha Dodi"* and *"Shalom Aleichem."* In our *zemiros,* we proclaim, *"Askinu seudoso* — I prepare the feast of perfect faith, the joy of the Holy King." What is the gift that our guest, the *Shechinah,* brings to His host, the Jewish home? The *kedushah* of Shabbos, the sanctity that makes every seventh day special and unique.

Once we understand the meaning of *mo'eid* as encounter, we have shed light on the juxtaposition of the last verses of *Parshas Emor.* Following the chapters describing the *Yamim Tovim* comes the command to bring "pure olive oil, pressed for lighting, to kindle the continual lamp *(ner tamid)."* Then comes the command to place the *lechem hapanim* — the twelve loaves of showbread — on the *shulchan.* "Every Shabbos you shall arrange it before Hashem, continually *(tamid)."*

The menorah, the showbread and the table all represent the continual presence of the *Shechinah* in our midst — the *mo'eid,* the encounter, between *Bnei Yisrael* and Hashem. *Emor* concludes with the story of the *megadef,* the blasphemer, whose sin caused the *Shechinah* to depart from the camp of Israel.

May our *mo'eid* with Hashem, our meeting with the Divine Presence on Shabbos and *Yom Tov,* kindle our menorah, sanctify our bread and our homes. May we also praise Hashem for the spirituality He instills in the *mo'eid,* which inspires us to greater heights of Torah learning and observance.

_____ *Rabbi Yitzchak Sladowsky*

I N THIS *PARSHAH,* WE FIND CONSTANT REFERENCES TO G-D'S DECLARA-tion, "I am the L-rd Who makes you holy." The *mishnah* relates that the world contains ten levels of sanctity, from *Eretz Yisrael* at the lowest end of the spectrum and the Holy of Holies in the Temple at the apex. Why does the *mishnah* need to point out that place *a* is holier than place *b* and place *b* is holier than place *c*? Why not simply state that the highest level of sanctity is found in the Holy of Holies?

Rav Yosef Dov Soloveitchik, *zt"l*, answers that the *mishnah* is teaching us that one can not attain the highest level of sanctity in a single giant step. A person can not jump from the lowest to the highest rung with one mighty thrust. Rather, one must start at the bottom and climb the ladder of *kedushah* step by step. The *mishnah's* lesson holds true for every aspect of life. One can not become a scholar without starting from the *Aleph-Beis,* nor can one achieve success in his business or profession without building from the bottom up. And this is certainly a *sine qua non* with respect to building character.

The *mishnah* also teaches us something else. Sometimes people are so overwhelmed by their efforts to achieve a particular goal and become convinced that it is beyond their capacity to achieve that they give up. The *mishnah* advises them not to look at the Holy of Holies, but rather look at each step along the way. Start with the lowest level and make your goal the next step, then the next and the next. By focusing on one level at a time, the task will seem less formidable and will be, therefore, more attainable.

The classic personification of this process is Rabbi Akiva, who, up until the age of 40, had never studied Torah. He observed that water will penetrate a rock by dripping on it slowly and constantly, and he adopted that approach for his Torah study. At the age of 40, he studied with a teacher who taught *Aleph-Beis* to children. From there he progressed to the next level and then the next, until he had learned the entire Torah. Had Rabbi Akiva tried to become an instant *talmid chacham* he may have failed from the outset.

Parshas Emor teaches that it is possible to attain even the loftiest of goals by ascending the ladder of success one rung at a time. While one should never lose sight of the ultimate goal, one should always focus on achieving the next level so as not to become intimidated and discouraged from making the effort.

_____ *Rabbi Maynard Hyman*

WHAT STANDS OUT, AT FIRST GLANCE, IN *PARSHAS EMOR* IS THE contrast in its cycle of events. The *parshah* begins with the regulations that guide the *kohanim* during the most devastating moments of a person's life, namely the loss of an immediate family member. We are reminded that no individual or class of individuals is spared the possibility of these life-shattering experiences.

The sons of Aharon, the *kohanim,* are ordered to not defile their priestly sanctity by coming into contact with a corpse. They may only contaminate themselves for seven close relatives: a wife, father, mother, son, daughter, brother and unmarried sister. But the *Kohein Gadol,* the High Priest, may not attend the funeral of even these immediate relatives.

After detailing the regulations concerning some possible occasions, this very same *parshah,* with only one chapter intervening, suddenly speaks of the most joyous, inspiring and uplifting holidays on the Jewish calendar. In addition to Shabbos, Yom Kippur and Rosh Hashanah, we are also treated to a review of the three pilgrimage Festivals of Pesach, Shavuos and Succos. How are we to understand the positioning of these two widely contrasting sections in the Torah portion?

Rabbi Mordechai Hakohein, in *Al Hatorah,* suggests the following answer. "These two sections were placed in close proximity," he explains, "to teach us not to give in to despair and hopelessness when misfortune occurs." Just as there are sad and depressing moments, by the same token there are also joyous and uplifting occasions as represented by the Jewish Festivals which we celebrate each year. Therefore, even in those moments when the sun sets and the thick darkness of gloom envelops us, we must make an effort to look forward with faith and hope to the dawning of a brighter and glorious new day. King David phrased it best when he declared in *Tehillim,* "You have changed for me my lament into dancing; you undid my sackcloth and girded me with gladness."

That this message of hope is expressed by the cycle of joyous Festivals expresses the idea that the antidote to despair is a greater devotion to Jewish observance. The Festivals recall the miracles that Hashem performed for our ancestors when they called out to Him. Likewise, we are reminded that "the Guardian of Israel neither slumbers nor sleeps."

The Jewish Festivals teach the eternal lesson that it is not Jewish to despair. We are not allowed to submit to any feelings of helplessness because this indicates a lack of faith. Our history tells us this, our survival affirms it, our faith demands it.

Rabbi Bertram Leff

PARSHAS EMOR CONTAINS THE MITZVAH OF SEFIRAS HA'OMER, THE seven-week count from Pesach to Shavuos. As the nexus between Pesach and Shavuos, this *mitzvah* teaches that the primary goal of our redemption from Egyptian slavery was *kabbalas Hatorah,* our acceptance of the Torah at Mount Sinai. The Exodus from Egypt was only a prerequisite for the servitude that the Jewish people would accept at Mount Sinai.

It is this concept that forms the basis for Rav Yosef Dov Soloveitchik's, *zt"l,* understanding of the dialogue between G-d and Moshe Rabbeinu. G-d commands Moshe "to bring the children of Israel out of Egypt," to which Moshe responds, "Who am I that I should go to Pharaoh and that I should bring forth the children of Israel out of Egypt?"

Moshe argues that he is not the right person for this mission. He had a speech impediment and felt he would have no influence on Pharaoh. The Lord answered him, "Do not worry, Moshe, for I will be with you."

But the dialogue does not end there. G-d informs Moshe that "this shall be the sign that I have sent you: when you have brought forth the people out of Egypt, you shall serve G-d on this mountain."

The Rav shows from this latter part of the verse that the purpose of G-d's freeing the Jewish nation from Egyptian slavery was not to create a political and social entity, but to establish "a kingdom of priests and a holy nation." To be a political leader, there were people more qualified than Moshe, but to be rebbe of the Jewish people, Moshe Rabbeinu was the most outstanding candidate. Only Moshe could lead the people to "serve G-d on this mountain."

The period of *sefiras ha'omer* offers an opportunity to journey each day toward the mountain of Sinai. Each day counted brings us closer towards Shavuos, strengthening our commitment to the Torah of Sinai. The Rav thus explains the Torah's repeated use of the word Shabbos in reference to *sefiras ha'omer.* Just as G-d created the physical world in six days and set aside the seventh day of Shabbos, to be a spiritual oasis, so must a Jew, during this expanded Shabbos, this seven-week period of *sefiras ha'omer,* create his own spiritual world.

This is the message of the prayer of *sefiras ha'omer.* "Master of the Universe, You commanded us to count the *omer* in order to purify us from our evil and defilement. Let there be purification for the souls of Your people Israel from their impurities. May *sefiras ha'omer* sanctify us with Your sublime Holiness."

פרשת בהר־בחוקותי
Parshas Behar-Bechukosai

_____ *Rabbi Hershel Schachter*

R AV YOSEF DOV SOLOVEITCHIK, *ZT"L,* TEACHES:
In the *haftarah* of *Parshas Behar,* the prophet Yirmiyahu records a conversation between G-d and himself. G-d tells him that his cousin, Chanamel, will approach him and offer him a piece of property — land that the prophet knew would soon be conquered by the Chaldeans. G-d instructs him to buy the land, and Yirmiyahu does so: "I purchased the field.... I recorded it in writing and sealed it, and I appointed witnesses.... I then took the purchase contract, the sealed one... and the open one, and gave the purchase contract to Baruch ben Neiriah."

Then: "I prayed to G-d after giving the purchase contract to Baruch ben Neiriah.... The city is given over to the hand of the Chaldeans who fight against it.... You told me, L-rd G-d, 'Purchase for yourself the field with money and appoint witnesses' — and the city is given over to the hand of the Chaldeans."

This is true, G-d responds, but the Jewish people will one day reclaim their land. "Purchase fields with money and record in writing and seal them, and appoint witnesses in the land of Binyamin and the outskirts of Jerusalem and in the cities of Judah, and in the cities of the mountain... for I will return their captives," declares G-d.

We see that first the prophet Yirmiyahu did that which he was commanded — to buy the field from Chanamel — even though this act was completely illogical. Only afterwards did he pray to G-d to explain to him the reason for the perplexing command he had just fulfilled. We find a similar incident with Avraham Avinu, who was commanded with regard to the *Akeidah,* which was completely illogical. Yet Avraham did not ask or protest or hesitate in fulfilling G-d's command. Only after he had fulfilled G-d's command did he pray to G-d to explain to him the reason behind it.

Rashi, at the end of *Parshas Vayeira,* quotes the words of the *midrash:* "Avraham said before [G-d], I will describe before You my complaint: Yesterday, You told me, '...for through Yitzchak will your progeny be called.' Then You reversed Yourself and said, 'Please take your son [and sacrifice him].' " Avraham did not ask G-d to explain the matter until after he had already fulfilled the command of G-d; when it was time to act, he was prepared to do the word of G-d even though, according to his understanding, it was completely illogical.

Such was the way of the prophets, and such should be the way of every believing Jew who accepts upon himself the yoke of the Kingdom of Heaven — to fulfill the commands of G-d, even at times when they appear to us to be completely illogical. In his prophecy, Yirmiyahu was commanded to write two contracts — an open one and a bound one. The distinction between them is that all the writing of the open one is revealed to the eye and is easily readable. But in a bound contract, all the writing is hidden, as one rolls up the document and stitches it up under the writing; it is impossible for any man to know what is written therein until the stitches are broken.

In life, be it the life of a single person or the life of an entire nation, when we wish to look into the future and know what will be at the end, there are many things that are easy for us to see from the start. This is symbolized by the open contract — the eventualities that are revealed to all.

But there are also many factors that are impossible for us to know from the start, and this is the symbolism of the sealed contract, for which G-d said to Yirmiyahu, "Is there anything hidden from Me?" We are obligated, therefore, to fulfill G-d's commands even if they come at times when they appear to be completely illogical. Because although human intellect is able to see a bit into the future, nonetheless, in life there is always the sealed book, whether in one's personal life or in communal life. And man is unable to truly know what is logical and what is illogical.

(Translated from Nefesh Harav)

A WELL-KNOWN RAV IN THE OLD COUNTRY ONCE VISITED A TOWN in the wintertime, staying as a guest in one of the Jewish homes, which were located on a hilltop. At the bottom of the hill was the town's _shul._ When the rav walked there for _Shacharis_ the next morning, he slipped a few times on the ice-covered ground and came to _shul_ with snow and mud covering his coat.

But to his surprise, the townspeople's coats were dry and clean. When he asked how, they told him that before the winter they tie a rope from the top of the hill to the _shul_ and use it as a railing so that no one falls down. "Now I understand," said the rav. "If one is tied to the top, he won't slip on his way down."

The story comes to mind because of the unique name of this _parshah,_ _Behar,_ On the Mountain. Not just any mountain, but Mount Sinai, where G-d gave the Torah to the Jewish nation. Jews have a special historical relationship with two mountains: Mount Sinai and Mount Moriah, the site of _Akeidas Yitzchak._ These two mountains are really one, says the _midrash._ Moriah was transplanted to the Sinai desert so that the Torah could be given on this precious place, the site of the _Akeidah._

Two mountains, Moriah, which represents the Jew's readiness to die for the sake of Heaven, and Sinai, which teaches that even martyrdom must come from within the confines of Torah law. Man's personal judgments, however well intentioned, can never replace the Torah's statutes. G-d forbid that man should decide when it is proper to give up his life, as recently happened in one group's attempt to reach "Heaven's Gate" through mass suicide.

Only G-d can decide what is and what is not true martyrdom. Torah and _Akeidah_ go hand in hand, Moriah and Sinai are one and the same.

There is another link. G-d blessed Avraham "because you... did not keep your only son from Me." But Avraham was halted by G-d's messenger. He did not go through with the _Akeidah._ What, then, was Avraham's great act?

Avraham's greatness stemmed from his subordinating his understanding to G-d's command. Following human logic, his sacrifice of

Yitzchak would have left Avraham with no heirs. No one would remain in the world to carry on his battle against idolatry and to spread the belief in One G-d.

But Avraham did not follow this logic, even though such a conclusion would have been for the sake of Heaven, because he understood that G-d also knew what he knew and had His own reasons for His instruction. Surely, G-d would not allow idolatry to triumph. Avraham knew he must not try to be more religious than G-d. That is why he was blessed with the promise that his descendants would conquer their enemies.

Let us do all we can to preserve the Torah, not according to our understanding, but according to the will of G-d as revealed in His Torah. The world offers us a choice. We can choose to be *behar Sinai,* choose to be tied to the top. Otherwise, the *midbar Sinai,* the wilderness of anarchy, will take over. May we choose to be *behar Sinai.*

_____ *Rabbi Herbert M. Bialik*

I MAGINE THE RANGE AND MAGNITUDE OF EMOTIONS SURVIVORS AND LIB-erators experienced as the Allied armies liberated the death and slave camps of World War II. That precious moment gave profound contemporary meaning to the verse, "Proclaim liberty throughout the land unto all her inhabitants."

Especially in Poland, survivors who tried to return to their former homes were often met with deadly hostility. A dear friend, in our Jewish Hospice Program, told how, after Liberation, he clandestinely led a group of two hundred survivors to freedom.

The Polish authorities would not readily grant their Jewish citizens exit permits. In order to escape from Poland, the two hundred posed as Greek Jews seeking repatriation to Greece. Our friend instructed this ragged group not to speak Yiddish, Polish, Russian, or any other regional language, lest they reveal their true identity.

Though none of them spoke Greek, the group's leader did speak Sephardic Hebrew, which is often spoken by Greek Jews. Confounded by the leader's language, the Polish military at the Czechoslovakia rail terminal was eager to have the group exit.

When they reached Bratislava, Czechoslovakia, they were stopped by Russian troops. An officer pointed to one of the members of the group and began questioning him in Russian. The man became frightened, since he did not speak Greek or anything that sounded foreign. However, he was familiar with the Hebrew prayer book. Hoping to fool the Russian officer, he looked him in the eye and spoke the opening words of a Sabbath prayer: *"Yikum purkan min shmaya,* May salvation come from Heaven."

The Russian officer continued the prayer, *"China v'chisda v'rachameim* — With grace, kindness and mercy." The officer then explained that he too was a Polish Jew forced into the Russian Army. He concluded by saying in Yiddish: "Perhaps some day we will meet in *Eretz Yisrael."*

Our generation has witnessed the process of purification that the Torah describes in relation to the *metzora,* the leper. The process consisted of taking two birds; one is slaughtered and the other bird is dipped into the blood of the slaughtered bird and released into the open sky. The living bird is designated as the bird of *deror,* liberty.

We have experienced the slaughtered bird of the Holocaust, but we have also seen how the Jewish people dipped its wings into the blood of the slaughtered bird, lifted itself out of the ashes and proclaimed itself the bird of liberty. Through the establishment of the State of Israel we have proclaimed *"deror,* liberty throughout the land and unto all her inhabitants."

May we merit to see the fulfillment of the verse of our *parshah:* "And each man shall return to his land and each man shall return to his family."

_____ *Mandell I. Ganchrow, M.D.*

A T THE CONCLUSION OF THE *TOCHACHAH* — THE SECTION WHEREIN G-d warns the Jewish people to stay within the bounds of His laws — the Torah states: "These are the decrees, ordinances and teachings that G-d gave on Sinai." The Torah then starts a new chapter dealing with voluntary contributions to the Temple.

Rabbi Samson Raphael Hirsch points out that this chronology signifies G-d's preference for adherence to His decrees, ordinances and teachings. The placement of voluntary contributions after them indicates that voluntary contributions can never adequately substitute for proper observance of basic laws.

Furthermore, the *midrash* states that one should refrain from making a pledge rather than making one and not redeeming it, far better to redeem your pledge. But the highest level, says Rabbi Yehudah, is *"mi she'eino nodeir kol ikar* — one who does not pledge at all," but instead simply brings his contributions to the Temple and sanctifies them there.

There are many reasons for pledging our time and finances to charitable causes, but too often we become susceptible to making commitments we can not fulfill. We are not honest with ourselves. The Rambam holds that a *neder* requires both an oral declaration and a commitment *beleiv:* both one's heart and his lips must be in synch. Words without a commitment do not constitute a valid *neder.*

The *parshah* starts with G-d's promise of reward for the Jewish people: *"Im bechukosai teileichu ve'es mitzvosai tishmeru* — If you follow My decrees and observe My commandments." If the second half of the verse refers to the *mitzvos,* asks the *midrash,* to what does the first half refer? *"Shetihiyu ameilim Batorah* — That you should study Torah intensively." Beside the standard obligation to study Torah, there is a higher obligation: to study Torah intensively.

Rav Moshe Feinstein, *zt"l,* applies the same principle to *mitzvos* themselves: they should be performed with intensity. If we do each *mitzvah* with all our power, he says, if we are willing to expend great energy on every one, we will influence others to see the importance of Torah and *mitzvos.*

The opposite of *ameilim* is superficiality. One great danger of the world in which many of us participate is the belief that by simply donating time and money towards holy institutions we can compensate for laxity in the laws and the *mitzvos.* After all, we do get great pleasure seeing our money directed toward Torah causes.

A person who devotes all his life to Torah study is like a servant in the palace of the king, says Reb Moshe Leib Misasov. Even when working in the king's chamber, he is permitted to carry on in a normal manner, for if he had to stand at attention in a three-piece suit, he would never accomplish anything.

We must act the same way before G-d. We must be *ameilim;* we must toil. We can not be satisfied by simply fulfilling the minimum requirements of the *mitzvos.*

One who is involved in worldly aspects, even if he does them *lesheim Shamayim,* upholding the beauty of the Torah in his worldly affairs, must still pay attention to be an *ameil Batorah* for fear that his standards in dealing with materialism and worldly pleasures might cause him to forget the One Who stands above him.

Before offering voluntary contributions of time and money, we must put emphasis on "the decrees, ordinances and teachings that G-d gave on Sinai." Let us continue to work and contribute to Torah causes. At the same time, let us strengthen our daily observance of Torah standards.

_____ *Rabbi Reuven P. Bulka*

A COVENANT IS AN "IF...THEN" RELATIONSHIP. IF *A* DOES THIS, *B WILL* do that. This is the relationship G-d forges with Israel at the outset of *Parshas Bechukosai* when He tells them, "If you walk in My statutes and keep My commandments and do them, then... the land will yield its produce and the trees of the field will yield their fruit.... And you will eat your bread to your satisfaction and you will dwell in your land in tranquility." Clearly, this arrangement seems to be covenantal: *If* the people follow G-d's word, then they will be rewarded with a bountiful yield to enjoy in tranquility.

But doesn't the Talmud teach that "there is no reward for the fulfillment of the *mitzvos* in this world"? How, then, are we to understand this arrangement?

Concerning the promise that "you will eat your bread to your satisfaction," Rashi, quoting the *midrash,* states that you will eat little, but the little that you eat will be blessed and will fill you. The blessing is one of quality, not quantity. This is the Torah's concept of ideal consumption: those who are outward-oriented are more likely to develop minimal needs and will be satisfied with the little they themselves eat. This blessing is dependent upon eating properly, in a value-imbued way. The fulfillment of these Torah guidelines insures the ultimate blessing: a community of caring citizens who share and look out for one another.

G-d introduces here not the notion of reward for adherence to *mitzvos*, but simple cause and effect. The effect of individuals abiding by the Torah and protecting the people and their environment is a society whose members appreciate the deep concern others have for them. The poor are not envious of the rich. The trees bear fruit because the individuals responsible for cultivating them do so sensitively.

Reward for adherence to the covenant is not this-worldly. This world simply produces consequences — good ones, certainly — for living a life of good deeds.

The Talmud teaches that those who mourn over Jerusalem will merit seeing her redemptive joy. Those who do not mourn over Jerusalem will not merit seeing her redemptive joy. No one can doubt the miraculous nature of our return to Jerusalem, which we celebrate on Yom Yerushalayim.

But let no one doubt the cause-and-effect component of our return either. Had we forgotten Yerushalayim, there would have been no foundation for this miracle. Through our remembering, the miracle became a possibility. The effect, the redemption, became a reality thanks in part to a cause, our remembering.

_____ *Rabbi Chaim Schertz*

T HE TALMUD OFFERS TWO INTERPRETATIONS THAT DESCRIBE THE chronology of G-d's revelation of His Torah to the Jewish nation. Rabbi Akiva maintains that the Torah in its entirety was revealed to Moshe at Sinai. G-d explained to Moshe not only the general principles of each *mitzvah,* but every minute detail of its explication. The laws of the Torah were then repeated to Moshe in the Sanctuary and, in the Book of *Devarim,* were repeated once more to the people at the plains of Mo'av.

Rabbi Yishmael, on the other hand, maintains that only the general laws of the Torah were told to Moshe at Sinai; their details were first described to him in the Sanctuary before being repeated at the plains of

Mo'av. The structure of the Book of *Vayikra* is used to resolve this debate. The contents of its last two *parshios, Behar* and *Bechukosai,* do not address the Levitical code, the dominant theme in the rest of the book.

Moreover, the text clearly states that the laws until *Behar* were given to Moshe in the Sanctuary. *Behar* begins with the laws given at Sinai and *Bechukosai* concludes with a declaration that all of these laws were given to Moshe at Sinai. Does this declaration include all the laws in the Book of *Vayikra* or just the laws in *Behar* and *Bechukosai?*

To answer this question, Rashi quotes the *Toras Kohanim* which delivers the position of Rabbi Akiva: All laws — general principles and details — were given to Moshe at Sinai. This is demonstrated by the first *mitzvah* listed in *Parshas Behar,* the laws of *Shemittah,* the Sabbatical year, which is specifically linked to Sinai. If only the general principle of this law was given at Sinai, its mention would be redundant, for this *mitzvah* was already presented in *Parshas Mishpatim.* The only point to ascribing this law to Sinai would be to point out the inclusion of details omitted in its first presentation.

To strengthen this argument, Rashi makes another point. The law of the Sabbatical year is not repeated in the Book of *Devarim.* This omission gives it unique status. *Shemittah* becomes the example par excellence of a commandment clearly enunciated in the Torah where both general principle and detail are eopenly ascribed to Sinai.

One could argue, of course, that, on the contrary, this omission makes *Shemittah* the exception rather than the rule. Indeed, the Ramban does just that. But Rashi treats this *mitzvah* as the standard-bearer for all others. Thus, the final verse of *Vayikra* is a declaration that applies to the whole book and not just the last two *parshios.*

_____ *Rabbi Shmuel Goldin*

_____

WE LIVE IN AN AGE OF SOUND BYTES, POWERFUL PHRASES THAT ARE quoted and requoted to simplistically convey an immediate, compelling message. However, the use of such phrases, often out of context, is not a new phenomenon. Consider a two-century-old example, rooted in American history. Engraved on the Liberty Bell in

Philadelphia is the well-known phrase "Proclaim Liberty throughout all the Land unto all the Inhabitants thereof." Taken from *Parshas Behar*, this phrase accurately conveys the aspirations of the United States as it strove to break the bonds of oppression and chart a bold new course toward freedom.

But the quotation is incomplete. A visit to the original Biblical text reveals that the sentence continues: "... a Jubilee year it shall be for you, and you shall return every man unto his heritage and every man unto his family you shall return." The entire text, detailing the laws of the Jubilee year, speaks of steps that will follow the proclamation of liberty. What then is the significance of the mandate to return to one's family and heritage? How does this return relate to the acquisition of liberty?

On a technical level, every word of the text carries great weight. From the phrase, "You shall return every man unto his heritage," our Sages learn that property reverts to its original owners on the Jubilee year. Likewise, "Every man unto his family you shall return" includes the indentured servant who had previously indicated his desire to remain in servitude, the Talmud explains. Even an individual who has clearly renounced his claim to freedom is released on the Jubilee year.

Yet, an additional explanation of the Biblical text can perhaps be proposed, an explanation that may have caused some consternation among this country's founding fathers. Through the laws of the Jubilee year, the Torah informs us that freedom can not be gained through a complete severance with the past. In order to chart a new course toward the future, the past, with all its complexities, must be reckoned with: lessons must be learned, successes cherished, failures confronted.

The Torah turns to the Jew who has sold himself into servitude because of poverty or thievery, and forces him to go free. "You can not run away from the past," instructs the Torah. "You must return to society and confront your failure." Likewise, the Torah instructs the property owner who has sold his cherished heritage, again because of poverty: "Learn from your errors, so that you will succeed tomorrow."

By speaking to these individuals, the Torah, as always, speaks to us all. "Brave new worlds" are alien to Jewish thought. As we strike off toward a new dawn, we take a simultaneous step back, into our own complex past. Therein lies the wealth of experience that will guide us in our emerging endeavors. A healthy respect for that past is the best insurance for the future.

The words engraved on the Liberty Bell tell only part of the story. Any proclamation of liberty must be accompanied by a sense of responsibility emerging from the past. Only then do we stand a chance of succeeding as individuals and as a people.

Sefer Bamidbar

פרשת במדבר
Parshas Bamidbar

Rabbi Eliyahu Safran

IN THE BEGINNING OF *BAMIDBAR*, THE TORAH PAINTS A CONTRASTING picture to that which took place in the *parshah* of *Korach*. There, Korach's "common sense rebellion," as Rav Yosef Dov Soloveitchik, *zt"l*, labels it, wrought havoc on the organized Jewish community.

But in *Bamidbar*, all was peaceful: "The children of Israel did all that G-d had commanded Moshe, that is how they camped according to their standards and that is how they traveled." The *midrash* comments that the Israelites distanced themselves from the *Mishkan* in order to allow the Levites to take their rightful place adjacent to the sanctuary.

That need not have been the case, the *Sefas Emes* points out. The Jewish people could have argued as logically and emotionally as Korach did. They, too, could have claimed that there were those who were more worthy than the Levites to stand near the *Mishkan*. Were all Levites of such superior stature? Was it not possible that among the non-Levites there were those more deserving of these coveted front-row seats?

But this did not occur. These arguments were not presented. The Jewish people understood and accepted that if these places were assigned by G-d, no switching could be done. They all assumed their designated positions and Divinely assigned roles.

It takes a combination of greatness and humility to discover and accept one's assigned role and responsibilities in life, and it takes a lifetime of effort to fulfill them. It is easier to usurp someone else's role, or to ask, as the more democratic among us might, "Why have roles altogether?"

But G-d not only assigned the Levites their role in the wilderness, He counted "the heads of the entire congregation of the children of Israel" in the wilderness as well — in that very wilderness where the Torah was given. G-d wants us to learn that only a humble Jew, who is barren as the wilderness of any vanity, is capable of receiving the Divine word and of accepting his assigned role and position.

The story is told of a man who was able to quote the Bible by heart but whose reputation in the community was questionable. One day , he confided a secret ambition to his grandfather. "More than anything else," he said, "I would like to go into the wilderness that our forefathers crossed, and then to Mount Sinai. I would like to climb the summit of the mountain and from there to read the Ten Commandments aloud. That would be the crowning achievement of my life."

His grandfather looked at him intently for a while and then said, "Instead of going to the wilderness and Mount Sinai to read the Ten Commandments, why not stay at home and observe them!"

_____ *Rabbi Hillel Klavan*

WITH RARE EXCEPTION, *PARSHAS BAMIDBAR* IS ALWAYS READ ON the Shabbos before the holiday of Shavuos. This arrangement is not mere coincidence, as there is a correlation between the theme of this *parshah* and the theme of Shavuos, the giving of the Torah. The *midrash* asks, Why does the Torah specify that G-d's conversation with Moshe took place in the Sinai Desert? "From this we learn," the *midrash* concludes, "that the Torah was given through three things: fire, water and desert."

The great sage, Rabbi Meir Shapiro, *zt"l,* understood this to mean that the Torah was given to *Klal Yisrael* as a covenant to be observed under all conditions and circumstances. Both as a people and as individuals we have been invested with the power to withstand all challenges to our faith and remain loyal to Hashem.

Avraham, the first Jew, withstood the test by fire when he preferred to be thrown into a fiery furnace rather than renounce his G-d. The entire Jewish people withstood the test by water when they followed Nachshon ben Aminadav into the Red Sea. In both of these instances, their tests were met with a single burst of faith. Sinai, however, represents a sustained loyalty to G-d and to His Torah. As the Jewish people traveled through the desert for forty years, they had to maintain their dedication to Hashem, and despite the difficulties and occasional lapses, they persevered and reached the Holy Land. Our people's acceptance of the Torah in the wilderness before they had a land of their own reveals a basic truth about the transcendence of Torah and the essential nature of Jewish peoplehood.

Living in the barren wasteland of the desert, where the winds of adversity blew in all directions, the Jews, as a nation, placed the Torah at the heart of their existence. The Tabernacle stood in the center of the camp, with the tribes camped around it, welcoming the *Shechinah* as the unifying and life-giving force of our people.

That the Torah was given to us in the wilderness also teaches that a Torah lifestyle does not depend on the territory upon which Jews find themselves. It continues to be in force regardless of where we live. Torah is not grounded upon a particular time, place or society, and therefore can not be limited to that particular time, place or society. Torah presupposes nothing. Societies and values must be built around it, not vice versa.

The Talmud relates that the prophet Ezra had arranged for the *Tochachah,* the stern warning that G-d places before the Jewish people, which is found in *Parshas Bechukosai,* to be read just before Shavuos. But, *Tosafos* points out, the readings were arranged so that the Shabbos of *Bamidbar* would act as a buffer between the *Tochachah* and Shavuos.

This proximity should serve as a reminder to us all. Though modern man lives in a period which is *bamidbar,* in a wilderness beset by the crosswinds of immorality and irresponsibility, marked by affluence and indulgence, plagued by the erosion of values and direction, he can still avoid the harsh implications of the *Tochachah.* By remembering that the formulation of our peoplehood, through our acceptance of the Torah, took place in a wilderness, we attain the proper perspective. We must embrace the holiday of Shavuos by acknowledging our unswerving loyalty to G-d's Torah during any time, place or circumstance.

W HY DO WE READ THE _PARSHAH_ OF _BAMIDBAR_ BEFORE THE FESTI-
val of Shavuos? According to one opinion, _Bamidbar_ is a
buffer between _Bechukosai,_ which contains the _Tochachah,_ the rebuke,
and Shavuos. I would like to suggest that there is an intrinsic connection between _Bamidbar_ on the one hand and Shavuos on the other.

Sefer Bamidbar is also known as _Chumash Hapekudim,_ the Book of
Censuses. A census is, indeed, the opening subject of the _parshah._
Three principles in conducting a census are guidelines for dedication to
Torah, the core idea of Shavuos.

First, the census teaches us that each individual must be counted
because each individual counts, because each person is different.
Just as the genetic makeup of every person is special, so too is the
inner being of each person — the soul — unique. Similarly, the Torah
of each person, both study and observance, are precious in the eyes
of Hashem on account of their uniqueness. Therefore, every Jew has
the responsibility to aspire to his fullest potential in study and observance.

Second, each person was counted and identified with his family. The
census teaches us the importance of family in Jewish identity, and in
the transmission of Torah. Faith in Hashem and _midos_ are derived initially from parents. This is why the commandment of honoring father
and mother is listed in the first tablet, which is dedicated to the _mitzvos_
between man and G-d. Bilam, the non-Jewish prophet, understood this
when he said, "How goodly are thy tents, O Jacob, thy dwellings, O
Israel."

Third, the person counted in the census was identified with the flag of
his tribe. Each tribe had its own symbol, testimony to its singularity. To
know a person you had to know him, his family and his tribe. The tribe
was an important ingredient in the makeup of each Jew.

The tribes, with the exceptions of Levi and Yehudah, do not have the
same significance today. But there remain tribal groups which provide
important ingredients to a Jew's makeup. These are the intermediate
groups, larger than a family and smaller than _Klal Yisrael,_ which say so

much about a Jew. Is a person *Sephardi* or *Ashkenazi*? Which *shul* does he attend on Shabbos? Which is his yeshiva and does he identify with it? Which are his communal and *chessed* organizations? These groupings and institutions are the tribes of today; they constitute the community about which our Rabbis say: "Do not separate yourself from the community."

Thus the censuses of *Bamidbar* teach us that the basic building blocks for a genuine Torah life and society are the unique individual, the family unit and significant communal groups.

פרשת נשא
Parshas Naso

_____ *Rabbi Milton H. Polin*

A RECENT ISSUE OF *THE JERUSALEM REPORT* CLAIMS THAT ONE IN three Israeli women have suffered some form of sexual harassment in the workplace. Yet, as only a handful of cases ever come to the police or the courts, the public is misled to believe that the issue is marginal.

Whatever the numbers, the fact is that sexual harassment is a problem both in Israel and in the United States. For the record, *Halachah* absolutely forbids sexual harassment, be it verbal or physical. Not only is it forbidden, but its sin is very grave. Commenting upon the juxtaposition of the law of the *nazir* and that of the *sotah,* our Sages tell us in *Shemos Rabbah:* G-d says to [the *nazir*], "You have vowed not to drink wine in order to distance yourself from sin. Do not say, 'I will eat grapes and no sin will befall me.' "

The *pasuk* in *Naso* is unequivocal: "All the days he is a *nazir* he shall not eat from anything that is made from the grapevine, from the seed to the skins." The Torah is not satisfied by the *nazir's* teetotalism; that alone is not enough of a preventative measure. He must stay away not only from wine but also from anything related to wine.

The *midrash* continues: Likewise, a woman is called a vine, for it says, "Thy wife shall be as a fruitful vine." G-d said, "Do not say, 'Since I am only forbidden to have sexual relations with a woman, I will take hold of her and not have sinned,' or 'I will embrace her and not have sinned,' or 'I will kiss her and not have sinned'... for just as the *nazir* who vowed not to drink wine must abstain from grapes... so also you are forbidden from even slightly touching any woman who is not your wife."

These limitations reflect a pattern in *Halachah.* The Men of the Great Assembly required the Sages to set "fences around the law" — additional restrictions that protect one from entering the dangerous area around sin. These fences have the status of Rabbinic law — with one exception. The restriction of the *nazir* is the only instance where a fence is explicitly prescribed by the Torah, giving it the status of Biblical law.

The *midrash,* by comparing *sotah* to *nazir,* considers the fence that surrounds sexual immorality to be on the same level as the one that protects the *nazir,* lending it the authority of Biblical law. Unfortunately, much of non-observant Jewry is permissive in matters of sexual morality. By abandoning the so-called "ritual laws" of the Torah, they have threatened the relevance of even the most elementary "moral laws." Sexual contact between two consenting adults has lost its stigma. Living together before marriage has become accepted (despite every study that shows it is poor preparation for marriage and results in a higher divorce rate). In a society that attaches so little importance to the sanctity of marriage, is it any wonder that sexual harassment is so rampant?

The Torah's prohibition of any sexual contact outside of marriage protects the dignity and sanctity of every person and is the best prevention of sexual harassment.

—————————————————————— *Rabbi Solomon F. Rybak*

A LTHOUGH *PARSHAS NASO* IS THE LONGEST SINGLE PORTION IN the cycle of Torah readings, a significant part of it is repetition. The Torah repeats the list of offerings brought by every one of the *nesi'im* at the dedication of the *Mishkan,* even though each brought the exact same offering. What could be the intent of this restatement, not just once or twice but twelve times? An all-encompassing statement such as, *"Vechein asu kol hanesi'im,"* would have sufficed.

Our Sages state, "One who reviews his studies one hundred times can not be compared to one who reviews his studies one hundred and one times." Rav Yosef Dov Soloveitchik understands the difference between these two types of students not in terms of quantity but in terms of quality. After reviewing a subject one hundred times, the student can be said to have mastered his lesson; an additional reading could be deemed insignificant.

But the student who nevertheless feels compelled to study the material one more time demonstrates his commitment to Torah study for its own sake — *Torah lishmah.* This extra time studying expresses a Jew's love for Torah and his satisfaction with having been selected as one of G-d's chosen. The extra reading transfers the entire learning experience from the realm of the intellectual to the realm of the spiritual. This kind of metaphysical sensation can be endlessly repeated by man. The number 101, selected by our Sages, merely serves as a metaphor for the infinite.

Talmud Torah, as an expression of our love, can be seen as a response to G-d's own overtures of love for the Jewish people. In the morning and evening blessings that are recited immediately before the *Shema* the *siddur* speaks of a "great love" and an "eternal love" — *ahavah rabbah* and *ahavas olam* — existing between G-d and Israel. This love resulted in our being given the Torah and commanded to observe the *mitzvos.* The Torah is G-d's and Israel's mutual expression of love for each other. Thus, when Shlomo Hamelech declared, *"Cholas ahavah ani* — I am sick with love," Rabbi Akiva proclaimed his *Shir Hashirim* to be *kodesh kodashim,* holy of holies.

The acceptance of prayer and sacrifices in the *Mishkan* and *Beis Hamikdash* can, likewise, be viewed as a demonstration of G-d's love for His people. In the *Amidah,* we petition G-d in the blessing of *"Retzei"* to always accept our prayers and sacrifices with love. The ultimate goal of every approach toward G-d is to evoke a loving response from him. Thus, Scripture, in repeating the actions of each individual *nasi,* does not reveal any additional information but rather reflects the enthusiasm that each one demonstrated. The greater the number of repetitions, the greater the affection.

P ARSHAS NASO CONCLUDES ON A HIGH NOTE, WITH THE DEDICATION
of the altar in the Tabernacle and a detailed description of the
offerings brought by the princes of the tribes of Israel. It is then followed
by the *parshah* of *Behaalosecha* which begins with the maintenance of
the Tabernacle's menorah. What is the reason for this juxtaposition?

Rashi explains: When Aharon saw the dedication of the princes, he
was filled with anguish, since both he and his tribe, the Levites, had
been excluded from bringing offerings. Hashem, however, said to him,
"By your life, yours is greater than theirs, for you shall kindle the menorah." But the Ramban is disturbed by Rashi's interpretation. Why is
servicing the menorah compensation for missing out on the dedication
of the altar?

Furthermore, the Torah is careful to itemize the gifts of each of the
princes. But why? The offering of each one was identical to that of the
next. Why didn't the Torah simply summarize and state that each one
brought the following gift?

Rav Solomon Breuer, *zt"l,* offers a meaningful interpretation. The
Torah purposefully repeats each of the princes' offerings to teach a
fundamental lesson — that twelve different men may offer the very
same gift to Hashem, yet each gift carries its own weight. "Judge the
donor according to the gift and the gift according to the donor." The
spirit and joy with which a gift is given determine its real value. Twelve
princes can bring the same offering and each bears its own significance
to Hashem. The Torah, in reiterating each offering, teaches us that at
that moment their hearts, thoughts and spirit were united with a solemn
vow, to place all their possessions in the service of Hashem and His
causes.

Regrettably, such feeling does not always find its way into our practice. Thus, according to Rashi, Hashem reassures Aharon, "Your task of
kindling the menorah is greater than theirs." The *midrash* notes, "You
are chosen for greater tasks. Sacrifices are offered only as long as the
Sanctuary stands, but the lights of the menorah are forever." The light
of the menorah represents the light of Torah. Aharon's daily mainte-

nance of the menorah served to keep the focus of *all* the service in the Tabernacle on Hashem above, on fealty to His word and to His law.

I would also make a connection between *Parshas Naso,* which is the largest *parshah* in the Torah, comprising 176 verses, and the 119th chapter of *Tehillim,* which also contains 176 verses and is the longest in *Tehillim.* The psalm carries the distinct title, "Torah, the Way of Life." It is the light of Torah which gives real purpose to our lives. Offerings and gifts may be of great significance, but the essence of our lives remains best expressed by David Hamelech, "Your word is a lamp unto my feet and a light unto my path."

_____ *Rabbi Edward Garsek*

P ARSHAS NASO TELLS OF THE INAUGURATION OF THE *MISHKAN* IN the wilderness: "It was on the day that Moshe finished erecting the Tabernacle, he anointed and sanctified it." Rashi asks why the Torah gives credit to Moshe for erecting the *Mishkan,* when Betzalel and Ohaliev had constructed it. In fact, many wise-hearted men and women contributed to the efforts that went into this wonderful architectural marvel. Why does the Torah attribute the *Mishkan* to Moshe alone?

Rashi explains: *"Lefi shemasar nafsho alav* — Because he *sacrificed* for it." Moshe Rabbeinu was *moseir nefesh* over each of the many minutiae that came with the construction of the *Mishkan.* He painstakingly followed the progress of its construction; it is, therefore, attributed to him. Many times we find this concept in the *Tanach.* The *Beis Hamikdash* is called *Sukkas David.* Though Shlomo Hamelech actually built it, it was David Hamelech who demonstrated the *mesiras nefesh* to build the Holy Temple.

At a *bris milah,* Eliyahu Hanavi is represented by the *kisei shel Eliyahu.* Because he had the *mesiras nefesh* to make sure that every Jewish child has a proper circumcision, even during times when fulfilling this *mitzvah* was punishable by death, he is honored at every *bris.*

And so it is with our *avodas hakodesh.* Even though we do not always see the end of our work, we must always strive to build, to teach and to sanctify. It is easy to become discouraged in the face of great odds. But with *mesiras nefesh,* with Hashem's help, we will prevail.

The reward we receive might not be in completing our objective, but simply in working toward it. This is a tremendous lesson — to put our greatest efforts into striving for, if not quite reaching, our goals. In that lies the achievement. As *Pirkei Avos* teaches, "The work is not yours to finish. But you are not free to neglect it."

_____ *Rabbi Nachum Muschel*

PARSHAS NASO HIGHLIGHTS THE *KOHEIN*'S ROLE IN COPING WITH SO-cial deviations that plague society. It is the *kohein* who must deal with the thief whose pangs of conscience make him seek forgiveness. It is the *kohein* who must address himself to the husband and wife when suspicions of infidelity threaten the foundation of their home. It is the *kohein* who has to react to the concerns of the person, who, over-whelmed by the allurement of society, tries to protect himself from sin by becoming a *nazir*.

In all these instances, the *kohein*'s task is to be one who atones. "*Vechiper hakohein,*" the Torah tells us. He is the one who repairs a rela-tionship. He is the one who restores lost trust or self-image. "*Vechiper hakohein*" — the *kohein* is an agent of forgiveness.

At the heart of *Parshas Naso,* however, is a totally different assign-ment entrusted to the *kohein*. Five verses at the center of the *parshah* compose the blessing that the *kohein* bestows upon the people of Israel to this day. As such, the *kohein* is presented with a new, most meaning-ful task. He is empowered: "*Koh sevarachu* — So shall you bless the children of Israel." Be an instrument for bringing G-d's blessing to the Jewish people, the Torah commands. Bestow this blessing with a full heart, with love, adding raised hands to accompany the words of your mouth. Begin this precious blessing with the word "*yevarechecha*" and conclude it with the word "*shalom.*"

The role here is no longer *kohein* as atoner, restorer of relationships, repairer of broken homes and broken hearts. Here, the *kohein* is called upon to be an agent of blessing, to act rather than to react, to offer "an ounce of prevention" rather than "a pound of cure."

A plethora of *midrashim* offer a variety of meanings to this word "*koh.*" The *Baal Haturim* notes that the numerical value of "*koh*" is twenty-five, reminiscent of the twenty-five letters that make up the first *pasuk* of *Kerias Shema.* *"Koh sevarachu"* also calls to mind the twenty-five times the Torah records the concept of blessing in association with G-d, and it recalls the twenty-five times that the word *shalom* appears in the Torah. *"Koh sevarachu"* clarifies the *kohein*'s most important mission: to be an agent of *berachah* and guidance — to make the Jew not just conscious of sin, but conscious of G-d.

Significantly, following the dedication of the *mizbei'ach* by the leaders of the twelve tribes, in which Aharon's role is diminished, the Torah details the *mitzvah* of lighting the menorah, at the start of *Parshas Behaalosecha.* Aharon's privilege is emphasized. "Yours is greater than theirs," Hashem tells him. The message to the *kohein* is revealing. An altar, a *mizbei'ach,* is for repairing, forgiving, bringing atonement.

The menorah, on the other hand, represents enlightenment, teaching, guidance. While the *mizbei'ach* uproots sin, the light of the menorah, as well as the *Birchas Kohanim,* prevents the Jew from falling into the abyss of sin to begin with.

Let the pitfalls of sin and strife be overwhelmed by blessings of light. And may we thus merit the result of *"veyaseim lecha shalom."*

פרשת בהעלותך
Parshas Behaalosecha

_____ *Rabbi Steven M. Dworken*

ONE FINDS A STRANGE MOMENT, WORTHY OF CONTEMPLATION AND explanation, in this *parshah.* The *Bnei Yisrael,* expressing bitterness over their fate in the wilderness, complain about the food they receive — the manna that rains down from the heavens each night. They reminisce about the better meals they enjoyed while slaves in Egypt. Moshe reacts uncharacteristically, lamenting his role. "Why have You acted so badly to Your servant?" he asks G-d. "Why have I not found favor in Your eyes that You placed the burden of this entire nation upon me?"

Could this be the same Moshe who defended the *Bnei Yisrael* with strength and rigor after their treacherous worship of the Golden Calf? The same Moshe who would not relent until G-d forgave the Jewish people for that sin?

G-d's reaction to the situation was to give them what they wanted. He sent them quail for an entire month and they gorged themselves on the meat until they died. This unique plague is the tragic story of *Kivros Hataavah,* the Graves of Desire. The nation was not guilty of murder or of idolatry at this time, only desire. "This portrays modern man," says Rav Yosef Dov Soloveitchik, *zt"l.* "This is the grave that man digs for himself — or better, the grave that desire digs for man."

After the Jews had received the Torah and constructed the Tabernacle, there was no longer any reason for them to remain in the wilderness. "There was no purpose to extend the sojourn any longer," said the Rav. "The final march into *Eretz Yisrael* could have been accomplished in only a few days. There was a mood of expectancy in the camp — the promise of G-d to Avraham was about to be fulfilled. Moshe told Yisro, 'We are traveling' in the present tense. Now, no delays, no waiting. He extended an invitation not just to Yisro but to the entire non-Jewish world to participate. Join our destiny; our triumphal march will also be yours."

But the lust brought everything to a halt. The crowd fell, seized by desire.

Why didn't Moshe pray for the *Bnei Yisrael* here as he had after the Golden Calf? Here we arrive at a fundamental and enlightening distinction between the two sins. "The Golden Calf," explains the Rav, "was the result of a great primitive fright. Though the people did violate the commandment prohibiting idolatry, there were mitigating circumstances. The people did not know why Moshe had not returned from the mountain and they were overwhelmed by terror and loneliness. They turned to idolatry as a substitute for Moshe."

Idolatry satisfies a need, misplaced though it may be. But the behavior of the people here is best characterized as paganism, which cries for boundless variety and insatiable desire. "It is," proclaims the Rav, "the antithesis of Judaism, which stands for limited enjoyment and the ability to withdraw, to retreat. Unlimited desire is man's worst trait; it is man reaching for the unreachable. The pagan's way of life is worse than the idolater's. An idol can not last. But paganism, being mad with desire with no controlling elements, gathering new goods before using the old, that is the opposite of the manna, which had limits."

It was this greed, this pagan way of life, that stopped the entire process of the complete redemption that awaited the Jewish people at that moment. It is this same behavior, perhaps, that continues to impede the redemption to this very day.

_____ *Rabbi Shlomo Krupka*

A T THE BEGINNING OF THIS WEEK'S *PARSHAH*, RASHI ASKS, "WHY IS the *parshah* of the menorah placed next to the *parshah* of the *nesi'im*," the princes who dedicated the Tabernacle at the end of *Parshas Naso*?

Rashi answers: Aharon was depressed that his tribe, Levi, was not given a role in this ceremony. G-d therefore told him, "Upon your life, your share is greater than theirs, for you light and prepare the menorah." The Ramban ascribes this consolation to a promise of a future Temple dedication, by Aharon's descendants, the *Chashmona'im,* after the miracle of Chanukah. In due time, his children would dedicate it all and bring the *mitzvah* of the Chanukah lights to the entire Jewish nation forever.

Rav Yosef Dov Soloveitchik, *zt"l,* takes a different approach in answering this question. How was it that Aharon was bothered in the first place? Was it not his job to offer upon the altar the sacrifices that the other tribes brought? Why did he feel shut out?

The Rav quotes the Rambam, "One may not bring a private incense offering on the inner altar." Nevertheless, the *nesi'im* were given a special exemption to do just that, to bring a special, private incense offering.

Aharon, for all his personal offerings both now and in the future, was never afforded this opportunity. He was only permitted to bring a voluntary *chatas* offering, but it was not accompanied by incense. Seeing the privilege given to the *nesi'im,* Aharon understood his limitation and was distressed. Hashem assuaged him with the menorah. The *mitzvah* of lighting the menorah is intrinsically tied to the *mitzvah* of offering the incense, in keeping with the verse, "When Aharon kindles the lamps, he shall bring [the incense] up in smoke."

Thus, says the Rav, the lighting of the menorah accomplishes two things. First, the actual *mitzvah* of the lighting, and second, the completion of the incense offering. If the incense is brought without the menorah being lit, the *mitzvah* is lacking. "Yours is greater than theirs," Hashem tells Aharon, for only through his lighting the menorah, therefore, was the incense offering of the *nesi'im* complete.

What is this bond between the incense and the menorah? Why is one dependent on the other? The answer is found within this *parshah.* At the beginning of *Naso, Bnei Yisrael* are about to enter the Land of Canaan. But the *parshah* ends with a sense of impending gloom. What happened to the dream of entering the Land? What caused this change?

Dreams, the Talmud tells us, follow the interpretations they are given. If a positive spin is given, a positive result will unfold; and, G-d forbid, vice versa. The Jews of the desert were fulfilling a dream. They had plenty of positive factors to focus on, but spoke only of the worst. Their petty complaints among themselves progressed to *lashon hara* about Moshe, and culminated in the following *parshah, Shelach,* with the spies speaking adversely about the Holy Land.

If you look for the worst, you will always find it even in Moshe and *Eretz Yisrael.* The Jews lost the dream and died in the desert. To guide us away from similar mistakes, the *parshah* begins with the *mitzvah* of the menorah, the symbol of wisdom. The incense, the Talmud tells us, was offered to atone for speaking *lashon hara* in private. But, as noted above, the incense offering was not complete without the prior lighting of the menorah. Only through wisdom will the atonement for *lashon hara* be complete. As Shlomo Hamelech states in *Aishes Chayil,* "Her mouth is opened in wisdom."

We must have the foresight to understand that speaking wisely, even in private, is the only remedy for *lashon hara.* Private discussions often burst forth into the public realm. Petty complaints, which mean nothing at first, can lead to disaster. This is a lesson for all of us and for all time. It applies to us at home, at work and especially at *shul.* If we adopt this principle, then our offerings, our prayers for success in all areas of life will be rewarded by the lighting of our internal menorah, the flame that glows within each of us.

_____ *Rabbi Harvey Well*

A CCORDING TO THE RAMBAN, *PARSHAS BEHAALOSECHA* STANDS AS an important transition between the two major themes of *Sefer Bamidbar.* The first ten chapters of *Bamidbar* deal mainly with the internal organization of *Klal Yisrael* — how they traveled and camped, the description of their banners, the location of the *Ohel Mo'eid.*

The second part of *Bamidbar* chronicles the events that happened to *Klal Yisrael* as they traveled — the story of the spies, the rebellion of Korach, the treachery of Balak and Bilam.

As such, this *parshah* clearly serves a most important function in the structure of the *sefer,* as a bridge between these two themes, between the life of the people as they were encamped around *Har Sinai* and their existence as a nation during their years of wandering in the desert.

As an aspect of this transition, we find a note as to how the people knew when to travel from one campsite to another. The *parshah* tells us that their signal was the *anan,* the cloud of glory that hovered above the *Mishkan.* When it rose, the people would travel; when the cloud settled, they stopped.

This cloud was not the only signal the people had. The Torah tells us that Moshe Rabbeinu was commanded to make trumpets with which to signal the people to travel. Moshe fashioned these trumpets from his own possessions. They were used only by Moshe and buried upon his death. Even his most trusted disciple, Yehoshua, could not use them, and used a *shofar* instead.

This information raises a series of questions: Why was a second signal needed? Why were these trumpets exclusive to Moshe? Why was Yehoshua given the *shofar* in order to perform the same function?

Every generation produces its own unique set of leaders, who are charged with the responsibility of guiding that generation in the ways of Torah and *mitzvos.* Each leader of Israel relates to the people of his generation in his own style. Moshe Rabbeinu did it through the trumpets. Yehoshua did it with the *shofar.* Rav Moshe Feinstein, *zt"l,* did it through his Torah and lectures. Each one of them did it in his own way, and *Klal Yisrael* was the richer for having them.

It would seem that our generation is still searching, still seeking that one special leader who can unite us, who can relate to us, who can draw us nearer to Torah and *mitzvos.* And who can do it with the understanding that our generation needs. May we merit such a blessing from the Creator and, in the midst of this great resurgence of Torah, grow and develop in both Torah and *mitzvos,* as well as unite and show the proper respect, one Jew to the next.

_____ *Rabbi Menachem Rosenfeld*

T HE *MITZVAH* OF LIGHTING THE MENORAH IS DESCRIBED IN THIS WEEK'S *parshah.* The lighting was to take place in a manner where all the lights were to be inclined towards the central shaft. In the *Sefer Iturei Torah* by Rabbi Aaron Yaakov Greenberg we find the comment that the light of the menorah is symbolic of knowledge. The number seven is representative of the seven branches of wisdom. The central shaft of the menorah represents Torah knowledge. But knowledge and wisdom is only valuable when directed toward the central shaft of Torah principles. To this end, the term employed in commanding Aharon to kindle the menorah, *"Behaalosecha,"* means, literally, "When you elevate." So, too, secular knowledge achieves inherent worth only when it is elevated.

This thought was often expressed by Rabbi Samson Raphael Hirsch in his essays on *Torah im derech eretz.* Rav Hirsch forcefully argued that secular knowledge was not to be shunned. On the contrary, "The times must be raised to the level of Torah, Torah must not be lowered to the times."

The *Kesav Sofer,* in his Torah commentary, analyzes the Sabbath blessing given by fathers to their sons: "May you be like Ephraim and Menashe." Why are these two role models chosen over all others?

The answer lies in the essence of the achievements of Ephraim and Menashe. Ephraim was the prototypical Torah scholar, while Menashe represented secular achievement. We pray that our children attain both realms, but, cautions the *Kesav Sofer,* we must remember that Yaakov "placed Ephraim before Menashe." Secular studies have value only when preceded by Torah *hashkafah* and spirit.

The Torah describes the menorah as consisting of one piece of pure gold. Torah and secular studies can not be artificially torn asunder. When they are one organic whole, dedicated to appreciating the spiritual dimension to all that exists, they truly form one unit which is pure and precious.

A simple but poignant description of how Torah and secular studies can form a perfect association is found in the writings of Rav Yitzchok Hutner, *zt"l.* A student was concerned about the propriety of his pursuit of a secular profession, notwithstanding his proficiency in Torah studies. The student was reassured by Rav Hutner that it is indeed possible to "rent two rooms" in one apartment. He explained the need to draw a circle around one's life, to place G-d in the middle of the circle, and then to broaden the circle with "points" of life.

The Torah tells us that Aharon fulfilled his obligation and, according to Rashi, "he did not change." The Vilna Gaon explains that the enthusiasm of Aharon never waned. He never felt that his *Avodas Hashem* was rote. Aharon could do the same *mitzvah* many times and still do it with freshness and vitality. We, too, must strive to live an integrated life, one where all our activities are directed to the central light of Torah. If we can attain this harmonious integration, we will achieve the menorah's ideal of "kindling an eternal light." It is this light that has illuminated the Jewish world. We await the time when this light will touch all of G-d's creations.

פרשת שלח
Parshas Shelach

_____ *Yisroel Epstein*

ASK ANY JEWISH CHILD, "WHO WERE THE *MERAGLIM*?" AND YOU WILL, no doubt, be referred to the events of *Parshas Shelach*. The *meraglim,* as everyone knows, were the twelve spies sent by Moshe Rabbeinu to report back on the Holy Land. But is it so? Reread the *parshah*. You will notice that the word *meraglim* never once appears in *Shelach*.

Years later, when Yehoshua sends spies into Canaan, the Torah refers to them as *meraglim*. Centuries earlier, when Yosef accused his brothers of spying on the land of Egypt, he too called them *meraglim*. But here the Torah says, "*Shelach lecha anashim veyasuru es eretz Canaan* — Send for yourselves men and they will explore the land of Canaan." Moshe refers to them as *tarim,* explorers, not *meraglim,* spies.

The root word *ragel* denotes slander and gossip. Yosef's brothers argued that they came to Egypt for the simple reason to buy food, but he pretends not to believe them. "*Meraglim atem,*" he declares; "*liros es ervas haaretz basem* — You are spies; you came to see the nakedness of the land." From Yosef's accusation we see that *meraglim* come to discover where a country is vulnerable, to plot strategy.

By contrast, the mission of the twelve emissaries sent by Moshe was simply to look over the land and report back. It was supposed to be an innocent mission. Their purpose was not to look for military advantages but *lasur es haaretz,* to explore the land. (One could argue that this word is the antecedent of the French-derived English word, "tour," which connotes an innocent sightseeing spree.)

220 / TORAH INSIGHTS

But that is not what happened. Moshe, recalling the incident at the beginning of *Devarim,* states that the men he sent went up to the land, "*vayeraglu osah.* " The twelve men were supposed to be *tarim,* but instead became the infamous *meraglim.*

There is nothing wrong with being a *meragel;* the term is not a negative one. Calev and Pinchas were both called *meraglim* when they were sent by Yehoshua on a mission of espionage. But for the men of *Parshas Shelach* the term is a slur, because by taking on the role of *meraglim* they betrayed their mission. They were not asked to proffer advice on whether or not to conquer the land. Yet they took it upon themselves to tell the Jewish nation of the powerful people who lived there and to conclude, "We will not be able to rise against the nation for it is stronger than us."

The lesson of the *meraglim* is a valuable one for every Jew. One is called upon to do many tasks in the course of a lifetime and the challenge is to know what that task is, what is called for at that moment — and not to waver from it. The key is to recognize when to report and when to advise, when to critique and when to encourage. By staying true to one's own mission, every person can achieve this personal *avodas Hashem* and plot his own path to the Promised Land.

_____ *Esther Wein*

W HEN THE SPIES RETURN FROM *ERETZ YISRAEL,* TERRIFIED BY THE gigantic proportions of the people, places and produce they saw, feeling unequal to the challenge that lay before them, they communicate their distress to the Jewish nation. The Jewish people, in turn, direct their frustration toward their leader. Moshe Rabbeinu, the supreme prophet of all time, who had taken the Jews from Egypt, split the Red Sea, and spoke G-d's word from atop Mount Sinai, was now under attack. The Jews doubted him and his prophecies. The suggestion was even made to return to Egypt under the authority of a new leader. What gave rise to such a challenge?

In *Parshas Behaalosecha,* the *Bnei Yisrael,* tired of the transcendent, spiritual life, sustained only by the manna, begin to mourn their plight and cry for meat. Moshe's response is uncharacteristic. When Hashem shows Moshe the retribution in store for the sinners, Rashi says, Moshe does not try to defend them or even pray for them, as he normally would. Rather, "the strength of Moshe waned." He cries, "I alone can not bear this entire nation."

In accordance with his plea, Moshe is commanded to assemble the Elders of Israel to share with them his *ruach hakodesh,* his Divine inspiration, and his responsibilities. This transfer creates the false illusion that Moshe is no longer a unique prophet, standing as the absolute mediator between *Bnei Yisrael* and Hashem. His status in the eyes of the Jewish people is diminished. This erroneous perception of Moshe causes Miriam and Aharon to question Moshe's behavior, specifically his separation from his wife. Why, they wonder, does Moshe conduct himself in a way not incumbent upon other prophets? Why does he assume celibacy for himself when it is forbidden to all of Israel, including prophets?

Hashem rebukes Aharon and Miraim for doubting Moshe, and immediately clarifies his standing. Despite what it may seem, Moshe remains unique and supreme among all prophets.

In *Parshas Shelach,* the challenge to Moshe's authority is on a broader scale. The people and their leaders declare that Moshe's mission to bring them into *Eretz Yisrael* as a free people can not be achieved. They feel misled. They lose faith in themselves and in Moshe.

But Moshe recognizes that the sin of the people saying, "We can't," has its origins in his declaration, "I can't." Moshe refuses G-d's offer to be the sole survivor and progenitor of a new Jewish nation and instead prays for the pardoning of the Jewish people. He pleads: Let not the nations say, "Because the L-rd was unable to bring his people into the land that He had sworn to them, therefore He has slain them in the wilderness." In other words, explains Rabbi Zalman Wein, do not let Moshe's saying, "I can't," which was a cause of *Bnei Yisrael*'s saying, "We can't," become the basis for the nations to say, "You can't."

Hashem's response is just. The people who said, "We can't," did not enter the land. However, the next generation, raised under the leadership of Moshe Rabbeinu, lived to experience the fulfillment of his prophecy. They entered the land knowing "*Moshe emes Vesaraso emes* — Moshe is true and his Torah is true."

Rabbi Benjamin Yudin

FOLLOWING THE SINS OF THE SPIES, THE _BNEI YISRAEL_ ARE INTRO-
duced to the _mitzvah_ of _tzitzis._ There is a connection between their
sin and this _mitzvah,_ notes Rav Samson Raphael Hirsch, just as there
was when Adam sinned by eating from the fruit of the Tree of Knowledge and G-d responded by designing clothing for him and Chavah.
When man shows himself to be a _bogeid,_ a transgressor, Rav Hirsch
explains, G-d responds by offering him a _beged,_ an article of clothing to
remind him of his frailty.

Moshe was told to send representatives _"veyasuru es eretz Canaan."_
After the debacle, the Jewish Nation was commanded to add _tzitzis_ to
their garments, in order that they remember G-d's command _"velo sa-
suru,_ and you will not follow [the desires of] your heart."

In his philosophical introduction to _Pirkei Avos,_ the Rambam identifies two types of religious individuals. One, the _chasid me'ulah,_ is naturally perfect; the other, the _moshel berucho,_ struggles, attaining perfection through constantly refining his character. These two prototypes of
man correlate to two forms of _mitzvos._ The _chukim,_ those _mitzvos_ that
man would not have initiated on his own, such as the forbidden foods
and _shatneitz;_ and _mitzvos sichlios,_ those commands that are within the
scope of human logic, such as robbery and murder.

In observing the _chukim,_ explains Rabbi Elazar ben Azariah, a Jew
should not say, "I have no desire to eat pork or lobster." Rather, one
should say, "I wish I could eat them, but I submit my will to G-d's." This
is the _chasid me'ulah_ component of man, the absolute acceptance of
G-d's laws.

With regard to _mitzvos sichlios,_ however, this acceptance is not sufficient. A Jew must incorporate these _mitzvos_ into his natural self. He
must work on himself and struggle until these _mitzvos_ become a true
reflection of who he is. An insightful comment by the Maharal exempli-
fies this idea. The Torah introduces the _mitzvah_ of lending another Jew
money with the words, _"Im kesef talveh es ami_ — If you lend my nation
money." Why does the Torah use the word _im,_ implying choice — when
we are obligated to do this _mitzvah?_

Parshas Shelach / 223

The Maharal explains that this *mitzvah* is fulfilled not simply through the actual lending of the money, but rather through a genuine desire to help another Jew by lending him money. This desire can not be mandated and it does not come easily. Drawing such emotions requires a natural inner struggle.

These two levels of observance are intertwined in the *tzitzis*. The white strings represent the pure, absolute acceptance of G-d's mandate. The blue strings of *techeiles* remind us of the sea, which reminds us of the sky, which, in turn, reminds us of G-d's Holy Throne. These strings represent a process, the struggle we must go through before reaching the Holy Throne.

Similarly, regarding *lashon hara,* it is not enough to simply abstain from character assassination, saying, "I wish I could say this, but the Torah prevents me." Rather, we must reach the point where *lashon hara* is instinctively abhorrent. As *Pirkei Avos* teaches, "Make His will your will." Your desires should be in line with G-d's.

The Mishnah teaches that the absence of *techeiles* in one's *tzitzis* does not impede the fulfillment of the *mitzvah*. Nonetheless, we ought to strive for the ideal. In our social behavior, the ideal is not to merely accept the law, but to integrate it into our very selves. As the blue of the *tzitzis* teaches us, it is not enough to do good; we must become good.

_____ *Rabbi Gedalia Dov Schwartz*

VARIOUS COMMENTATORS HAVE EXAMINED THE SIN OF THE *MERAGalim,* the treacherous spies, whose slanderous report on the Holy Land caused the Jewish people to fear entering the land and subsequently wander in the desert for forty years. One central question raised by the commentators revolves around the verse that describes the nation's retraction. The people "rose early in the morning and went to the top of the mountain, saying, 'We are here, and we will go up to the place that G-d said, for we have sinned.' "

Why, the commentators ask, did repentance not remove, or at least mitigate, celestial punishment? The people admitted their sin. If recognition of one's transgression is a basic dimension of the repentance process, why was their demonstration of repentance not accepted?

The Torah anthology, *Iturei Torah,* relates that the Gerer Rebbe, Rabbi Avraham Mordechai, *zt"l,* once visited Rabbi Dovid Goldman, *zt"l,* the rebbe of Kielce, and asked him this very question. Why was the *teshuvah* of the Jewish people not accepted?

Rabbi Dovid explained that had there been, in fact, an authentic recognition of sin, their repentance would surely have been effective. But one needs to read the verse carefully to understand the people's words. They did not say, "We will go up to *the place that G-d said,* for we have sinned." Rather, the verse is properly read: "We will go up to the place, *for G-d said we have sinned."* The phrase "G-d said" modifies the second half of their declaration, not the first, explained Rabbi Dovid. In other words, they did not admit their own guilt, but merely accepted the fact that Hashem considered them to have sinned. As a basis for *teshuvah,* this acknowledgment can not be considered a true act of repentance.

This novel interpretation has great relevance today when *Klal Yisrael* is locked in an inner struggle concerning the supremacy of Torah in our national and individual lives. We are surrounded by forces of assimilation and intermarriage. The traditions of our faith are ignored by a large percentage of our fellow Jews. In order to stem the tide, the Jewish community must recognize the "sins" of the past. Jewish communal leaders must acknowledge both in word and deed that all Jewish identification and continuity can not be forthcoming unless there is a strong commitment to the *halachic* framework of Jewish practice and observance.

How can this essential component of Jewish survival be strengthened? The answer is Jewish education in day schools established in every Jewish community. The sin of the past is that for a long period of time day-school education was an orphan, neglected and even spurned by a large segment of the Jewish community. We have unfortunately learned our lesson as we face the alienation of many of our co-religionists from the Torah of Sinai.

If we are to enter the Promised Land, which will be evidence of the triumph of Judaism in our society, we must reaffirm the pledge we took at Mount Sinai. We will thus be able to leave behind the spiritual exile that threatens to engulf us.

PARSHAS *SHELACH* RECOUNTS ONE OF THE MAJOR TRAGEDIES DUR-
ing the Israelites' saga in the desert. The hand-picked leaders of
the twelve tribes are sent to tour the Promised Land and upon returning
to the nation they report: "We will not be able to overcome the inhabitants of Canaan" and conquer the land. Hearing this, the nation of Israel
immediately became depressed. Ignoring Yehoshua and Calev's positive account and encouragement, they resigned themselves to failure,
demanding, "Let us head back and return to Egypt."

These pivotal words, displaying a lack of faith in G-d's ability to bring
them to the land as He had promised, had tragic consequences — the
generation of Jews, who had left Egypt through the Mighty Hand of G-d,
would now not enter the Promised Land. One group, however, retracted
these words and tried to make amends. They awoke the next morning
and ventured on their own to Canaan, acknowledging that they were
doing so "because we have sinned."

But the Almighty does not react positively to their move. Moshe
admonishes them, saying, "Why do you transgress the word of G-d?
You will not succeed. Do not go up, because G-d is not in your midst."
Once G-d had forbade their entry, they could not enter.

But why? Now, suddenly, G-d does not want them to enter the land? If
their repentance was sincere, why did He reject it?

Moshe's words address this question: "Because G-d is not in your
midst." This comment describes the nature of their repentance — G-d is
not in your midst; you have not internalized what you are doing. What
you are expressing verbally and exhibiting externally, says Moshe, is
not flowing from the essence of your existence. It is not "in your midst."

The desire of this group to repent flowed from an incomplete process.
Yes, they felt regret for what was said. Yes they felt a desire to right the
wrong. But the regret remained a superficial expression of remorse,
rather than a deeper desire to change.

In our century, as well, the doomsayers and pessimists said "*lo
nuchal*" — we can not do it. We will never see *halachic* Judaism take
root, let alone flourish, in America. Observance of the *Shulchan Aruch*

is unpopular and obsolete. Yet the Jewish people stepped up and frustrated that prognosis, as evidenced by the proliferation of yeshivos, day schools, outreach movements, *daf yomi* classes and more.

Nonetheless, we must still ask ourselves the question, "Is G-d in our midst?" Despite all our wonderful accomplishments, have we forgotten to internalize our relationship to G-d? Do our successes lack sufficient follow-through and a quest for further growth? Are we complacent?

The answer must be a resounding "No!" We must constantly renew our efforts as individual Jews, as Jewish communities and as a Jewish nation to internalize and deepen our understanding of *Yiddishkeit* and our commitment to its observance. May we all be granted the strength to continue to grow both individually and collectively so that our very selves reflect the Presence of G-d.

פרשת קרח
Parshas Korach

_____ *Rabbi David Stavsky*

A YOUNG NCSYER RECENTLY WROTE: "FOR THE FIRST TIME EVER, I felt a true Shabbat — and it wasn't just a tingle at the last minutes of Shabbat. It was tears on Friday night after your skit with Baruch, it was *davening* with deep *kavanah,* it was the sensation of sitting down with someone my age on Shabbat afternoon to learn *Gemara,* it was the singing during *shalosh seudos* and feeling the presence of Hashem. Most of all, it was coming to the reality of how seventeen years of my life were wasted and the reality of how stupid I was to even consider going to a college where I would not be able to get an extensive Jewish education."

These words may surprise many people today. Who would have thought that some young people can find authenticity of life in G-d and in Torah? But it happens just the same. Today we find the son who rebels against his father, just as his father rebelled against his spiritual father, his teacher.

One finds precedent for this in *Parshas Korach.* Moshe is confronted with a revolution. He has a serious rebellion on his hands. Korach, jealous of Moshe and Aharon, challenges their leadership. Like all revolutionaries, Korach appears as a saint instead of a sinner. In a brilliant analysis, Rav Yosef Dov Soloveitchik, *zt"l,* calls Korach's revolt a "common sense" rebellion. Korach rhetorically asks if a house full of *sifrei Torah* needs a *mezuzah* on its doorpost. After all, if the house contains the entire Torah, why the need for a *mezuzah,* which contains only several verses?

/ TORAH INSIGHTS

Korach masquerades as an honest everyman arguing that "all in the community are holy." His is not a lust for power but a populist appeal to egalitarianism, affirming "the right of each Jew or group of Jews to follow their own individual judgment."

Moshe turns to G-d and says, in effect, "You choose." G-d does, and Korach and his 250 cohorts are suddenly, supernaturally, swallowed into the earth. Ecology, Torah-style. Getting rid of waste, Torah-style.

The tale seems to end there, but one may be surprised to learn in the following *parshah, "Uvenei Korach lo meisu* — Korach's children did not die." Why not? They, too, were part of the rebellion. But they were spared, because, Rashi notes, they did *teshuvah* as the conflict became more serious. Theirs was a different type of revolution: Korach's kids' revolution. A *kiddush Hashem* revolution. A positive and beautiful revolution, not of jealousy or power-mongering, but of repentance and spiritual growth. To this end, every Rosh Hashanah, just before the sounding of the *shofar,* we recite the very psalm that Korach's children sung when they did *teshuvah.*

Moreover, the subject of this *parshah's haftarah* is the great prophet, Shmuel, who breathed spirit into the young Jewish nation and established its crown. Why is his story chosen? Because Shmuel Hanavi is descended from Evyasar, son of Korach. How is it possible that such a great figure of the Jewish nation is a descendant of Korach?

This is the power of *teshuvah. "Kechu imachem devarim veshuvu el Hashem,"* advises the prophet Hoshei'a. "Take words with you" — words of *teshuvah* — "and return to G-d." *Devarim* can also be understood as *mitzvos* and good deeds. Take them with you. Become activists, participate in the spiritual awakening of our time, and return to G-d.

_____ *Rabbi Alan J. Yuter*

N OT EVERYTHING THAT OCCURRED TO OUR ANCESTORS IN THE wilderness is recorded in the Torah. Our Torah is not a mundane diary, but an eternal teaching — the lessons of the past forever informing our ever-changing present. The Korach incident anticipates the challenge faced by Torah Jewry today.

The Torah reports that Korach and his cohorts, "stood up in the presence of Moshe...and assembled themselves (*vayikahalu*) over Moshe and over Aharon and said to them, '[This matter of communal leadership] is too great for you, for the entire community is entirely sacred and Hashem is among them, and why do you lift yourselves over the community (*kahal*) of Hashem?' "

Korach makes the egalitarian argument. To Korach, all Israel is identical and their equality is intuitive, a matter of common sense and conventional consensus. Rav Yosef Dov Soloveitchik describes Korach as the exemplar of the "common sense" revolt against Torah authority. He is the populist pretender to power.

But while Korah's rhetoric is egalitarian, his agenda is not. His words reveal his true intention. He challenges Moshe and Aharon: "Why do you lift yourselves over the community of Hashem?" Indeed it is Korach who wants to rule over others. It is no accident that Maimonides defines idolatry as a religious ideology invented by the unscrupulous to manipulate and dominate others.

Torah sanctity — *kedushah* — is only attained through the *mitzvos,* the commands of the Commander. In the Shabbos *kiddush,* we ask Hashem, "*Kadesheinu bemitzvosecha* — Sanctify us with Your commandments." The blessing formula, "*asher kideshanu bemitzvosav,*" thanks Hashem for sanctifying us with His commandments. When we say the concluding paragraph of *Kri'as Shema,* we remind ourselves that we become *kedoshim,* holy objects, by remembering to perform the Commander's commands.

According to the Torah, everyone's role and destiny is distinct, and thus special and sacred. But to Korach, everyone is the same. Nothing is sacred or special. The Torah teaches that Korach's common sense revolt against Torah authority is an insidious, but ultimately answerable, challenge to Torah. Those who appeal to the popular consensus do so in order to use, abuse and dominate others.

Moshe, the most modest of all men, is jealous only for *kedushah,* for the sanctity of the individual enshrined by the commands of the Commander. When Korach and his crowd refuse to "go up" to address Moshe, they go down, swallowed into the ground, marking the futility of the common sense revolt. Our Sages teach that voices came forth from the ground saying, "Moshe and his Torah are truth." In death, Korach has the integrity to concede that spirituality and sanctity are acquired by following the Torah's prescription.

May we merit to find the words to spread this message to the Jews who see themselves as participants in *bris goral,* Rav Soloveitchik's term for those who share Jewish destiny, and raise them to the sanctity of *bris Sinai.*

_____ *Rabbi Marc Penner*

THE REBELLION OF KORACH AND HIS FOLLOWERS BRINGS OUT A SIDE of Moshe Rabbeinu that has not yet been seen. Moshe's role is usually that of caring shepherd and intercessor for *Klal Yisrael* when they sin. On their journey from *Mitzrayim* to *Eretz Yisrael,* Moshe always pleads with Hashem to be understanding and merciful, to forgive the offenses committed against Him.

Now, however, Moshe's attitude seems to change. When Korach questions his authority, Moshe seeks only justice! Why, asks Rabbeinu Bachya, does Moshe respond differently than he did during the sin of the Golden Calf and the sin of the Spies, when G-d's supremacy was challenged? Is it possible that Moshe is more protective of his own honor than of Hashem's?

Undoubtedly, the Jew's faith in Hashem, which should have remained firm after all they had witnessed during the Exodus, was sorely lacking during the sin of the Golden Calf and the sin of the Spies. These two sins surely mark two of the lowest moments in our people's collective history.

These situations, orchestrated by Hashem, gave the Jewish people opportunities to succeed and grow. Whether at the shores of Yam Suf, the foot of Sinai, or the border of Israel, *Klal Yisrael* is challenged by Hashem to rely on Him and Him alone. These circumstances can be viewed as tests from Hashem, tests that the Jews failed one hundred percent, causing the sinful behavior that followed.

Yet, in their defense, the Jewish people perceived themselves during those periods as being in a state of national crisis. Was it easy for a nation so dependent on Moshe to deal with the possibility of continuing on in the wilderness without his leadership? Was it easy for a people, unaccustomed to fighting, to envision conquering the land of Israel?

They may have done poorly on these exams, but even the process of failing can be a source of future strength. Moshe, therefore, pleads again and again with Hashem to give them another chance. Korach and his followers, though, did not deserve that second chance.

It is one thing to face a challenge and fail. But to create a crisis, to sow the seeds of disunity within the Jewish people, to generate strife and unnecessarily challenge the leadership of the Jewish people — these sins can not be excused or forgiven. Korach took his personal agenda and planted it on the national stage. He put *Klal Yisrael* at risk. This type of threat can not be overlooked or tolerated.

_____ *Rabbi Yitzchak Meir Goodman*

WHEN HASHEM TELLS MOSHE TO DEPART FROM THE NATION OF Israel so that He can destroy them, Moshe responds, "If one man sins, will You rage at the entire people?" Rashi explains: Human kings, who do not know exactly who is guilty, will punish the masses for the crimes of a few. But, asks Moshe of G-d, do You do likewise?

Well said, G-d answers. I do know and will make known who is guilty and who is innocent. The Biblical commentators are astonished. How does G-d "change His mind"? What could He have discovered from the argument of a human being that He did not know before?

In his volume, *Yitzpon Layesharim Toshiyah,* Rav Yitzchak Pinchas Goldvasser maintains that Hashem operated with a simple logic: if the honor of a human king allows him to destroy many for the crimes of a few, how much more so should the honor of the King of the Universe justify such an annihilation. *Kiddush Hashem* justifies such a decision.

Moshe responds that he views it the other way around: G-d's singling out the guilty and sparing the innocent would be a far greater *kiddush Hashem* before the eyes of all who survive. This is a feat no human king could accomplish under such circumstances. Nonetheless, the original question remains: surely G-d knew this argument as well; so what did Moshe contribute to "change G-d's mind"?

There is a clear Talmudic precedent for this. In cases where two interpretations of an event or situation are possible, first a human interpretation is established in this world, and then the Heavenly Court acts accordingly. The Talmud relates that Rabbah bar Shila once met Eliyahu Hanavi, who told him that though G-d would repeat the various maxims of the great *Tanna'im* of the Talmud, he would never mention the great Rav Meir by name. Why? Because he had studied from Elisha ben Avuyah, who turned to heresy.

Rabbah bar Shila was dismayed. Rav Meir, he argued, is like one who eats a pomegranate — he enjoys the fruit, but throws away the shell (for Rav Meir was able to glean Torah knowledge from his mentor while ignoring any improper influence of Elisha ben Avuyah). Hearing this reasoning, Eliyahu reported that G-d had begun to quote Rav Meir. The decision as to whether Rav Meir was justified in studying from Elisha ben Avuyah was first determined by his human colleagues. Had they deemed his behavior improper, he would have remained on G-d's "blacklist."

But once they declared that they had no objection and knew Rav Meir was capable of handling Elisha ben Avuyah without becoming in any way blemished, this affected the Heavenly attitude, and Rav Meir's reputation was rehabilitated.

Kiddush Hashem, as well, is entirely a matter of how humans react to a situation. Until Moshe registered his human response and attitude, G-d followed the logic that a complete annihilation was justifiable. Once Moshe declared that the other approach would create a still greater *kiddush Hashem* in the eyes of the Jewish community, G-d acted on the logic of His servant Moshe.

_____ *Rabbi Howard S. Joseph*

KORACH, A LEVITE, A COUSIN OF MOSHE, LEADS A REVOLT AGAINST Moshe and Aharon. Martin Buber explains Korach's rebellion as based upon a distortion of G-d's summons to become holy — *"Kedoshim tihiyu."* Rather than view Divinely mandated holiness as a challenge, hope or request, Korach baldly states, "For the entire community, all of them, are holy, and the Lord is in their midst." Holiness is presented as an already established fact. Consequently, argues Korach, that being the case, there is no need for Moshe and Aharon's leadership, nor is there need for the instructions and commandments allegedly delivered from G-d.

"Why do you exalt yourselves over G-d's community?" Korach demands. The people stood at Sinai, were addressed by G-d, and have the Ark and Tablets in the Sanctuary. G-d is "on their side" if not in their midst. They do not need guidance, instruction, laws and commandments. Whatever they do will be holy because they are holy. This "insolent self-assertion," as Buber calls it, is a great temptation for those who move on the trail of holiness. Self-righteousness, triumphalism, sacred arrogance are the dangers and pitfalls that mark their path.

Further reflection on this story leads us to ask for the foundation of Korach's position. As often is the case, there is a partial truth embedded in his position that is the source of his danger and destructive potential. Korach knew that there exists an Ancestral Covenant — the *Bris Avos,* as Rav Yosef Dov Soloveitchik, *zt"l,* taught — which G-d struck with the fathers and mothers of Israel, and that they are a consecrated, holy people because of this covenant. Moshe himself taught the principle, "You are a nation holy unto the Lord your G-d."

However, as the Rav explained, this early Ancestral Covenant is followed by a second covenant at Mount Sinai, where the nation redeemed from Egypt gathered to hear the word of G-d. It is from the Ancestral Covenant that we derive our strong sense of family belonging and common destiny: we are the children of the fathers and mothers of Israel. As members of the same family, we care for each other, rejoice in each other's successes, and cry over each other's tragedies.

The Sinai Covenant, on the other hand, is of a different kind. It is one of learning and doing: specifically, to learn to do that which was commanded to us by G-d. We are bidden to strive for personal holiness through the commandments. Holiness is not a given but something to achieve.

Korach was not entirely wrong. He articulated his position on the basis of an important facet of the Jewish soul: Ancestral Covenant consciousness. That is his redeeming feature. In fact, Korach's descendants were righteous Levites who sang and officiated at the Jerusalem Temple. The Ancestral Covenant consciousness is the basis of all of Judaism. Without it there can be no Sinai Covenant. Korach's descendants learned well from their ancestor the importance of the Ancestral Covenant and eventually found their way into an understanding of the Sinai teachings.

Many Jews today are Korach Jews. Their main link to Judaism is a deep appreciation for the historical experiences of our people. They are strongly aware of our unique destiny, a lesson reaffirmed by the events of our time: the Holocaust, the destruction of our ancient communities in numerous lands, the migrations to new communities, and, of course, the building of the State of Israel. These Jews may have forgotten the Sinai Covenant, the traditions and observances of Judaism, but they have not disregarded the Ancestral Covenant.

Other Jews, however, are in need of Korach's message. About them we would say "*Halevai* — If only it were so!" If only they had some Ancestral Covenant consciousness. These are Jews who think of themselves as being like everyone else, as having no unique destiny, as having little, or nothing, in common with other Jews. *Halevai* that they should at least think like Korach. Then their children might have a chance to be counted among the future generations of our people.

While the Ancestral Covenant is the foundation of our identity, it needs the nourishment of the Sinai Covenant. Through Torah study, those who have lost even the Ancestral consciousness can be inspired to see the beauty of our covenantal traditions and reconnect to our destiny.

פרשת חקת
Parshas Chukas

_____ *Rabbi Rafael Grossman*

THE TORAH BEGINS THE LAW OF THE *PARAH ADUMAH,* THE RED HEIFER, with the assertion, "This is the statute of the Torah." The *parah adumah* is burned, its ashes mixed with water and used to cleanse "whoever touches the corpse of any human being." Contact with the dead causes defilement and excludes one from entering holy places or participating in sanctified rituals.

Why does death defile? How do the ashes of the red heifer cleanse this defilement? Rashi states, "Because Satan and the nations of the world taunt Israel saying, 'What is this command and what reason is there in it?' It is therefore called a statute — it is a decree from before Me; you have no right to question it."

The *midrash* furthers this principle with the tale of a heathen who came before Rabbi Yochanan ben Zakkai asserting, "The rites you perform in connection with the red heifer smell of witchcraft."

The Rabbi asked him, "Have you ever been possessed by a demon?"

The heathen said no.

"Have you ever seen a man who was possessed by a demon?"

The heathen answered yes.

"What do you do for him?" Rabbi Yochanan ben Zakai wanted to know.

"We bring roots and make them smoke beneath him, then throw water upon him and the demon is exorcised."

Rabbi Yochanan ben Zakkai replied, "Let your ears hear what comes out of your mouth. The spirit of defilement is also an unclean spirit. We sprinkle on it the waters of purification and it is exorcised."

The word used by the *midrash* for demon is *tazazis,* which can also mean perturbation. The "demon" in Rabbi Yochanan ben Zakai's response to the heathen can be seen as the disturbed, angry feelings frequently felt by one who is confronted with death.

"Man relegates the knowledge of his inevitable end to the subconscious," wrote Sigmund Freud. "Only when confronted with the reality of death does man react." This reaction takes on diverse forms. For some it is denial; for others, fierce anger. We try to explain away death: "He died because the doctors erred"; "He worked too hard"; "He was ill" — as if to say that death is caused by reasons from which one can escape.

This extraordinary law can thus be seen as Hashem's response to all who attempt to rationalize death. We are commanded "to take a heifer, completely red, whole, which has no blemish, upon which never came a yoke" — a living being without impairment, which has never known the burden of labor. Before the eyes of one who has been confronted with death, the symbol of perfection and moral immutability is destroyed. He now knows that man is incapable of achieving immortality without the Immortal One.

Upon hearing this dialogue between Rabbi Yochanan and the heathen, the Rabbi's disciples questioned him. "The heathen you put off easily, but what do you say to us?"

He replied, "Neither does the dead defile nor does water purify, but the Holy One, Blessed is He, said, 'It is a statute I have laid down, a decree I have decreed, and you are not authorized to violate My decree.' "

A response to the non-believer's perturbation over death is that his treatment is a therapeutic form of exorcism, a catharsis for his anger and grief. But to the believer it is simply a matter of accepting that Hashem, the Giver of life, determines by His decree who shall live and who shall die. This is the essence of Rabbi Yochanan ben Zakkai's words, "Neither does the dead defile nor does water purify." He taught that our thoughts and feelings defile, while the acceptance of Hashem's decree — even if it be death — cleanses.

"He who grieves excessively over his dead, weeps for another," states the Talmud in *Mo'eid Katan.* I suspect that "another" is the bereaved himself. The Torah Jew does not deny death but seeks to defy it.

Committing life to the wellsprings of Torah relegates death to irrelevancy and forms another link in a chain of eternal service to G-d, "Who has given us the Torah of truth and has planted everlasting life in our midst."

_____ *Rabbi Walter S. Wurzburger*

THE RITES OF PURIFICATION MANDATED FOR AN INDIVIDUAL WHO HAS come into contact with a deceased person defy rational explanation. They serve as the classical illustration of *chukim*, laws we observe without our being able to fathom their reason.

The *midrash* nonetheless seeks to explain the choice of a heifer's ashes for restoring individuals to ritual purity. In the words of *Pesikta DeRav Kehana*: "Let the heifer atone for the sin of the Golden Calf." But the *midrash* is still perplexing. What links atonement for the sin of the Golden Calf with the rites of purification for defilement from a corpse?

Rav Yosef Dov Soloveitchik, the Rav, *zt"l*, observed that while ritual purification is usually attained through immersion in a *mikvah*, the impurity induced by contact with a corpse, as described in *Chukas*, is an altogether different story. It can not be removed by our own efforts at purification. Rather, it requires supernatural assistance, symbolized by the necessity for the waters containing the ashes to be sprinkled by another ritually pure person.

Why is there such a contrast between the different types of purification? Unlike any other source of impurity, death confronts us with the ultimate challenge. Our sense of the worthwhileness of life is shattered when we contemplate the inevitable end of our finite existence. The values and ideals we cherish become meaningless as we confront the limitations of our very being.

We can extricate ourselves from this malaise only when we recognize that a Divine purpose is served by our finite existence. Thus, the *midrash* maintains, observing the *chok* of the red heifer helps us recover our sense of meaning and purpose. We must erase the last vestiges of our trust and faith in any agency other than G-d. As long as we seek substitutes for the living G-d, we are in no position to aim for a worthwhile human existence.

Any attempt to place our trust and faith in any partial value, force or institution constitutes idolatry. The Rav frequently pointed out that the sin of idolatry is by no means limited to the worshiping of statues or graven images. In more subtle forms it is an omnipresent spiritual threat. What have changed are merely the objects of worship. Though we no longer prostrate ourselves before figures made of gold, silver, stone or wood, we still practice idolatry whenever we elevate any force or value, however important, into an absolute. Thus modern man has elevated science, nationalism, economic or historical determinism, *et cetera,* into the supreme powers controlling our destiny.

Because idolatry represents the absolutization of particular values, we can understand why the Torah mandates that the ashes of purification be obtained by burning a heifer of uniformly red color, which has never borne a yoke. The ashes from such a heifer remind us that we must not commit the idolatry of placing absolute faith or trust in any agency, power or value other than G-d, if we wish to restore our spiritual health.

The *haftarah* for *Parshas Chukas* also demonstrates the tragedy that results from absolutizing a partial value. Yiftach sacrificed his daughter because he had vowed that whomever he would meet first upon his victorious return from the battle would be offered to G-d. Yiftach treated his vow as an absolute. His simplistic one-issue mentality blinded him from seeing that there are other norms and principles — such as respecting the sanctity of life — that must be observed. The life of his daughter should have superseded the value of keeping his vow. In the words of the Kotzker Rebbe, at times, even the performance of a *mitzvah* may degenerate into a form of idolatry.

Let us not be like those who do not see the forest for the trees. We must follow the prescription of *Tehillim* 19:9 and view G-d's Torah in its totality in order to restore the human soul.

_____ *Rabbi Jacob Reiner*

P ARSHAS CHUKAS OPENS WITH THE CLASSIC ILLUSTRATION OF A *CHOK,* a biblical imperative that defies all human logic and rationale — the *parah adumah.* This red heifer was slaughtered, reduced to ash, mixed with water, and used to purify those who came into contact with the dead and became ritually impure. Ironically, while the impure person is purified, the person who purified him, by sprinkling the water upon him, becomes impure.

Not only is this law incomprehensible, but, as Rashi comments, we do not even have permission to seek an explanation — a rather peculiar notion, as it seems to contradict the Jewish approach requiring us to study and interpret. The Rabbinic statement that there are "seventy faces of Torah" implies a freedom, or perhaps an obligation, to probe and understand.

If we were created and blessed with the capacity to intellectualize and comprehend, should we not utilize these Divine gifts that are ours? What, then, is the function of a *chok,* and what role does it play in the panorama of Jewish observance?

There is always the danger that in emphasizing the power of the intellect, one may be inclined to view comprehension as the determinant of observance — observing only what one understands. This approach is totally unacceptable. The authority of a *mitzvah* lies not in our understanding of it, but in its being stated in the Torah.

There are a number of safeguards incorporated in the Torah whose purpose is to protect the *mitzvos* and their observance. Jews believe in reward and punishment, for example. The Rambam lists this as a fundamental Jewish belief. Yet, with little exception, the Torah does not specify the reward for each *mitzvah.* This deliberate omission prevents us from using our intellect to try and determine which *mitzvos* are more important than others, a judgment which may impair our commitment to all the *mitzvos* equally.

The *chok* plays a similar role. Every *mitzvah* has a purpose that adds meaning to our lives. The rationale of the *chok,* however, is kept from us, demanding our unquestioned commitment, regardless of whether or not we understand it. The *chok* is a continuous reminder that the authority of the *mitzvah* and our obligation to observe it come from the word of G-d.

When our ancestors were introduced to the Torah, their response was, "*Naaseh venishma.*" *Naaseh* — first and foremost, we will accept and observe the Torah. Then *venishma* — we will commit ourselves to study and understand it.

A T THE END OF *PARSHAS CHUKAS,* THE TORAH DESCRIBES TWO battles that the Jewish people fought en route to the Land of Israel. The first battle took place with Sichon, king of Emori, who did not permit the Jews to pass through his land. The Jews were victorious and conquered much of the land of Emori.

Next, Og, king of Bashan, prepared to do battle with the Jews. At that point in time, one would expect the people of Israel to be confident, following their decisive victory over Emori. But this was not the case. Rather, "G-d said to Moshe, Do not be afraid of him, because I have given him and his people and his land to you, and you will do to him what you did to Sichon."

Why was G-d's reassurance necessary? Why did Moshe fear battling Og?

Rashi explains Moshe's fear as stemming from an earlier role that Og had played. According to the *midrash,* Og was the one who is described in the Torah as the messenger who ran from the battlefield and informed Avraham that his nephew, Lot, had been taken captive during the War of the Four Kings and the Five Kings.

Moshe was afraid that Og would be rewarded at this decisive moment for his earlier act of kindness and be granted a victory over the Jews. Thus G-d needed to reassure Moshe that the Jewish people would prevail.

The Maharal further clarifies Moshe's fear — and G-d's subsequent reassurance — with a quote from the Talmud: "The height of Moshe was ten cubits. He took an ax ten cubits long, leaped ten cubits in the air, and struck [Og] on the ankle, killing him." According to the Maharal, Og's height was the source of Moshe's fear. How, Moshe wondered, could he defeat this giant? This was G-d's reassurance: through a desperate leap and a simple strike on the ankle, Moshe defeated Og.

Victory does not always go to the biggest or the strongest, the Maharal tells us. Rather, G-d's help and supervision are the only factors in determining our fates. Though our enemies seem formidable and our task insurmountable, a small leap of faith is all we need to claim our victory.

THE REGULATIONS OF THE *PARAH ADUMAH,* THE RED HEIFER, HAVE long been regarded as the paradigm of *chukim,* those commandments that, on the surface, have no rational explanation. Certainly, the contradictory quality of the *parah adumah*'s ashes, which are *metaher es hatemei'im umetamei es hatehorim* — which purify the impure and render impure the pure — are a perfect example of this genre of statutes and justify the introductory clause, *"Zos chukas Hatorah."* This is the *chok,* the statute par excellence, of the Torah.

Yet, Rav Yosef Dov Soloveitchik, *zt"l,* points out that the phrase *"Zos chukas Hatorah"* applies not merely to the laws of the red heifer, but rather instructs that every law of the Torah, no matter how perfectly rational it seems, has within it a measure of *chok,* a measure of the inexplicable.

Consider the institution of marriage. Is it a perfectly natural occurrence for two people of different genders, with distinct personalities and backgrounds, interests and intellect, to forgo their individual ambitions and merge into a new entity? Today's society seems to illustrate that the opposite, remaining single, is an equally sane and rewarding alternative.

Consider also the commandment to honor one's parents. Certainly this seems to be a proper and understandable obligation. But consider the extent of its application. If a parent were to publicly humiliate a child or throw his money into the sea, the child is obligated to not oppose the parent. The well-known Talmudic paradigm of honoring one's parents is the gentile Dama ben Nesina, who refused to disturb his father's sleep and, in so doing, forfeited a great fortune. Are these really sane expressions of honoring one's parents?

Today's society is setting its own standards of ethical and moral behavior in consonance with its understanding of right and wrong. We are unfortunate witnesses to its errors. What is equally, if not more, disturbing is that once convinced that an ethical and moral life can be led as taught by Western culture, one feels no need to turn to Judaism for guidance. Such individuals are thus unfortunately lost to Jewry as well as to themselves.

The Divine Imperative, and not Kant's Moral Imperative or any other, can be the only criterion that governs our actions. Those *tehorim* who study Torah, yet choose to follow their own rationale (and rationalizations) when making life decisions, can clearly become *tamei*. Only those who realize that Torah is the only guide to life can aspire to *taharah*.

This is why the *korban pesach*, with its many *chukim*, is the logical symbol of our nation's liberation. For only when we completely accept G-d's dictums, the seemingly irrational with the rational, can we be liberated from thoughts and influences that enslave us. Only then can we become true *ovdei Hashem*, servants of the Almighty.

פרשת בלק
Parshas Balak

Rabbi Moshe S. Gorelik

WHILE BLESSING ISRAEL, BILAM CRIES OUT, "MAY I DIE THE DEATH OF the upright!" — a reference to Avraham, Yitzchak and Yaakov. The Hebrew word for upright is *yashar,* which can also be translated as just, straight or honest. The Torah uses this word in several contexts. Hashem is described as "*tzaddik veyashar* — righteous and upright." Jews are instructed to do "*hayashar vehatov* — what is upright and good." The nation of Israel is also named Yeshurun.

What is the significance of this word, *yashar?* How does it differ from *tzaddik?*

In his work, *Haameik Davar,* the Netziv — Rabbi Naftali Zvi Yehudah Berlin, dean of the yeshiva of Volozhin in the nineteenth century — devotes his introduction to the Book of *Bereishis* to the study of this word, *yashar.* Why does Bilam specifically call our forefathers *yesharim?* the Netziv asks. Because, he answers, *yesharim* are on a higher plane than *tzaddikim.*

The Talmud states that in the period just before the destruction of the second *Beis Hamikdash,* Jews occupied themselves with Torah, *mitzvos* and good deeds. "Why was it destroyed? Because at the time there was causeless hatred." The Netziv explains: "They were righteous, pious and engrossed in Torah study, but they were not *yesharim* in the ways of the world." They were unaccepting of those who did not appear to reach their standard and this led to *sinas chinam,* causeless hatred, among the Jewish people.

The Talmud also teaches that Jerusalem was destroyed because Jews adhered to the letter of the law and did not raise their standard above the law. What is the implication of this statement?

There are two dimensions to piety. The first, represented by the word *tzaddik,* implies strict adherence to the laws of the *Shulchan Aruch.* A *tzaddik* is meticulously observant. But while one may be scrupulously attentive to the laws of the Torah, he may still overlook the Torah's ethical substratum. The *tzaddik* may pay special attention to the application of the law, while remaining insensitive to the ethical quality of the *mitzvah.*

Being *yashar,* on the other hand, denotes strict adherence to the moral values as well as the basic observance of the commandments. *Yashar* implies the integration of law and morality, a commitment to the ideals and values symbolized by the law. The Jews of the Second Temple era may have observed the laws rigorously, but they failed to conduct themselves according to the ethical and moral imperative of the *mitzvos.* Torah life possesses religious significance only when it transcends narrow legalisms, only when a person internalizes its moral qualities and ethical values and responds to events and challenges accordingly. Only then does he transcend *tzidkus.* Only then is he *yashar.*

This message is far reaching. In an era such as ours, this admonition is extremely relevant. Neither intellectual dialectics nor devout obedience to the laws is religiously meaningful unless their moral and ethical character is intact. During the nineteenth century, Rabbi Yisroel Salanter and his disciples decried the absence of a total commitment to Torah morals and ethics even among pious Jews. The *mussar* movement strove to restore to religious life such virtues as integrity, compassion, sensitivity, tolerance, uprightness, honesty and respect. A bifurcation between morality and law abuses the religious character of Judaism.

Were one to capsulate the concept of Torah piety, an appropriate motto would be: *Frumkeit* without *menschlichkeit* is not *Yiddishkeit.*

_____ *Rabbi Baruch Taub*

A CCORDING TO RASHI AND THE RAMBAN, A SIGNIFICANT PORTION OF Bilam's prophecy depicts the Messianic era. The Ramban, in fact, understands this to be the entire thrust of the prophecy, a theme developed by later commentaries. The *Sefer Hachaim,* for example, interprets the verse, "When [Israel] kneels down and rests like a lion, who will stir it up?" to mean that when a generation experiences mounting distress, their sense of futility is indicative of the impending redemption. This *pasuk*'s message was of such significance that our Sages wanted to incorporate Bilam's prophecy into *Krias Shema.*

In a related depiction of the Messianic era, the Talmud tells of the prophet Yeshayahu cursing the Jewish people with eighteen curses. He was not satisfied, however, until he said, "The youth shall pride themselves over the elders, and the base over the honorable." This means that the opinion of those who are devoid of *mitzvos* will take priority over that of those who are filled with *mitzvos.*

A glaring question confronts us. Did Yeshayahu have his heart set against *Bnei Yisrael* with such passion that he needed this last and harshest curse to ease his wrath? It is obvious that the prophet had other intentions.

Yeshayahu understood that this last curse, depicting a generation of unmitigated *chutzpah,* will be a precursor to the *Mashiach,* as is pointed out in the *Mishnah* that insolence will be widespread in the days leading up to his arrival. Yeshayahu, in his vision, saw the abject despair of *Bnei Yisrael* at the end of days. He saw the breakdown of society in the most disgraceful fashion. Nonetheless, since he knew that in its wake the *Mashiach* would appear and rescue the Jewish people from the brink of disaster, he was relieved and comforted.

The famed Chassidic master, Rabbi Levi Yitzchak of Berdichev, saw the very same idea in the final words of the Tishah B'Av elegies, which liken the end of days to a woman giving birth. Though the labor pains are excruciating and the woman screams out in pain, her family, hearing her cries, anticipates the imminent birth of a child and the pleasures that they hope to derive from the blessed new addition.

The 17th of Tammuz is the anniversary of Moshe Rabbeinu's smashing the two *Luchos* when he witnessed the Jewish nation worshiping the Golden Calf. But while the *Luchos* were broken, the *Sefas Emes* points out, their holy letters returned to the Heavens, and when *Bnei Yisrael* will be worthy the first *Luchos* will again illuminate the world. In essence, the 17th of Tammuz is a *Yom Tov.*

Appropriately, this *parshah,* with Bilam's prophecy, should serve to inject the Messianic dream into our hearts, in order that we not fall into total despair during the upcoming Three Weeks, which brought about the most tragic events of our nation's history. By combining our mourning during this period with a rededication to the quality of our observance, we are assured that the signs of redemption are tangible and that the period of our exile is concluding.

_____ *Rabbi Aaron Gruman*

WHEN IT COMES TO PROPHECY, OUR SAGES COMPARE BILAM TO Moshe Rabbeinu: "Never again has there arisen in Israel a prophet like Moshe. But among the gentiles one did arise. Who is this? Bilam, son of Be'or." Regarding character traits, however, our Sages compare Bilam with Avraham Avinu: "A generous eye, a humble spirit and an undemanding soul, these are the characteristics of the disciples of Avraham; An evil eye, a haughty spirit and a demanding soul, these are the characteristics of the disciples of Bilam."

Where did our Sages see evidence of Bilam's haughty spirit? Under which similar circumstances did Avraham Avinu display a humble temperament?

Rabbi Meir Bergman in his work, *Shaarei Orah,* points to a somewhat puzzling statement of the Talmud: "Whoever establishes a set place for prayer, the G-d of Avraham will come to his aid, and when he dies they will say about him, 'What a humble man, what a pious man. He is a disciple of Avraham Avinu.' And from where do we know that Avraham Avinu had a set place for prayer? From the verse, 'And Avraham arose in the morning to the place that he had stood [prayed] earlier.' "

Certainly maintaining a set place for prayer is admirable, but why heap such effusive praise on its practitioner?

We return to Bilam. Balak enlists him to curse the Jewish people. Bilam's initial attempt fails. His reaction? Let's try again from somewhere else. Round two: same result. Bilam's reaction? Let's try yet another location. Does Bilam really think that his failure is caused by a particular site being unworthy? Does it not dawn on him that perhaps it is his prayer that is lacking, or that he himself is inadequate?

Arrogance, the *mishnah* in *Avos* teaches, is the source of Bilam's blindness.

Not so Avraham Avinu. After his valiant efforts to rescind G-d's decree to destroy Sodom did not bear fruit, Avraham Avinu returns to pray. He returns to the very same spot where the previous prayer went unanswered. Perhaps the failure was mine, muses Avraham Avinu. Did I pray with enough *kavannah*? Was there sufficient depth and meaning to my words? Humility, the *mishnah* teaches, allows for serious introspection. Can I do better next time?

Kevi'as makom, establishing for oneself a place for prayer, refers to more than a physical seat in the synagogue. It represents a commitment to *tefillah* that states, "It is not the *shul* I attend or the spot I occupy that determines successful prayer. It is my ability to constantly dig deeper and sharpen my focus internally." Of such a person we can surely say, "What a humble man, what a pious man. He is a disciple of Avraham Avinu."

_____ *Rabbi Simon Benzaquen*

MOAV SAID TO THE ELDERS OF MIDYAN, "NOW THE ISRAELITE COMmunity will lick up everything around us, just as the bull licks up the vegetation in the field." Rashi, drawing from the *Midrash Tanchuma,* asks: Since Moav and Midyan were implacable enemies, how is it that Moav decided to seek advice from Midyan?

Rashi explains: Moav had witnessed how the people of Israel were winning wars in an unnatural way and concluded that Israel's leader must be a great strategist of war. Moav wished to uncover the leadership qualities that Moshe possessed which made him so effective. Since Moshe grew up in Midyan, Moav naturally turned to Midyan for information.

Upon investigation, the Midyanites concluded that Moshe's strength lay in his power of speech. So Moav decided to counteract him by engaging a man whose power also came through speech — Bilam.

How did the Midyanites arrive at this conclusion? All the great acts that Moshe did on behalf of the Children of Israel came after he left Midyan. Albeit he fought off the shepherds on behalf of the daughters of Yisro, that brief act pales compared to all that was brought upon the Egyptians.

Moreover, even in Egypt, Moshe's supposed power of speech was not evident. All the plagues inflicted upon the Egyptians began with Moshe stretching out his staff; the Torah never mentions that Moshe said anything to bring on the plagues. In fact, Moshe only used words to pray for Egypt. Why did Midyan credit Moshe's speech?

The Midyanites knew that Moshe had a speech impediment. Nonetheless, every time he spoke to Pharaoh and demanded, "Let my people go," his words made a great impression on Pharaoh, and had G-d not hardened Pharaoh's heart at the last minute each time, Pharaoh would have succumbed to Moshe's demands. This could only be explained, the Midyanites reasoned, if Moshe's authority was based in his ability to bless and to curse.

The Moavites, who did not know of this speech impediment, assumed that Moshe's power was based on his ability to galvanize the nation and sway Pharaoh with his oratory powers. This was a skill that they assumed was developed at a young age, from his days in Midyan. But the Midyanites, who knew of Moshe's speech defect, understood that Moshe did not possess the verbal ability to influence others. They believed, instead, that his success rested on his power to bless or curse.

When the Moavites heard this theory from the Midyanites, they sought to enlist the services of a man whose power was also based on the ability to bless and to curse. But their theory was entirely wrong. As G-d tells Moshe: "Who gave man a mouth? Who makes a person dumb or deaf? Who gives a person sight or makes him blind? Is it not I, G-d? Now go! I will be with your mouth and teach you what to say."

Moshe's power was not based on any ability to bless or curse. His power came strictly from Hashem. G-d further communicated this message to Bilam with a verbal exchange between him and his donkey. Why was it necessary for G-d to change the nature of the donkey and make it talk? In order to teach Bilam something that should have been obvious to him — and to us: that G-d alone controls the power of speech and He alone controls blessing and curse.

פרשת פנחס
Parshas Pinchas

THIS WEEK'S *PARSHAH* BEGINS WITH PINCHAS BEING REWARDED FOR HIS act of zealotry, recorded at the end of *Parshas Balak*. G-d grants him and all his descendants entry into the priesthood and, say the commentaries, all future High Priests descended from him as well.

Why the priesthood? Contrast the defining characteristic of Pinchas's grandfather, Aharon, the first High Priest, who is described as an *oheiv shalom verodeif shalom* — a lover and pursuer of peace — with Pinchas's defining characteristic, his zealotry, and G-d's common gift of the priesthood becomes more difficult to understand. Aharon avoided controversy; he even accommodated the construction of the Golden Calf. Pinchas did the opposite. He reacted violently to a situation to which both Moshe and Aharon did not respond.

Pinchas's unwillingness to compromise, which receives Divine sanction in this *parshah*, is deemed a weakness by the *midrash* in another incident. In the book of *Shoftim*, Yiftach vows to sacrifice to G-d the first thing that walks out of the door of his home should he be successful in his battle with the Ammonites. Tragically, that was his daughter. Though he could have had his vow annulled by Pinchas, Yiftach, the conquering hero, would not go to him. Nor would Pinchas, the High Priest, go to Yiftach, an ignorant commoner. Consequently, his daughter was not saved. She was doomed by an unwillingness to meet in the middle.

The disparity between these two approaches is analyzed by Rav Yosef Dov Soloveitchik, *zt"l,* who describes the incompatibility of *chessed* and

250 / TORAH INSIGHTS

emes. In his masterful essay, "A Eulogy for the Talner Rebbe," the Rav defines the essence of *chessed* as universal love — a love without reason, one that knows no bounds. The person of *chessed* does not ask for moral credentials from the recipients of his love; he simply gives it.

Emes, on the other hand, is strict justice; the man of truth gives nothing gratuitously, rewarding only in proportion to the other's merits and denying love to those not deserving. In his view, there can be no compromise with sin. This total commitment to *emes* is what produces a zealot. "Ultimate reconciliation of the conflict between *chessed* and *emes* can only be found in G-d," writes the Rav, "man may find only a relative solution to the problem, depending upon the temperament and outlook of the person."

The priesthood, as it reflects Jewish religious leadership, requires a combination of the qualities of both Aharon and Pinchas. The chronology of the High Priesthood, with Aharon, the personification of *chessed*, chosen initially, followed and modified by the infusion of the zealot, Pinchas, suggests that all-encompassing love is the primary approach.

Hillel, in *Pirkei Avos*, advises one to be a disciple of Aharon — loving peace, pursuing peace, loving people and bringing them closer to Torah. One would be hard pressed to find a similarly strong recommendation to become a zealot. On the same note, the Talmud in *Sanhedrin* debates the relative merits of settling disputes through arbitration versus settling them through a strict application of the law. Maimonides concludes that a court that always opts for arbitration is praiseworthy.

In his essay, "The Torah Way of Justice," the Rav explains why. *Din*, law, produces justice but not social harmony, while arbitration promotes both reconciliation and righteousness. Clearly, if judges of the court are advised to balance strict justice with accommodation, then the primary role of the priest should be to promote *chessed* with a leavening of zealotry.

_____ *Rabbi David Weinberger*

ONE OF THE MORE DIFFICULT SECTIONS OF THE TORAH IS THE story of the zealot, Pinchas. The greatest leaders of Israel, Moshe and Aharon, are aware of the despicable behavior of one of the tribal heads, yet do nothing to reprimand or disgrace him. Along comes a "man of the flock" and avenges Hashem's wrath. The plague destroying *Klal Yisrael* ceases. Apparently, Pinchas acted properly, for Hashem rewards him with "a covenant of peace." But why didn't Pinchas consult Israel's leadership before engaging in such a serious action?

Rashi, at the end of *Parshas Balak*, comments that Pinchas did seek their advice but Moshe had forgotten the law until Pinchas reminded him of the principle, "Zealots may slay him." Moshe responded that he who revealed the law should also carry it out. Pinchas was motivated by the pure, selfless concern of averting a catastrophic *chillul Hashem*, a desecration of G-d's Name. When there is desecration of the Divine, one cannot be complacent. One must react, lest one become numb to the atrocities that surround us.

Pinchas's zealousness is clearly not the normative behavior that we should emulate. Who among us can be so brazenly confident that his intentions are one hundred percent pure? In addition, the *halachah* that "zealots may slay him" is true only within a particular set of circumstances. Yet, in a society as decadent as ours, if one does not conduct himself inwardly, among his children and family, with zealousness, one jeopardizes his and their spiritual equilibrium.

Our Sages teach that among those present when Pharaoh convened a meeting of his advisors to decide the fate of the Jewish people was Iyov, who did not comment one way or the other. For his silence, he was punished with incredible pain and suffering. One may not be silent at a time when human suffering is taking place. There is a Yiddish idiom: "*Az iz tut vei, shriet mahn* — If it hurts, you must scream." Even if in the long run our scream won't make a difference, it is essential to speak out and impart the proper values to ourselves and our loved ones, lest we become desensitized. Although we can not be zealots in every regard, there is a most definite area where zealotry applies to us all.

The Talmud relates that the wicked Turnusrufus asked the great Rabbi Akiva, "If Hashem loves the poor, why doesn't He sustain them?"

Rabbi Akiva responded, In order to allow us to be spared purgatory by giving them charity. Hashem permits us to join in doing His work for our spiritual benefit. In areas such as *bikur cholim*, *tzedakah* and *talmud Torah* we can be and should be zealots. So much needs to be done in areas of public service, but often only a few are doing the job. In communal life, there is much room for a modern-day Pinchas.

The Torah says that Pinchas "took a spear (*romach*) in hand." A great rebbe once noted that the word *romach* can refer to the *remach eivarim*, the 248 limbs of the human body. In order to live up to the zealotry of Pinchas, one must plunge his entire body into Divine service.

The lesson of Pinchas is a relevant one. We dare not be complacent when we see an immoral society around us. We must react from within and speak out with the clarion call of Torah values. In all areas of life there is ample room for many zealots to do the work that must be accomplished and thereby merit the greatest of blessings, being *mekadeish Sheim Shamayim*, sanctifying the Name of Heaven.

_____ *Rabbi David J. Radinsky*

PINCHAS, THE SON OF ELAZAR, THE SON OF AHARON THE HIGH PRIEST, turns aside the wrath of G-d when he takes the law into his hands and kills Zimri, prince of the tribe of Shimon, and Cozbi, a Midyanite princess, who were involved in an immoral sexual act in the sight of Moshe and the people of Israel. G-d praises Pinchas's act and rewards him with His "covenant of peace" and the promise that his descendants will have everlasting membership in the priesthood.

Contrast this with the fate of Aharon's two oldest sons, Nadav and Avihu, who were killed by G-d when they brought an unauthorized fire offering during the dedication of the Tabernacle. The exact nature of Nadav and Avihu's sin is a matter of dispute among our Sages. One opinion states that they were killed because they decided a matter of Jewish law in the presence of their teachers, Moshe and Aharon, without consulting them.

But Pinchas also decided a matter of Jewish law in the presence of his teachers, Moshe and Aharon, without consulting them, and he was not killed by G-d. To the contrary, he is praised and rewarded by G-d. What is the difference between Pinchas's act and Nadav and Avihu's act? Why is Pinchas rewarded and Nadav and Avihu killed?

Nadav and Avihu's transgression was in the area of commandments between G-d and man. On their own, they modified a G-d-given ritual, neglecting to consult their teachers to determine if their modification was permissible. All the commandments concerning the ritual offerings are *chukim*, commandments whose reasons are not revealed to us. They are decrees from G-d and we must follow them to the letter. There is no room for personal initiative and modification. Only complete obedience to the decrees of G-d will bring us closer to Him.

Because Nadav and Avihu tampered with these unknowable laws before the entire congregation, G-d had to make an example of them and punish them with death. G-d does not show favoritism; even great men are punished when they sin. If improvisation in the sacrificial service would be overlooked, in time, pagan elements would eventually seep in as well.

Pinchas, too, violated commandments of the Torah. Not only did he decide the law without consulting his teachers, but he also killed two people. Indeed, we find criticism of him in the Talmud Yerushalmi: "They would have excommunicated him were it not for the Holy Spirit, which jumped up and said that he and his descendants would have a covenant of everlasting priesthood."

The Talmud Bavli explains that Pinchas dared to act without first receiving permission from Moshe because when there is a desecration of G-d's name, one does not give honor to his teacher. Moshe and Aharon did not act. They cried at the entrance to the Tabernacle. They did not know how to respond to this ghastly act of immorality, perhaps, as some of our Sages suggest, because Moshe himself had married a Midyanite. An act of gross immorality that threatened to undermine the very basis of Jewish family life was being performed in public by a prince of Israel and no one was doing anything about it. This was a great desecration of G-d's name, which could have brought destruction upon the entire people. Pinchas, therefore, killed two people to prevent this plague.

His act was risky, though. Had Zimri killed Pinchas first, it would be seen as self-defense and well within halachic bounds. No court would have convicted Zimri of murder.

The practical lesson we learn is that Pinchas's action was unique, a one-of-a-kind emergency measure that can only be justified in the context of his time and place. Unlike Nadav and Avihu, Pinchas was rewarded because he stepped in during a national emergency and saved the people from disaster. Nonetheless, we should never imitate his actions. Even Pinchas would have been condemned by the religious authorities of his day had G-d Himself not come to his defense. Even though the fate of Nadav and Avihu and that of Pinchas were very different, the conclusion that we draw from their actions is the same: No one is above the law.

_____ *Rabbi Joseph Radinsky*

IN *PARSHAS PINCHAS*, YEHOSHUA IS CHOSEN TO BE THE LEADER OF THE Jewish people. What were the characteristics of Yehoshua that made him the worthy successor of his teacher Moshe?

Jewish tradition requires leaders who can bring out the best in others, as the Torah describes it, "one who will lead them out and bring them in." Moshe, in asking G-d to appoint a new leader, says, "You are the G-d of the spirits of all flesh." Moshe prayed, says the *midrash,* "Sovereign of the universe, You know the minds of all men and how the mind of one man differs from that of another. Appoint over them a leader who will be able to bear with the differing minds of every one of Your children."

In other words, Moshe prays that Hashem choose a leader who is able to bring out the best in others. A leader who brings out the worst in others by polarizing the community has not done his job. This principle is found in sports. Very rarely do you find a baseball manager or a football coach who was a star player. The reason managers and coaches are successful is not because they were brilliant players (most weren't), but because they know how to bring out the best in others.

The Torah describes the pre-Messianic era as being led by a dog. What does this mean? When a dog and its master go out for a walk, the dog usually runs ahead. It appears that the dog is leading the man, but every once in a while, the dog looks back toward its master to see which way to go.

Unfortunately, many leaders of today's societies do not lead. They just look back every once in a while to see in which direction those they are supposed to be leading want them to go.

A successful leader must do what he thinks is right and not act based on what the polls are saying. He must have noble goals and set proper standards. A real leader teaches by example; his method is, as the Torah puts it, to "go out before them and come in before them." A leader must tolerate the foibles and errors of the people he leads. Often, a leader must bear the problems until he is able to solve them.

But some leaders equate tolerance with approval and can not lead because they always divide the people. Yehoshua was chosen as leader of the Jewish people because his actions united them and did not divide them. He brought out the best in them. He set the standards and knew when to tolerate and when to disapprove.

This is the type of leadership we always need. Charisma and brilliance may be nice, but other things are far more important.

_____ *Rabbi Shlomo Caplan*

PINCHAS, THE HERO OF THIS *PARSHAH*, IS THE PARADIGM OF THE JEWISH zealot. An analysis of his actions and motives reveals the parameters of zealotry.

The Torah states that Hashem rewarded Pinchas with His "covenant of peace." What does this mean? We know that Hashem responds to our actions *midah keneged midah* — measure for measure. So if Pinchas acted violently, killing Zimri and the Midyanite woman with whom he had sinned, why did Hashem reward him with a covenant of *peace*?

The Midrash, *Yalkut Shimoni*, elaborates on Pinchas's fate: "Rabbi Shimon ben Lakish said, Pinchas is Eliyahu Hanavi. *Hakadosh Baruch Hu* said to him, You made peace between Me and My sons; in the future you too will be the one to make peace between Me and My sons, as it says, 'Behold I will send to you Eliyahu the prophet... and he will return the hearts of the fathers to their sons.' "

As the *midrash* sees it, G-d viewed Pinchas's behavior not as violent but as peaceful — a reconciliation between Hashem and His sons, a motion to restore the deep fondness that characterizes the relationship of G-d and His people. This is the proper model of zealotry.

The Talmud explains the verse in *Tehillim*, "*Vayaamod Pinchas vayifallel* — Pinchas quarreled with Hashem": "The angels sought to push him away but Hashem said to them, Leave him. He is a zealot the son of a zealot, an assuager of wrath the son of an assuager of wrath."

Pinchas argued with G-d not to punish *Bnei Yisrael* because of the sin of Zimri. Only as a last resort, when arguing with G-d failed, did Pinchas kill in order to assuage the wrath of G-d. Pinchas's zealousness arose from his great love of *Klal Yisrael*. His love prompted him to go to bat for them, to quarrel with Hashem for them. Thus his genealogy is traced by the verse: "Pinchas the son of Elazar the son of Aharon." Aharon was Judaism's great peacemaker, "a lover of peace and a pursuer of peace." Pinchas shared his grandfather's traits. Just as Aharon sought to turn back the wrath of Hashem during the rebellion of Korach, so too Pinchas sought to turn back the wrath of Hashem by killing Zimri and the Midyanite woman.

Pinchas could have been killed during his attack on Zimri, the Talmud records. Yet, he was willing to risk his life for *Klal Yisrael*.

Someone once asked Rav Yosef Chaim Sonnenfeld the first Chief Rabbi of Jerusalem, why he was so sharp in his castigation of the secularists. Isn't the role of a pious man to advocate on behalf of all the Jewish people?

Rav Sonnenfeld responded: "I only take this approach when speaking to the people involved directly in order to make it clear to them that their behavior is unacceptable. However, every day I say *Tehillim* and cry to Hashem on their behalf."

The true zealot is a student of Aharon Hakohein, who loves *Klal Yisrael*, who advocates on behalf of *Klal Yisrael*, and who resorts to zealousness only as a last resort to restore peace between Hashem and His children.

פרשת מטות־מסעי
Parshas Matos-Masei

_____ *Dr. Rivkah T. Blau*

A S THE JEWISH PEOPLE PREPARE TO CONQUER AND DIVIDE THE LAND
of Israel, two groups approach Moshe with diametrical requests.
One group is referred to as *bnei*, the sons of, and the other as *bnos*, the
daughters of. The *Bnei Gad* and *Bnei Reuvein* did not want to cross over
into the land of Canaan with the other tribes of Israel, preferring instead
to remain on the other side of the Jordan and settle its fertile land,
newly conquered from the kingdoms of Sichon and Og. Meanwhile, the
bnos Tzelaphechad had the opposite concern — that their family would
lose its share in the land of Israel because their father died leaving no
male heirs.

In her masterful analysis of the deal between the *Bnei Gad* and *Bnei
Reuven* and Moshe, Nechama Leibowitz, a"h, demonstrates, through a
careful reading of the text, that the two tribes were concerned with their
material standing in the new land, in contrast with Moshe, who spoke of
a Divine mission. Though they volunteered to lead the way into the
land of Canaan, their offer was merely a quid pro quo: they would
contribute to the conquest of the land in return for the region they
desired. "We will build pens for our flocks and cities for our children,"
they told Moshe, "and then we will arm ourselves and go up before
the children of Israel." They mention their cattle before their children,
Rashi points out, and are corrected by Moshe, who tries to set their
priorities straight.

In contrast, the *bnos Tzelaphechad* did want a share in the Holy Land

and presented their arguments before Moshe as to why they should have it. Moshe could not answer and had to bring their claim before G-d, who ruled in the daughters' favor. They inherited their father's portion and were only asked to marry within their own tribe so that the land would not transfer to another tribe. The Talmud interprets this request as a recommendation, not a requirement, and their desire to comply as a reflection of their righteousness.

The *midrash* makes two points regarding the behavior of the *bnos Tzelaphechad*. One, they were extraordinary women, wise and righteous, and all five are named — individually — on the *midrash's* list of the 23 great Jewish women of the *Tanach*. Two, on a general level, the women of that generation fenced in the breaches that the men had created. The two terrible sins of the Jews in the wilderness, the worshiping of the Golden Calf and the episode of the Spies, were committed by men, not women. It was the men who did not want to enter the land of Canaan, while the women loved the land.

Both approaches teach us that the behavior of the *bnos Tzelaphechad* is the antidote to the mentality of the *Bnei Gad* and *Bnei Reuven*. These unique women serve as role models for all generations and as representatives of the overall commitment of Jewish women.

_____ *Emanuel J. Adler*

PARSHAS MATOS BEGINS WITH MOSHE RABBEINU INSTRUCTING THE heads of the Jewish tribes: "This is the word (*Zeh hadavar*) that G-d commanded." Rashi, quoting the *Sifri*, points out that while other prophets generally use the phrase, *Koh amar Hashem* — So said G-d — Moshe uses the superior phrase, *Zeh hadavar*. What is the significance of the words *zeh hadavar* that indicates a higher level of prophecy?

Moreover, why does the *Sifri* wait until this *parshah*, which discusses the laws of vows, to make this observation when the phrase *zeh hadavar* appears earlier in the Torah?

The *Sefas Emes* distinguishes between the roots of these two phrases. *Amirah*, he points out, is external to the message; it is reportage, narrative. *Dibur*, on the other hand, is intrinsic to the message;

in a sense it is the message itself. Unlike *amirah*, which is merely the physical act of saying something, *dibur* connotes influence and causation. A *dibur* penetrates the ear of the listener with its message. The *koach hadibur*, the power of speech, is often referred to as the *koach hachibur*, the power to unite speaker and listener in purposeful communication.

To most of His prophets, G-d merely told a narrative, which could be communicated through dreams and riddles. But to Moshe Rabbeinu, G-d spoke "mouth to mouth and in a vision not in riddles." Rashi explains that the vision was the *dibur* itself. The message was so real that Moshe could actually see it.

Just as communication between G-d and His prophets was on either the informational level (*koh amar*) or the instrumental level (*zeh hadavar*), so too communication between people can take these two forms. People can talk, relating facts and events to each other, but they can also *speak* — in a manner that has a profound effect on the listener.

The paradigm of human speech that has a tangible effect is the *neder*, where by pronouncing the words, "This is prohibited to me," a person actually transforms an ordinary object into a prohibited object. Words have consequences. "*Lo yacheil devaro*," the Torah commands, "He shall not break his word." He shall not allow his *dibur* to become *chullin*, unholy, or worse, profane.

By using the words *zeh hadavar* in detailing the laws of *neder*, the Torah reminds us that we have the ability to elevate our speech to the highest level of holiness, just as Moshe reached the highest level of communication, of *dibur*, with the Creator.

We live in an age of communication unparalleled in the history of the world. The War of 1812 continued to be fought in the United States for weeks after the Treaty of Ghent was signed in Europe. Today, the entire text of that treaty can be faxed or e-mailed in a matter of seconds. The global village has a communications system so sophisticated that most of its instruments were unknown only twenty years ago.

Yet, humanity has failed miserably in using this technology to elevate the content of its communications. It is obvious that society has rendered its speech *chullin*. Unholy, and even profane, messages are transmitted into our living rooms daily. Though they are sometimes disguised as such, these are not mere narratives, words of *koh amar*. These are ideas intended to have an effect, expressions of *zeh hadavar*. As Marshall McLuhan said so prophetically thirty years ago, the medium is the message. We, as Jews, can utilize that which G-d gave us — namely, the Torah — to elevate our communications, our *dibur*, to heightened levels of spirituality.

In the Talmud *Berachos*, Rabbi Ami says that one is responsible to read each verse of the weekly Torah portion three times, twice in Hebrew and once in *targum*, translation, "even '*Ataros Vedivon*.' " This verse, "*Ataros Vedivon*," in *Parshas Matos*, has no translation; it is merely a list of certain cities on the east bank of the Jordan River. Nevertheless, Rabbi Ami instructs us to read the verse a third time. Why?

Obviously, the recitation of these words a third time has an intrinsic value. The mere reading of words of Torah, in a manner that would suggest *amirah*, is actually *dibur*, having a profound effect on the person speaking as well as the person listening. Communications of Torah, on any level, raise us spiritually; they are the polar opposites of "*Lo yacheil devaro*."

As we begin the Nine Days, let us not view this period as merely a time during which we eat dairy meals and refrain from swimming. Let us use this period to transcend the empty communications that surround us and rededicate ourselves to the highest form of communication possible, the study of Torah, and thereby hasten the coming of *Mashiach Tzidkeinu*.

 *Rabbi Avigdor Slatus*

I N *PARSHAS MATOS*, THE TRIBES OF GAD AND REUVEN APPROACH MOSHE and request that their inheritance in the Holy Land be apportioned from the lands of Sichon and Og, in Trans-Jordan.

Their abundance of cattle and sheep necessitated that they seek land conducive to grazing. Moshe agrees. He only objects to their implications that they will not join the rest of *Klal Yisrael* in conquering *Eretz Yisrael*. Their absence, Moshe knew, would dramatically discourage the other tribes and result in a repetition of the sin of the spies, who, forty years earlier, discouraged *Bnei Yisrael* from entering the Promised Land.

But once *Bnei Gad* and *Bnei Reuven* commit themselves to be vanguards, leading the other tribes in battle, Moshe wholeheartedly grants their request and gives them possession of their desired property. Without a doubt, Moshe did not consent to their proposal without first receiving the approval of Hashem. Indeed, the land of Trans-Jordan was not meant to lie fallow.

Centuries earlier, our patriarch, Yaakov, remained apart from his family on the other side of the river and was confronted by the angel of Eisav. Why was he there? The Talmud explains that he returned to retrieve some small jars he had forgotten. Why would these insignificant jars impel Yaakov to jeopardize his safety and return alone for them? What possible value could these containers have possessed that justified his abandoning his family, even for a few moments, to get them back?

Rav Eliyahu Dessler, *zt"l,* explains that every trait and talent, every natural affinity and propensity that one has is but a tool presented by Hashem for one's worldly mission. Earthly possessions are made available to man as instruments for Divine service. They enable us to fulfill the purpose for which we are created.

The tribes of Gad and Reuven recognized that their herds and flock were entrusted to them by Hashem, and it was necessary for them to sacrifice their portion in the Land of Israel and take up residence in Trans-Jordan in order that the animals be well cared for.

In doing so, they followed the path of Yaakov Avinu, who understood that even worthless jars have value if they are viewed as a means to Heavenly service. Of the many challenges that face the Jewish people, one of the greatest is the material affluence available to us. For centuries, Jews remained faithful to Torah principles despite poverty and hardships.

Today, however, we are challenged to do just the opposite — to discover the beauty and sanctity of authentic Torah Judaism despite wealth and comfort. The many opportunities that are now available to Jews and Jewish communities are tools for fulfilling our Heavenly mission, to love and serve Hashem with loyalty and sincerity.

IN THE *PARSHAH* OF *MATOS*, G-D COMMANDS MOSHE TO "EXACT THE vengeance of the children of Israel upon the Midyanites," for their aggression toward the Jewish nation. This would be Moshe's last mission. Afterwards, G-d tells him, "You will be gathered to your people" in death.

It would seem advantageous for Moshe to have delayed the war against Midyan as long as possible. But Moshe immediately exhorts the Jewish people "to exact the vengeance of G-d upon Midyan." Rashi, quoting the *midrash,* remarks that even though Moshe knew that his death would follow the completion of this matter, he carried it out with joy and did not delay. A leader, especially one who leads the Jewish people, must overlook personal advantages — even if it means relinquishing his life. Moshe was asked to demonstrate for all generations the position of Jewish leadership.

Although Hashem referred to this war as "the vengeance of the children of Israel," Moshe calls it "the vengeance of G-d." Rashi explains that "one who stands before Israel is considered to be standing before G-d." The Jewish people represent G-d in this world, and those who harm them are displaying a lack of faith in G-d. To carry the designation Jew is to be a representative of G-d.

Thus, Moshe presents G-d's command to the Jewish people as a lesson for all Jews to know that their purpose in life is primarily to represent the existence of G-d. To defend the honor of the children of Israel is to carry out the *mitzvah* of sanctifying G-d's name.

Rashi offers two reasons why Midyan, and not Moav, is singled out for revenge by Israel. The Moavites were afraid of what the Jewish people might do to them. They were genuinely frightened by the prospects of being conquered by this new nation. So they recruited the Midyanites to help them. But Midyan had no reason to become involved in a fight that wasn't theirs. Additionally, two great figures would emerge from Moav: Ruth and Na'amah the Ammonite. Midyan, though, offered no redeeming future benefits to Israel.

We learn from the war with Midyan that a country which offers nothing of value to our nation, and seeks only recognition for itself and is ready to abuse the name of G-d for this purpose, has no reason to exist and must be made an example for the rest of the world. Moshe, at the same time, has to become the example of the selfless leader of the Jews, whose only thrust is to make the Jewish people a G-dly nation.

_____ *Rabbi Pinchas Herman*

I N *PARSHAS MASEI*, HASHEM COMMANDS MOSHE RABBEINU TO ESTAB-
lish cities of refuge, safe havens for those who kill unintentionally, or even intentionally if their cases are still being decided by the Supreme Court. The Talmud tells us that the *Bnei Yisrael* built wide, paved roads leading to these cities and had signposts marking the way so that these hunted people (they were fair game to the deceased's next-of-kin) could quickly and easily reach safety without having to stop and ask directions.

Today, we have no actual cities of refuge. Nonetheless, the Lubavitcher Rebbe, *zt"l,* writes, the Torah's message is eternal and the notion of these cities remains relevant. Many Jews are at a crossroads in their lives. One road is the path of Torah and *mitzvos*, which assures a fulfilled life both spiritually and materially. The other road, devoid of Torah and *mitzvos*, leads to assimilation, discontent and spiritual frustration.

The job of rabbis and laypeople alike is to be like the signposts leading to these cities — clearly marking the Path of Life, showing people that this is their refuge, the way that will bring them toward fulfillment. If we have an obligation to help our brothers and sisters with their material needs through the *mitzvah* of *tzedakah*, how much more so do we have an obligation to help all Jews with their spiritual needs, regardless of their observance, knowledge and affiliation.

A *chassid* of Rav Sholom Dov Ber of Lubavitch once inquired of the Rebbe why he spent so much of his time with simple, unlearned Jews. The Rebbe asked the *chassid* — a jeweler by trade — if he had any gems with him. The *chassid* emptied a bag of stones on the table. The Rebbe looked at them and picked out the largest one, "Is this the most precious stone you have?" he asked. The *chassid* shook his head.

"Actually," he said, pointing out a small, uncut diamond, "this is the most precious. Once it is cut and polished properly, its brilliance will be appreciated by all. With all due respect, Rebbe, when it comes to diamonds you have to be an expert."

"Precisely," said the Rebbe. "When it comes to *neshamos* you also have to be an expert."

As we observe the Three Weeks that lead up to Tishah B'Av, let us reflect on our obligation to provide this spiritual safe haven for all Jews. The Talmud tells us that the *Beis Hamikdash* was destroyed because of *sinas chinam*, senseless hatred. By employing *ahavas chinam*, senseless love, instead, we will turn the day of Tishah B'Av to a day of rejoicing with the building of the final *Beis Hamikdash*.

❧ Sefer Devarim

פרשת דברים
Parshas Devarim

_____ *Rabbi I. Nathan Bamberger*

PRIOR TO THIS SHABBOS, WE HAVE COMPLETED A FAST DAY, SHIVAH Asar B'Tamuz, and experienced three weeks of mourning. Now we observe the Shabbos that precedes the saddest day of the year, Tishah B'Av.

The commentators point out that three prophets used the word *eichah*. First, Moshe Rabbeinu employs it in *Parshas Devarim*: "Eichah — How can I alone carry your difficulties, your burdens and your quarrels?" The prophet Yirmiyahu begins the book of *Lamentations*, which we chant on Tishah B'Av evening: "Eichah — Behold, how the city sits desolate, a city once filled with people." Finally, the prophet Yeshayahu, in the *haftarah* for Shabbos Chazon, laments over the city of Jerusalem: "Eichah — How she has become a harlot."

We may well ponder the meaning of this unique expression, used by three of our greatest prophets. What did they envision in this word, which they used to describe the terrible situation that had befallen the Jewish people, the land of Israel and the holy city of Jerusalem? What does *eichah* signify that it became the hallmark of devastation, destruction and despair? The word, its meaning, as well as the tune we use to chant the book of *Eichah* have become so ingrained in the soul of our people that we tremble when we hear the word.

The Maharal of Prague, in his work, *Netzach Yisrael*, provides an insightful interpretation. The word *eichah*, he explains, actually dates back to Adam. After Adam sinned by eating from the Tree of Knowledge he heard the sound of Hashem approaching him in the Garden of Eden. "And Hashem called out to Adam and said, 'Ayekah — Where are you?' "

Obviously Hashem knew where Adam was, the Maharal explains. He was saying something else through the word ayekah, which, spelled in Hebrew, can also be pronounced eichah. Eichah — How could you, Adam, My creation, have fallen so fast and sinned? What happened that you could not withstand temptation and thus lost the great opportunity devised for you? How could you make such a mistake for which future generations will have to grieve and suffer? This was the question G-d posed to Adam by asking, "Ayekah?"

Thus, when the three prophets looked at the terrible condition of the Jewish people, they remembered the first eichah. Our teacher Moshe, after leading the Jewish people out of Egypt and guiding them for forty years through the wilderness, questions the behavior of the people. How can they be so lighthearted and so quarrelsome? Am Yisrael, who saw miracles in Egypt, at the Red Sea, and in battles with vicious enemies, who were saved each time, still had not mastered the lesson of eichah. Said our teacher Moshe: I mourn for them!

The prophet Yirmiyahu, in a similar vein, questions the people about the city of Jerusalem, the city that Hashem had chosen for Himself, where His holy Temple stood. How could they not have taken pride in this city? "Eichah," says the prophet, I mourn for you and for your actions which have caused this glorious city to become desolate and abandoned.

The prophet Yeshayahu joins in these lamentations using the same word: Eichah — Woe unto you for disregarding and neglecting the Torah and her teachings.

However, amid all the doom and gloom of the Nine Days, Shabbos Chazon and Tishah B'Av, we do find words of hope, faith and promise, which recognize the bright future that is in store for us. The Mashiach is born on Tishah B'Av. With his arrival, eichah will be changed back to ayekah — Where are you? — a call to the Jewish people, wherever they are, to return to our ancient homeland.

Tishah B'Av is not all black. Just as a rose is the most beautiful flower and can come in many shades from pure white to very dark, still there is no black rose. Each rose has a drop of water within its flower — a tear signifying not only our eternal mourning over our long exile, but also symbolizing our unwavering belief in the final redemption and restoration of our people, our land and our city of Jerusalem to their former glory. In the words of Yeshayahu: "Zion shall be redeemed with justice and her returnees with righteousness."

_____ *Rabbi Yisroel Miller*

THE TORAH RECORDS THAT, BEFORE HIS DEATH, MOSHE "SPOKE TO ALL Israel beyond the Jordan, in the wilderness, in Aravah, opposite Suph, between Paran and Tophel and Lavan and Chatzeiros and Di Zahav."

What is this lengthy list of locations? Rashi, citing the *midrash*, explains that these are reminders of the various places where the Jews angered G-d. They are referenced here, in Moshe's farewell address to the nation, as reproof for their past sins. For example, "in the wilderness" can not be taken literally, as they were no longer in the wilderness but in the plains of Mo'av about to enter the Holy Land. Moreover, Rabbi Yochanan points out, places with names like Tophel and Lavan are not recorded anywhere in the text; they are instead names meant to signify the place where the Jewish people "criticized (*taphlu*) the manna, which is white (*lavan*)."

Nonetheless, the Talmudic principle that "a verse does not depart completely from its simple meaning" indicates that these were real places. What then is the plain meaning behind these names?

Rav Samson Raphael Hirsch suggests that when Moshe reviewed the events of their forty years in the wilderness, pointing out to the Jewish people the errors of their past in order that they glean lessons for the future, the people responded by giving names to various landmarks around the plains of Mo'av. By turning these landmarks into national historic monuments, the lessons associated with them would not be forgotten.

"These names," writes Rav Hirsch, "testify to national lapses, and by bringing to mind these errors of the past, were to awaken firm resolutions for a purer, more loyal future."

This pattern is an extension of the principle of the *mitzvah* of *tzitzis*, of which it is written: "You shall look at them, and remember all the *mitzvos* of the L-rd, and you shall do them." Simply staring at the *tzitzis* will not automatically remind one of G-d's commands; nonetheless, the Torah tells us to use *tzitzis* as a reminder, to consciously look at a tangible object for the purpose of becoming inspired to an abstract idea.

In this week's *haftarah*, G-d laments, "The ox knows its owner, and the donkey its master's trough, but Israel does not know. My people do not reflect." Rav Avigdor Miller points out that the prophet's unfavorable contrast of the Jewish nation's detachment from G-d to the loyalty of farm animals seems unfair. After all, oxen and donkeys act from instinct, not free will. Thus, they don't really make a conscious effort to know their owner.

But the prophet is teaching that we are to make use of the opportunity for inspiration by watching the loyal ox and donkey, just as *Mishlei* urges the lazy man to take lessons from the industrious ant. The mind is guided by Torah knowledge; but the heart is awakened by concrete examples — even when they tell us truths we already know.

The Talmud states "All who mourn over Jerusalem will merit to see its rejoicing." Still, many Jews find it difficult to relate to the spirit of Tishah B'Av. They do not have instinctive feelings of bereavement over the loss of the Temple, whose beauty they never saw and whose sanctity they never felt. But even without immediate feeling, as long as we are loyal to the rituals of the day, to the concrete acts of mourning, eventually our inner spirits will be uplifted and we will come to experience the ultimate rejoicing of *Klal Yisrael*.

_____ *Rabbi Bertram Leff*

THE FIRST CHAPTER OF THE BOOK OF *DEVARIM* CONTAINS MOSHE'S review of past events in the history of the Children of Israel. After their sojourn at Mount Sinai, G-d commands the Israelites, "Enough of your dwelling by this mountain. Turn yourselves around and journey.... See I have given the land before you. Come and possess the land that Hashem swore to your forefathers."

The land of Israel would have been theirs without opposition, without even a battle, Moshe reminds them. But, unfortunately, this did not happen — because of the disastrous mission of the spies.

However, Moshe's narrative seems a bit odd. After recounting the command to posses the land, but before talking of the spies, Moshe interjects with a passage mandating the appointment of the *shoftim*, judges, in the Holy Land, and the establishment of a judiciary system there. We are left to ask why Moshe interrupted the logical sequence of historical events with this directive.

Nachmanides teaches that with the receiving of the Torah at Mount Sinai and the appointment of the judges "we were ready to enter the land." Moshe's interjection teaches us that the institution of courts of justice was a prerequisite to our possession of the land of Israel and the fulfillment of the promise given to Avraham, Yitzchak and Yaakov.

Rav Yosef Dov Soloveitchik, *zt"l*, understood this concept as the connection between *Parshas Devarim* and the *haftarah* of Shabbos Chazon. In the time of the prophet Isaiah, the judicial system was corrupt and the judges, the leaders of the nation at that time, had forsaken their Divine role as the guardians of "*tzedakah umishpat* — righteousness and justice." The destruction of the Jewish State was therefore inevitable, as the *haftarah* proclaims: "Zion shall be redeemed with justice and her returnees with righteousness."

This principle is also found in our daily prayers, the Rav points out. In the *Amidah*, we pray to G-d "to gather our exiles from the four corners of the earth" and return our people to their sovereign homeland, *Eretz Yisrael*. The next blessing should logically be, "And to Jerusalem, Your city, may You return in compassion.... May You rebuild it soon in our days and speedily establish the throne of David within it." But it is not. Immediately following the prayer for the ingathering of the exiles we ask Hashem, "Return our judges as in earliest times .... Blessed are You, Hashem, the King Who loves righteousness and justice."

The sequence of these blessings proclaims that the gathering of the exiles and the establishment of a sovereign Jewish State with Jerusalem as its eternal capital can not have any permanence unless there is a judicial system within which justice and righteousness can flourish.

We are the generation that was blessed to see the establishment of the sovereign State of Israel. *Medinat Yisrael* is the fulfillment of our prayers and dreams. But in order for our Jewish homeland to flourish as a Jewish State, justice and righteousness must dominate both the government and the lives of individual Jews. No man, religious or secular, is above the law, which stems from the ideal of *tzedakah umishpat*. If we allow individuals, as well as government representatives, to be disloyal to the tenets of justice and righteousness, our future as a people in a sovereign state is jeopardized. We all have the obligation to preach and practice *tzedakah umishpat* so that Zion may be redeemed speedily in our days.

פרשת ואתחנן
Parshas Va'eschanan

_____ *Rabbi Jacob J. Schacter*

R AV YOSEF DOV SOLOVEITCHIK, *ZT"L*, USED TO SPEND TISHAH B'AV
morning delivering a brief *shiur* followed by a multihour recitation
and analysis of the *Kinos.* In 1974, his *shiur* was devoted to an analysis
of the verses in *Parshas Va'eschanan* that compose the Torah reading
for that day.

The Talmud in *Megillah* (31b) brings four opinions as to what should
be read. All four understood, of course, that the Torah reading should
correspond to the central themes of the day, but differed on precisely
which theme should be chosen.

The first opinion felt that linking Tishah B'Av to the *Tochachah* —
G-d's warning to the Jewish people of what would befall them should
they stray from observing His commands — would be the most appropriate selection.

The next two opinions suggest invoking the story of the *meraglim,* as
that event stamped Tishah B'Av with the marks of tragedy at the very
dawn of our national history. When the *meraglim* returned from their
reconnaissance mission with a deleterious report on the Holy Land, the
verse tells us that "the nation cried out on that night," to which the
Talmud states, "*That night* was the night of Tishah B'Av" (*Taanis* 29a).

The fourth and final opinion, Abaye's choice of the fourth chapter of
Devarim, is the one we follow. Why? Rav Soloveitchik pointed to several
themes contained in these verses that render them timely on this day.

Exile: "And G-d will scatter you among the nations" is not simply the Jews' dislocation from their ancestral land, explained the Rav. G-d promised to scatter them over the entire globe. This came as a direct result of the Temple's destruction.

Re-enactment: "When you will have children and grandchildren and grow old in the land, you will then act destructively" implies that the first generation to enter the land will not degenerate into idolaters; only later generations will. The basic human emotion of gratitude felt toward a benefactor — especially a Divine one — prevented the original inheritors of the Holy Land from straying. But that feeling is not passed on from one generation to the next because, said the Rav, "Man is basically a forgetful being, not only intellectually but also emotionally." One's sense of gratitude diminishes — and ultimately expires — with the passage of time. It is for precisely this reason, he noted, that Judaism stresses the concept of personally re-experiencing history, whether through the Pesach *seder* or the recital of *Kinos* on Tishah B'Av. At the *seder,* each Jew speaks of the time *"betzeisi mimitzrayim* — when I left Egypt"; during *Kinos,* each Jew speaks of the time *"betzeisi miyerushalayim* — when I left Jerusalem." Both statements are made in the first person, singular.

Redemption: "You will, in the end, return to the L-rd your G-d and heed His voice." This is not just a prediction, states the Rambam, but an absolute promise: G-d will insure that we return to Him. No matter how far we stray, no matter how distant and alienated we become, we will somehow always feel a mysterious longing to return to G-d (*Hilchos Teshuvah* 7:5).

And when we do, it will be, as the verse says, "for all eternity." This too is an appropriate lesson for Tishah B'Av. May it be fulfilled soon and in our days.

 *Rabbi David Movsas*

V A'ESCHANAN CONFRONTS US WITH AN APPARENT REDUNDANCY. SEVeral admonitions throughout the *parshah* command us to observe the laws taught by Moshe. Then, toward the end of the *parshah,* we are told, "And you shall do that which is right and good in the eyes of G-d."

What new instructions does this verse add? Surely, doing what is "right and good" is a part of the numerous injunctions already presented. If one observes all the commandments and prohibitions set forth in the Torah, does he not accomplish what is "right and good in the eyes of G-d"? What new obligation does this verse apply?

Both Rashi and the Ramban understand this verse to denote a level of behavior that is *lifnim mishuras hadin,* above the letter of the law. To appreciate the full spirit of the law, one needs to read between the lines of the Torah, and one who does this shows a sincere desire to observe Hashem's bidding.

The story is told of a poor man who came to the Brisker Rav on *erev Pesach* with a question. Could he use milk instead of wine for the four cups at the *seder*? The Brisker Rav didn't reply. Instead he took five rubles from his pocket and gave them to the man. The Rav's wife wondered why he had given the man so much money. "Wouldn't one ruble have been enough for wine?" she asked.

"True," the Brisker Rav answered, "but if he was planning on drinking milk throughout the *seder,* that means he has no money for meat either. I gave him enough for both wine and meat." The Brisker Rav combined keen perception with adherence to the spirit of the law, for though he could have answered the poor man's question, he went the extra mile to ensure that the poor man would fulfill the *mitzvos* of Pesach as well as enjoy its festive spirit.

A similar precept is encapsulated in the verse, "You shall be holy, for I the L-rd your G-d am holy." It is possible, the Ramban comments, for a person to keep the letter of the law while violating its spirit, thus becoming a *naval birshus Hatorah* — a degenerate within the confines of the Torah. The Torah commands us to be holy, to sanctify ourselves even in those circumstances that are permitted according to the strict interpretation of the law.

These two verses complement each other. "You shall be holy" tells us to take a step back in order to uphold the spirit of the law. It tells us that even though a certain act seems permitted, we must nevertheless demonstrate self-restraint to prevent the spirit of the law from being violated. In doing so we become holy.

At the same time, "You shall do that which is right and good" tells us to take a step forward in order to promote the spirit of the law. Though we may find ourselves in situations where we feel we can sit back and not get involved, the spirit of the Torah demands that we take initiative and get involved.

The Talmud states that Jerusalem was destroyed because her inhabitants failed to raise their standard of behavior above the letter of the law. It is therefore fitting that *Va'eschanan* is always read on Shabbos Nachamu, the Shabbos of Comfort, which follows Tishah B'Av. If we live up to the message of this *parshah* by doing what is "right and good in the eyes of G-d," we will be deserving of redemption and merit the rebuilding of the Temple.

_____ *Rabbi Moshe David Tendler*

> *"Guard (i.e., study) and do (i.e., live by) my commandments*
> *... then the nations of the world will affirm that we are a wise,*
> *understanding, great nation."*
>
> *Va'eschanan* [4:6]

> *"Israel sinned twofold, she was punished twofold and will be*
> *consoled twofold, as it is written: 'Nachamu, nachamu ami.' "*
>
> *Yalkut Yeshayahu* [40:445]

WHAT IS MEANT BY TWOFOLD (*KIFLAYIM*)? TWO TIMES WHAT? SURELY a better term would be "sinned greatly, grievously, terribly, extensively."

The term twofold harbors within it an important lesson. Transgressions blemish the potential moral and ethical characteristics that we are all capable of developing within our spiritual beings. However, there are some *aveiros* that also degrade the image of G-d within us. Such sinful acts blur the distinction between man and the other creatures of the world. We sin *kiflayim*, twofold.

Jewish family life, with its code of sexual morality, has been the distinguishing mark of the Jew throughout the centuries. Of course, there were individuals in every generation who fell prey to secular values, even in the realm of sexual morality. What distinguishes our generation is that there is a driving force to legalize and ultimately sanctify that which our Torah designates as an abomination. This movement will destroy our humanity and the image of G-d in which we were created. This is the twofold sin that plagues contemporary society. Such behavior will ultimately lead to the twofold punishment in which our humanity will be diminished.

In this week's *haftarah* we are consoled by Hashem twofold. *"Nachamu, nachamu ami, yomar Elokeichem"* — We will once again become a holy nation. We need only to resume the lifestyle ordained for us by Hashem — a lifestyle that all nations know to be a source of wisdom and understanding of perfection in the eyes of G-d and man.

The *haftarah* records a rhetorical question [40:25]: "To whom can you compare our G-d?" Indeed do compare! Place our Torah lifestyle, family life, business ethics, social responsibilities alongside the value system of secular humanism. There is no comparison. Secular humanism has led to the moral decay of American society and a spiritual holocaust that continues to have a negative influence on contemporary Jewish life. Torah values are our only *nechamah,* the ultimate consolation in our struggle to fulfill our mission as a kingdom of priests and a holy people.

> *"Is there a great nation that has righteous decrees and ordinances to compare to this entire Torah that I place before you this day?"*
>
> Va'eschanan [4:8]

> *"Let them hear My words so that they shall learn to be in awe of Me all the days that they live on the earth and they shall teach their children."*
>
> Va'eschanan [4:10]

_____ *Rabbi Joel Landau*

W HEN THE PROPHET YIRMIYAHU DESCRIBES THE INIQUITIES OF THE Jewish people, he says, "Jerusalem has sinned a sin." The prophet Yishayahu, referring to the Jews' suffering, says, "She has received double for all her sins." And when Yishayahu speaks about redemption, he says, "Comfort, comfort my people." The double nature of these verses ("sinned a sin"; "double for all her sins"; "comfort, comfort") emphasizes that man constantly functions on two levels, spiritual and physical, the Midrash observes. Everything we do impacts on both our relationship with G-d and our relationship with the world around us.

This concept also applies to the Jews as a nation. Just like the individual Jew, the Jewish people constantly function on these two levels. On the one hand, our national focus is toward our relationship with G-d alone, as articulated by the infamous Bilam: "Behold, it is a nation that dwells in solitude, not to be reckoned among the nations." On the other hand, as Yishayahu puts it, we are mandated to be a "light unto the nations."

The sins of the Jewish people, both as a nation and as individuals, also occur on these same two levels. G-d conveys through Yishayahu, "Children have I raised and exalted, but have rebelled against Me.... They have forsaken Hashem, they have angered the Holy One of Israel and have turned their back to Him."

At the same time, the prophet declares, "How the faithful city has become a harlot. She had been full of justice, but now murderers.... Your princes are... associates of thieves, each of them loves bribery."

Sins against G-d; crimes against man.

Divine punishment was thus dealt measure for measure. G-d severs His relationship with us. "Your worthless meal-offering... is an incense of abomination to Me.... My soul detests your new moons and holidays.... When you spread your hands in prayer, I will hide My eyes from you... I will not listen," G-d declares through the prophet.

On the physical level, he declares, "Your country is desolate, your cities burned with fire. As for your land, strangers consume its yield."

Fortunately, we are told, the redemption shall share these dimensions. Our spirituality will be restored and "the Glory of Hashem will be revealed and all flesh together will see that the mouth of Hashem has spoken."

So, too, our physicality will be restored: "As for your ruins and desolations... you will now become crowded with inhabitants.... For Hashem will comfort Zion.... He will make her wilderness like Eden... joy and gladness will be found there, thanksgiving and the sound of music."

Too many of us lose sight of the importance of our dual role and responsibilities as Jews. Instead, many people focus on either a man–man relationship or a man–G-d relationship. This approach is clearly wrong. Judaism is a package deal. In order to be a good Jew, it is essential to perfect a relationship with G-d as well as one with fellow men. It may be possible to be a good person without being a good Jew, but one can not be a good Jew without being a good person. Only when this concept is internalized can our redemption materialize.

פרשת עקב
Parshas Eikev

_____ *Rabbi Steven Pruzansky*

PRAYER IS ESSENTIAL TO THE JEWISH EXPERIENCE AND IS, MORE-over, a fundamental human need. Every culture has some type of prayer, but Jewish *tefillah* differs substantially from what the world perceives as prayer. The Biblical basis for the *mitzvah* of *tefillah* is found in *Parshas Eikev*, in the verse read twice daily in the second paragraph of the *Shema:* "If you pay careful heed to My commandments... to serve Him with all your heart." "What is *avodah shebeleiv*, service of the heart?" ask our Sages. "Prayer." What is the purpose of prayer? In what sense is it "service of the heart"?

Prayer is most commonly perceived as an outpouring of feeling and emotion, a turn to G-d in times of personal distress and suffering and, certainly, *tefillah* incorporates this aspect of prayer. Most of the *tefillos* by individuals recorded in *Tanach* — Avraham on behalf of Avimelech; Moshe on behalf of Miriam — were supplications. But to construe *tefillah* as merely petitions and requests, as beseeching the Almighty for salvation from trials and tribulations is to render *tefillah* unrecognizable in a uniquely Jewish context. This is borne out by one observation and one *halachah.*

Our daily prayers consist mainly of praises of G-d, not petitions. The morning blessings and the paeans of *Pesukei Dezimra* contain no personal requests, but rather extol the qualities of the Creator. And the quintessential prayer, the *Shemoneh Esrei,* similarly values blessings of praise more than petitions, for while supplications predominate, the *halachah* is that if one fails to concentrate during the first blessings of praise, the entire *tefillah* must be repeated. This *halachah* applies to no other *berachah*, suggesting that the primary blessings are those of praise.

Furthermore, Rav Yosef Dov Soloveitchik once explained in the name of his grandfather, Rav Chaim Soloveitchik, that the loss of concentration referred to above means a lack of focus on the meaning of the words. If one's concentration is so deficient, however, that one is not even mindful that he or she is standing before G-d in prayer, then there is no act of *tefillah* at all — and the prayer requirement has not been fulfilled.

It would seem then that the purpose of *tefillah* is, ultimately, to stand before G-d and recite His praises. *Tefillah* thus affords us the thrice-daily opportunity to reiterate truisms about G-d, the world He created, and our place in it. We ask for our needs only insofar as they will facilitate our service of G-d. Paradoxically, the existence of our personal needs forces us to acknowledge G-d and makes us even more aware of His presence. It is therefore understandable that many *Rishonim* define *avodah shebeleiv* as "service of the intellect" and not "of the heart," because *tefillah* removes us from the world of the mundane and petty and brings us into the world of objective ideas and values, and the recognition of G-d.

Through the repetition of these ideas, we perfect our minds and souls, we learn "what G-d asks of us," and we become His beloved servants. It behooves us to appreciate the opportunity of prayer, to enhance our moments of prayer, and to beautify our places of prayer. Prayer is our link to the Divine Creator and His world of truth. Conducted properly, prayer ennobles our people and makes us worthy of His protective hand and ultimate redemption, speedily and in our days.

_____ *Rabbi Tobias Roth*

THERE IS A DIFFERENCE BETWEEN AN EVENT'S SEQUENCE AND ITS interpretation. This notion is illustrated through a verse in *Parshas Eikev*, which refers to the manna that the children of Israel began receiving four decades earlier. In the book of *Shemos* we read how the children of Israel were hungry and complained to Moshe, who brought their complaints before G-d. G-d had the heavens rain down manna from the sky, which should have impressed the young Jewish nation.

But the manna seemed to bring only trouble. The Jews went out to collect it on Shabbos when they were told explicitly not to; they took more than their share and it rotted; they complained that they were bored of it and asked for meat. Questions abound. Why did the Jewish people have to complain for food before G-d provided it for them? Why did they disregard instructions on how to deal with it? Why were they not grateful for it? Why did they beg for meat?

The text offers no interpretations of these events as they unfold. Only forty years later, in Moshe's final message to the Jewish people, does he offer some insight into this strange bread: "[G-d] made it difficult for you and made you go hungry; then he fed you the manna which you did not know of and your fathers did not know of, in order to show you that man does not live by bread alone, but man lives by everything that comes from G-d's mouth."

The purpose of the manna was not mere physical sustenance. It was provided — after a waiting period — as a builder of character, to see if the children of Israel had it in them to rely only on G-d. In this area they struggled. Still, why does Moshe wait forty years to reveal the manna's deeper implications?

Because the Jewish people would not have understood these implications without experiencing them. Manna, Moshe tells the children of Israel, was a substance for which "you could find no parallel in your own past experience, nor in that of your forefathers," writes Rav Samson Raphael Hirsch. Without a frame of reference, the Jewish people could not have appreciated G-d's message. The *interpretation* of the manna could come only after its entire *sequence* was played out, after forty years of wandering in the wilderness with only G-d to protect them and provide for them.

Many of us have the tendency to predict the aftermath of an event immediately after it happens. Whether any of these prophetic pronouncements will come to pass remains to be seen. But if history has taught us anything, it is that they will be minimally true at best. Once we understand and accept that only time will confirm an interpretation with which we wish to color an event, is there anything we can say with certainty?

Only the conclusion that Moshe reached after explaining the manna: "Remember the L-rd your G-d, for He is the One Who gives you strength."

<hr>

"**A**ND IT WILL BE, IF YOU HEARKEN DILIGENTLY TO MY COMMANDS that I command you today to love Hashem your G-d and to serve Him with all your heart and with all your soul. Then I will give the rain of your land in its time, the early rain and the late rain, and you will gather in your grain and your wine and your oil."

These verses indicate that our service of Hashem "with all our heart and soul" will cause our agricultural efforts — and by extension, all our materialistic toil — to be blessed with success. The *mishnah* in *Avos* emphasizes this ideal: "Pleasing is Torah with *derech eretz* [a wordly occupation], for the efforts of both causes sin to be forgotten. And any Torah that is not accompanied by work will become nullified in the end and lead to sin."

In the Talmud, Rabbi Yishmael champions this position. "*Hanheig bahem minhag derech eretz* — Combine them [words of Torah] with a worldly occupation." This simple strategy presents an incredible challenge. For Torah study, according to Rav Chaim Volozhin, must be your pursuit during all free moments, and Torah ethics must be reflected in all of your conduct as you are pursuing your livelihood.

Nonetheless, Rabbi Yishmael's view is forcefully challenged by Rabbi Shimon bar Yochai. "Is it possible," he asks, for one to be beholden to the agricultural cycle of plowing, sowing, harvesting, and processing and still have time to study properly? "What will become of Torah?!" cries Rabbi Shimon bar Yochai.

Which view do we accept? Abaye remarks that many followed Rabbi Yishmael and succeeded, while many followed Rabbi Shimon bar Yochai and did not succeed. And Rava, the Talmud informs us, told his students to look after their livelihoods during the planting and harvest seasons and not report to the study hall.

Parshas Eikev / 285

The Rambam, as interpreted by many Sages, maintains that the view of Rabbi Yishmael is the approach for the majority of people. Nonetheless, a select few, who understand the sacrifices and responsibilities entailed, may opt for the view of Rabbi Shimon bar Yochai and expect to be supported by the community as they dedicate themselves to the study of Torah.

That is our situation today: a majority of working Torah Jews combined with a cadre of Torah scholars. It behooves us to stress to the world of Rabbi Shimon bar Yochai how much respect is needed for the world of Rabbi Yishmael. As one of the greatest sages of *Eretz Yisrael* commented to one of his contemporaries after listening to him tell a group of yeshiva students that their studies during the war put them, too, on the front lines: "*Richtig. Aber ich bin zicher as zei dafen nit goimel benchin nochen milchamah* — You're right. But I'm sure they don't have to *bench 'Gomel'* after the war."

It is also our obligation to educate and persuade the world of Rabbi Yishmael to appreciate how crucial it is for *Klal Yisrael* to have the world of Rabbi Shimon bar Yochai. The phenomenal growth of *kollelim* across the country has strengthened each and every community by raising the general level of observance and learning. Moreover, we must reject any camp that sees only its own point of view and refuses to acknowledge the validity of other positions. Our Sages recognized and appreciated both points of view.

_____ *Rabbi Michael D. Shmidman*

PARSHAS EIKEV BEGINS ON A HIGH NOTE. "*AND IT WILL BE,* IF YOU listen to these judgments and you observe and do them .... [G-d] will love you and bless you and multiply you."

Our Sages tell us that this opening word, "*Vehayah* — And it will be," portends good news. It therefore follows that joy and happiness await those who hearken to and observe the ordinances of the Torah. Happiness does not result from being free to do whatever one wants, with no thought to the consequences and absolved of accountability. This type of behavior may give one a charge, a quick high — but not a joy of lasting significance. Good times don't always bring about happy days.

"*Vehayah eikev tishme'un* — And it will be, if you listen": What is the source of happiness? Listening to G-d's instruction, following a course of discipline that fulfills a Divinely mandated responsibility. When our behavior is true to our calling, based on our potential and talent, when we make meaningful contributions to society — then we experience real, lasting happiness.

Rashi provides another insight into the joy of *mitzvos,* based on another interpretation of the word *eikev.* "If you heed the lighter commandments — those that people tread upon with their heel (*akavav*)." In many instances of everyday life, in so many facets of human relations, we neglect or simply fail to see opportunities that make life more pleasant, more satisfying, more enriching, more ennobling — because we fail to recognize the importance of what we could have done.

How many of these possible and potential "lighter" *mitzvos* have we tread upon during the past year? Think of the telephone calls we should have made, the thank-you notes we should have written, the visits we should have taken, the classes we should have attended, the *minyanim* we should have prayed with.

These are some of the *mitzvos kalos* that we so often neglect, but from which we could reap such great rewards of satisfaction, joy and camaraderie if we only paid them more attention. If you want to bring joy into your life and the lives of others, listen to and perform those simple *mitzvos* that we tend to tread upon, that we think of as insignificant and thus don't give the proper due.

Along the same lines, there are *mitzvos* that have "footsteps behind them." We often fail to realize that good deeds bring about results well after the time that the good deed is performed. A *mitzvah* may have long-lasting consequences. Bring a new person to *shul,* invite a newcomer for a Shabbos meal — the ramifications may last forever. Look at lasting friendships that are the result of one act of kindness or one simple introduction.

We often refer to *ikvasa demeshicha* — the footsteps of *Mashiach* — to describe our times. We feel redemption coming closer. If we live a life of "*Vehayah eikev tishme'un*" in all its many facets, we hope to hear soon and in our time the footsteps of *Mashiach.*

פרשת ראה
Parshas Re'eih

_____ *Rabbi Yitzchok Rosenberg*

PARSHAS RE'EIH BEGINS WITH MOSHE'S UNEQUIVOCAL DECLARATION to the Jewish nation: "See I place before you this day a blessing and a curse. The blessing, if you listen to the commands of the L-rd your G-d ...." Presented with such a clear-cut contrast, why is it that so many of our people choose to cast aside the blessing to forgo the benefits and rewards of the Torah?

Among the many *mitzvos* outlined in this *parshah* is the *mitzvah* of *maaser sheini*. Unlike the other portions of one's produce which were separated and given away — to the *kohein*, the *leivi*, the poor — this tithe was brought to Yerushalayim and eaten there by its owner. But what about the farmer who lived a great distance from the Holy City and could not transport all his food there? How was he to fulfill his obligation?

The Torah provides for him too: "*Vechi yirbeh mimcha haderech ki lo suchal se'eiso ki yirchak mimcha hamakom* — If the journey is too long for you, for you are not able to carry [your burden], for the place is too far from you," the *pasuk* commands, "*Venasatah bakasef, vetzartah hakesef beyadcha, vehalachta el hamakom* — Then you shall exchange it for money and bind the money in your hand and go to the place that the L-rd your G-d will choose." There, in Yerushalayim, he could use the money to purchase other food to substitute for his own.

The Arizal offers a novel interpretation, pertinent to modern times, by rendering these two verses thus: "*Vechi yirbeh mimcha haderech*" — If the path of Torah and *mitzvos* becomes distant to you; *"ki lo suchal se'eiso"* — for you are unable to bear its burden; *"ki yirchak mimcha hamakom"* — for the Eternal G-d seems far from you; *"venasatah bakasef"* — then it is evident that you have given yourself over to materialism.

What then is the remedy for one stuck in this predicament? *"Ve-tzarta hakesef beyadcha"* — bind the materialism in your hand, reestablish your mastery over the material world; *"vehalachta el Hamakom"* — and walk toward the Eternal G-d. Once you have reasserted yourself against the physical world and not allowed yourself to be swallowed up by it, you will be able to travel toward G-d and follow the path of Torah and *mitzvos.*

Elul is a month during which Hashem is compared to a king who walks through the fields visiting his subjects. It is a time when the king is most approachable, when supplications are most acceptable. No appointment necessary.

Elul is also a month during which we turn inward for introspection and change. As we approach the new year, what better time to bind the materialism in our hands, to reestablish our dominance over our possessions, to reorient our priorities —*"vehalachta el Hamakom"* — and travel along the path of Torah and *mitzvos* toward the Eternal G-d.

_____ *Rabbi Elchonon Zohn*

THE *PARSHAH* BEGINS WITH MOSHE'S ARTICULATION OF THE CHOICE and challenge facing each member of *Klal Yisrael,* "See, I place before you today blessing and curse." Moshe then adds, "The blessing, that you will listen to the commands of Hashem your G-d; and the curse, if you will not listen to the commands of Hashem your G-d."

These words are not only simple cause-and-effect, if you listen, then you will be blessed, but literal, explains Rav Samson Raphael Hirsch and the *Ohr Hachaim.* Moshe Rabbeinu is defining the blessing as Torah observance, and the curse as abandonment of Torah values.

Moreover, Moshe's message contains much more than definitions of blessing and curse. By using the word *Re'eih* — See — Moshe informs us of our capacity to perceive his words as a visual reality. Seeing is believing. We can learn a Torah concept and see its blessing, and we can hear an opinion contrary to Torah and sense its inherent curse, as if the blessing and curse were unfolding before our eyes.

"Who is a wise man?" The Talmud tells us, "One who can see the future." Why does one actually have to see the future to be wise? Wouldn't knowing the future be just as enlightening?

Rav Mordechai Gifter explains. A man is deciding whether or not to take his umbrella with him as he leaves his home. He knows that the forecast is for rain. He looks out the window and sees that it is dark and overcast, but not yet raining, and the thought of carrying around an umbrella, coupled with the memory of all the umbrellas he's left on trains, deters him from taking one. Nevertheless, if he walks outside and sees a few drops of rain on the front steps, he will go back inside and fetch the umbrella. Visual perception makes all the difference.

Many times we can predict the future, but if we can't visualize it we won't act upon that knowledge. Moshe tells us *Re'eih,* we are capable of this level of perception when equating blessing and curse with acceptance and rejection of a Torah way of life. A beautiful illustration of this is found in the verse, "You are children of Hashem your G-d; do not cut yourselves and do not make a bald spot between your eyes for the dead." The first part of this verse provides the rationale for the second part, the prohibition against self-mutilation.

Can one be so devastated by the loss of a loved one, so filled with a sense of abandonment and dread for the future that he is driven to mutilate himself? Certainly one might. However, when one lives with a visual perception of Hashem as a loving parent, both to him and the deceased, he could not harm himself. How blessed is one who sees his relationship with Hashem in such a way. What a blessing it is to feel such comfort, trust and security at the most despairing moments of life.

Later in the *parshah* we are commanded to tithe our produce. Our Sages tell us, "*Aseir bishvil shetisasheir* — Tithe so that you will become wealthy." This wealth, explains Rav Shimon Schwab, *zt"l,* based on a comment by the Rambam, follows the *mishnah* in *Avos:* "Who is wealthy? He who is content with his lot." By giving to others through tithing, one develops a contentment that is the blessing of true wealth.

Many of us look for *berachos* from *tzaddikim*. That certainly has its place and value. But let us remember that the ultimate *berachah* is available to us by listening to the Torah, observing its *mitzvos* and living by its values. We also have the ability to see the inherent blessing even in the Torah's most esoteric concepts. The key is, "that you will listen."

_____ *Rabbi Avraham Feigelstock*

I N *PARSHAS RE'EIH*, G-D TELLS THE JEWISH PEOPLE, "SEE, I PUT BEFORE you today blessing and curse." The blessing will go to those who keep the Torah and its *mitzvos*. The curse, G-d forbid, will affect those who do not heed the Torah. G-d uses the term *see*, and not the term *listen*. One might have expected G-d to say, "*Listen*, I will explain to you how to achieve blessing and avoid curse." Why does G-d say, "*Re'eih* — See"?

Our Rabbis teach that hearing can not be compared to seeing. When a person hears something, he does not always believe it. Perhaps he didn't hear clearly or the message was not passed to him accurately. He can challenge that which he heard.

But unlike hearing, seeing is absolute. A person who sees something accepts it as fact. He sees it with his own eyes and can not deny it. If you tell him it isn't true, he will insist that it is.

All too often we coast through life without focusing on the reason for our existence. We fail to give meaning and purpose to our lives. G-d, therefore, chooses His words carefully, instructing us, "See" — focus and comprehend — "I have put before you blessing." Understand what will bring blessing, purpose and meaning to your lives. Discover challenges and opportunities in life that will be beneficial to you. If you look carefully, you will find meaning in life.

Another lesson is learned from the phrase "that *I* put before you today." The word *I* is written *anochi,* an uncommon term. The word *ani* is most often used. Why then did G-d choose to use the word *anochi* here?

Because *anochi* reminds us of the first of the Ten Commandments, which begins "*Anochi Hashem Elokecha* — I am Hashem your G-d." G-d began by introducing Himself to the Jews as the G-d Who delivered us from Egypt. With these words He assured us that wherever a Jew might be, even in exile, G-d is there together with him and will ultimately redeem him from his suffering. There is Divine providence in the world and G-d will never forsake His people.

Additional significance is found in the word *nosein,* translated above as "put." G-d puts the opportunity for blessing and curse before us and allows us to choose. But *nosein* stems from the word *matanah,* a gift. If we focus carefully on all that happens to us during our lifetimes, we will recognize all the gifts we have received from G-d. Even the challenges of life are gifts given to us as opportunities to elevate ourselves and grow to greater spiritual heights.

G-d stresses that He has put this knowledge "before us," indicating that we are in control of our individual and collective destinies. It is we who determine what our future will be. Will it be a blessing or, G-d forbid, a curse?

It all depends upon how we perceive life. If we take the challenges that are presented to us as opportunities to grow spiritually, then our lives become a blessing. But if we view events from a negative perspective, seeing any inconvenience as an unwelcome burden, then life becomes a curse.

G-d teaches us how to maintain this positive attitude that will bring blessing to our lives. He said, "See, I put before you *today* blessing and curse." All too often we become overwhelmed by all the challenges that we have to take on and all the obstacles that we must overcome. G-d gives us sound advice: *hayom* — today! Take it one day at a time. Focus on each day's challenges and you will not become overwhelmed. But do keep focused and never allow the truth to fade away.

_____ *Rabbi Moshe Stern*

DESCRIBING, IN *PARSHAS RE'EIH,* THE *MITZVAH* OF GIVING CHARITY TO the poor, the Torah tells us, "You shall surely give him, and your heart should not feel bad when you give him." Why would the Torah suspect that one *would* feel bad upon helping a poor person? How can doing a *mitzvah* leave a bad taste in one's mouth? What causes such a reaction? More important, how can we avoid having such feelings ourselves?

In the *mishnah* in *Avos*, Rabbi Shimon said, "If three have eaten at the same table and have not spoken words of Torah, it is as if they have eaten of offerings to the dead idols." Obviously, such a gathering mandates that words of Torah be exchanged. If a person eats alone or even with someone else, the *Chasam Sofer* explains, it is possible that neither one has any Torah knowledge. But with three people at the table, surely one is capable of explaining some point in the Torah to the others. How then is it possible that no one speaks words of Torah at such a gathering?

In answering, the *Chasam Sofer* points to a Talmudic passage that discusses the composition of the *Birkas Hamazon,* which these three will say at the conclusion of their meal. The first blessing was instituted by Moshe Rabbeinu, the second blessing was instituted by Yehoshua, the third blessing was instituted by Kings David and Shlomo, and the fourth and final blessing was instituted by the Men of the Great Assembly at Yavneh.

We do indeed presume, says the *Chasam Sofer,* that one of these three at the table is familiar with this statement of the Talmud. Thus, he reasons, inasmuch as the *Birkas Hamazon* contains all elements of Torah — Moshe's blessing representing *Chumash;* Yehoshua's blessing representing *Neviim;* David and Shlomo's blessing representing *Kesuvim;* and the final blessing representing the Oral Tradition — what need is there to add other words of Torah?

It is due to this laxity that their meal is so poorly judged. This laxity is what can cause one to dislike the *mitzvos.* Those who seek to circumvent any aspect of observance will ultimately find their observance trivialized. People who seek to avoid doing *mitzvos* or look for loopholes are the same people who, when they actually do the *mitzvah,* do so half-heartedly, feeling bad in the process.

Even when it comes to something as natural as giving to the poor, a person who has not properly trained himself in the proper performance of *mitzvos* may find that he resents helping out. We must encourage and educate ourselves to do more, not less, which will result in our enhanced enjoyment of the *mitzvos.*

פרשת שופטים
Parshas Shoftim

_____ *Rabbi Yaacov Haber*

ACH OF US HAS STOOD, AT DIFFERENT POINTS IN OUR LIVES, ON THE threshold of a great endeavor. Whether entering a marriage or a new career or the lifetime commitment of parenthood, we become at such times very thoughtful, resolving to build a home of charity and peace, to find fulfillment in the workplace, to "always be there" for the children.

Then something happens. Reality sets in and the demands of the moment cloud our view of the big picture. The nitty-gritty of life overwhelms us. We find ourselves asking, What happened to this marriage, this job, these children? Where did I go wrong?

The conflict between idealism and reality is as old as the ancient kings of Israel, who provide a telling image in *Parshas Shoftim.* G-d commands the king of Israel to carry a *Sefer Torah* with him wherever he goes. The nation's leader can never be seen without the Torah close to his heart. When he convenes his ministry and meets with his officers, he must have his Torah with him. As he marches onto the battlefield, he must carry his Torah. Even as he strolls through the marketplace, the king must never be separated from his Torah.

But that's not all. The king of Israel is commanded to keep a second *Sefer Torah* locked away in his treasury, never to be seen with him. A curious *halachah*? No, a fitting solution to a practical problem. Since the king carries his Torah everywhere, the air and elements he exposes it to take their toll. Gradually, letters crack, fade, fall off. So slow is this process that the king may not realize that the Torah he is carrying is not the same one he set out with at the start of his reign.

G-d tells the king, therefore, Don't rely on this Torah alone. Keep a pristine copy in the treasury, not to be exposed to the winds and wars of life. Let its characters remain intact. While your cradled Torah fades and cracks, your treasured Torah will stay sharp and flawless. From time to time, the king is told, bring your public Torah into your inner chambers. Open both and put them side by side on a table. Don't just compare them, correct them. Review and renew your standards. Do not allow the faded Torah to become the standard for you and your people.

This check-and-correct process applies to us today as well. Every one of us fashions a set of principles, a personal *Sefer Torah* by which to live, unbiased and untainted by the winds and wars of life. But as we go through life, our principles begin to fade, crack and fall apart. So the Torah gives us good advice: Go back into your inner chamber for reflection. Compare and correct. Life is full of challenges and pitfalls, and we're only human. But our original standard is Divine and is to be treasured and called upon for review and renewal, enabling us to go out once again with the clarity of our youth.

The *kabbalists* teach that first thoughts are holy. Inscribe those idealistic thoughts not on parchment, but on your heart. Treasure them, refer to them, for in them lies the secret to G-dliness and growth.

_____ *Rabbi Alan Kalinsky*

I T IS APPROPRIATE THAT THE *PARSHAH* OF *SHOFTIM*, THE *PARSHAH* OF Jewish leadership, is read during the month of Elul, the month of *teshuvah.* An understanding and appreciation of the roles and responsibilities of leadership enable our desire to come closer to Hashem and empower us to rededicate ourselves to His service.

The *parshah* begins with the command to establish a judicial system and "*Tzeddek, tzeddek tirdof,*" to "pursue perfect honesty," in the words of Rav Aryeh Kaplan, *zt"l,* it is not enough to rely on the rulings of a judicial system; the whole nation must be involved in the pursuit of justice for society to function correctly.

We as a people have been blessed throughout our history with leaders who have had vision, determination and compassion, whose concern for fellow Jews set an example for their fellow Jews and brought the nation closer to G-d and His Torah.

The Torah then describes for us the laws and purpose of the monarchy. What is the king's role?

As soon as the land of Israel was conquered and settled, the Jewish people were responsible to fulfill the command, "Appoint over yourselves a king whom the L-rd your G-d will choose." "Over yourselves," the Talmud explains, denotes "that his fear shall be upon you." The Jews have a responsibility to show honor and respect for their king and his position, for he keeps the nation from being "a flock without a shepherd."

Nevertheless, the Torah warns, he may not overindulge himself with too many possessions or too many wives, "so that they will not turn his heart away" from his Divine mission. The king's position makes him the supreme role model for the Jewish people, a role he and they have to safeguard.

For this reason, the king is also commanded to write for himself two *Sifrei Torah,* one which he carried with him at all times and one which he kept in his treasury. "And he will read from [the Torah] all the days of his life in order that he will learn to fear the L-rd his G-d, to guard all the words of this Torah... to do them." This verse, says the *Sifri,* informs us that study leads to fear of G-d, which in turn leads to service and performance of *mitzvos.* By continually reviewing the Torah, the king reminds himself daily that he does not possess supreme power, but serves at the pleasure of the Divine King of kings. He thus sets an example for the entire nation.

In our time, one need not be a king to follow the Torah and serve as a role model. Jewish leadership requires individuals who live a proper Torah lifestyle, who pursue perfect honesty, and who can transmit our sacred values to those who do not yet possess them. Such individuals are especially needed in our times when American Jewish leadership is challenged by the tremendous inroads that assimilation and intermarriage have made within our community.

The concern that our ancestors had, that the Jewish people would have a king just like the nations that surrounded them, echoes once again in Jewish history. We have the benefit of the experiences of those who came before us and we must utilize their examples to ensure that all our actions and motives are directed by Hashem's Torah. In doing so, we will create in the years ahead Jewish leaders who will be able to bring about the final redemption of our people.

_____ *Rabbi Melvin Granatstein*

P ARSHAS SHOFTIM BEGINS WITH THE JEWISH NATION'S OBLIGATION TO appoint judges and officers, establishing requirements for the governance of the Jewish polity. The Torah presents the overall requirement to execute true justice. Not only shall you "not pervert justice, show favoritism and take bribes," but, in a positive vein, "Justice, justice shall you pursue."

Why is the word *tzeddek,* justice, repeated in this refrain? Rashi writes that this repetition instructs us to "seek after the most competent court." In other words, justice is a qualitative value. Not only must we seek a just and honest verdict, but we also must be sure that the court's deliberations are of the highest standards. The results must be just, and the process producing those results must be just, too. As Reb Menachem Mendel of Kotsk sums up, the doubling of *tzeddek* teaches that both means and ends must be honest and fair.

In this spirit we can understand why bribery is forbidden even if its purpose is to see that justice be done. For even if a bribe does not pervert the verdict, it clearly perverts and invalidates the process.

Included in this theme of government is the *mitzvah* of appointing a king. The Torah states, "When you say, 'I want to appoint a king over myself as is the custom of the nations around me,' you shall indeed designate a king whom G-d will choose." There are many ambiguities here. Is the Torah making kingship obligatory or optional? The Rambam adopts the position that it is obligatory to appoint a king. But if it is obligatory, why does it have to await "when you will say I want to appoint a king"?

The Netziv in his *Haameik Davar* explains: "The governance of the state turns upon whether it is to be a monarchy or a state governed by the consent of the nation and her elected representatives .... This matter can not be determined by the force of a positive commandment." Rather, the Netziv insists, the designation of a king depends upon the consent of the nation and the nature of government generally. This explains why three hundred years pass after the death of Yehoshua before a king is appointed over Israel.

The requirement for the consent of the governed should not be viewed as disconnected from the initial issues dealt with in our *parshah*. On the contrary, this demonstrates the Torah's insistence upon both lawful process and result, both means and end. "Justice, justice shall you pursue" is both a juridical requirement in the Jewish polity and an administrative requirement.

The Jewish state is not to be built upon force but rather on lawful consent. What this means for us is that Jewish communal conduct must be imbued with a sensibility that respects civilized process, values persons and contends appropriately with the autonomy of every Jew. This path assures that not only are our goals from the Torah, but even our processes shed luster upon the Torah.

_____ *Rabbi Mark Cohn*

PARSHAS SHOFTIM DISCUSSES THE APPOINTMENT OF A KING OVER *Eretz Yisrael*. Unlike most national rulers, our king must refrain from indulging in the excesses common to his contemporaries. The Torah teaches, "Only he will not have too many horses ... and he will not have too many wives ... and he shall not greatly increase gold and silver for himself." The reason given by the Torah for these prohibitions is in order that he should remain humble, lest he forget that even a Jewish king is still a servant of G-d.

Obviously, this *mitzvah* can only be performed when the Jewish people have returned, in their entirety, to *Eretz Yisrael*. Yet, there remains a beautiful lesson that applies to this day. The *Sheim Meshmuel* explains that every person has the spirituality of an entire world within him or herself. It is the job of each of us to rule over that world and to protect that potential spiritual growth. This world comprises the body, the spirit and the intelligence — all three of which are referred to in the *parshah*.

The king's need to limit his wealth corresponds to the individual's need to control his intellect. Just as money is only a means and not an end in itself, so, too, intellect is a tool to be used for spiritual wisdom and understanding, not something to be exercised for any purpose.

The prohibition against horses corresponds to a need to control the spirit of man, the source of arrogance. As we learn in *Avos,* "Be exceedingly humble in spirit." (The Torah is warning us not to "get on our high horse"!)

Finally, the king's limitation on wives shows a need to control the desires of the body. Every individual must control his physical desires, lest he become consumed by them and drawn away from G-d.

The Torah not only gives the king these prohibitions but also gives him one more *mitzvah* to help him avoid falling into the trap of excess: "And he shall write two copies of this Torah ... and it shall be with him and he shall read from it all the days of his life, so that he will learn to fear Hashem, his G-d, to observe all the words of this Torah and these decrees and do them."

This timeless directive applies to us all. In order to avoid the temptations of the body, spirit and intellect, it is essential that every individual Jew dedicate himself to the study of Torah. For, in the words of the *parshah,* only through the study of Torah will one "learn to fear Hashem ... observe all the words of the Torah ... to do them."

May it be the will of *Hakadosh Baruch Hu* that we all live our lives with the understanding that we are all like kings, shapers of our own spiritual destinies, and that, like kings, we must be careful to keep our priorities straight and our mission clear.

פרשת כי תצא
Parshas Ki Seitzei

_____ *Rabbi Yitzchok Adler*

T O A GENERATION SUCH AS OURS, A GENERATION ENGAGED IN A FIERCE
battle against the forces of acculturation, assimilation and intermarriage, the opening passages of *Parshas Ki Seitzei* seem antithetical.
The Torah teaches the procedure for a Jewish soldier to consummate
his desire for an *eishes yefas to'ar,* a non-Jewish woman captured in war.

What's going on here? While synagogues and outreach centers are
spending untold sums of money to protect the integrity of the modern
Jewish family, *Parshas Ki Seitzei* opens with a Torah-sponsored avenue
for a weary Jewish man to marry a non-Jewish woman. Is battle fatigue
a justifiable excuse for welcoming a non-Jew into the traditional Jewish
home? Has the Torah conceded defeat in the face of passion?

My rosh yeshiva, Rabbi Meir Belsky, addressed this very concern
twenty-five years ago, long before "continuity" was the mantra of Jewish organizations. He used the example of *eishes yefas to'ar* to illustrate
what can happen when a Jew — even an observant and dedicated Jew
— seeks special accommodations for his unique needs. He spoke of
those Jews who are "looking for a *heter.* "

How a question is asked, when it is asked, to whom it is asked and by
whom it is asked all weigh in on the answer one receives. To any given
question, many reasonable answers are possible, even acceptable. The
Torah is not a monolith, bereft of flexibility. Rather, *Halachah* provides for
similiar cases, a polyglot of options, that work together to create a structure within which the Jewish community is expected to live and prosper.

Sometimes one seeks the counsel of great rabbis because he does not know what to do. Other times, one knows exactly what he wants to do but needs a *heter* in order to proceed. This *parshah* of the *eishes yefas to'ar* tells the story of a soldier who knows precisely the proper thing to do but seeks permission to do what he believes is tolerable under his specific circumstances. Still, his actions have consequences.

Rashi notes the sequence of the *parshah*. It opens with this *halachah*, then proceeds immediately to the law of the firstborn son of a wife who is hated, and then to the law of the rebellious son. Rashi comments that the last two situations result directly from the sanctioning of the first. The lack of love between parents and the rebellion of a child stem from a marriage that never should have happened. Had this battle-fatigued soldier sought support from within the disciplines of tradition rather than from a special dispensation given in the spirit of compassion and tolerance, his long term well-being would have been infinitely more secure and satisfying. His determination to be in total control — to seek the *heter* he desired — planted the seed of his ultimate unhappiness.

It is important for every Jew to have a close and meaningful relationship with a mentor who is a scholar. The mentor's role is not only to tell the student what he wants to hear but what he needs to hear. In seeking spiritual guidance, a Jew is mandated to pursue truth and wholesomeness. To do so, he must not attempt to sway the verdict in favor of his preferred answer. This does not mean that there is only one correct answer to every question. What it does mean, though, is that in order for the answer to be proper, the conditions under which it is asked must also be proper.

_____ *Rabbi Joseph Eisen*

THE AMMONITE AND MO'AVITE MAY NEVER ENTER THE JEWISH NATION says the Torah, "because they did not greet you with bread and water on your way out of Egypt, and because they hired Bilam ... to curse you." The commentaries find perplexing the combination of these two reasons for banning these nations from the Jewish people forever.

Why does the Torah first list the seemingly lesser of these two evils? Furthermore, how can the Torah hold Ammon and Mo'av accountable for not extending their land and hospitality to *Klal Yisrael,* who was, at the time, their archenemy?

To understand the severity of Ammon and Mo'av's action, the Ramban points out, one must remember that they owed an enormous debt of gratitude to the Jewish nation. Only through the merit of Avraham Avinu did Lot and his two daughters — the mothers of Ammon and Mo'av — escape the total destruction of Sodom and Amorrah. Ammon and Mo'av owed their very existence to our Patriarch, Avraham, and hence, to his descendants.

Ammon and Mo'av were obligated to recognize and appreciate their legacy. By not extending the most common decency, by not providing bread and water to starving men, women and children, people to whom they owed their lives, they revealed their essence: they were consummate ingrates. Their character trait of ungratefulness must be rejected and never be integrated into the Jewish nation. Hatred, even attempts at annihilation, can eventually be eradicated. But ingratitude is a character flaw in wicked people which can rarely be altered.

When Avraham Avinu was charting the destiny of the Jewish people, he sent his emissary, Eliezer, to his own family to find an appropriate match for his son, Yitzchak. The reason, explains Rav Avraham Pam, is because *midos tovos,* good character traits, are inherited through family.

Given the proper atmosphere and education, philosophical errors and lack of commitment can be reversed. However, good *midos* — such as *hakaras hatov,* recognizing acts of kindness — are an integral part of one's soul.

In preparation for the High Holy Days, let us try to develop this outstanding *midah* of *hakaras hatov,* which will bring us closer to our fellow men and to Hashem.

_____ *Rabbi Ephraim Kanarfogel*

PARSHAS KI SEITZEI, WITH ITS PANOPLY OF 74 *MITZVOS* (MORE THAN ANY other single *parshah*), affords us an excellent opportunity to review the way that we categorize *mitzvos.* Typically, we distinguish between *mitzvos bein adam lachaveiro* (concerning man and his neighbor) and *mitzvos bein adam Lamakom* (concerning man and G-d). Or, one could say, between those *mitzvos* that are also expressions of basic morality, and those whose sole motivation is Divine imperative.

These distinctions have their roots in venerable rabbinic sources and are quite useful. Nonetheless, we sometimes tend to employ these distinctions too sharply. For example, most would consider charity to be a classic *mitzvah bein adam lachaveiro.*

The *Sefer Hachinuch* argues, however, that this *mitzvah* has significant *bein adam Lamakom* dimensions. Had the Almighty wished to distribute the resources and assets of His world in a perfectly equitable manner so that all people would have equal amounts, He certainly could have done so. Rather, the Almighty wished to inculcate within His people the great importance of doing acts of kindness and showing compassion to others. Thus, charity clearly has an aspect of *bein adam Lamakom* as well.

Two *mitzvos* in *Ki Seitzei* can also be understood in this manner. The requirement to build a *maakeh,* a porch or parapet, around a flat roof so that "you should not cause bloodshed in your home," lest someone fall off, would appear to be a *mitzvah bein adam lachaveiro.* Yet, in putting up a *maakeh,* one recites a blessing, and the Rambam indicates that one does not make a blessing on any *mitzvah* that is *bein adam lachaveiro.* This would suggest that a *maakeh* is not exclusively in this category.

This may be because once the roof is complete, even before people are actually able to go up on it, the Torah commands that a *maakeh* be erected. It would be insufficient to simply prevent anyone from going on the roof. The requirement of a *maakeh* is not just to protect people; it fulfills a Divine imperative, which sensitizes us even further.

Similarly, the *mitzvah* of maintaining honest weights and measures would seem to be a simple case of treating fellow humans fairly. But it is juxtaposed with the story of Amaleik's attack on Israel, and the Midrash notes a connection — if a person is dishonest in business, he exposes himself to attack.

The Netziv wonders about this connection. How could Amaleik be the symbolic punishment for corrupt weights and measures if the Jews did not engage in any commerce while in the desert?

The Netziv explains that one who cheats in weights and measures does not do so for personal gain. Rather, he manifests a lack of faith in the Almighty by expressing doubt that Hashem supports and sustains people according to His will. The Talmud even suggests that this is a form of idolatry.

Amaleik attacked the Jewish people because they expressed doubts about whether the Almighty would continue to sustain them in the desert — the same sin that a dishonest businessman engages in. This sin is another example of how a *mitzvah bein adam lachaveiro* is, at its root, a *mitzvah bein adam Lamakom,* and demonstrates once again how observing even those *mitzvos* that appear to be simple rules of social conduct achieves the highest levels of Divine service.

_____ *Rabbi Bertram Leff*

IN REFERENCE TO WAR, THE TORAH EMPHASIZES THE WORD *MACHANEH,* camp. The Torah commands, "When you go out to encamp against your enemies, you shall guard against anything evil ... for Hashem, your G-d, walks in the midst of your camp to rescue you and to deliver your enemies before you so that your camp shall be holy."

Rav Yosef Dov Soloveitchik, *zt"l,* distinguishes between *machaneh,* camp, and *eidah,* congregation. Camp and congregation are two distinct sociological phenomena. A camp is formed in the face of a common enemy, who engenders fear and creates the need for self-defense. "When you go out to encamp against your enemies" — the camp is established when people feel helpless and must join together to battle the enemy.

An *eidah,* a congregation, on the other hand, shares a common ideology, and is nourished by love rather than fear. A congregation expresses man's powerful spirit. In a Jewish context, the *eidah* is grounded in the teachings of Sinai, a holy nation committed to a Divine destiny. In order for the nation of Israel to fulfill its Divine mission and destiny, "your camp shall become holy." This *machaneh,* this camp, must develop into an *eidah.* It must become holy.

It is this notion of encampment that unites the beginning of our *parshah,* "When you will go out to war against your enemies," with its conclusion, "Remember what Amaleik did to you .... Wipe out the memory of Amaleik from under the heavens — do not forget."

Throughout our history we have united as a camp against our enemies, the Amalekites of the world. But too often we have failed to advance from there to become a holy congregation. No doubt our unity in the face of Amaleik is part of our destiny. But, as the Rav defined it, it is a destiny of fate not a destiny of faith — not the destiny of an *eidah*.

Even when *eidah* overtakes *machaneh*, it is possible for that congregation to maintain a negative ideology, such as the Spies and the followers of Korach. Though formed for ill purposes, the Torah nonetheless refers to each of these groups as an *eidah*.

We must be vigilant to insure that our *eidah* is a holy *eidah*, with a Divine ideology, not one filled with the evil that destroys us. The Jewish community is concerned with the crisis of Jewish continuity. The solution is to unite not only as a *machaneh* but as an *eidah*, a holy congregation committed to the destiny of faith — a faith rooted in Torah and *mitzvos*. Such a covenant stems not from fear but from love, the love of G-d and the Jewish people.

פרשת כי תבוא
Parshas Ki Savo

_____ Rabbi Haskel Lookstein

THE TOCHACHAH, G-D'S STERN WARNING TO THE JEWISH PEOPLE OF what will befall them should they stray from His commands, appears twice in the Torah, first in *Parshas Bechukosai* and again in *Parshas Ki Savo.* This follows the ruling of the prophet Ezra, "that they read the curses in *Toras Kohanim* before Atzeres [Shavuos] and the ones in *Mishneh Torah* before Rosh Hashanah."

The link between the *Tochachah* and Shavuos — the anniversary of our acceptance of the Torah — is readily understandable. But what accounts for the connection between the *Tochachah* and the start of the new year?

The new year includes Yom Kippur, Rav Yosef Dov Soloveitchik, *zt"l,* notes, which is also *zeman matan Toraseinu* — it is the date on which Moshe brought down the second set of *luchos* from Sinai.

But there is a difference between the two *Tochachos,* Abaye points out in the Talmud *Megillah.* The first *Tochachah* is stated in the plural and delivered by Moshe from the mouth of G-d. The second *Tochachah* is stated in the singular and delivered by Moshe on his own. How is it that the second *Tochachah* was delivered independently by Moshe? *Tosafos* answers that he did so with *ruach hakodesh* — the words still came from G-d.

The Rav suggests another, textual answer. The *Tochachah* in *Ki Savo* concludes, "These are the words of the covenant... besides the covenant that was executed with [the Jewish people] at Choreiv." The *Tochachah* is referred to as a covenant between Israel and G-d, an oath taken by the Jewish people that they maintain the Torah in its entirety. When the second set of *luchos* was delivered to replace the first, they called for a new oath to be administered along with them.

In the first *Tochachah,* G-d establishes His covenant with all of Israel. Although Moshe delivered the words, G-d is considered to have administered the oath to the entire Jewish people — including Moshe. In the second *Tochachah,* however, Moshe made the covenant, one-on-one, with each member of *Klal Yisrael.* Though he did so with *ruach hakodesh,* he is considered to be the administrator of the oath.

There is another critical difference between the two *Tochachos.* The contents of the first *Tochachah* are fierce, sharp and awesome, yet end with words of hope, consolation and encouragement. Redemption will come. Despite the harshness, there will be a bright future.

The *Tochachah* in *Ki Savo* is radically different. There is no happy ending. Is one to conclude, therefore, that there is no hope? Will there be endless suffering? Will redemption never come?

The answer, says the Rav, is in *Parshas Nitzavim:* "And it will come to pass when all of these things will happen ... you will return to the L-rd your G-d ... and G-d will return the captives and have mercy on you." But why is this promise of hope and consolation postponed? Why is it not stated at the end of the *Tochachah* itself?

The Rav finds the answer in an insight of the Ramban. The *Tochachah* in *Bechukosai* presages the destruction of the First Temple, which drove the Jewish people into an exile lasting seventy years, as promised by the prophet Yirmiyahu. But the destruction of the Second Temple and its consequent exile came with no such promise. This is the curse of the second *Tochachah.* No time limit is provided. Israel will not be redeemed except through repentance, declares the Rambam. Yet the Torah does guarantee that we will, ultimately, repent "and you will return to the L-rd your G-d."

This is a further reason for reading the *Tochachah* now, as we observe the penitential season. We do *teshuvah* not merely for our own shortcomings, but also to hasten the redemption of all Israel. May we be successful this year in this dual mission for our personal benefit and for the well-being of the State of Israel and all the people of Israel.

A S WE APPROACH ROSH HASHANAH, THE DAY OF JUDGMENT, MANY of us begin a battle within ourselves. On the one hand, we understand intellectually the need to reflect on our lives and on our lifestyles. On the other hand, the inertia of our "being" curtails deep reflection and, consequently, often prevents change.

An insight offered in _Parshas Ki Savo_ provides an extra measure of motivation to become "new and improved" for the New Year. The Torah gives us 248 "positive" commandments and 365 "negative" commandments. While it is without question that we owe unswerving loyalty to each and every _mitzvah_, nonetheless, Hashem chose to emphasize certain _mitzvos_. In _Parshas Ki Savo_, Hashem proscribes twelve actions with the statements, "Cursed is the one who . . ."

Not only are these twelve actions prohibited, but the one who transgresses them carries the label "cursed"! The last of these curses is given to someone "who does not fortify the words of the Torah to ensure their fulfillment." In the Talmud Yerushalmi, Rabbi Shimon ben Tachlifa understands this verse to refer to the need to establish a _beis din,_ a religious court of justice.

The Ramban adds that fortification includes the establishment of a king and a _beis din_ who have the ability and the power to strengthen Torah observances among those who are not presently upholding its precepts.

The _beis din's_ role is amplified by a passage in the Talmud which explains that before each of these curses was stated to _Klal Yisrael,_ as they stood on Mount Grizim and Mount Eival, a blessing was given to those who fulfill these _mitzvos_. Not only does one fulfill a _mitzvah_ by observing these commands, but he is also labeled "blessed" by G-d.

The _Chafetz Chaim_ emphasizes the unique opportunity each Jew is presented in his own community. By generously supporting the day schools, yeshivos and _kollelim_ in one's community, one receives the badge of honor "blessed."

Moreover, this opportunity begets an awesome responsibility. We can and must reach out to all of our brethren who have not been fortunate enough to experience and explore the beauty of Torah and its way of life. We must support outreach organizations not just with our money, but also with our time and effort. We must bring our fellow Jews into our homes and show them the beauty of a Torah lifestyle.

With this badge of honor, the G-dly label of "blessed," as motivation, we can break the inertia of our "being" and take monumental strides toward fortifying the Torah and its observances among *acheinu bnei Yisrael.* We can then approach Rosh Hashanah with more hope that we will merit the seal of life.

_____ *Rabbi David Rebibo*

ONE OF THE HALLMARKS OF OUR TORAH IS ITS CAPACITY TO YIELD new meanings and fresh insights every week. In *Parshas Ki Savo,* after a description of the *mitzvah* of *bikkurim* — the first fruits that were brought to Jerusalem and given to the *kohein* — the verse concludes: "You shall rejoice in all the good that Hashem your G-d gave you and your family — you and the Levite and the proselyte in your midst."

We are expected to perform this *mitzvah* with joy and enthusiasm. But how can this be? How can the Torah order us to rejoice in performing any *mitzvah*? Happiness often comes spontaneously and is difficult to orchestrate. Is it that simple to be happy? Happiness is rare. Often, we witness people who have every reason to be happy, yet are not, and others who seem to be lacking, but are, in fact, happy.

The Rambam writes that by observing this *mitzvah* man becomes accustomed to acting generously, by sharing and learning to limit his desire for possessions. A person can reach this supreme goal only through an inner feeling of happiness and goodness of the heart. Likewise, a lack of happiness will cause him to forsake Hashem's will.

We mistakenly consider a happy life to be one without problems. Certainly happiness does not depend on the multiplication of material possessions. A man with three cars is not three times as happy as a man with one car.

Rav Zaks, in his work, *Zeved Tov,* reminds us that material wealth does not always bring blessings with it. At times, the opposite is true. Therefore, "you shall rejoice in all the good that Hashem your G-d gave you and your family — you and the Levite and the proselyte in your midst." By sharing one's bounty with the Levites and the needy, one can reach a state of happiness.

A true perspective on our possessions serves to remind us that they are given to us in trust, to use not only for our own pleasures but also in the service of others. The fact is that when we give, we give nothing that we ourselves have not already received.

_____ *Rabbi Mordechai Yehuda Tropp*

ASK ANY COMMITTED JEWISH TEENAGER HOW HE WOULD RESPOND TO A Holocaust denier and you will see him defending the absolute truth of events that he never witnessed. From where does this strength come?

Rav Yosef Dov Soloveitchik, *zt"l,* explains that the Jewish religious experience requires a consciousness of time. A slave is not attuned to the nuances of time's passage, because his time belongs to the will and whim of his master. A free person, however, observes time and masters its use for his own advancement.

In order to achieve this mastery, one must comprehend three dimensions of time: past, present and future. Thus, time awareness consists of retrospection, appreciation and anticipation.

Parshas Ki Savo repeats the *mitzvah* of delivering first fruits to the Holy Temple in Jerusalem and introduces a related *mitzvah, mikra bikkurim.* Upon presenting the *kohein* with his basket of fruits, the pilgrim recites a selection from our *parshah:*

> A wandering Aramean was my father, and he descended to Egypt.... And the Egyptians mistreated us and tormented us.... But we cried out to Hashem, G-d of our fathers...and He extracted us from Egypt with a strong Hand.... Then He brought us to this place, and he gave us this land, a land flowing with milk and honey. And now, behold I have brought the first fruits of the land that You, Hashem, have given me.

Then after this praise, the *Sefer Hachinuch* writes, he asks G-d to continue bestowing blessings upon him and his family.

This declaration amalgamates all three dimensions of time. It recalls the past straits of our nation with the story of our descent to Egypt; it acknowledges G-d's present benevolence to us in the Land of Israel with its lush produce; and it ends by beseeching Hashem to extend his blessings upon us in the future.

From this *mitzvah* we draw a stunning conclusion: the Torah *does* consider us capable of affirming the veracity of events that occurred to our forefathers thousands of years ago, even though we did not personally witness them. We can make this declaration because our collective Jewish memory comes alive. And in so doing, we increase our faith in Hashem and our fervor for His service.

Contemporary experience bears this out. The Rav viewed our binding cord to *Eretz Yisrael,* for example, as explicable only in terms of Jewish experiential memory.

Likewise, in his *shiurim,* the Rav would vividly dramatize the study of Talmud as an actual multigenerational meeting between the teacher, the class, the *Tanna'im,* the *Amora'im* and the *Rishonim.* Rashi and Rambam would argue their different views of Rav Yochanan's opinion. Rav Chaim Brisker would then arrive to defend Rambam from the severest attacks. Anyone who attended Rav Soloveitchik's *shiur* vividly recalls this confrontation of the sages.

This vivid Jewish memory sustains many segments of *Klal Yisrael.* One rabbi told me of his mother's recollections of her work in an umbrella factory more than fifty years ago. On Passover, her Jewish co-workers would bring in matzah sandwiches — with ham. They had forgotten *kashrus* but remembered Pesach. It is surely the children and grandchildren of such *Yidden* who return to the fold. As long as there is a sustained Jewish memory, there remains a spark of *Yiddishkeit* to ignite. Should these embers go out, G-d forbid, outreach becomes exponentially more difficult.

Those who are already Torah observant are equally challenged to make Moshe Rabbeinu, Rabbi Akiva and Sara Schenirer come alive to deliver their special messages to us in a vibrant and resonant way. Let us use the means we have to recognize and promote positive and substantive Jewish memories in ourselves as well as in our wandering Jewish brethren.

Through proper recognition of our past, we empower ourselves to use the present in order to pave the way for the glorious Jewish future that awaits us, as individuals and as a people. To quote the popular Jewish radio personality, Nachum Segal, "Remember the past, live the present and trust the future."

פרשת נצבים־וילך
Parshas Netzavim-Vayeilech

_____ *Rabbi David Algaze*

" **Y**OU ARE STANDING HERE TODAY, ALL OF YOU TO ENTER INTO THE
covenant of Hashem your G-d .... Not with you alone do I make
this covenant and this oath, but with whoever is here with us, standing today before Hashem our G-d, and with whoever is not here with us today."

These dramatic words encapsulate the special relationship every Jew
has with G-d's covenant and usher in the Jew's everlasting duty to
uphold it. The Torah states unequivocally that the covenant is binding
even on "whoever is not here with us today," the future generations of
Israel. But how can that be? How can a person be responsible for a
commitment he did not actually make and never approved of?

In his commentary on the Torah, *Akeidat Yitzchak,* Rav Yitzchak Ara-
ma raises this question, explaining that, indeed, such a commitment
should not be legally binding. "The fathers have eaten sour grapes and
the teeth of the children are set on edge?" asks the prophet Yechezkel.
"By My Name, says the L-rd, the soul that sins — it [alone] will perish."

Apparently, there is no connection between the deeds of parents and
the responsibilities of their offspring. How can a child, who does not
suffer for his parents' misdeeds, be bound by their oaths?

The *Akeidat Yitzchak,* therefore, suggests another explanation, that
"G-d's love for Israel is not dependent on the latter's material existence
but is a lasting natural phenomenon so strong that its cancellation is
inconceivable." Just as nature dictates that a person would not abandon
his identity, "so too it is inconceivable that this nation would ever

detach itself from G-d and His laws in any manner, because this is a law of their nature which is stronger and more significant than an oath."

There is an element in the Jewish soul which is intimately connected to Hashem and to His Torah. As our Sages say, "Israel, Torah and Hashem are one." The observance of the Torah's laws is not just a matter of choice but rather is a healthy expression of a Jew's deeper nature. Abandoning this commitment is as harmful to a Jew as ignoring his psychological constitution.

This understanding of Jewish nature is in line with the rule that allows the *beth din* to punish a recalcitrant husband until he agrees to divorce his wife. Though such a *get* should be invalid since the Torah requires that it be given voluntarily, this divorce is legitimate. Why?

The Rambam explains that deep in the husband's heart is a desire to do the right thing. Were it not for his *yeitzer hara* holding him back, he would divorce his wife. By punishing the husband we merely remove the obstacle that prevents him from doing what he truly wishes to do. Similarly, built into a Jew's nature is a desire to connect to Hashem and obey His laws. Only the presence of disturbing influences, which plague us with psychological barriers and distractions, prevents us from achieving our spiritual potential.

This notion can well explain the return of so many Jews to our tradition and has ramifications for our work in outreach as well. The soul of every Jew possesses characteristics that were infused at Sinai and in the subconscious of every Jew, the *Akeidat Yitzchak* maintains, lies an awareness of that commitment made long ago. That memory is part of a Jew's being and can not be erased without his sense of identity being lost. Our commitment to Torah was not made by others but by ourselves. In the depth of our subconscious lies an unshakable memory and feeling that stems from another, more enlightened spiritual age.

_____ *Rabbi Gershon C. Gewirtz*

W E HAVE LEARNED FROM OUR REVERED TEACHER, RAV YOSEF DOV Soloveitchik, *zt"l,* that "G-d demands not tribute from man, but man himself," and that "total and unreserved offering of soul and body — that is the foundation of Judaism." Contemplation of such expectation, let alone its realization, may engender a sense of being overwhelmed. How, indeed, can anyone even aspire to such awesome heights of spirituality? Is such achievement attainable on any level?

In *Parshas Nitzavim,* as part of Moshe's final discourse, the children of Israel are told the following:

> This mandate that I am prescribing to you today is not too mysterious or remote from you. It's not in heaven, that you should say, "Who shall go up to heaven and bring it to us that we can hear it and keep it?"... It is something that is very close to you. It is in your mouth and in your heart, so that you can keep it.

Relying upon a statement in Tractate *Eruvin,* Rashi teaches that if "this mandate," i.e., Torah and *mitzvos* were in the heavens, each of us would be obligated to ascend to the heavens to retrieve it. On the face of it, the task Rashi describes is simply impossible. How could Torah demand and expect that we scale the heavens? Indeed, it is ludicrous to the point of possibly undermining any rational and thoughtful commitment to Torah at all.

Rav Avraham of Sachatshav, *zt"l,* however, provides resolution to our dilemma. He teaches that each of us is, in effect, G-d's representative in this life and it is our mission to fulfill His will as expressed in His *mitzvos.* Consequently, we are granted by G-d whatever strength and ability necessary to fulfill our tasks. Were it essential to ascend the heavens, this too would have been possible for us. As, however, in point of fact such is not the case, we must view every apparent obstacle to our fulfillment of Torah as a challenge that can be faced and overcome. Indeed, every challenge becomes an opportunity for spiritual growth and renewed commitment.

When the Rav teaches that "G-d demands...man himself," representing a "total and unreserved offering of soul and body," this too "is not in heaven;...it is [indeed]...in your heart." It is in our hearts if we but will it to be so.

This challenge is anything but trivial and the resulting spiritual growth-potential approaches the infinite. It is necessarily worthy of our attention and our efforts. As we approach the coming Days of Awe, may we align the will of our hearts with the will of the Almighty, and be deserving of His eternal blessing.

A S MOSHE WARNS _BNEI YISRAEL_ TO BE LOYAL TO _HAKADOSH BARUCH Hu_ and avoid His wrath, he concludes one segment with a well-known _pasuk:_ "Those which are hidden belong to Hashem our G-d, while those that are revealed belong to us and to our children (_lanu ulevaneinu_) forever, to do all the words of this Torah." This _pasuk_ is recited on Yom Kippur in the _Viduy_ section of each _tefillah._ The words _"lanu ulevaneinu"_ are graced with dots on all of their letters. This phenomenon appears several times in the Torah. What exactly is the significance of the dots? What do they convey to us?

Rav Yosef Dov Soloveitchik, _zt"l,_ once suggested that in ancient civilizations all forms of written communication were etchings in stone. If an error was made or the writer intended to alert the reader that something should not be taken too seriously, it was much too difficult to erase the word or the phrase. Placing a simple dot upon the letter or word was the technique used to highlight the error or to sensitize you to an alternate reading of that word.

Apparently, the Rav explained, this is the purpose of the dots in the Torah as well. In _Parshas Vayishlach,_ the Torah discusses the encounter between Eisav and Yaakov. It reads "_Vayichabkeihu vayishakeihu,_" literally translated, "He embraced and kissed him." Rashi, however, translates _vayishakeihu_ as "He bit him." What alerted Rashi to this? The word _vayishakeihu_ has dots on each of its letters, suggesting that you not take the text literally. Instead of a _nishikah,_ a kiss, this was a _nishichah,_ a bite.

A second example is found in _Parshas Behaalosecha_ in conjunction with the eligibility to offer _pesach sheini._ The Torah states, "If any man is ritually unclean by [coming into contact with] a corpse or is on a far-away (_rechokah_) journey" when it is time to bring the _korban pesach,_ he is eligible to bring a _pesach sheini._ The _mishnah_ in _Pesachim_ records a dispute between Rabbi Akiva, who says _rechokah_ implies he is a half-day's journey from Jerusalem, and Rabbi Eliezer, who believes that as long as he is outside the Temple court, he is considered "far away." Explaining Rabbi Eliezer's opinion, Rabbi Yosi adds, "That is why a dot appears above the letter _hei._"

The word *rechokah* seems to be modifying the word journey. Hence, Rabbi Akiva would be correct that one must be a specific geographic distance from Jerusalem to be eligible to bring *pesach sheini*. However, if you drop the *hei* the word reads *rachok,* which is modifying the word *ish* at the beginning of the *pasuk.* In other words, it is the person who is "far away" — physically he may be standing right outside the *Mikdash,* but mentally and spiritually he is not yet prepared to bring a *korban pesach* on that day. Consequently, we offer him a second opportunity the following month.

Our *pasuk* conveys the notion that the realm of the hidden belongs exclusively to G-d — why young children succumb to cancer, why national disasters suddenly wreak havoc on entire communities. But there are certain things that we believe are "revealed" and these are given "to us and to our children." We believe that we can comprehend the cause and effect of certain social, economic or historical events.

But the dots indicate that even that which we believe is open and revealed truly rests in the hands of *Hakadosh Baruch Hu.* As we approach the High Holy Days we indeed recognize that both *hanistaros and haniglos* are in the hands of Hashem our G-d.

_____ *Rabbi Doniel Z. Kramer*

T HE *PARSHAH* OF *NITZAVIM* IS ALWAYS READ ON THE SHABBOS BEFORE Rosh Hashanah. *Nitzavim* means standing, and the first verse appropriately sums up the mood of the day: "All of you are standing this day before the L-rd your G-d."

As we prepare for the High Holy Days and the beginning of the recitation of *selichos,* the penitential prayers, the portion bids us to repent. G-d tells us, "I have placed before you life and death" — and urges us, "You shall choose life." Make the commitment to repent and to live in a manner that will be worthy of judgment for a renewed life.

This year, along with *Nitzavim,* we read a second *parshah, Vayeilech. Vayeilech* comes from the Hebrew word, go. In sharp contrast to the standing of *Nitzavim, Vayeilech* represents movement. The combination of these two *parshios* teaches us our greatest lesson — to both stand still and move on. We must not only stand and take stock of what we have accomplished, the Lubavitcher Rebbe, *zt'l,* taught, but also move forward and commit ourselves to making the coming year a productive one.

As we enter the twenty-first century on the secular calendar, there is tremendous potential for change and redemption. This is not a time to be standing still. Observant and committed Jews especially must make the commitment to diligently work for *tikkun olam,* to be exemplars of purity of thought and action in order to help perfect the world under the sovereignty of the Almighty. If all Jews live their lives in a pristine and holy state, the resulting *kiddush Hashem* will infuse the world with holiness.

The world, says Rabbi Eliezer in the Talmud, was created on the 25th day of Elul. Six days later, the first day of the month of Tishrei, marked the creation of the first human being. The 25th day of Elul is also the anniversary of the creation of the Second Holy Temple, which allowed God's presence to be manifested in this world. The Book of *Nechemiah* recounts the many efforts made by his foes to prevent the rebuilding of the Temple, but he persevered, and after fifty-two days, the building was completed.

In our Holy Land, Israel, we face the same challenge that Nechemiah did: building a sanctuary for G-d in an environment in which so many seek to thwart that work. Our call is to ensure that the holiness of the State of Israel is fully resurrected. Our prayer is to see in this year the fulfillment of the prophecy of Yeshayahu: "The year of redemption has come."

Through our commitment to live lives of holiness and purity, we can ensure the fulfillment of the prophet's promise. May the entire House of Israel be privileged to witness the Messianic redemption and ingathering of Israel and the spreading of the tabernacle of peace over Jerusalem and the entire world.

_____ *Rabbi Ralph Pelcovitz*

E VERY *SEDRAH* SHOULD HAVE, AS THE WORD IMPLIES, A *SEDER,* AN order. Yet to anyone examining *Parshas Vayeilech,* it seems to lack a thematic unity. The opening chapter heads in several directions.

Verses that focus on Yehoshua's succession of Moshe Rabbeinu wind themselves around verses describing the *mitzvah* of *"Hakheil"* — the assembling of the entire Jewish nation on Succos of every Sabbatical year — and G-d's dire declaration about Israel's future.

But what may seem superficially to be incongruous is in reality teaching us a most important lesson. In these verses we find a subtle blending of two forces: the leader and the people. Leader and people are inexorably intertwined and both must be prepared, instructed and inspired. Both must be encouraged and cautioned. As a leader, Yehoshua's future will be wound around that of his people because any leader will only be as effective as the people he leads allow him to be. Winston Churchill once said regarding his historic role during the Second World War, "It is not I who inspired. The free world had a lion heart. I but had the good fortune to be called upon to give the roar."

The mission of the Jewish people and the translation of Torah principles into their everyday lives is the responsibility of both the leader and the nation. Hence the introduction of the *mitzvah* of *Hakheil,* when the king reads from the Torah before all the Jews "that they may hear, that they may learn and revere the L-rd their G-d and be careful to observe all the words of this Torah."

The Jewish people need to constantly renew their awareness of their role as "a kingdom of priests and a holy nation." It is not enough to do *mitzvos* by rote. One must hear and learn and understand the Torah, one must fill himself with awe for the Almighty, and one must raise this understanding and awe to the practical level by carefully observing the words of the Torah.

The *mitzvah* of *Hakheil* includes everyone; men, women and children. This *mitzvah* serves to reinforce a Jew's understanding that his obligation goes beyond individual responsibility. The Torah demands that he assume responsibility on a national level as well.

As the Jewish people were about to enter the Promised Land, where their status as a nation would be complete, they needed this notion of collective responsibility implanted in their consciousness. It was this which the leader Yehoshua was charged to preserve and teach.

Rekindling this awareness is particularly timely on *Shabbos Shuvah,* between Rosh Hashanah and Yom Kippur. At this time of atonement and assessment, each Jew must be cognizant of the dual role he plays as both a *yachid* and as a member of the *tzibur*. Only by developing both roles, by focusing on his individual development while also accepting the responsibilities of the community, can he realize his full potential as a Jew.

Another link between *Parshas Vayeilech* and *Shabbos Shuvah* is the verse that refers to the Torah as *"hashirah hazos* — this song." A wise man once wrote that much can be learned from an orchestra wherein a group of musicians, each proficient in his chosen instrument, play together, humbly lending their talents to each other so that the composition is properly and beautifully played.

The song that is the Torah demands no less. One must set aside his ego and submerge himself in the *klal,* giving of his talent and proficiency to cooperate with other Jews and create the collective character of *Klal Yisrael.*

"We often visit with others," a philosopher once remarked. "When was the last time we visited with ourselves?" On *Shabbos Shuvah* we visit with ourselves and with others. *Teshuvah* means return — a return to self-responsibility and a return to one's roots within the Jewish nation.

Having achieved this return, one can echo the words of the *Shunamis,* "I dwell in the midst of my people." I possess the self-confidence, the self-identity and the recognition of my destiny. May the new year be one of *Achdus Yisrael* and may Hashem grant His people and all mankind a *shenas chaim veshalom.*

_____ Rabbi Baruch A. Poupko

R AV YISROEL SALANTER ONCE REMARKED: *"AMOL, LOIFT MEN TZU TON a mitzveh mit azah impit vos me ken choirev machen de gantze velt* — At times, people run to do a *mitzvah* with such zeal that it is possible to destroy a whole world in the process."

A *Chassidic* tale tells of two *chassidim* who were agonizing over the challenge of doing *teshuvah* during the month of Elul. One said, "I can't eat or sleep when I think about my sins of this past year."

His friend responded, "I'm not as worried about my sins as I am about my *mitzvos.* I know what my sins are and I am able to ask a Merciful G-d for forgiveness. But how can I begin to identify the sins I did, thinking they were *mitzvos*?"

In *Parshas Vayeilech,* we find a hint of this danger when Moshe confronts the Jewish people. "You were rebels before G-d (*im Hashem*)," he admonishes them. Alternately, one can translate this verse as, "You were rebels *with* G-d." In your passion for serving G-d you committed grievous sins.

Isn't this the lesson of history? Do we deny that there were many in the past who introduced innovations not supported by *Halachah,* whose motivation and sincere desire was to insure the continuity of Judaism in their communities? There is no doubt that they thought that their adherence to new trends was a *mitzvah.* But how misguided and destructive was the outcome.

At the same time, we can not ignore the destructive actions of some of the zealots within our midst. Rav Yosef Dov Soloveitchik, *zt"l,* once commented, "The zealot's life is quite simple — no hardships confront him. He has no doubts to resolve. He is not challenged by painful doubts or difficult choices. For him there are very few questions and no regrets. For him there is only black and white."

The *Chafetz Chaim, zt"l,* was once asked how one can determine if one's actions are consistent with the teachings of the Torah. He replied, quoting the verse, *"Derachecha? Darchei noam!* Are these the ways of Your Torah? Only if they are ways of pleasantness!"

During these days of introspection, in our earnest search for *teshuvah,* let us focus not only on our sins, but also on what we perceive to be *mitzvos.* In that way, may our prayers be accepted by our Merciful Father in Heaven.

פרשת האזינו
Parshas Ha'azinu

_____ Rabbi Daniel H. Mehlman

THE *PARSHAH* DESCRIBES HOW MOSHE PREPARED TO TAKE LEAVE OF the Jewish people. Presenting a highly emotional farewell song, Moshe states, "It [the Torah] is not an empty teaching for you; for it is your life." Moshe's point is emphatic: a Jew without Torah lives a void existence. Torah is our *eitz chaim,* our tree of life. It is our very existence.

These past few weeks have been uplifting ones for all Jewry. Our individual and collective spirituality were heightened as we experienced Rosh Hashanah and Yom Kippur, and these feelings will surely continue as we eagerly await the holiday of Succos. But what will happen after these spiritual days pass? What will continue to nurture our spirituality, influence our behavior and inspire our religious growth? Don't we need a constant force to motivate us in this direction?

This is exactly Moshe's final point to the Jewish people — "For it is your life" — the Torah and only the Torah will keep the Jewish people alive.

Rav Yosef Dov Soloveitchik, *zt"l,* echoes this principle in his explanation of the verse, "And a king ruled in Yeshurun," which refers to Moshe Rabbeinu's leadership of the Jewish nation. Moshe played a unique role, the role of king-teacher. A king-teacher, explains the Rav, engages the intellect of the people. He is responsible for analyzing, classifying, clarifying and transmitting the details of *Halachah* with precision. He teaches texts and conceptualized thinking, reconciling seeming contra-

Parshas Ha'azinu / 321

dictions and formulating underlying principles. In short, he emphasizes *limud,* study, as a primary means of identifying with G-d.

How so? The Rav explains that his intellectual pursuit is based upon the conviction that the human mind reflects in some way the infinite mind of G-d. To know the Torah is to identify with G-d's knowledge and, in effect, to identify with G-d Himself.

There is also a second type of teacher, whom the Rav calls the saint-teacher. He is the one who communicates through the heart, focusing on the invisible soul of the Torah. This teacher encourages his students to become emotionally involved with the Torah. He expresses the need to feel, not only to understand, the Torah's mission. He teaches not just texts but the art of cleansing one's heart of unworthy sentiments, uncouth emotions and selfish desires. This teacher breeds a society of intense personal piety and subliminal closeness to G-d.

Reflecting upon Moshe's message, "For it is your life," one understands well the Rav's point. To enhance our personal lives as well as our communal impact on world Jewry, we need to capture the attributes of both the king-teacher and the saint-teacher to form a unique, complete Jewish personality. Our aim, on the one hand, must be to emphasize scholarship, to increase our intellectual capacity through intensive Torah study. At the same time, we must strive to come closer to one another, to achieve a greater state of national *achdus* through love and understanding.

The Rav's words are a clarion call to all Jewry. His message is especially important in an age plagued by both ambivalence and disharmony. As we prepare for the holiday of Succos and step behind G-d's protective shield may this message go forth and may we merit the day when we all sit in G-d's Tabernacle in unity and tranquillity.

_____ Rabbi Stuart J. Rosen

"WHEN I CALL OUT THE NAME OF HASHEM, ASCRIBE GREATNESS to our G-d." This calling out, according to the Malbim and Rabbi Chaim of Volozhin, is one of Torah. Anyone who keeps the Torah and learns it, learns the Name of Hashem, and the Divine Presence rests upon him.

A community calling out Hashem's Name through study and prayer, produces the greatest broadcast of G-d's greatness. This is the task of the Jewish people, writes the Malbim — to publicize G-d's sovereignty in the world, to acknowledge that the laws of nature are subject to His will, and that the Torah is the medium for this acknowledgment. Every time we call out His Name, we ascribe greatness to our G-d.

In *Parshas Haazinu,* Moshe calls upon the Heaven and Earth and the Children of Israel to proclaim G-d's greatness. Though G-d set the laws of nature and rarely interferes with them, He continues to orchestrate the world's every detail.

When we keep the Torah, Hashem dwells in our midst and His supervision becomes obvious. If, however, we do not fulfill the Torah, Hashem does not dwell in our midst and turns His countenance away from us. Subsequently, we do not feel His supervision.

Moshe cries out to Heaven and Earth, "When Israel keeps the Torah, influence them with goodness, with great wonder, until it is obvious to all that even the laws of nature are in the Hands of Hashem. And if they should forsake the Torah, then it will seem as though there is no supervision from Hashem. It will seem as if only nature is at play."

Our task is clear: To the extent that we return to Torah learning and Torah living, the closer we will come to a wonderful existence that goes beyond the simple laws of nature. Returning to Torah is realizing our unique Jewish identity. We must proclaim and declare our special relationship with Hashem.

We must also take extra care in reciting the blessing before Torah study. The Temple was destroyed because the Jewish people "left my Torah." How could that be when Torah study was so widespread? the Sages asked.

Even thought they learned Torah, we are informed, they didn't learn for the sake of learning. Rather, they learned Torah like any other subject. They did not recite a blessing upon learning Torah — proof that the Torah was not important in their eyes. Thus their learning could not protect them.

Torah study is the declaration of G-d's Name. We must not learn Torah out of idle curiosity or for intellectual stimulation, but rather to ascribe greatness to the One Who created the universe. We must learn Torah as a spiritual pursuit, and in doing so "ascribe greatness to our G-d."

THE FOCUS OF THE ENTIRE PERIOD FROM ELUL THROUGH TISHREI IS *teshuvah*. During this period Hashem seeks our return to Him. Throughout the year we struggle to perform Hashem's commands and fight off the urges, habits and rationalizations that lead us to sin and distance us from Him. But in order to do *teshuvah,* we must uncover why we fail in the first place. Do we fully understand the adversary we battle? What is sin?

In an illuminating essay on the nature of sin, Rabbi Adin Steinsaltz, *shlit"a,* points out that while the Hebrew language has many names for sin, as well as many categories of sin, the concept in and of itself is never fully developed. Usually, points out Rav Steinsaltz, sin is understood as the negation of *mitzvah.* The Torah consists of "positive" and "negative" commandments — what to do and what not to do — and sin, therefore, means doing what one shouldn't or not doing what one should. In both cases, though, sin is simply the opposite of something — not an entity in and of itself.

To better understand sin, we need to better understand how Judaism regards *mitzvos.* Rav Steinsaltz offers several ideas.

Mitzvos are Divine commands; therefore, they require our obedience as a sign that we accept the "yoke of Heaven" and recognize that all we have is from Hashem. Sin, therefore, is an act of rebellion against Hashem. The "leader" of the rebellion could be other gods, other men, or one's own will. But sin is a revolt nonetheless.

Doing *mitzvos* can also be viewed as doing things the way they were meant to be done — the "Golden Mean," as Maimonides would put it. As a source in *Zohar* writes, the *mitzvos* reflect Hashem's good counsel to humankind on how best to live. Sin is a deviation from this path — and a violation of nature.

Yet another understanding of *mitzvos* is that they are a means of rectifying the world, as it says in the *Aleinu* prayer, "to repair the world within the Kingdom of G-d." The world was created incomplete and our role as Jews is to help complete it. Sin is a failure to rectify something — or worse, an addition to the problems of the world.

With sin comprising all of these — rebellion, deviation, destruction — why do we still sin?

The answer may be found in *Bereishis*. After rejecting Cain's offering, G-d tells Cain, "Why have you become depressed? Surely, if you improve yourself, your spirit will be lifted; but if you will not improve yourself, sin crouches at the door."

Rabbi Ovadiah ben Yaakov Sforno suggests that G-d is encouraging Cain to make the necessary changes to make his offering acceptable. On the other hand, G-d informs Cain (and by extension, all of us) that if he does not strive to improve himself, the evil inclination lies in wait, "crouching at the door" — ready to capitalize on man's weakness and vulnerability. Our enemy is our own stubbornness, our own arrogance, our own foolish unwillingness to resist the temptation of sin and dedicate ourselves completely to the Creator's will.

Teshuvah is that process by which we renew our spiritual closeness to G-d which enables us to perform *mitzvos* and avoid sin. The Sforno's remedy to sin is to recognize that "man is stronger than the inclination to sin and can conquer it because he possesses the strength of the Divine image within him." The battles against sin, which we will fight in the year to come, will still be harsh. But if knowledge is power, we are much better equipped to do more *mitzvos* and avoid *aveiros,* because we know what the obstacles are.

·ↅ Yamim Tovim

יום טוב
Yom Tov

_____ *Rabbi Abraham Mandelbaum*

I N *PARSHAS EMOR,* WE ENCOUNTER THE JEWISH HOLIDAYS BEING chronicled for the first time. As a matter of fact, this chapter is often referred to as *Parshas Hamo'adim* — the Chapter of the Holidays. An in-depth analysis of the chapter will reveal the essence of Judaism.

The five holidays, Pesach, Shavuos, Rosh Hashanah, Yom Kippur and Succos can be conveniently and theologically divided into two categories — the universal and the covenantal. Pesach, Shavuos and Succos, according to Rav Yosef Dov Soloveitchik, *zt"l,* can be properly described as covenantal holidays. These three pilgrimage Festivals represent three historic events that changed the course of Jewish history.

Pesach — *zeman cheiruseinu,* the season of our freedom — commemorates the betrothal of G-d (*chassan*) and the Jewish people (*kallah*). Shavuos — *zeman matan Toraseinu,* the season of our acquiring the Torah — represents the actual marriage between G-d and the Jewish people. Finally, the festival of Succos — *zeman simchaseinu,* the season of our rejoicing — celebrates the intimate joy of *yichud,* the consummation of the relationship between G-d and the Jewish people. The fragile *succah* symbolizes the sacredness of space, which completes the relationship that began at Pesach.

The Jew that best represents this covenantal experience is Moshe Rabbeinu. This larger-than-life figure is the ultimate guardian and protector of Jewish interests and causes. He is the one who willingly and unhesitatingly killed an Egyptian who was beating a Jew to death. He is the one who defended the Jewish people from extinction after the sin of the Golden Calf.

Moshe is the quintessential leader and prophet of the Jewish people — always ready, willing and able to defend and protect the honor of *Klal Yisrael.* He is our liberator, our legislator, our teacher, our defender, our shepherd — who tends to his flock with love, empathy and respect.

In contradistinction to these pilgrimage and parochial festivals are two universal holidays. Rosh Hashanah and Yom Kippur commemorate G-d's sovereignty and G-d's judgment of mankind. Though some Jews observe only these two holidays, they have nothing to do with the Jewish people *per se.* These holidays represent not the parochial interests of the Jews, but the cosmic and universal concerns of mankind. In the words of the prophet, Malachi, "Do we not have one father for all of mankind?"

Universalism is an indispensable component of the Jewish faith. As such, Avraham Avinu, Avraham *our* father, is also *av hamon goyim,* the spiritual father of all mankind. When the wayward cities of Sodom and Amorrah were threatened with Divine retribution and annihilation, Avraham, the universal Jew, courageously intervened on their behalf and prayed for their survival. He challenged the Almighty because he felt the pain and anguish of humanity crying to him for defense and protection.

According to Rav Soloveitchik, "Avraham did not appear in the historical arena in order to free the Jews from universal obligations. On the contrary, the Sinaitic covenant enhances the universal norm and elevates it to greater heights. It adds more norms to those obligatory upon all members of mankind."

Moshe taught the Jews to imitate G-d, *imitatio dei,* to "be holy, because I the Lord, your G-d, am holy." The Jewish people are mandated through the Sinaitic covenant to reach for the ideal of being "a kingdom of priests and holy nation." But Avraham Avinu propagated the seven Noachide laws for all peoples, rooted in the universal *imago dei* (G-d's image), the source of man's dignity and respect.

Many religiously committed Jews are indifferent to the concerns of the larger, non-Jewish society. They choose to concentrate on the Mosaic model of parochialism. They are very content to live in isolated communities with a total disregard, and even contempt, for the gentile world. The problems which afflict the gentile world are irrelevant and of no concern to them. Insulation and isolation are their slogans.

But the holistic Torah Jew is enjoined to emulate both Avraham Avinu, the archetype universalistic Jew, and Moshe Rabbeinu, the incomparable covenantal Jew.

Authentic Judaism postulates that those in the Jewish world who seek to bring us back to the mentality of Jewish isolation and suffering have not learned the message of Rosh Hashanah and Yom Kippur. At the same time, those who abandon the depth of commitment to Jewish historical intimacy in the name of universalism have not learned the lesson of Pesach, Shavuos and Succos, which form the total Jewish festival year — to live as a full Jew and to live in both rhythms, in the framework of Jewish history and in the framework of creation.

ראש השנה
Rosh Hashanah

_____ *Rabbi Tzvi Hersh Weinreb*

"**I**T IS A NEW YEAR. WE MUST BE READY TO SURRENDER OUR MATERIAL comforts to foster our religious ideals."

Such a statement in a Rosh Hashanah sermon would not surprise us. But suppose we heard the following: "It is a new year; we must be willing to surrender our spiritual growth to foster our religious principles." We would find such a statement incredible. We would not easily believe that there are religious objectives that require spiritual sacrifices. What might these sacrifices be? And what objectives will justify them?

There are years when Rosh Hashanah falls on Shabbos. Biblically, the *shofar* is to be blown on Shabbos as on weekdays. Our Sages, however, postponed the *shofar* blowing on Shabbos out of the concern that one might carry the *shofar* four cubits in a public domain which would violate the Shabbos. Under certain circumstances, the Rabbis are authorized to suspend one *mitzvah* in order to protect another.

Rabbi Meir Simcha of Dvinsk is troubled by this readiness to forgo the *mitzvah* of *shofar*. Yes, he writes in *Meshech Chochmah,* our Sages were technically within their rights when they suspended the *shofar* blowing on Shabbos, but why were they not concerned with the spiritual benefits that the *shofar* helps us to obtain? After all, the Talmud teaches that "a year which does not begin with the *shofar* blast will witness evil tidings before its end." Can we risk omitting a ritual of such cosmic potency? And what about the *zikaron* function of the *shofar,* its mystical ability to bring each of us to the forefront of G-d's memory, as it were?

We are taught that the *shofar* brings us to the innermost sanctum. We are taught that the *shofar* confounds the Satan. Can we relinquish our access to such a powerful metaphysical force, just to avoid the remote possibility of *chillul Shabbos*?

We might supplement Rabbi Meir Simcha's questions with some of our own. What about the psychological benefits of the *shofar*? Surely it shatters our moral complacency, filling us with awe. Maimonides sees the *shofar* as an alarm capable of arousing us from our deepest spiritual slumber. Do the implausible odds of a single Shabbos infraction justify trading off all of these undeniable spiritual benefits?

Rabbi Meir Simcha's answer is most provocative. Our willingness to forgo personal, spiritual advantage in the interest of G-d's Sabbath is indeed of greater merit than all the aforementioned benefits. Shabbos is G-d's own possession, stored in His treasure house. We yield our spiritual growth and all of the mystical *shofar* force before this higher objective, His Sabbath.

The subtext to Rabbi Meir Simcha's commentary is evident and incisive. Sometimes our search for spirituality is guided by selfish motives. It is often nothing more than an egoistic quest for a "spiritual high" or a mystical "peak experience." Our Sages advise us to be willing to relinquish the *shofar* "high" in favor of G-d's tranquil Shabbos.

This teaching has special relevance for our new beginning at this time of year. Can we resolve to surrender the "selfish" spiritual benefits of our familiar Shabbos table and instead endure the probing, perhaps cynical questions of guests who are ignorant of Shabbos? Can we commit to one less hour of intellectually stimulating personal Torah learning and instead teach "boring" basics of Judaism to a beginner?

Let us ponder these and similar questions when Rosh Hashanah coincides with Shabbos, as we "listen" to the silent *shofar*.

_____ *Rabbi Hershel Billet*

THE *AMMORA* REISH LAKISH DISTINGUISHES BETWEEN TWO TYPES OF repentance. One, called *teshuvah meiyirah,* is motivated by awe and reduces the level of severity of the transgressor's sins. The other, called *teshuvah mei'ahavah,* is motivated by love and actually trans-forms the sins into merits.

Rav Yosef Dov Soloveitchik, *zt"l,* expounds upon these two types of repentance. The Rambam in *Hilchos Teshuvah* describes a *teshuvah* of sudden change, of total catharsis through which a sinner, who was but yesterday despised by Hashem, eradicates the past and instantly as-sumes a new identity, becoming a close friend of Hashem. This form of repentance is *tikkun hara,* repairing the evil.

The other form of repentance is not instantaneous, but part of a process. Rather than totally abandoning the past, one takes the energy he used to err and redirects it to do good. In this form of *teshuvah,* the sinner does not assume a new identity. Instead he takes a new road in life, utilizing all of his skills to gradually develop a new relationship with Hashem. The Rav refers to this move as *ha'alas hara,* elevating the evil.

Likewise, Rav Avraham Y. Kook, *zt"l,* contrasts *teshuvah pisomis,* sudden change, with *teshuvah hadragis,* gradual change. Sudden change is the equivalent of *tikkun hara* and can be identified also with Reish Lakish's *teshuvah meiyirah.* It can not wipe the slate perfectly clean because little effort was put into the defining moment of repentance. Gradual change, however, is the equivalent of *ha'alas hara* and can be identified with *teshuvah mei'ahavah.* This form of repentance, the result of a long cleansing process, transforms the energy of sin into merit.

These two methods of *teshuvah* are found in numerous Talmudic examples. Reish Lakish himself was a notorious bandit who repented his ways and dedicated long hours to Torah study. Through hard work he channeled his energy, previously used for evil, toward good, becom-ing one of the great rabbis of the Talmud and the editor of the Jerusalem Talmud — an example of *teshuvah mei'ahavah.*

On the other hand, the *Tanna*-turned-heretic Elisha ben Avuyah is an example of *teshuvah meiyirah.* He was once riding on his horse on Shabbos and talking with his student, the *Tanna* Rabbi Meir, who walked alongside. "Repent," Rabbi Meir told him.

Elisha ben Avuyah replied that a Heavenly voice told him that the gates of repentance were open to all but him. Nevertheless, Rabbi Meir insisted that as long as one is alive it is never too late to repent. Elisha cried and his soul departed from him, whereupon Rabbi Meir declared him a *baal teshuvah.*

"Some acquire the World to Come in an instant," the Talmud declares. Whether we repent instantly or gradually, whether we are motivated by fear and awe or by love, there is always time and opportunity for us to obtain forgiveness and develop ourselves and our relationship with Hashem.

Let us seize these opportunities on this *Yom Hadin* of Rosh Hashanah.

_____ *Yisroel Epstein*

ALL THE FASCINATION THAT SURROUNDED THE OMINOUS Y2K PROBLEM has got me thinking about computers and how they work. The language of the computer, its code, is absurdly simple. Computer code is written in ones and zeros — that's it. Long strands of numbers composed of these two digits represent every command inside that miraculous little box that sits on nearly every desk in homes and offices across the world. All the graphics, documents, spreadsheets, databases, e-mails — all of it is distilled inside the hard drive into ones and zeros.

The simplicity of computer code presents a philosophical bombshell: Ones and zeros. Something and nothing. An accurate representation of life itself — a huge computer program that boils down to a collection of something and nothing. Practically, this synthesis provides us with a useful framework to better understand our nature — our own code — and how we can reprogram it to better ourselves for the coming year.

On Rosh Hashanah all of us want to be better Jews, to increase our observance and to minimize our sins. We are in the *mood* to change. Yet for many of us even the changes we do manage to implement come undone by November or December. What's a responsible Jew to do?

Rav Chaim Friedlander, *zt"l,* the Ponovizher *mashgiach,* addresses this predicament in his *sefer, Sifsei Chaim.* "Teshuvah," he writes, "is not simply a 'resolution' not to fail again .... A person should not mislead himself that 'Yesterday and the day before I was not in order, but from now on I will be in order' — for he has failed many times. And why suddenly will he not fail again? If he shuts his eyes to this, he will surely not succeed, G-d forbid."

Rav Friedlander goes on to explain that change is about carving out a different path. *Teshuvah* can not be simply intellectualized or emotionalized. Otherwise it remains this vague, ephemeral notion — it isn't real. We must make it real. And we can do so only with tangible, structural changes. We too quickly comfort ourselves with grand thoughts but no immediate, tangible action.

This is the lesson of the ones and the zeros. This is *our* Y2K problem. We must reprogram the hard drive; otherwise the system will fail again and again. It will continue to crash as it always has.

How does one reprogram the system? By changing the zeros to ones. By taking real steps to add value where it was previously missing. It is not enough to say, "I will learn more." Instead, pick up the phone, call a friend and agree to meet at the synagogue fifteen minutes before services to study. Now you have a time, a place and a partner. Not an idea. A reality.

It is not enough to say, "I must pray better." Go out and buy an ArtScroll *siddur* and open your eyes to the English while you read the Hebrew, so that you understand the words you are saying during prayer.

The level at which we make these changes is not as important as insuring that some changes are made. The goal is not to go from zero to sixty — just from zero to one. We must take the empty pieces of our lives and fill them with something.

With Rosh Hashanah upon us, we are getting a jumpstart on the Y2K hoopla. Let us not simply rededicate ourselves but reprogram ourselves to take seriously our mission, to do the necessary small things that elevate the zeros to ones, and to become the Holy Nation that G-d expects us to become and that we are assuredly capable of becoming.

יום כפור
Yom Kippur

_____ *Rabbi Efrem Schwalb*

YOM KIPPUR IS A TIME WHEN *TESHUVAH,* REPENTANCE, IS ON EVERY Jew's mind. We all have personality flaws and deficiencies of religious observance that we would like to remedy, but it is extremely hard to effect changes in these areas. If we want to repent properly and effect these positive changes, the Talmud and the *baalei mussar* instruct us to perform a self-examination, to measure where we stand based on the past year, and to determine practical strategies for improvement in the coming year.

For many Jews, this self-evaluation process is particularly frustrating because invariably, after following this process and having thoughts of repentance, thoughts of improvement, we find ourselves repeating mistakes and ending up in the same position where we started. How many times have we promised ourselves, "I won't do that again. I will improve." And then, at the first opportunity, we find ourselves right back where we started, unable to put those good intentions into practice.

Thus, we ask ourselves a fundamental question: Why bother? Why go through this process of introspection if it rarely succeeds in bringing about the intended changes? Is there any value in our good intentions if they do not lead to real change?

Many people believe that thoughts of repentance alone, without a transformation of those thoughts into practice, are meaningless. This is not true. The Talmud is clear that we should never underestimate these thoughts. If a man says to a woman, "Be betrothed to me on the condition that I am righteous," she is considered betrothed — even if he is known to be a wicked person, because perhaps, at the time, he had thoughts of repentance in his heart.

How can this be so? Because sincere thoughts of repentance have tremendous power. They can transform a person from evil to righteous even without any actual acts of penitence.

In his book, *Oros Hateshuvah,* Rav Avraham Yitzchak Kook, *zt"l,* expounds on this theme. He writes: "The thought of repentance is that which reveals the depth of will, and the strength of the soul is revealed by means of these thoughts in the fullness of its splendor.... Actually, even the slightest thought of repentance effects great salvation .... Since the thought is bound with sanctity and with the desire for repentance, there is nothing to fear. Most assuredly, G-d, Blessed is He, will provide all the ways whereby perfect repentance ... can be achieved."

Thoughts of repentance are meaningful because they demonstrate that we have not given up hope. A good intention is a beginning, and beginnings are very difficult. Indeed, as Rav Kook explains, intertwined with our noble thoughts is the possibility, even probability, of correcting our faults. Our actions will follow our good intentions. As we plan for next year, let us not underestimate our thoughts. Let us never become so frustrated that we give up hope in improving ourselves and moving closer to Hashem. May we have repentant thoughts and may Hashem bless us with the ability to transform those thoughts into action.

סוכות
Succos

_____ *Rabbi Edward Davis*

I N THE *HALACHOS* OF SUCCOS, A CLEAR DISTINCTION IS MADE BETWEEN
the walls of the *succah* and its covering, the *schach*. The Rama holds
that one must first build the walls of the *succah* prior to arranging the
schach atop them. If one reverses the order and puts the *schach* up first
(upon a frame, for example) and then places the walls around it, it is
debatable whether he has built a kosher *succah*. While some permit
using this *succah* to fulfill the *mitzvah,* others disqualify it.

While the crux of this dispute lies in the complexities of the Talmudic
discourse, perhaps one can glean from it a certain symbolic insight into
the meaning of the *succah* and the holiday of Succos.

The walls of the *succah* must be strong enough to withstand normal
weather conditions. But the *schach* above must not be piled on so thick
as to lock out the elements. The walls of the *succah* represent the
barrier between us, the Jewish people, and the nations of the world, who
are outside the *succah*. The walls must be strong; we must be protected
from all outside forces and influences. Only when fortified in such a
manner is it possible to develop a relationship with Hashem.

But our *succah* can not be so self-contained that rays of spirituality
from above can not penetrate it. The *schach* must be sparse enough to
allow in sunlight.

The first time the Torah notes the building of *succos* is when Yaakov
and Eisav part company following their peaceful reunion. Eisav wishes
to travel with Yaakov, but Yaakov begs off. After Eisav returns to Sei'ir,

Yaakov builds *succos* for his animals and even calls the area Succos. Immediately thereafter, Yaakov's family must deal with Shechem. Dealing with this outside threat was not easy; the family was not of one voice on how to handle it. The separation between the young Jewish nation and her enemies had been breached and needed to be strengthened.

The Talmud relates that the non-Jewish world failed to prove themselves worthy of a special relationship with G-d. They bolted from the *succah*. Was it because they could not tolerate the *succah* or because the *succah* could not tolerate them?

The *succah* not only consummates our special union with G-d, but also upholds our unique station as G-d's chosen people — to the exclusion of the non-Jewish world. All three pilgrimage Festivals — Succos, Pesach, Shavuos — contain this theme: the exclusion of the non-Jew as a prerequisite to our becoming close to the Almighty.

The need for the *succah*'s walls to be established before the *schach* is in place highlights the importance of establishing ourselves as a unique nation, not one that emulates the ways of the non-Jewish world. Once that is accomplished, we can reach for higher levels of holiness and develop our relationship with Hashem, thereby earning his eternal protection.

_____ *Rabbi Aryeh Scheinberg*

O NCE EVERY SEVEN YEARS, ON THE FIRST DAY OF CHOL HAMO'EID Succos, men, women and children were assembled to hear the king of Israel read sections of *Sefer Devarim*. The *Sefer Hachinuch* states that the reason for this *mitzvah* of "Hakheil" was to emphasize the centrality of Torah in our personal and national lives. This assembly would lead to a national yearning to study Torah. According to the Talmud, this *mitzvah* also emphasized the primacy of the family in Torah study and in transmitting Torah to each new generation.

But why here? Why, on Succos, does the Torah mandate teaching these fundamentals of Jewish existence — the centrality of Torah and the primacy of family in Torah study? Wouldn't this gathering be more appropriate on, say, Shavuos?

The Torah calls the nation of Israel, Yeshurun — a name that means "straightforward." The verse states, "He became king in Yeshurun when the leaders of the nation gathered — the tribes of Israel in unity." This name, notes the *Sefas Emes,* reflects Israel's mission toward the nations of the world. By promoting an upright lifestyle in a world of injustice, Israel will one day merit to see all men adopt their ways.

But this verse requires something else: "The tribes of Israel in unity." How does Israel accomplish this often elusive goal of unity? The answer lies in the previous verse: "Moshe commanded us the Torah, an inheritance of the congregation of Yaakov."

There is no greater unifying force among Jews than Torah. Despite our differences, all Jews share the heritage of Torah. Every Jew, even the most unlearned, has a portion in Torah, writes the *Sefas Emes.* Unity through Torah knowledge enables us to bring light unto the nations. But history, and particularly the American experience, has demonstrated, that when we concern and involve ourselves with this universal mandate to bring the Sinai message to all, we are most apt to ignore the particular responsibility of teaching Torah to our own. This neglect leads to confusion and disunity. To bring water to others to drink while our own families are parched and thirsty is unacceptable for G-d's messengers.

The Talmud tells the story of Reb Nechonia, who was known as a digger of wells. This man would dig wells and trenches so that the thousands of Jews who made the pilgrimage to the Temple before the Festivals would have water to drink. Yet, sadly, his only son died from thirst. Is this not symbolic of our people?

We dug wells for the world to drink from our waters of Torah. Our psalms are sung in the houses of worship of other peoples; our legal concepts have helped shape the law of many nations; our social doctrines inspire the most advanced, liberal thinking of this or any time; our prophets and their demands for social and moral justice are eagerly read by the entire world; our Hebrew tongue and its Biblical expression have influenced the literature of all western civilizations; our Sages have enriched the spiritual life of all mankind. And yet our own children do not drink from our wells, but instead die of thirst.

Thus, it is on Succos, precisely the time that we bring sacrifices for other nations, that we must emphasize the national interest — the centrality of Torah and the primacy of family in Torah study. Family and nation studying Torah gives us the strength to carry forth the waters of Torah to quench a thirsty world.

_____ *Rabbi Ephraim H. Sturm*

MANKIND, RECOGNIZING THE FRAILTIES OF LIFE, SEEKS SECURITY. IN the State of Israel, diplomats, politicians and citizens demand secure borders. On these shores, we seek economic stability. Our parents and grandparents drummed into us the need to save for the *"elterer yurin."* Airlines, government buildings — even some elementary schools — have security checks. We seek medical security through insurance plans. Old-timers look back with nostalgia at an earlier age when people did not need deadbolt locks and alarm systems to feel secure in their own homes.

To appreciate the message of Succos in our age of insecurity we turn to two themes: the joy of the harvest and the acknowledgment of the clouds of glory that shielded the Jewish nation in the wilderness.

In an agricultural society the farmer plows the land, seeds it, tends it, fertilizes it and weeds it to achieve fiscal security. His fellow men do the same in other endeavors and through other methods. But after all human efforts have been expended, the crops and their profits, which represent security, are only achieved through the beneficence of the Creator who controls the rain, the sun and the world market. Succos tells us that after doing all that is expected of us, real security remains a special gift from Above.

"Not with strength and not with power, but with My Spirit," G-d tells us through the prophet: Physical security can not be achieved exclusively through might. In addition to courage, sacrifice and sophisticated weaponry, we need the catalytic factor of G-d's Spirit. Succos addresses this issue by reminding us that for forty years of desert wandering amid hostile nations and marauding bands we were protected and given physical security by the *annanei hakavod,* the clouds of glory.

Today, though we are not privileged to physically perceive these clouds of glory, we see them through the eyes of faith and belief. When a *chassid* told the Kotzker Rebbe that another Rebbe is visited in his *succah* by the seven giants of Jewish history known as the *Ushpizen,* the Kotzker told him that he, too, clearly sees these guests in his *succah* — through eyes of faith.

King David attests to the protective powers of the invisible clouds of glory: "Let all the nations praise Hashem, let all the people laud Him, for His kindness to us." The sweet singer of Israel tells the nations of the world that they and they alone know all the secret plans that they made to destroy us which were frustrated and aborted by G-d's intervention — by the hidden clouds of glory.

Therein lies the secret of Succos — a festival attesting to the Jewish faith in Hashem to provide a comprehensive package of security which we symbolize by leaving our homes, our citadels of security, to live under the stars and the protection of the invisible clouds of glory.

שמיני עצרת־שמחת תורה
Shemini Atzeres-Simchas Torah

Rabbi Tzvi Flaum

ONE OF THE MOST OUTSTANDING THEMES OF THE SUCCOS FESTIVAL
is the unity that should prevail among all factions of the Jewish
people. This unity, says the Midrash, is represented in the four species,
which we are instructed to hold together each day of Succos, except
Shabbos.

These varied species represent the entire gamut of our nation, each
one alluding to a different type of Jew, from the _esrog,_ which combines
a pleasant taste and aroma, representing the _"esrog_ Jew," one accomplished in Torah scholarship and good deeds, down to the _aravah,_
which has neither taste not smell, representing the _"aravah_ Jew," one
unlearned and empty of kindness. "Let them all be bound together,"
says Hashem, "and they will atone for one another."

Shemini Atzeres portrays an even greater degree of unification
among Jews. In contrast to the seven days of Succos, during which a
total of seventy oxen — corresponding to the seventy nations of the
world — were sacrificed in the _Beis Hamikdash,_ on Shemini Atzeres
only one ox, representing the Jewish people, was sacrificed. This lone
offering, says Rashi, served as a farewell party between the Jewish
people and G-d, Who declares, _"Kasheh Alai preidaschem_ — Your parting is difficult for Me."

Some commentaries, however, interpret _preidaschem_ — your parting
— as the separation and divisiveness among Jews themselves. This lack
of unity perturbs Hashem. The single offering on Shemini Atzeres

serves as a unifying agent for *Klal Yisrael*. Though the *Beis Hamikdash* does not exist today and animal sacrifices are not offered, our annual reading of the *parshah* that details these offerings sends a message that is relevant to us at all times and in all places.

Moreover, the unity manifest in the four species is not a total unity. The *mitzvah* is to take four distinct species; the differences among them are readily noticeable and each retains its particular identity. It is only the *mitzvah* of bringing them together that forms their unification. The unity represented by Shemini Atzeres is different. On this day there is one ox sacrificed, one animal. This is not the unification of separate parts, but one single entity.

The impact of this innate unity should be felt by all Jews in the days and weeks ahead. When the rejoicing and unity of the *Yom Tov* leaves, there should be no fear that the Jewish unity will also dissipate. The solidified unity of Shemini Atzeres will certainly have a lasting effect.

Even after the culmination of the *Yom Tov* it is important that Jews cooperate in a unified and peaceful fashion. Now, more than ever before, Jews who recognize the authenticity of Torah must join hands in a concerted effort to stem the rising tide of assimilation, intermarriage and other ills facing world Jewry today. This can only be accomplished through a cohesive Torah unit dedicated to the perpetuation of Torah-true Judaism through reinforced Torah study and observance of *mitzvos*.

When the *preidaschem* element, the divisiveness among Jews, is minimized and we all work peacefully toward one goal — "to serve Him with one accord" — we will evoke Hashem's supreme blessing. As Rabbi Shimon bar Charlafta declared: "The Almighty found no other vessel that contains blessings for the Jewish people other than peace, as it is written, 'The Almighty shall give strength to His people; and the Almighty shall bless His people with peace.' "

_____ *Rabbi Alfred Cohen*

T HE HOLIDAY CELEBRATES, ONCE AGAIN, THE COMPLETION OF THE yearly cycle of the Torah reading. The last few verses of the Torah recount the death of Moshe Rabbeinu, the outstanding individual in

Jewish history, the lawgiver, the central figure in the mighty drama of the Jewish Exodus and their forty-year sojourn in the wilderness.

Recalling all the incidents in his life, which would one choose to illustrate his greatness? He negotiated with Pharaoh, mightiest ruler in the world. He urged the nation of fleeing slaves into the Red Sea. He bore with the Jewish people in their sorrow and pain and through their bitter denunciations of him when their water was bitter and their food lacking. He ascended Mount Sinai to receive the Tablets of the Torah.

The *Midrash Rabbah* sets the scene: On the eve of the Exodus, Moshe is coordinating all the activities attendant upon the departure of some three million people from Egypt. He must answer questions, field royal emissaries, attend to myriad details. To which responsibility did he turn first?

The Midrash tells us. "Why did Moshe merit [to be the one to give the Torah and lead the Jews out of Egypt]? While all the Israelites were busy [taking] the silver and gold of Egypt, Moshe was going through the city for three days and nights to find the coffin of Yosef."

Hundreds of years earlier, Yosef, as he lay dying, made the Jews promise they would take his bones with them when they left Egypt. With the momentous moment of the Exodus imminent, Moshe put all his efforts into upholding this vow and finding Yosef's casket, which had been hidden by the Egyptians centuries earlier. But there was a problem: no one knew where the casket was.

Enter Serach bas Asher, Yaakov's granddaughter, a woman two hundred years old, who ran into Moshe. Their conversation began with small talk, but Moshe, busy as he was, did not rush off. It was she who knew where to find Yosef's body — it had been brought to the Nile and sunk there. Moshe went to the river and after he prayed for a while, the coffin floated to the surface. Moshe carried it on his back on his way to lead the Jews out of bondage.

Picture that! Moshe Rabbeinu carrying a coffin while the other Jews cart off gold and silver. This summarizes the essence of Moshe's uniqueness and greatness. His concern for the important things in life qualified him to be the first leader of the Jewish people.

America is a youth-oriented society, adulating youthful vigor. Kennedy used to play football on the White House lawn and Clinton makes sure he is photographed jogging. But Judaism respects old age, reveres the achievements of a lifetime of toil. Judaism also teaches that it is not the external trappings of glory that count but rather concern for others.

Surely we must ask ourselves how a Harvard graduate, a man with a Ph.D. from a prestigious university, could be the Unabomber. How could someone of that background and training kill so many people? All his years of education led to — murder? As we extol the brilliant scientists and the youthful technocrats, we must ask ourselves: Is this the right way?

No. This is not the way of Judaism. Judaism states that even the most important person in the nation must take the time to be politely attentive to an old lady. Judaism also teaches that although everyone else may be busy amassing a fortune of gold and silver, the truly wise person concerns himself with keeping a centuries-old code of conduct. As we finish reading the Torah and then begin again, let us remind ourselves of these timeless lessons and use this holiday as an opportunity for improvement and growth.

_____ *Rabbi Donald Bixon*

R AV GEDALIAH SCHORR, *ZT"L,* WRITES IN HIS *SEFER, OHR GEDALIAHU* that the three pilgrim Festivals correspond to our three Patriarchs — Pesach to Avraham, Shavuos to Yitzchak and Succos to Yaakov. The *midrash* teaches that each of the Festivals merits a blessing from the Patriarch associated with it: Pesach provides the world with the blessing for grain, Shavuos the blessing for fruit and Succos the blessing for rain. Each of these blessings are for material concerns. Nevertheless, explains Rav Schorr, they influence our spirituality as well.

But what about Shemini Atzeres? Which Patriarch is represented by this holiday? What blessing is brought to the world from this Festival?

The *Sefas Emes* explains that Shemini Atzeres corresponds to Moshe Rabbeinu. This is evident from the *Midrash Rabbah* at the beginning of *Parshas Vezos Haberachah:*

> Each of them began [his prayer] at the place where his predecessor had left off. How? Avraham blessed Yitzchak, for it is written, "And Avraham gave all that he had to Yitzchak." When Yitzchak

was about to bless Yaakov he said, "I will begin from the place where my father left off. My father left off at [the word] 'Give,' I will begin with 'Give,'" for it is written, "May God give you." And with what did Yitzchak conclude? With "calling," as it is written, "And Yitzchak called Yaakov, and blessed him." When Yaakov was about to bless the tribes he said, "I [too] will begin with 'calling,'" as it is written, "And Yaakov called his sons." And with what did he conclude? With, "And this is," as it is written, "And this is what their father said to them." When Moshe was about to bless Israel he said, "I therefore will begin 'And this is,'" as it is written, "And this is the blessing."

The strength of each blessing, according to this *midrash*, builds from one to the next. Each generation takes part in adding to the blessing. Where one generation leaves off, the other continues.

Shemini Atzeres comes as a continuation of Succos, which is the third of the three pilgrim Festivals. This is alluded to, writes Rav Schorr, in a *pasuk* in *Vezos Haberachah*: "Moshe commanded the Torah to us, an inheritance of the congregation of Yaakov." Yaakov, who is associated with Succos, has a direct alliance to Torah. Moshe, who is associated with Shemini Atzeres, is the "next generation" and is charged with the dissemination of Torah.

Blessings build from generation to generation and represent Jewish continuity and the process of our *mesorah*. Each blessing of the *midrash* could only have been given had the previous blessing been given first. If there was no Succos there would be no Shemini Atzeres. Shemini Atzeres is, therefore, the Festival of continuity, and there is no greater course of continuity among the Jewish people than the perpetuation of Torah.

The blessing of Shemini Atzeres, consequently, is *birkas Hatorah*. On the surface this seems to be inconsistent with the blessings of the other Festivals, which are all material blessings. But all these blessings are part of a *mesorah*. Had there been no blessing from Yaakov, there could be no blessing from Moshe either.

Similarly, if the blessings of grain, fruit and rain were not bestowed upon *Klal Yisrael*, the blessing of Torah would not take effect either. In the new year, may we continue to merit all of these blessings from the *Ribbono Shel Olam*.

חנוכה
Chanukah

_____ *Rabbi Yaacov Haber*

THINKING RECENTLY ABOUT CHANUKAH, A NEW IDEA OCCURRED TO ME. Chanukah, the Festival of Lights, occurs at the darkest time of the year (in the Northern Hemisphere). It occurs at a time when you would least expect it. This is an important characteristic of Judaism — light and holiness occur where one least expects them.

Remember the origin of Chanukah: The Greeks were conquering the world, with their ideas as well as their armies, and were bringing a modern, practical, "enlightened" philosophy to the world. Resistance to this came from where one would have least expected it, from a small group of people, without military power, without weapons, who went into the streets against the Greek rule and were victorious!

I am reminded of a story of a man in Jerusalem, Reb Yehuda Holtzman. He was not a rabbi, not a *dayan,* just a humble Jew in Meah Shearim known as "Yehuda the *Blecher,*" since he made *blechs* (metal covers placed on the stove before Shabbos). There was an American who was in the habit of spending Shabbos with him. He told the story that Reb Yehuda had the custom of making *Kiddush* on *challah,* rather than wine, every Friday evening.

At first he thought that Reb Yehuda might be allergic to wine, but no, on Saturday morning Reb Yehuda would drink wine at *Kiddush.* He did not ask him about this, until one Friday evening, some years later, Reb Yehuda's wife brought him a bottle of wine, which he then used for *Kiddush.* My friend could not contain his curiosity any longer and asked him the reason for this. He answered, "I'll tell you. There's no deep kabbalistic reason. It's very simple." He told him the following story.

Twenty-five years earlier, during the British Mandate, a friend of Reb Yehuda had a serious illness for which the only known cure would cost five thousand pounds sterling, a fortune in those days. He had absolutely no idea how he would raise the money, and came to Reb Yehuda for advice.

Reb Yehuda said to him, "Go ahead and borrow the money, and I'll repay it for you." For he had calculated that if he did without wine at *Kiddush* on Friday evening for twenty-five years, he would be able, with the money saved, to repay the whole debt. And that is what happened. And on that very Shabbos, the twenty-five years ended, and he could go back to having wine for *Kiddush.*

Holiness is found in the most unexpected places. Often it is found coming from people who are quiet and humble — people who have an abiding sense of commitment.

There is a custom, among some people, of turning off the lights when they light the menorah at Chanukah. This emphasizes the idea of light coming forth from darkness, and holiness appearing where it is least expected.

_____ *Rabbi Howard Wolk*

THE TALMUD POSES THE FAMOUS QUERY, "*MAI CHANUKAH?*" WHAT is Chanukah? The Talmud goes on to relate the basic outline of the story: the victory of the Maccabees, culminating in the public lighting of the seven-branched menorah in the *Beis Hamikdash.* "*Naaseh bo neis,*" the Talmud exclaims, a miracle happened and the small flask of oil kept the menorah burning for eight full days. The following year, on the first anniversary of the event, the festival of Chanukah was formally instituted by our Sages.

But why institute a holiday just because of a miracle? Since when were Jews so impressed by miracles that they responded by instituting holidays? To those who don't see G-d as actively involved in the goings-on of the world, a miracle is imposing. But to the Jewish people? Our perspective is that both miracles and nature are equal revelations of

G-d's mastery over the world. Every day Hashem renews the creative process. The sun rises; a baby is born. There are daily, miraculous reminders of the ongoing creative forces of Hashem.

Furthermore, miracles happened regularly in Temple times. *Pirkei Avos* enumerates the ten miracles that occurred daily in the *Beis Hamikdash,* yet no holiday was ever established to commemorate them. Why Chanukah? *Mai Chanukah?*

My rebbe, Rav Moshe Tendler, *shlit"a,* explains that the message of Chanukah is to live up to our potential. The Chanukah miracle shows us that a little oil had more in it than we had suspected. So too, every Jew, even the smallest "flask," contains the energy to give more light than one might imagine. This message is reflected in the singular *halachic* measures that our Sages instituted for this holiday. According to *Halachah,* a pauper must even sell the shirt off his back to purchase oil for the menorah.

Why this requirement? Someone who is destitute is exempt from other *mitzvos;* he does not have to place a *mezuzah* on his door or buy a pair of *tefillin.* But for the sake of the Chanukah lights he has no excuse. He must fulfill the *mitzvah* of *hadlakas neiros* no matter what. Why such a demand?

Because the Chanukah flame exhorts us to have no small dreams. Mediocrity is the antithesis of the Chanukah obligation. We have no excuses. Sell the shirt off your back if necessary, but proclaim to all that the Chanukah lights burn bright, that we believe Hashem expects us to live up to our full potential. That full potential is realized by Yosef in Egypt. From the dungeons of a foreign country, he rises to the second-highest position in the land.

Likewise, in the *haftarah* of *Parshas Mikeitz,* Shlomo Hamelech decides the fate of a baby whom two women are claiming as their child. The *Tanach* tells us: "And all Israel heard the judgment that the king had judged and they feared the king, for they saw that the wisdom of G-d was in him, to do justice." The people saw the greatness imbued in Shlomo as he too realized his full potential.

May the lesson of Chanukah lead us to great accomplishments and the realization of our potential as the *Am Hanivchar.*

פורים
Purim

_____ *Rabbi Menachem Genack*

T HE ARIZAL WRITES OF A CONNECTION BETWEEN PURIM AND YOM
Hakipurim — *yom ke-Purim,* a day like Purim — an association
that, on its face, is difficult to understand. No two days on the Jewish
calendar are more dissimilar than these two: Yom Kippur is a day of
solemnity, awe, introspection and fasting, while Purim is a day of
frivolity, raucousness, drinking and feasting. What common denominator links these two days, which seem to represent antithetical moods
and perspectives?

The Rav, Rav Yosef Dov Soloveitchik, *zt"l,* points to the central role
that a lottery plays in each of these days. At the center of the Temple's
Yom Hakipurim service were two goats, similar in every respect but
one; their destiny. One goat went *Lahashem,* sacrificed to G-d, its blood
sprinkled inside the Holy of Holies. The other went *La'azazeil,* thrown
ignominiously off a cliff in a desolate area far from the Temple. Who
determined which goat would be sacrificed in the Temple and which
would be sent into the wilderness? The *Kohein Gadol* did, by drawing
lots.

Purim, which literally means "lots," also centers around a lottery —
the one Haman conducted to choose the date upon which he would
liquidate all the Jews. The story of Purim is on its surface capricious,
wherein a king kills his wife on the advice of his minister and subsequently hangs his minister on the advice of his next wife. Everything
seems like mere happenstance.

But behind these events, unseen by most of the participants, lies G-d's will, which silently but inexorably guides the storyline. G-d's veiled hand is symbolized by the lack of any mention of His name in the entire *Megillah,* the only book of the Bible to completely leave out the name of G-d.

Nevertheless, our tradition holds that the oft-repeated word *hamelech,* the king, in the *Megillah,* does not refer only to King Achashveirosh, but also to the King — G-d, Who controls the events in history from behind the scenes. This belief runs counter to the nefarious ideology of Amaleik and its scion, Haman, that there is no Divine order or purpose in life, and specifically that the Jewish people have no historical mission.

Purim, therefore, understood in its proper context, is like Yom Hakipurim, confronting us Jews with our frailty and vulnerability. Throughout life, a Jew is buffeted by harsh, haphazard events, but the person of faith recognizes G-d's hand in otherwise erratic events, and in doing so achieves salvation.

Both Yom Hakipurim and Purim celebrate the same fundamental religious theme, namely, that what seems like a lottery, like the result of a historical "uncertainty principle," is, from G-d's omniscient perspective, meaningful and thereby redeeming. This outlook is nurtured by our commitment to Torah, the blueprint for all creation and the affirmation of G-d's constant connection to and intimate concern for the Jewish people and mankind.

It is interesting to note that both Yom Hakipurim and Purim commemorate days of the giving of the Torah. On Yom Kippur, the second tablets were given after the first had been shattered by Moshe. Purim, our Rabbis tell us, is when the Jews accepted the Torah, with a full heart, for at Sinai they were coerced as G-d lifted Mount Sinai above the heads of the Jewish people. Only from the sacred wellsprings of Torah can we achieve the understanding, to give meaning to the events that seem chaotic and harshly fickle, but are in reality part of a Divine higher order.

שבת הגדול
Shabbos Hagadol

_____ *Rabbi Benjamin Blech*

W HAT MAKES A SHABBOS WORTHY OF BEING CALLED *HAGADOL*?
For a Jew, the adjective *gadol* defines the age at which he or she becomes counted as a full-fledged member of our people. It marks a turning point in one's life, representing the change from child to adult. More significantly, it is the moment when one moves from dependence to independence, from being *someich al shulchan aviv* to being *someich al shulchan atzmo.* Human beings begin their lives totally dependent upon their parents, but as years pass, maturity and growth demand the ability to learn to stand on one's own two feet. A grown-up, a *gadol,* is someone responsible for his actions.

To understand the theological principle implicit in this idea, according to Rav Yosef Dov Soloveitchik, *zt"l,* is to grasp the significance of the very first *mitzvah* given to Avraham Avinu, the *mitzvah* of *bris milah.* *Milah* represents the covenant between G-d and man. What is striking, however, is its seeming expression of disrespect to the Almighty Himself and His method of creation. Imagine being presented a bouquet of flowers from a friend and immediately snipping off a few petals to improve its appearance. Yet, the first thing we do after receiving the Divine blessing of a newborn son is to alter what G-d created and presented to us.

To change what G-d made seems a great sin, but only if we suppose that He created a perfect world; a perfect world precludes any efforts at improvement. But clearly this is not the way in which

354 / TORAH INSIGHTS

the Creator decided to fashion His world. Instead, He decided to limit His role with the additional Name of Shakai, which, according to our Sages, refers to the One *she'omer dai,* the One Who said, "Enough."

G-d intentionally left the world imperfect. For what reason? Because, answers the Rav, only an imperfect world leaves room for man to become a partner with G-d in perfecting it. In fact this is the very name G-d used when introducing the *mitzvah* of *milah.* He tells Avraham, "I am Keil Shakai, walk before Me and be perfect." The Jew is told to demonstrate his belief in the mandate for partnership with G-d, an act referred to as a *bris,* a covenant, implying by that very word the concept of shared responsibility.

More remarkable still, the *mitzvah* is to be performed on the eight day of the child's life, symbolizing that after the first seven days of creation, on the eighth day, G-d asks man to complete the world and bring perfection through his efforts.

G-d does not do everything for us. We are not meant to always be *someich al shulchan avinu.* Human beings who reach the status of *gadol* must be big enough to act on their own, to initiate, to take charge without merely waiting for our Father in Heaven to accomplish everything for us. In Egypt, our people watched as G-d punished the Egyptians, but they played no role in the process — until the tenth of Nissan. On that Shabbos, each family was commanded to take a lamb — an animal deified by the ancient Egyptians — to be slaughtered. The Jewish people had to explain their intentions to their Egyptian neighbors and collectively demonstrated for the first time that their faith in G-d did not imply abandonment of their own role in the historic drama of the redemption. This was the first Shabbos Hagadol.

Believing that G-d promises redemption is not equivalent to leaving everything in His hands. In an imperfect world, we too must play a role in assuming our mission as partners with the Almighty to bring the *Geulah.* The original Shabbos Hagadol was not so much the Great Shabbos as the Shabbos on which every one of our people became a *gadol,* prepared, via sacrifice, personal example and partnership with G-d, to perfect this world and hasten the day of the *Geulah.*

SHABBOS HAGADOL SIGNIFIES THE BEGINNING OF THE *BNEI YISRAEL'S* liberation. According to the Talmud, it was on Shabbos, the tenth of Nissan, that the *Bnei Yisrael* rose up and defied that which Egypt deified. Unimpeded by the Egyptians, they freely fulfilled the will of Hashem: "On the tenth of this month, each of them shall take a lamb to a family, a lamb to a household."

Moshe Rabbeinu's previous apprehensions about Egyptian retaliation went unrealized. If liberty is the power to do as one pleases, then on that Great Shabbos, the *Bnei Yisrael,* at last, experienced liberty.

Liberty, however, represents only half of the equation. With liberty comes the responsibility to follow Hashem's charge to choose a lifestyle that is holy, right and good. And Hashem teaches the *Bnei Yisrael* this second, perhaps even more essential element in a very striking way. The *Bnei Yisrael* were instructed to spend the first night of their redemption, the fifteenth of Nissan, confined to their homes. After slaughtering the Paschal lamb, the *Bnei Yisrael* framed their homes and their very lives with the *mitzvah* of painting their doorways — through which they could not exit — with its blood. Why did Hashem begin the Exodus with a night of forced residence?

The Mishnah tells us that seven days prior to Yom Kippur, the *Kohein Gadol* was sequestered in a chamber in the Temple to prepare him for his duties on Yom Kippur. The Talmud asks whether that chamber required a *mezuzah.* The Sages say that it did because it served as a dwelling for the *Kohein Gadol.* Rabbi Yehudah disagrees. He says that since the *Kohein Gadol* is forced to remain in the chamber, it is not a bona fide residence and does not require a *mezuzah.*

Perhaps the Sages believe that a forced residence is nonetheless a bona fide residence, because as long as one has the freedom to choose to frame one's house and one's life with *mitzvah,* one still holds the freedom of self-determination. Thus, many *halachic* authorities rule that even a jail cell requires a *mezuzah,* assuming that the prisoner who lives there enjoys basic religious freedoms.

On Shabbos Hagadol, Hashem empowered the *Bnei Yisrael* with the liberty of free motion and free choice. On the night of Pesach, sealed in their crowded homes, the *Bnei Yisrael* learned that the essence of freedom lies more in our ability to choose, than in our ability to move. And that moment of realization, that moment of *mitzvah*, marks the true beginning of our redemption.

פסח
Pesach

_____ *Rabbi Raphael B. Butler*

THE CENTRAL THEME OF THE PESACH SEDER IS THE FULFILLMENT OF the *mitzvah*, "And you shall tell your child on that day" of G-d's miraculous rescue of the Jewish people from Egypt. Pesach, in general, and the seder, in particular, present an opportunity to explore one of the basic foundations of Judaism: belief in the guiding hand of G-d. By recounting the Jew's redemption from Egypt we can reflect on trends in Jewish history and the *Yad Hashem* — the Hand of G-d — implicit in every response to every challenge against our nation.

Curiously, however, the *Haggadah* begins not with the story of our Exodus from Egypt, but with our enslavement there: "*Avadim hayinu Lepar'oh Bemitzrayim* — We were slaves to Pharaoh in Egypt."

Wouldn't it be more appropriate to begin with our recollection of the original Pesach with the story of redemption, rather than that of enslavement? While we gain great insight into Jewish life in exile by reviewing our national enslavement — we learn, for example, that *Bnei Yisrael* prevented acculturation by keeping their Hebrew names and distinct dress — should that be the focus of the initial statement of the evening? How is that germane to the story of redemption?

The *Sfas Emes* asks us on the seder night to ponder G-d's design in sending us to Egypt. He explains that we must begin the story of redemption with the story of servitude, because the anguish of slavery evolved into an appreciation of G-d and an ability to become closer to Him. Without the experience of servitude, we never would have become the *Am Hanivchar*, G-d's Chosen People.

Had we been alive in Egypt at the time of the enslavement, we probably would not have seen the redeeming quality of the experience. We would have cried, "Why is G-d putting us through this?" What good can come out of years of terror and pain? Little would we realize that enslavement is the first step toward becoming as one with G-d.

A Torah scholar once told me that he spends significant time at the seder recounting his personal "slavery" — his years of suffering in Europe during the Second World War. He uses the seder to recount before family and friends the miracles that were born from the pains of life. He points to the hand of G-d that led him to freedom, to build a family and a life out of the ashes of Europe.

Pesach is a time, therefore, to reflect upon the moments of anguish in our national history and, with long-term perspective, appreciate the message of hope in every challenge to our national and personal survival. Just as slavery ultimately turned into redemption under the hand of G-d, so too every personal and communal challenge should be looked upon as a contemporary opportunity for reaching ever closer toward *Hakadosh Baruch Hu*.

 *Rabbi Pinchas Stolper*

THE JEWISH NATION WAS BORN ON PESACH — A BIRTH UNLIKE ANY other, uniting G-d, the Torah and *Am Yisrael* in an unbreakable, eternal relationship. This relationship is best symbolized in the manner in which G-d chose to give the Jews His Torah.

The Torah describes the words of the Ten Commandments as "*charus al haluchos*" — inscribed on the Tablets. Our Sages teach: "Do not pronounce it *charus*, inscribed; instead, pronounce it *cheirus*, freedom — freedom from the Angel of Death." What is the purpose of this change in pronunciation? What is the connection between the Ten Commandments and the Angel of Death?

The Talmud instructs a person who witnesses the *yetzias neshamah* — the soul's departure from the body, that is, the moment of death — of a fellow Jew, to tear his clothing. "To what is this comparable? To a Torah scroll that is burned."

Rav Yitzchok Hutner, zt"l, points out the halachah that one who witnesses the destruction of a Sefer Torah must tear his clothing twice — once for the parchment that was destroyed, and again for the writing. As the Talmud compares a human life to a Sefer Torah, Rav Hutner reasons, it is apparent that an analogy exists between the soul within the body and the letters upon the parchment. One can compare the human body to the parchment of a Torah scroll, his soul to its letters. Just as the letters of the Torah are distinct from the parchment upon which they are written, so too a person's soul is distinct from his body.

This distinction, however, does not apply to the inscription on the Tablets of the Ten Commandments. These letters are charus, chiseled through the stone, not ink atop parchment. Once chiseled, these letters become an intrinsic part of the stone. They can be neither erased nor separated.

Similarly, these chiseled letters represent the special relationship between the Torah and Israel that began with the Exodus and culminated at Sinai, a relationship in which the two can not be separated, in which one constitutes an intrinsic part of the other. "Yisrael Ve'oraisa chad hu — Israel and the Torah are one." They constitute an eternal unity.

This unique, eternal relationship explains the message of the Sages in reading the word charus, inscribed, as cheirus, freedom. The relationship between Am Yisrael and the Torah is so permanent that it creates a freedom. What kind of freedom? Freedom from the Angel of Death. The Covenant Israel achieved through the Tablets created an eternal relationship with G-d and Torah that is not subject to physical death. The body, the nation of Israel, and its soul, the Torah, are eternal; the two can not be separated. Every person who attaches himself to Klal Yisrael achieves eternal life.

_____ *Rabbi Bertram Leff*

D URING THIS FESTIVAL OF PESACH, WE COMMIT OURSELVES TO THE fulfillment of the mitzvah of sipur yetzias Mitzrayim, retelling the story of our Exodus from Egypt. We study the Torah text and the commentaries of our Sages at the seder table. We seek to understand the purpose of the Exodus. Obviously, for the Israelites, the Exodus was their liberation from bondage. But what did Pharaoh and the Egyptians learn from the miraculous events and their encounter with the G-d of Israel?

Prior to the Exodus, Pharaoh considered himself divine. He proclaimed, "Who is Hashem that I should heed His voice? I do not know the G-d of Israel." The plagues and miracles of the Exodus, explained Rav Yosef Dov Soloveitchik, *zt"l*, came to teach Pharaoh and the citizens of Egypt that there is a G-d Who is not only Master of the universe but also the Guide and Determiner of history.

G-d could have freed the Israelites in one sweeping act of coercion. But Hashem's plan of plagues, signs and wonders had an important purpose: "In order to show you My strength, and that My name may be declared throughout the world." It wasn't enough to just liberate the Jewish people; G-d had to be recognized, acknowledged. His Presence had to be unequivocally established.

The verse in *Sefer Devarim* states, "Hashem took us out of Egypt with a strong Hand, with an outstretched Arm, with great awesomeness and with signs and with wonders." What does "great awesomeness" refer to? "*Gilui Shechinah* — the Revelation of G-d's Presence," our Sages respond in the *midrash* quoted in the *Haggadah*. It was the manifestation of G-d's Presence, which Pharaoh and the Egyptians had to acknowledge and which led to the Exodus from Egypt.

The Rav understood that this was the underlining reason for Moshe's request to Pharaoh that the Jews leave Egypt for three days in order to serve G-d. Why ask for only three days when the request could have been for total liberation?

This was Pharaoh's test. Pharaoh would only have allowed the Jews to leave Egypt, to worship Hashem even for a short time, if he recognized the existence and the sovereignty of G-d. The granting of a three-day release would symbolize that Pharaoh was no longer a non-believer. His recognition of G-d would eventually lead to the complete liberation of the Israelites.

The importance of *gilui Shechinah*, the Revelation of G-d, which both Israel and Egypt learned from the Exodus, must be incorporated into the spiritual lives of every generation of Jews. We underscore this need not only through our annual observance of the Festival of Pesach, but every week during our Shabbos experience. When we proclaim in the

Kiddush that Shabbos is *"zeicher le'yitzias Mitzrayim* — a memorial to the Exodus from Egypt," the very lesson of *mora gadol* is implied. The Presence of G-d, the *gilui Shechinah*, in our individual and national lives is affirmed by our observance of the Shabbos.

For six days we utilize the Divine gift of *melachah* — creative work — to indicate our right to master the world that G-d has given us. But on Shabbos we reaffirm the lesson of Pesach: that G-d is the real Master and that His *Shechinah*, His Presence, governs our Jewish existence. This teaching of Passover shapes us as a people and strengthens our commitment to Torah and *mitzvos*. May we adopt this awareness from the Pesach seder and carry it with us throughout the year.

_____ *Rabbi Raymond Harari*

WE CELEBRATE THE HOLIDAY OF PASSOVER BY JOINING OUR FAMILIES and friends at the seder table. From the seder's outset, most of us look forward to the time we will eat, and though the actual meal is delayed until relatively late into the night's festivities, lessons about what our attitude toward meals and eating should be abound from the very moment we sit at the table.

The seder begins with the recitation of *Kiddush*, despite the fact that the meal will not follow for some time. Next, after tasting the *karpas* and breaking the matzah, we invite all disadvantaged Jews to join us as we read the *Haggadah* and retell the story of our exodus from Egypt. All this takes place before the meal is eaten — not after or during the meal. Why?

Clearly, the Passover seder provides a lesson in the etiquette of eating. All year long, we recite blessings before and after eating, and, in doing so, we raise the physical act of eating to a higher plane. On Passover night, however, we display how a truly Jewish meal is organized.

One who sits down to eat, particularly on a holiday, must first acknowledge that the Jewish people, like this day, have been sanctified by G-d. Furthermore, a meal must be preceded by the recognition that the poor always have a place at our table. Though we do not follow the practice of one of the Babylonian *Amora'im*, who would recite daily the invitation to the poor, *"Ha lachma anya,"* we do say these words on Passover night to single out one of the critical components of every meal. Indeed, Maimonides writes that if no poor person attends one's festival meal, his feast is simply for the purpose of filling his stomach.

Even after *Kiddush* has been recited and an invitation to the poor has been tendered, we are still not ready for the actual meal. *Divrei Torah* and songs of slavery and redemption take precedence over our appetites.

If we perform the seder correctly, we have eaten at least one meal during the year the way it ought to be eaten. In this sense, the seder shares common ground with other *mitzvos* and practices throughout the year. For example, it is incumbent upon each of us to repent our sins every day. Nevertheless, certain days of the year have been set aside for particular emphasis on repentance.

Likewise, the need to remind ourselves of our sanctity as G-d's chosen people, our responsibility to the poor, and our obligation to engage in the study of Torah before tending to our physical needs is a daily challenge. One night during the year is set aside to highlight these duties.

Rabbi Ilan Feldman

A MAJOR DIMENSION OF THE PESACH EXPERIENCE — PROBABLY A more prominent feature in our post-industrial society than ever before — is the elimination of *chametz* from our homes during Pesach. Preparing for Pesach is a daunting task, and warrants a holiday just to celebrate its successful completion! As we enjoy our *chametz*-free *Yom Tov,* having struggled through these agonizing preparatory days, we ought to absorb some of the impressions that the elimination process is meant to leave with us.

One interesting *halachah* we come across in our obligation of searching for the *chametz* pertains to *chametz shenafal alav mapoles* — *chametz* that is inaccessible because it is buried under a heavy object. One is not required to search for and destroy this *chametz*, but may rely instead upon his verbal nullification to resolve any problems posed by its existence on his property. The lesson presented by this *halachah* is far reaching. *Chametz* is the representation of the *yeitzer hara*, man's evil impulse. Thus, while we are required to mount a frontal assault against the *yeitzer hara* in the guise of *chametz*, we know too well that we will fall short in our desire to reach every nook and cranny.

Just as some of the *chametz* in our possession may be impossible to destroy, the complete elimination of our evil inclinations is beyond our grasp as humans. In such cases, we must rely on help from Above to complete the task. Divine assistance will come in response to our prayers, our verbal nullification of the *yeitzer hara*, as we ask G-d each morning to "compel our inclination to be dedicated to You."

A passage from *Mishlei* reinforces the concept that the Almighty completes the task of spiritual soul-cleansing begun in earnest by us mere mortals: "*Ner Hashem nishmas adam chopeis kol chadrei baten* — The lamp of G-d searches the innermost chambers of man's soul." It is for us to begin the duty of self-cleansing, aware that G-d is our partner in completing the task.

_____ *Rabbi Efraim Davidson*

A BSOLUTE FREEDOM EXISTS ONLY WITHIN THE BOUNDARIES OF ABSOLUTE servitude — this is the message of Pesach. Hashem commands us to be grateful to Him for delivering us from slavery in Egypt and orders us to express that gratitude by enlisting as His servants. "For the children of Israel are servants to Me; they are My servants, whom I have taken out of the land of Egypt. I am Hashem, your G-d."

This is not mere flowery language. We truly must be obedient servants to a powerful and demanding Master. At the same time, Pesach is *zeman cheiruseinu*, the time of our freedom. We are no longer subject to the murderous whims of a flesh-and-blood despot. We are free. But how can we be free if we remain servants? Servitude implies dependence. Freedom implies independence.

The lesson of Pesach is that our servitude is a necessary prerequisite for our freedom. A slave serves a master because he depends on the master — for food and drink, for physical well-being, for a wife and family, for his education. All aspects of a servant's identity depend on the allowance and validation of his master.

Rav Yerucham Levovitz, *zt"l*, the Mirrer *mashgiach*, teaches that this is how we become slaves. Our happiness becomes dependent upon elements that exist outside ourselves, important as they may be. We hinge our self-identity on what we do and what we have, rather than on what we are. We ought not to depend on anything outside ourselves for happiness and self-esteem. This is true even if one loses a loved one, a job, a sense of accomplishment. Fundamental as these are, the independent soul relies on none of them, but remains the creation of Hashem, totally free from all else. This sense of self-possession can only be had when one thoroughly understands that the only reality is Hashem. "He is our G-d; nothing else exists." The persecution of Egypt is temporary and external; only Hashem and His Torah are permanent.

Victor Frankl describes seeing Jews in the camps who did not let the German oppressors define their character. These Jews chose to be ethical, thoughtful, even happy, despite their inhumane environment. When all else was stripped away, they were left with themselves and Hashem. This is real freedom.

Just as external sources of misery are not real, so too external sources of happiness are illusory. Those many important things which make up life — family, income, study, community, recreation — can and should bring about a great sense of pleasure, accomplishment and satisfaction. However, one is only free when he realizes that his relationship with Hashem transcends all else.

One is absolutely free when he places his entire self in the service of the One True Source. The Torah and the principles of *mussar*, with the proper *halachic* application in each of our lives, is how that service is defined for each of us. And with that absolute servitude comes absolute freedom.

_____ *Rabbi David Hirsch*

T HESE DAYS, IT SEEMS THAT EVERY PHONE CALL (PARTICULARLY THE one arriving at dinner time) contains another appeal for charity. It is difficult to find a piece of "real" mail amid the bounty of solicitations that arrive daily. Even our e-mail boxes, a symbol of our fledgling computer literacy, store frequent pleas for charity. How do we respond to these pleas? We train our children to put a coin every day, or before Shabbos, into the *pushkah*, but have we honestly developed a similar regimen for ourselves?

Three times a year, on the eighth day of Pesach, the second day of Shavuos, and Shemini Atzeres, we read the same Torah portion — a discussion of the relationship one must have with the poor: "If there shall be a destitute person among you, any of your brethren in any of your cities, in the land that Hashem, your G-d, gives you, you shall not harden your heart or close your hand to your destitute brother. Rather, you shall open your hand to him; you shall lend him his requirement, whatever is lacking to him."

The Torah is specific. One must override his natural inclination to deny or even limit the gift. One of the first words in a young child's burgeoning vocabulary is "mine," and even as adults, we feel that we have labored long hours and endured tremendous hardships to feed, clothe and educate our families. Confronted with a request for charity, we very often regress to this yelp from our childhood.

The Torah continues: "You shall surely give him, and let your heart not feel bad when you give him, for in return for this matter, Hashem your G-d will bless you in all your deeds and in your every undertaking."

"You shall *surely give*" signals Hashem's awareness that it takes extra effort to overcome the disinclination to part with our possessions. Hashem also reminds us, with a double expression, that the reward is commensurate with the effort. Repeating the words of *Tehillim* every day in our prayers, we beg Hashem for graciousness and generosity: "Open Your hand, and satisfy the needs of every living creature."

It is ironic that while we have no qualms in beseeching Hashem for assistance, our spirituality often dissipates when the doorbell rings or the phone call beckons. For with a closed fist, one can neither give nor receive. If we don't give to our fellow man, we cut off our ability to receive from Hashem.

We read during the Torah portion on the eighth day of Pesach, that we "shall not appear before Hashem empty-handed — every one [must bring] according to what he can give, according to the blessing that Hashem your G-d gives you." We are reminded amid our own celebration, that if we have not provided for the poor among us, we are lacking.

Today, unfortunately, we are not privileged to live in a time where there is a Temple for us to travel to. We do not come to Jerusalem each year with our first fruits, our sacrifices, or our tithes. Nevertheless, we can open our hands and we can open our hearts. Instead of feeling pinched or squeezed at the next request for charity, however inconvenient, let us try to reach a little deeper. For unlike other forms of exercise, this spiritual workout offers a maximum yield.

_____ *Rabbi Moshe Shulman*

*Z*EMAN CHEIRUSEINU, THE TIME OF OUR FREEDOM, IS THE ESSENTIAL theme of the holiday of Pesach. Still, one must understand what *cheirus* means, for the Jewish concept of freedom is very different from its secular counterpart. In the language and culture of the Western "free" world, freedom is the opposite of slavery; it means freedom from physical labor, freedom from limitations imposed by others, freedom to do what you want, to say what you want, to be whom you want. To the extent that society places limitations on us, society limits our freedom.

The Jewish notion of freedom is very different. In Judaism, freedom is inexorably connected to the moral responsibilities that accompany not physical opportunities but spiritual ones. For a Jew, freedom denotes a higher purpose in life. The Jewish people became free on Pesach when we became a new nation, with a new purpose and a new direction. The essence of Pesach is the celebration of that spiritual freedom.

This freedom connects Pesach to Shavuos. Through the counting of the *omer*, we link the two holidays, as our spiritual freedom was not complete until the giving of the Torah seven weeks later. When we accepted upon ourselves a new lifestyle through a commitment to the laws and values of the Torah, we achieved true freedom.

Our Sages allude to this notion when they say, regarding the Ten Commandments, which the Torah describes as *charus*, engraved, in the tablet's stone, "Do not read it *charus* but *cheirus*" — freedom. The greatest freedom is the ability to carry out the will of the Creator through the study of His Torah.

Throughout the history of our people the question has been raised: How can we celebrate the festival of freedom while living in the Diaspora, often under intense persecution and affliction? For how many centuries did the Jewish people live in societies that seriously curtailed their rights and their freedoms, yet continued to celebrate Pesach? Was this not a contradiction?

Indeed, if one understands freedom in a physical sense, perhaps it would have been a contradiction. In fact, if one looks at physical freedom, the Exodus itself did not permanently change our status, for we may yet again be enslaved, as was the case after the Babylonian exile. We must therefore look at freedom in spiritual terms. Once the Torah was given, once the identity of the Jewish people became linked to the laws of the Torah, then freedom is eternal. Freedom that stems from pride in our spiritual mission can never be taken away from the Jew, ever.

Our Sages teach, "There is no free man except the one who is involved in Torah." If the deeper meaning of Pesach is the pride at being able to follow the Almighty's Torah, then what better way to internalize and understand the profound meaning of freedom than the diligent study of the Almighty's greatest gift: the Torah itself.

Celebrate the real Pesach and experience what true Jewish freedom is all about through the study of Torah.

יום העצמאות
Yom Ha'atzma'ut

_____ *Rabbi Morey Schwartz*

JUST AS PESACH BEHOOVES US TO REFLECT ON HOW *YETZIAS MITZRAYIM* impacts upon our contemporary lives, so too *Yom Ha'atzma'ut* gives us reason to reflect upon the vital role *Medinat Yisrael* plays in our lives.

At a Mizrachi convention, some forty years ago, Rav Yosef Dov Soloveitchik, *zt"l*, compared the work of Mizrachi to the life of Yosef. Yosef was concerned about the future of *Bnei Yisrael*. He believed that their national destiny was about to take a turn and dreamed about how they could prepare for the new civilization on the horizon. His brothers, on the other hand, saw their future as a continuation of the present. They would forever remain in their father's home, generation after generation.

Yosef dreamed of the stars, the moon, the sun. He had visions of grandiose technical advancements, challenges to their heritage and solutions to those challenges. The brothers said, in effect, "That's not our business to figure out; that's G-d's domain." Clearly, G-d led history forward according to Yosef's position. Preparation for Jewish survival in a new and alien society was imperative.

At the dawn of the 20th century, many Jews saw the future of the Jewish people merely as a continuation of the present. Thousands of Jews wanted nothing to do with the winds of advancement. The new world did not interest them at all. Others, however, could not sit back. Seeing destruction on the horizon, they knew intuitively to move forward, to establish the foundations of *Medinat Yisrael*, to advance the physical and spiritual survival of *Klal Yisrael*.

Just as Yosef dealt with the Egyptians, with whom he had very little in common, in order to secure the survival of his family, so too the policy of religious Zionists has always been to find common ground with secular Jews, with whom we have much more in common for the sake of Jewish survival.

And yet, although Yosef's insights maintained the survival of the house of Israel, he is introduced to us with the words, "Yosef brought disparaging gossip about [his brothers] to their father." But did he mean to be disparaging, or rather to be corrective, to point out the inappropriate shortcomings of his brothers, the founding fathers of the Jewish nation?

Perhaps religious Zionists should not make waves with those who refuse to recognize the sacred value of *Medinat Yisrael*. After all, the Torah admonishes us not to gossip. On the other hand, the Torah states, "Do not stand idly by while your neighbor bleeds."

It is time for religious Zionists to come forward and reclaim our position as the uniting force of *Klal Yisrael*. We must again have a voice. *Klal Yisrael* is bleeding. We must speak out against actions and positions coming from both the right and the left, which impede the ongoing development of *Medinat Yisrael* as the modern manifestation of the prayers and dreams of Jews throughout the centuries, *reishis tzemichas geulaseinu*.

_____ *Rabbi Mark Dratch*

THE FRENCH SOCIOLOGIST CLAUDE LEVI-STRAUSS REPORTED THAT he once came upon a tribe that claimed to have the ability to see the planet Venus in broad daylight. This seemed to him totally implausible. But upon further research, astronomers confirmed that, considering the amount of light that the planet emitted, such a sighting was conceivable. Levi-Strauss later recorded that he subsequently found old treatises on navigation that indicated that western sailors, at one time, were able to see Venus in full daylight. Perhaps we could too, if only we knew how.

What is true of the physical world is true of the spiritual world as well. The beauty of Shabbos, the aura of prayer, the radiance of Torah and the presence of Hashem in our lives are all right before us. We could see them — if only we knew how.

Spiritual vision is not universal. Consider: Avraham and Yitzchak left for the *Akeidah* accompanied by two lads, Yishmael and Eliezer. The *midrash* recounts that when they reached Mount Moriah, Avraham turned to Yitzchak and asked, "My son, do you see what I see?"

"Yes," responded Yitzchak.

Avraham turned to the two others and asked, "Do you see what I see?"

They answered no.

Avraham instructed the two to stay with the donkey while he and Yitzchak ascended the mountain, "since donkeys do not see and you do not see." Avraham called that place Hashem Yireh, "as it is said to this day, in the mount where the Lord is seen." Only those with spiritual insight merit ascending to Divine heights.

As we celebrate the anniversary of the State of Israel, we have the opportunity to reaffirm our vision of G-d's role in its establishment. Reb Dovid Cohen, *zt"l*, the famed *nazir* of Jerusalem, put it well in his comment on the phrase in our prayers, "May our eyes behold Your return to Zion." It is not only G-d's return to Zion for which we pray, but for our ability to see and appreciate His presence at the time of that return as well.

We, who are proud religious Zionists, believe firmly in G-d's role in the modern Zionist enterprise, whether we consider the establishment of the State as "the beginning of the messianic redemption" or simply acknowledge the great Divine kindness that the creation of the State represents. But many of us have lost our sense of spiritual vision. The euphoria of 1948 and of 1967 has waned. Partisan politics and personal proclivities have muffled our religious and spiritual connections to the land and the state.

Dr. Norman Lamm, in his essay, "The Face of G-d: Thoughts on the Holocaust," describes our present challenge. While the Holocaust was a period of *hester panim*, Divine concealment, he wrote, the establishment of the State of Israel was a period of *nesias panim*, in which G-d turns toward us, giving us "the opportunity to return G-d's glance, to fill our lives with meaning and not emptiness, with providence and not chance, with destiny and not fate."

May this Yom Ha'atzma'ut be an opportunity to renew our vision and to reopen our eyes. As the prophet Yeshayahu promised, "Lift up your eyes round about, and see: They all are gathered together, and come to you.... Then you shall see and be radiant. And your heart shall throb and be enlarged."

שבועות
Shavuos

_____ *Rabbi Bernard Rosensweig*

S HAVUOS COMMEMORATES THE GIVING OF THE TORAH AT MOUNT SINAI
Judaism ultimately stands upon our affirmation of the events at
Sinai — that G-d, in a manner that we mortals may find difficult to
understand, appeared to the people of Israel at a particular time and
place and gave us the Torah to illuminate our lives for all generations.
The *Aseres Hadibros*, the Ten Commandments, are the start of the
revelation.

The first commandment begins: "I am the L-rd your G-d Who took
you out of the land of Egypt, out of the house of bondage." Rav Avraham Ibn Ezra records a question posed to him by Rav Yehudah Halevi:
Why did G-d reveal himself to the Jewish people with this description?
Why not say, "I am the L-rd your G-d Who created heaven and earth"?

Ibn Ezra answers with the classic phrase, *"Eino domeh shemi'ah
lere'iyah* — What one hears is not comparable to what one sees." The
story of Creation was something the Israelites had only heard of, an
event handed down to them as part of their national tradition. But they
had personally experienced the Exodus from Egypt. The impact of their
redemption, more than any other event, served to affirm their belief in
the One, living G-d of Israel.

One can also understand the distinction between these two descriptions another way. To describe G-d as the Creator of heaven and earth
is, in effect, to describe Him as the G-d of Nature. But to characterize
G-d as the Redeemer of Israel is to declare that He is the G-d of History.

This was one of the great contributions of Judaism to the understanding of G-d. In giving the Torah, G-d wished to impress upon the children of Israel that He is not only the Creator of the physical world, but that He also guides and directs the destinies of men and nations. G-d is involved in the lives of every person and every country. The implication is clear: We are not alone; G-d cares for us and will never abandon us.

Rav Yosef Dov Soloveitchik, zt"l, responding to Rav Yehuda Halevi's question, provides a beautiful insight. In this world, the Rav says, G-d manifests Himself on two levels. On one level, G-d is the King of the Universe. "Reign over all the universe in Your glory," Jews declare in their prayers. On another level, G-d is "King of Israel and her Redeemer." G-d is, at once, King of the universe and also, especially, King of Israel.

In creating the universe, G-d did not create a special relationship with the Jewish people; that first came as a result of the Exodus from Egypt.

G-d's identification as Redeemer of Israel has far-reaching consequences. It imposes a singular responsibility upon the Jewish people in human history. G-d chose us, not for greater accolade, but for greater responsibility; not only to be guardians of His Torah, but, by accepting a regimen of 613 mitzvos, to be living embodiments of its values and demands. To be a Jew is to live a responsible Jewish lifestyle and to sanctify G-d's Name every day in every arena of life. At the same time, G-d redeems us in every generation and reaffirms His commitment to us as Melech Yisrael, the G-d of Israel.

_____ *Rabbi Moshe J. Yeres*

ONE OF THE LINCHPINS OF THE JEWISH FAITH, PRESENTED BY RABBI Yehudah Halevi in the *Kuzari*, is Hashem's revelation to over six hundred thousand Israelites. Judaism is not based on hearsay or philosophical speculation. Nor does it rest on the oracle or a divination received by a single "prophet." Rather, *Am Yisrael* in its entirety witnessed, directly and openly, many miracles of Hashem, both in Egypt and in the wilderness of Sinai.

The most significant of these miracles, theologically and religiously, was G-d's revelation to us of the Torah, commonly referred to as *ma-amad Har Sinai*, which we celebrate on this holiday of Shavuos.

The Torah makes it patently clear that G-d's magnificent performance was visible to all of *Klal Yisrael*, His words heard by the entire people. We are told: "All the people perceived the thunder and lightning and the sound of the *shofar*." This marvelous and awe-inspiring spectacle of G-d appearing to a vast audience of direct and immediate witnesses remains unique in the history of world religions. As the *Kuzari* notes, it would be close to impossible to fabricate such a tale and claim that so many people could vouch for it.

Just as importantly, the Midrashic literature paints a picture of not only *Bnei Yisrael* being witness to this seminal event. The revelation at Sinai was heard around the world. Not one animal moved, not one person spoke, not one blade of grass rustled while G-d uttered those epic commandments. The entire world, too, served as eternal witnesses to these magical moments at Sinai.

However, one ought not forget that immediately subsequent to the public proclamation of the Ten Commandments, the Israelites sinned with the Golden Calf, resulting in the smashing of the two tablets by Moshe. Rashi suggests that, ironically, the *luchos* were destined to be broken specifically because of the public fanfare that accompanied their reception. And the longevity accorded to the second set of *luchos* was due primarily to their being received in a non-ostentatious manner.

If so, why did Hashem choose to present the Ten Commandments in such a public forum? And why is this story the focus of our Torah reading on Shavuos?

Rav Yosef Dov Soloveitchik, *zt"l*, suggests that, though G-d was aware of the consequences, it was nevertheless essential that He state the Ten Commandments — and by extension the entire Torah — openly, so that all the nations of the world would become exposed and sensitized to our religious beliefs, tenets and laws. As significant as the Torah was for *Klal Yisrael*, it needed to be enunciated publicly for the rest of mankind.

The Rav adds that the two events described by the Torah immediately prior to the Sinaitic Revelation are the arrival of Yisro to the Israelite camp and the attack on Israel by Amaleik. Both of these heard of Hashem's miracles. Yisro heard and joined the cause, impressed by G-d's law. Amaleik heard and came to weaken and destroy the nation. The Torah was proclaimed not only for *Klal Yisrael* but also for all of the Yisros of the world, and even for the Amaleiks.

Our obligation, as proud inheritors of Sinai's legacy, is to spread and share the moral and ethical ideals of our faith with the family of man. We tend to view Shavuos, *zeman mattan Toraseinu*, in a parochial fashion, linking it with Jewish religious commitment as is indeed implied by the words spoken at Sinai, *"Naaseh venishma."* Yet, Shavuos is also the holiday that enabled us to become the *ohr lagoyim*, setting the moral and ethical standards for the world.

To be a religious Jew, one must accept both the ritual and the ethical components of our faith equally. One can not be divorced from the other. Facing G-d, we need to be as ritually righteous as possible; facing mankind — both Jew and non-Jew — we need to present a faith of ethical rectitude and upright morality, for our goal in this life is to allow Hashem's word to enter this world.

_____ *Rabbi Zalman Posner*

T HE FABLED WISE SON OF THE *HAGGADAH* NOTES THE DIFFERENT categories of *mitzvos* — *eidos*, *chukim* and *mishpatim*. *Eidos* are testimonial commandments, reminders of great events in our history. *Chukim* are inexplicable, trans-rational commandments; they are observed simply because they are the law of G-d.

The third type, *mishpatim*, are the rational commands that every society subscribes to, such as honor your father and mother, have an honest business, treat people respectfully. So obvious are *mishpatim* to any civilized society that one wonders: Why does the Torah need to identify them and place them on par with the other *mitzvos*?

As the 19th century was ending, man began to feel confident that he could solve all human problems. Diseases that had brought dread and death began to be cured. Science could boast of many successes. But as the 20th century comes to a close, man is not as confident. Walk on the moon? Easy. Transplant hearts? No problem. But define right from wrong, good from evil? Whoa. No easy answers to those questions.

The Ten Commandments include some obviously simple directives. Ask any kindergarten child and he will tell you, "Don't take someone else's crayon." "Don't hurt anyone." Aren't these commandments superfluous? Hardly. As science continues to answer many questions, it still can not demonstrate that killing and stealing are evil.

"Science makes no value judgments," we are told. This insight is a 20th century product. How to make an atom bomb? No problem. Whether to drop it on a city? That's someone else's decision, the scientist will say. But don't scientists make moral decisions? Don't they have families, raise children? What values do they teach them? A scientist once told me, "I'm a scientist two percent of the time. The rest of the time I'm a slob like everyone else."

But the Jews have Sinai to turn to. What does Sinai say to the 21st century? There is good and there is evil, and man must not create his own moral code to distinguish between the two. Society can not determine good and evil. After all, the Soviet Union and Nazi Germany were "societies." They had "codes." Everything the Nazis and Bolsheviks did was according to their "laws."

The Talmud says that man's evil impulse does not urge him at the outset to worship idols. Instead it breaks him down slowly. It says, "Do this," and the next day, "Do that," until it finally urges idolatry.

The Lubavitcher Rebbe, zt"l, suggests that the yeitzer hara often begins by urging us to do mitzvos we agree with. We then become arbiters over what we do and come to violate those mitzvos we do not understand or agree with. We can not be trusted to accurately ascertain right from wrong. Our definitions of right and wrong must instead come from a Source apart from man, higher than man. And that Source spoke to us through the Torah.

The wise son recognizes that every mitzvah, even the mishpatim, even the ones that seem so logical that they need no mention — "Do not kill"; "Do not steal" — need the Torah's imperative to be valid. Otherwise, they too will eventually be corrupted.

_____ *Rabbi Moshe Sokol*

T HE REVELATION AT MOUNT SINAI, WHICH WE CELEBRATE ON SHAVUOS, enabled each Jew to hear G-d's voice amid the miraculous thunder, lightning and sounds of the *shofar*. How is it, then, that it took no more than three days following their departure from Sinai for corruption to set in? As the verse states, "And they journeyed from G-d's mountain three days. . . . And the nation were as murmurers, speaking evil in the ears of the Lord."

The sin of the Golden Calf, which took place at Sinai itself, may have involved a subtle theological error, as some commentators urge. But how we are to understand their "murmuring" and evil speech — that seems to be plain bad behavior. How did the spiritual high of Sinai evaporate so rapidly?

One explanation may rest on a distinction between two forms of love, which I shall call external love and internal love.

External love strikes from without. Powerful circumstances ensnare a person, leading him or her to fall in love. These circumstances can be superficial, such as great beauty or charm, or they can be deeper personality traits. But in either case, the effect is immediate and powerful, the person is smitten overwhelmingly with love. The second form of love is internal. Internal love grows slowly, over time, as two persons get to know each other. As time goes by, they increasingly appreciate each other's strengths, and each new phase of the relationship calls forth a different, deeper, response. Their love grows incrementally.

Internal love is based on increased knowledge and understanding of the other. It is also internalized through the daily routines of a life together, from making a morning cup of coffee to putting the toothpaste cap back on. These two forms of love may characterize not only interpersonal relationships, but also the relationship between humans and G-d. G-d's presence at Sinai was so overwhelming to *Bnei Yisrael* that they were captured by love for Him.

But this was only an external form of love, a spiritual high not yet integrated into their lives. They had not yet painstakingly worked to deepen their understanding of G-d, nor had they taken the many steps necessary to integrate that spiritual insight into the daily routines of their lives. Therefore, three days into their journey, the spiritual high evaporated in the desert sun.

Rabbi Levi Yitzchak of Berditchev, in his *Kedushas Levi*, explains that great spiritual achievements must be captured in restraint, or they vanish. Hashem wanted *Bnei Yisrael* to control their passion at the mountain, and to thereby, paradoxically, sustain it.

The Torah is not only about spiritual insight and passion, but also — perhaps even more so — about internalizing and integrating that spirituality through the routines and disciplines of a commanded life. The experience at Sinai was G-d's voice; but what G-d spoke was the language of law. Law without the experience of G-d's voice is empty; the experience of G-d's voice without the Law is evanescent.

On Shavuos we celebrate both.

תשעה באב

Tishah B'Av

_____ *Rabbi Bernard E. Rothman*

A BOUT TWO HUNDRED YEARS AGO, WHEN THE RENOWNED EMPEROR Napoleon Bonaparte visited the Land of Israel, he stopped at a synagogue and was surprised to see all the Jews praying while sitting on the floor instead of in their seats. Told he had come on a special day, one on which the Jews mourned the destruction of their Holy Temple, he asked, "When was the Temple destroyed?"

"Over seventeen hundred years ago," came the answer.

Napoleon's reaction was historic: "A nation that still mourns a Temple that was destroyed seventeen centuries ago is destined to witness its rebuilding."

Napoleon was probably unaware that he was echoing the words of our Sages, who said, "Whoever mourns over Jerusalem merits seeing its rebuilding."

At the end of *Makkos*, the Talmud records the story of Rabbi Akiva who, together with his colleagues, visited the site of the Temple ruins, There they saw a fox exiting the Holy of Holies. Seeing such degradation of the holiest of sites, the Rabbis cried. But Rabbi Akiva laughed.

"Why do you laugh?" they asked him.

"Now that the prophecy of Uriah has been fulfilled," Rabbi Akiva answered (referring to the verse, "Zion will be plowed like a field"), "it is certain that the prophecy of Zechariah will be fulfilled" and Jerusalem will be restored to her former glory.

In the *Kinos* service of Tishah B'Av, a day of mourning over the destruction of both Temples, the tragic deaths of the *asarah harugei malchus*, the ten martyrs, is commemorated in the special *kinah*, "*Arzei Halevanon*." Why is this elegy included in the Tishah B'Av service? What is the connection between the Temples' destruction and the horrific deaths of Rabbi Akiva, Rabbi Chanina ben Tradyon and their colleagues?

Rav Yosef Dov Soloveitchik, *zt"l*, notes that we commemorate the loss of these ten great scholars twice annually, once on Tishah B'Av and again on Yom Kippur during the moving *tefillah*, "*Eileh Ezkerah*." What is the connection between these two *tefillos* and the days on which they are said?

On Tishah B'Av, the Rav answers, our nation commemorates the loss of these martyrs to impress upon us that "the death of the righteous is as great a tragedy as the destruction of the Holy Temple." On Yom Kippur we are reminded of a different lesson, that "*misas tzaddikim mechaperim* — the death of the righteous atones" for the sins of the entire nation.

To each of us who studied with the Rav, to each of us who was inspired by his brilliant teaching and his insightful, charismatic leadership, his passing was like the destruction of the *Beis Hamikdash*. Similarly, the death of the Lubavitcher Rebbe, *zt"l*, a driving force in building *Yiddishkeit* throughout the world, had a profound impact upon so many whose lives he affected. But at the same time, we need to remember that the loss of these righteous giants, along with the loss of Rav Shlomo Zalman Auerbach, *zt"l*, and Rav Shimon Schwab, *zt"l*, provide expiation for our generation.

May the merit of these *tzaddikim* atone for all of us and may we personally be blessed to see the complete redemption of our people and the rebuilding of the *Beis Hamikdash*.

ৎৡ Contributors

Abramson, Rabbi Alan M., Congregation Anshei Motele, Chicago, IL.

Adler, Emanuel J., National Associate Vice President, Orthodox Union.

Adler, Rabbi Elchanan, Rosh Yeshiva, RIETS, Yeshiva University, New York, NY.

Adler, Rabbi Yitzchok, Beth David Synagogue, West Hartford, CT.

Adler, Rabbi Yosef, Congregation Rinat Yisrael, Teaneck, NJ.

Algaze, Rabbi David, Congregation Havurat Yisrael, Forest Hills, NY.

Angel, Rabbi Marc D., Congregation Shearith Israel, New York, NY.

Aranov, Rabbi Saul, Beth Israel Synagogue, Halifax, Canada.

Auman, Rabbi Kenneth, Young Israel of Flatbush, Brooklyn, NY.

Azose, Rabbi Michael, Sephardic Congregation, Evanston, IL.

Balk, Rabbi Hanan, Congregation Agudas Israel, Cincinnati, OH.

Bamberger, Rabbi I. Nathan, Rabbi Emeritus, Kingsbridge Heights Jewish Center, Bronx, NY.

Baum, Rabbi Shalom, Congregation Ahavath Achim, Fairfield, CT.

Benzaquen, Rabbi Simon, Sephardic Bikur Holim Congregation, Seattle, WA.

Berkowitz, Rabbi Yehoshua, Congregation Shaarei Tefila, Los Angeles, CA.

Berman, Julius, Honorary President, Orthodox Union.

Bialik, Rabbi Herbert M., Congregation Agudath Achim, Bradley Beach, NJ.

Bieler, Rabbi Jack, Kemp Mill Synagogue, Silver Spring, MD.

Billet, Rabbi Hershel, Young Israel of Woodmere, Woodmere, NY.

Billet, Rookie, Assistant Principal, Stella K. Abraham H. S. for Girls, Hewlett Bay Park, NY.

Bixon, Rabbi Donald, Young Israel of Miami Beach, Miami Beach, FL.

Blau, Dr. Rivkah T., Jewish Educator, New York, NY.

Blau, Rabbi Yosef, Mashgiach Ruchani, RIETS, Yeshiva University, New York, NY.

Blech, Rabbi Benjamin, Rabbi Emeritus, Young Israel of Oceanside, Oceanside, NY.

Block, Rabbi Robert D., The Roslyn Synagogue, Roslyn Heights, NY.

Bogopulsky, Rabbi Avram, Beth Jacob Congregation, San Diego, CA.

Bomzer, Rabbi Moshe, Beth Abraham Jacob Congregation, Albany., NY.

Borow, Rabbi Aaron, Rabbi Emeritus, Nusach Hari – B'nai Zion Congregation, University City, MO.

Brander, Rabbi Kenneth, Boca Raton Synagogue, Boca Raton, FL.

Breitowitz, Rabbi Yitzchok A., Congregation Ahavas Torah – Woodside Synagogue, Silver Spring, MD.

Bulka, Rabbi Reuven P., Congregation Machzikei Hadas, Ottawa, Canada.

Burg, Rabbi Melvin I., Congregation Pri Eitz Chaim – Ocean Avenue Jewish Center, Brooklyn, NY.

Bush, Rabbi Asher, Congregation Ahavat Yisrael, Wesley Hills, NY.

Butler, Rabbi Raphael B., Executive Vice President, Orthodox Union.

Caplan, Rabbi Shlomo, Congregation Beth HaMedrash of Overlook Park, Philadelphia, PA.

Charlop, Rabbi Zevulun, Dean of RIETS, Yeshiva University, New York, NY, Rabbi, Young Israel of Mosholu Parkway, Bronx, NY.

Chinn, Rabbi Yitzchak, Congregation Gemilas Chesed, McKeesport, PA.

Cohen, Rabbi Alfred, Congregation Ohav Yisrael, Monsey, NY.

Cohen, Rabbi Daniel, Young Israel of West Hartford, West Hartford, CT.

Cohn, Rabbi Mark, Executive Director, Southern Region, Orthodox Union.

Crandall, Rabbi Shlomo, Bnai Torah, Indianapolis, IN.

Davidson, Rabbi Efraim, Jewish Educator, Atlanta, GA.

Davis, Rabbi Edward, Young Israel of Hollywood and Ft. Lauderdale, Ft. Lauderdale, FL.

Diament, Nathan J., Director, Institute for Public Affairs, Orthodox Union.

Dratch, Rabbi Mark, Congregation Agudath Sholom, Stamford, CT.

Dworken, Rabbi Steven M., Executive Vice President, Rabbinical Council of America, NY.

Ehrenberg, Betty, Director, International Affairs & Communal Relations, Institute for Public Affairs, (IPA) Orthodox Union.

Eisen, Rabbi Joseph, Congregation Bnai Israel of Midwood, Brooklyn, NY.

Epstein, Yisroel, Associate Editor, Torah Insights.

Faskowitz, Rabbi Moshe, Torah Center of Hillcrest, Hillcrest, NY.

Feigelstock, Rabbi Avraham, Eitz Chaim Congregation, Richmond, British

Columbia, Canada.

Feldman, Rabbi Ilan, Congregation Beth Jacob, Atlanta, GA.

Feuerstein, Rabbi Mordecai E., Suburban Torah Center, Livingston, NJ.

Fine, Rabbi Michael, Congregation Machzikeh Hadas, Scranton, PA.

Finkelstein, Rabbi Joel, Anshei Sphard-Beth El Emeth Congregation, Memphis, TN.

Flaum, Rabbi Tzvi, Congregation Kneseth Israel, Far Rockaway, NY.

Frank, Rabbi Moshe, Congregation Ezrath Israel, Ellenville, NY.

Freundel, Rabbi Barry, Congregation Kesher Israel, Washington, DC.

Friedman, Rabbi Yosef, Congregation Bnai Israel, Norfolk, VA.

Ganchrow, Mandell I., M.D., President, Orthodox Union.

Gans, Rabbi Moshe, Congregation Machane Chodosh, Forest Hills, NY.

Garsek, Rabbi Edward, Etz Chayim Congregation, Toledo, OH.

Genack, Rabbi Menachem, Rabbinic Administrator Kashruth Department, Orthodox Union, Congregation Shomrei Emunah, Englewood, NJ.

Gewirtz, Rabbi Gershon C., Young Israel of Brookline, Brookline, MA.

Glass, Rabbi Jonathan, Congregation Beth Israel, New Orleans, LA.

Goldin, Rabbi Shmuel, Congregation Ahavath Torah, Englewood, NJ.

Goodman, Rabbi Yitzchak Meir, Young Israel of Far Rockaway, Far Rockaway, NY.

Gorelik, Rabbi Moshe S., Young Israel of North Bellmore, No. Bellmore, NY.

Granatstein, Rabbi Melvin, Green Road Synagogue, Beachwood, OH.

Green, Rabbi Mordechai, Adas Israel Congregation, Hamilton, Ontario, Canada.

Greenberg, Rabbi Jacob J., Congregation Beth Tikvah Knesseth Israel, Brooklyn, NY.

Grossman, Rabbi Rafael, Baron Hirsch Synagogue, Memphis, TN.

Gruman, Rabbi Aaron, Congregation Toras Emes, East Windsor, NJ.

Grunblatt, Rabbi Joseph, Queens Jewish Center, Forest Hills, NY.

Haber, Rabbi Yaacov, Congregation Bais Torah, Monsey, NY, Director, Jewish Education, Orthodox Union.

Hain, Rabbi Kenneth N., Congregation Beth Shalom, Lawrence, NY.

Halbfinger, Rabbi Abraham, Congregation Kadimah Toras Moshe, Brighton, MA.

Harari, Rabbi Raymond, Congregation Kol Israel, Brooklyn, NY.

Hartman, Rabbi Barry, Ahavath Achim Synagogue, New Bedford, MA.

Hauer, Rabbi Moshe, Bnai Jacob Congregation, Baltimore, MD.

Hecht, Rabbi Yehoshua S., Beth Israel Synagogue of Westport / Norwalk, CT.

Herman, Rabbi Pinchas, Congregation Sharei Israel, Raleigh, NC.

Herring, Rabbi Basil, Atlantic Beach Jewish Center, Atlantic Beach, NY.

Herzog, Rabbi Jerome, Rabbi Emeritus, Knesseth Israel Congregation, Minneapolis, MN.

Hirsch, Rabbi David, Fleetwood Synagogue, Mt. Vernon, NY.

Hochberg, Rabbi Shlomo, Young Israel of Jamaica Estates, Jamaica Estates, NY.

Hollander, Rabbi Dovid Dov, Hebrew Alliance of Brighton Beach, Brooklyn, NY.

Holzer, Rabbi Emanuel, Chairman Rabbinic Kashruth Commission, Rabbinical Council of America.

Horowitz, Rabbi Jonathan, Congregation Beth Israel, Schenectady, NY.

Horowitz, Rabbi Shlomo, Hebrew Academy of Tidewater, Virginia Beach, VA.

Hyman, Rabbi Maynard, Beth Sholom Synagogue, Chattanooga, TN.

Joseph, Rabbi Howard S., Spanish Portuguese Congregation, Montreal, Canada.

Kahane, Rabbi Nachman, Young Israel of the Old City, Jerusalem, Israel.

Kalinsky, Rabbi Alan, West Coast Regional Director, Orthodox Union, Los Angeles, CA.

Kanarfogel, Rabbi Ephraim, Congregation Beth Aaron, Teaneck, NJ.

Kasinetz, Rabbi Moshe A., Rabbi Emeritus, Suburban Torah Center, Livingston, NJ.

Kilimnick, Rabbi Shaya, Congregation Beth Sholom, Rochester, NY.

Klavan, Rabbi Hillel, Congregation Ohev Sholom Talmud Torah, Washington, DC.

Kletenik, Rabbi Moshe, Congregation Bikhur Cholim Machzikay Hadath, Seattle, WA.

Korobkin, Rabbi Daniel, Congregations Sons of Israel, Allentown, PA.

Kramer, Rabbi Doniel Z., Director, United Jewish Communities, UJA Rabbinic Cabinet.

Kranz, Rabbi Herzel, Silver Spring Jewish Center, Silver Spring, MD.

Krauss, Esther, Principal, Ma'ayanot High School for Girls, Teaneck, NJ.

Krupka, Rabbi Moshe D., National Director of Synagogue Services,

Orthodox Union.

Krupka, Rabbi Shlomo, Congregation Etz Chaim, Livingston, NJ.

Kupchik, Rabbi Abraham, Congregation Beth-El, Long Beach, NY.

Kutner, Rabbi Howard, Congregation Beth Israel, Omaha, NE.

Labaton, Rabbi Ezra, Congregation Magen David, West Deal, NJ.

Landau, Rabbi Chaim, Congregation Ner Tamid, Baltimore, MD.

Landau, Rabbi Joel, Congregation Beth Jacob, Irvine, CA.

Landman, Rabbi Leo, Congregation Talmud Torah of Flatbush, Brooklyn, NY.

Leff, Gloria C., Faculty member, Jewish Studies, Hebrew Academy of the Five Towns and Rockaway (HAFTR) High School, Cedarhurst, NY.

Leff, Rabbi Bertram, Editor, Torah Insights.

Levin, Rabbi A. Mark, Director, Rabbinic Services, RIETS, Yeshiva University, New York, NY.

Levine, Michelle, PHD, Biblical Studies, New York University.

Levovitz, Rabbi Pesach, Rabbi Emeritus, Congregation Sons of Israel, Lakewood, NJ.

Lew, Rabbi Elazar, Kashruth Department, Orthodox Union.

Lookstein, Rabbi Haskel, Congregation Kehilath Jeshurun, New York, NY.

Luban, Rabbi Yaakov, Ohr Torah Congregation, Edison, NJ.

Mandelbaum, Rabbi Abraham D., Rabbi Emeritus, Congregation Ahavat Yisrael, Hewlett, NY.

Marcus, Rabbi Alvin M., Rabbi Emeritus, Ahavas Achim Bnai Jacob and David, West Orange, NJ.

Marcus, Rabbi Elihu, Executive Assistant to the President, Touro College.

Marcus, Rabbi Raphael, Congregation B'nai Torah, Toronto, Canada.

Marder, Rabbi Chaim, Hebrew Institute of White Plains, White Plains, NY.

Mehlman, Rabbi Daniel H., Lido Beach Synagogue, Lido Beach, NY.

Miller, Rabbi Nisson Dov, Congregation Etz Chaim, Sharon, MA.

Miller, Rabbi Yisroel, Congregation Poale Zedeck, Pittsburgh, PA.

Mintz, Rabbi Adam, Lincoln Square Synagogue, New York, NY.

Morduchowitz, Rabbi Moshe, West Side Institutional Synagogue, New York, NY.

Movsas, Rabbi David, Congregation Shaare Zedek, West New York, NJ.

Muschel, Rabbi Nachum, Congregation Hadar, Dean Emeritus of Yeshivat Hadar Avraham Tzvi (ASHAR), Monsey, NY.

Muskin, Rabbi Elazar, Young Israel of Century City, Los Angeles, CA.

Oberstein, Rabbi Leonard, Randallstown Synagogue Center, Randallstown, MD.

Ozarowski, Rabbi Joseph S., Elmont Jewish Center, Elmont, NY.

Pelcovitz, Rabbi Ralph, Rabbi Emeritus, Congregation Kneseth Israel, Far Rockaway, NY.

Penner, Rabbi Marc, Young Israel of Holliswood/Holliswood Jewish Center, Holliswood, NY.

Polakoff, Rabbi Dale, Great Neck Synagogue, Great Neck, NY.

Polin, Rabbi Milton H., Rabbi Emeritus, Kingsway Jewish Center, Brooklyn, NY.

Pollak, Rabbi Yaakov, Congregation Shomrei Emunah, Brooklyn, NY.

Posner, Rabbi Zalman, Congregation Shearith Israel, Nashville, TN.

Poupko, Rabbi Baruch A., Congregation Shaare Torah, Pittsburgh, PA.

Pruzansky, Rabbi Steven, Congregation Bnai Yeshurun, Teaneck, NJ.

Radinsky, Rabbi David J., Congregation Brith Shalom Beth Israel, Charleston, SC.

Radinsky, Rabbi Joseph, United Orthodox Synagogue, Houston, TX.

Rakowitz, Rabbi Myron, Sephardic Jewish Center of Canarsie, Brooklyn, NY.

Rebibo, Rabbi David, Congregation Beth Joseph, Phoenix, AZ.

Reiner, Rabbi Jacob, Congregation Ohav Zedek, Belle Harbor, NY.

Ron, Rabbi Zvi, Congregation Kneseth Beth Israel, Richmond, VA.

Rosen, Rabbi Stuart J., Knesset Israel Torah Center, Sacramento, CA.

Rosenberg, Rabbi Moshe, Congregation Etz Chaim, Kew Garden Hills, NY.

Rosenberg, Rabbi Yitzchok, Director, Education Programs, Orthodox Union.

Rosenblatt, Rabbi Jonathan I., Riverdale Jewish Center, Riverdale, NY.

Rosenfeld, Rabbi Menachem, Congregation Ahavat Achim, Fairlawn, NJ.

Rosensweig, Rabbi Bernard, Rabbi Emeritus, Congregation Adath Jeshurun, Kew Gardens, NY.

Roth, Rabbi Tobias, Congregation Brothers of Israel, Elberon, NJ.

Rothman, Rabbi Bernard E., Congregation Sons of Israel, Cherry Hill, NJ.

Rubenstein, Rabbi Jacob S., Young Israel of Scarsdale, Scarsdale, NY.

Rybak, Rabbi Solomon F., Congregation Adas Israel, Passaic, NJ.

Sackett, Rabbi Shaya, Congregation Degel Israel, Lancaster, PA.

Safran, Rabbi Eliyahu, Rabbinic Coordinator, Kashruth Dept, Orthodox Union.

Samuels, Rabbi Benjamin, Congregation Shaarei Tefillah, Newton Centre, MA.

Schachter, Rabbi Hershel, Rosh Kollel of RIETS, Yeshiva University, New York, NY.

Schacter, Rabbi Jacob J., The Jewish Center, New York, NY.

Scheinberg, Rabbi Aryeh, Congregation Rodfei Sholom, San Antonio, TX.

Schertz, Rabbi Chaim, Congregation Kesher Israel, Harrisburg, PA.

Schnaidman, Rabbi Mordecai, Mt. Sinai Jewish Center, New York, NY.

Schonfeld, Rabbi Fabian, Young Israel of Kew Garden Hills, Kew Garden Hills, NY.

Schonfeld, Rabbi Yoel, Assistant to the Rabbi, Young Israel of Kew Garden Hills, NY, Rabbinic Coordinator, Orthodox Union.

Schreier, Rabbi Max N., Avenue N Jewish Center, Brooklyn, NY.

Schwalb, Rabbi Efrem, Utopia Jewish Center, Hillcrest, NY.

Schwartz, Rabbi Allen, Ohav Zedek Congregation, New York, NY.

Schwartz, Rabbi Gedalia Dov, Av Beth Din, Chicago Rabbinical Council and Rabbinical Council of America.

Schwartz, Rabbi Morey, Congregation Beth Israel Abraham and Voliner, Overland Park, KS.

Schwartzberg, Rabbi Ronald, Congregation Ahavas Achim, Highland Park, NJ.

Shapiro, Rabbi Mordekai, Congregation Ohr Torah, North Woodmere, NY.

Shmidman, Rabbi Michael D., Congregation Orach Chaim, New York, NY.

Shore, Rabbi Evan, Young Israel Shaarei Torah, Syracuse, NY.

Shulman, Rabbi Moshe, Congregation Shaaray Shomayim, Toronto, Canada.

Shulman, Rabbi Nisson E., Prominent Author and Lecturer.

Sladowsky, Rabbi Yitzchak, Forest Park Jewish Center, Glendale, NY.

Slatus, Rabbi Avigdor, Congregation Bnai Brith Jacob, Savannah, GA.

Slepoy, Rabbi Ephraim, Beth Israel Synagogue, Longmeadow, MA.

Sokol, Rabbi Moshe, Yavneh Minyan of Flatbush, Brooklyn, NY.

Sonnenschein, Rabbi Gershon, Congregation Kodimoh, Springfield, MA.

Stavsky, Rabbi David, Congregation Beth Jacob, Columbus, OH.

Steinmetz, Rabbi Chaim, Congregation Tifereth Beth David Jerusalem, Montreal, Canada.

Stern, Rabbi Moshe, Congregation Shaarei Tefillah, Toronto, Canada.

Stolper, Rabbi Pinchas, Senior Executive, Orthodox Union.

Sturm, Rabbi Ephraim, Executive Vice President Emeritus, National Council of Young Israel.

Sugarman, Rabbi Marvin, Shaarey Zedek Congregation, North Hollywood, CA.

Taub, Rabbi Baruch, Beth Avraham Yosef Congregation, Toronto, Canada.

Tendler, Rabbi Moshe Dovid, Community Synagogue of Monsey, Monsey, NY., Rosh Yeshiva, RIETS, Yeshiva University, New York, NY.

Tessler, Rabbi Joel, Congregation Beth Shalom, Potomac, MD.

Tradburks, Rabbi Reuven, Kehillat Shaarei Torah, Toronto, Ontario, Canada.

Tropp, Rabbi Mordechai Yehuda, Regional Director, New Jersey Region — Etz Chaim, NCSY, Orthodox Union.

Vale, Rabbi Asher, Manhattan Beach Jewish Center, Brooklyn, NY.

Viener, Rabbi Yosef, Agudas Yisrael of Flatbush, Brooklyn, NY.

Wagner, Rabbi Feivel, Young Israel of Forest Hills, Forest Hills, NY.

Wakslak, Rabbi Chaim, Young Israel of Long Beach, Long Beach, NY.

Weil, Rabbi Steven, Young Israel of Oak Park, Oak Park, MI.

Wein, Esther, Lecturer, Jewish Renaissance Center, New York, NY.

Wein, Rabbi Berel, Rabbi Emeritus, Congregation Bais Torah, Suffern, NY.

Weinberger, Rabbi David, Congregation Shaaray Tefila, Lawrence, NY.

Weinreb, Rabbi Tzvi Hersh, Congregation Shomrei Emunah, Baltimore, MD.

Weiss, Rabbi Abner, Beth Jacob Congregation, Beverly Hills, CA.

Welcher, Rabbi Herschel, Congregation Ahavas Yisrael, Kew Garden Hills, NY.

Well, Rabbi Harvey, Or Torah Congregation, Skokie, IL.

Wolk, Rabbi Howard, Congregation Shaare Tefilla, Dallas, TX.

Wurzburger, Rabbi Walter S., Rabbi Emeritus, Congregation Shaaray Tefila, Lawrence, NY.

Yeres, Rabbi Moshe J., Community Hebrew Academy of Toronto, Toronto, Canada.

Yudin, Rabbi Benjamin, Congregation Shomrei Torah, Fair Lawn, NJ.

Yuter, Rabbi Alan J., Congregation Israel, Springfield, NJ.

Zack, Rabbi Howard, Beth Jacob Congregation, Oakland, CA.

Zeitz, Rabbi Mordecai E., Congregation Beth Tikvah, Montreal, Canada.

Zierler, Rabbi Lawrence S., Jewish Community Center of Cleveland, Beachwood, OH.

Zohn, Rabbi Elchonon, Director, Chevra Kadisha of Queens, NY.